THE
MAKING
OF
OREGON

TWO CENTURIES OF OREGON GEOGRAPHY

by

Samuel N. Dicken

Emeritus Professor of Geography
University of Oregon

and

Emily F. Dicken

Volume I: THE MAKING OF OREGON:
A Study in Historical Geography

Volume II: OREGON DIVIDED:
A Regional Geography

THE MAKING OF OREGON

A STUDY IN HISTORICAL GEOGRAPHY

SAMUEL N. DICKEN
Emeritus Professor of Geography
University of Oregon

EMILY F. DICKEN

Oregon Historical Society
Portland, Oregon
1979

LC 79-89087
ISBN 0-87595 — 63-9
(volume one)
ISBN 0-87595-074-4
(two volume series)
Oregon Historical Society
Portland, Oregon
©1979

CONTENTS

FOREWORD   xi

PREFACE   xiii

CHAPTER 1   1
EARLY PERCEPTIONS OF OREGON   Fact and Fancy – Pro and Con. Points of View.
                                        Oregon as Seen in the East. The Oregon Ques-
                                        tion in Congress. Missionaries and Indians.
                                        Books and Guides. Place Names.

CHAPTER 2   14
OREGON FROM THE AIR – OVERVIEW AND   Willamette Valley. Klamath Mountains. Coast
PREVIEW   Range. Cascade Range. Basin-Range. High Lava
                                        Plains. The Owyhee Upland. Blue Mountains.
                                        Deschutes-Umatilla Plateau. Summary.

CHAPTER 3   35
THE IMPACT OF THE INDIANS ON OREGON   How the Indians Came to Oregon. Indian Con-
                                        tributions. The Indian Population. Indian
                                        Resource Areas. Tribal Distribution, 1840:
                                        Western Oregon and the Lower Columbia;
                                        Eastern Oregon. Summary.

CHAPTER 4   48
EXPLORATION OF OREGON TO 1840   Exploration by Sea. Exploration by Land. Lewis
                                        and Clark. Astoria. Hudson's Bay Company Ex-
                                        plorers and Traders. Eastern Oregon. The Ore-
                                        gon Map to 1840. Summary.

CHAPTER 5   64
EARLY SETTLEMENT, 1840–1850   Lieutenant Charles Wilkes. John H. Frost. Cap-
                                        tain John C. Frémont. Lieutenant Neil M.
                                        Howison. Sources of Immigrants. Why Did the
                                        People Migrate to Oregon? The Way West. The
                                        Migration Accelerated. Scarcity of Game and
                                        Wild Fruits. Diseases in Oregon. The Indian
                                        Problem in the 1840s. Agriculture. Transporta-

tion: Boats, Trails, and Roads. Political Divisions. Land Ownership. The California Gold Rush. Oregon Population in 1850. The Rival Towns. Summary.

CHAPTER 6   84
   EXPANDING SETTLEMENT, 1850–1870

The Oregon Gold Rushes: The Klamath Mountains; the Blue Mountains. The Civil War. Indian Wars. Population Growth and Areal Expansion. Agriculture. Manufacturing. Transport. Land Ownership and Land Surveys: Surveys and Maps. Summary.

CHAPTER 7   105
   THE RAILROAD-BUILDING ERA, 1870–1900

Population; Indians. Railroads. Railroad Construction. Urban and Interurban Lines. Roads. Rivers and Harbors. Agriculture: Crops; Agricultural Technology; Irrigation; Livestock. The Grub Lands. Fisheries. Mining. Manufacturing. Exports and Imports. Mapping. Comments on Oregon at the Turn of the Century. Impact of Development.

CHAPTER 8   134
   AUTOMOBILES, HOMESTEADS, AND LUMBER BOOMS, 1900–1930

Population. Homesteading. Automobiles and Roads: Road Maps. Railroads and Interurbans. Topographic Mapping. Agriculture: Agricultural Technology; Cropland and Crops; Livestock. Fisheries. Mining. Manufacturing: Lumbering. Summary.

CHAPTER 9   157
   DEPRESSION AND RECOVERY, 1930–1950

Population. Transportation. A Breakthrough in Mapping. Agriculture. Fisheries. Mining. Manufacturing. Impact.

CHAPTER 10   170
   URBANIZATION AND SUBURBANIZATION, 1950–1978

Population. Suburbanization. Housing. Energy. Transportation. Forests. Agriculture. Fisheries. Minerals. Manufacturing. Tourism, Recreation, and Retirement. Impact on the Land.

NOTES   191

INDEX   198

ILLUSTRATIONS

1.1   Cape Blanco.   2

1.2   Oregon coast near Cape Ferrelo.   3

1.3   Airphoto of Astoria and Columbia   4
      River entrance.

1.4   Map, Gerhard F. Müller's of Russian   5
      discoveries on the Northwest Coast.

1.5   Map, S. Lewis' of "Louisiana," 1804.   6

1.6   Map, Louisiana Purchase and the   7
      Oregon Country.

1.7   Map, Lee and Frost's of Oregon, 1844. 9

2.1   Map, landform regions.   15

2.2   Map, "Oregon from the air."   16

2.3   Portland.   17

2.4   Willamette Valley near Wilsonville.   18

2.5   Salem.   19

2.6   Grants Pass and Rogue River.   20

2.7   Rogue River at Gold Beach.   21

2.8   Cape Perpetua.   23

2.9   Tillamook.   25

2.10 Relief model of the Cascade Range   27
      (vicinity of Mt. Hood) and part of
      Deschutes-Umatilla Plateau.

2.11 Abert Rim, Lake County.   29

2.12 Owyhee Reservoir.   30

2.13 Blue Mountains between La Grande   32
      and Pendleton.

2.14 Columbia Gorge at Crown Point.   34

3.1   Map, probable Indian migration   36
      routes across land bridge.

3.2   Indians catching a wild horse.   37

3.3   Stephen H. Meek.   38

3.4   Indian dugout canoe.   39

3.5   Indians dip-netting salmon at Celilo   40
      Falls.

3.6   Rocky benches at Neptune State   41
      Park.

3.7   Map, Indian tribes, 1840–1850.   42

3.8   Indian plank house.   44

3.9   Indian tepee.   45

4.1   Map, William Broughton's chart of   49
      lower Columbia River, 1789.

4.2   Map, routes of the principal land ex-   50
      plorers of Oregon to 1843.

4.3   Map, part of Captain William Clark's   51
      of the Oregon Country, 1810.

4.4 Map, part of William Clark's of lower Columbia River. 53

4.5 Map, route followed by Robert Stuart from Astoria to the East in 1812–1813. 54

4.6 Map, Peter Skene Ogden's fur-trading expeditions to eastern Oregon in 1827–1828 and 1828–1829. 59

4.7 Map, Bonneville's *Territory West of the Rocky Mountains*, 1837. 61

4.8 Map, J. J. Abert's *Map of the Territory of Oregon*, 1838. 62

5.1 Map, Oregon Country in 1843. 65

5.2 Map, Lt. Charles Wilkes' of Oregon Territory, 1841. 66

5.3 Early road on Neahkahnie Mountain. 67

5.4 Map, eastern United States showing sources of Oregon immigrants, 1840–1850. 69

5.5 Map, Barlow Road between The Dalles and Oregon City, 1846. 70

5.6 Artist's scene of covered wagons on Barlow Road. 73

5.7 Sketch of Fort Vancouver. 75

5.8 Early steamer on Snake River. 76

5.9 Map, population by counties, 1850. 79

5.10 Population pyramid, 1850. 80

5.11 An early log cabin. 82

6.1 Map, population by counties, 1870. 85

6.2 Map, gold-mining regions. 86

6.3 Panning for gold, Whisky Run, Coos County. 87

6.4 Hydraulic gold mining near Medford. 88

6.5 Map, Indian reservations and important Indian battles. 90

6.6 Diagram, Willamette Valley towns and transportation routes, 1870. 91

6.7 Map, roads and settlements of the northern Willamette Valley, 1860. 97

6.8 Map, the Donation Land Claims of western Oregon. 98

6.9 Map, Donation Land Claims in northern part of French Prairie. 100

6.10 Map, Land Office township map. 101

6.11 Map, U.S. Coast Survey map of the lower Columbia River, 1868. 102

7.1 Map, population by counties, 1900. 106

7.2 Population pyramid, 1880. 107

7.3 Map, Railroad Survey, 1855. 109

7.4 Map, railroad and wagon road land grants. 110

7.5 Passenger train, Oregon and California Railroad, 1870. 112

7.6 Map, railroads, 1900. 113

7.7 Horse-car line, Portland, 1888. 114

7.8 Jetties at entrance of Siuslaw River. 116

7.9 Map, wheat acreage, 1899. 118

7.10 Horse-drawn combine, eastern Oregon. 119

7.11 Map, irrigated areas, 1900. 120

7.12 Map, value of livestock, 1899. 121

7.13 Early cattle ranch near Roseburg. 122

7.14 Map, sheep (lambs and ewes), 1899. 123

7.15 Sheepherder and flock. 124

7.16 Map, cattle trails in Oregon and adjacent states.   125

7.17 Fish wheel, Columbia River.   127

7.18 Map, principal flour-mill cities, 1870–1900.   129

7.19 Map, J. K. Gill, 1878.   130

7.20 Map, Klamath Sheet, U.S. Geological Survey, 1889.   132

8.1 Map, population changes, 1900–1930.   135

8.2 Map, population, 1930.   136

8.3 Automobile and tractor on a road.   138

8.4 Map, improved roads, 1930.   141

8.5 Map, Willamette Valley interurbans, 1915.   142

8.6 Artist's view of Bayocean resort and Tillamook Bay.   145

8.7 Map, cropland, 1929.   146

8.8 Combines in Gilliam County.   147

8.9 Map, irrigated areas, 1935.   148

8.10 Map, wheat acreage, 1929.   149

8.11 Map, dairy cows, 1929.   150

8.12 Gold dredge, Sumpter, Oregon.   152

8.13 Map, sawmill locations, 1930.   154

8.14 Early lumber mill.   155

9.1 Map, population, showing percentage gains and losses, 1940–1950.   158

9.2 Diagram, size order of towns and cities in the Willamette Valley, 1950.   159

9.3 Population pyramid, 1940.   160

9.4 Early resort hotel, Gearhart.   162

9.5 Tillamook Plain, 1939.   163

9.6 Map, harvested cropland, 1949.   165

9.7 Map, acres of irrigated land, 1949.   166

9.8 Map, value added by manufacturing, 1947.   168

10.1 Map, Portland's urbanized zones, 1940 and 1975.   171

10.2 Map, changes in Oregon's population, 1950–1975.   172

10.3 Map, occupied mobile homes, 1974.   175

10.4 Map, power plants and transmission lines, 1971.   176

10.5 Power relay station, The Dalles.   177

10.6 Map, geothermal lease and lease application areas.   178

10.7 Graph, timber harvest, 1954–1974.   180

10.8 Map, changes in log production, 1951–1973.   181

10.9 Map, two fragmented farms, Willamette Valley.   182

10.10 Map, value added by manufacturing, 1972.   185

10.11 Map, outward movement of industries from Portland's central area.   186

To
CHARLES

FOREWORD

Too often we read history with an awareness of place names but with little sense of place. Conversely, we read geography with a reasonably clear perception of place and the relationship of places, but the people we encounter are abstractions and statistical summaries. Sam and Emily Dicken have brought history and geography together. They people the landscape we call Oregon with flesh-and-blood men and women who occupy places and who experience, exploit, change and are changed by the place they have come to believe they possess.

In an early chapter, which, like a prologue from a Shakespearean play, reveals the outlines of the plot, the Dickens take their readers on an imaginary airplane flight over the entire state, giving them a sense of the whole and its component parts, a kind of omniscience denied to the people who play the roles in the historico-geographical drama. The people in the real world of the Dickens' drama have no such perception of wholeness. They are confined strictly to their place in time. They see Oregon in fragments, with the distortion of the partial view. In consequence they are sometimes buffeted and broken by the land they seek to conquer, and they frequently direct their Lilliputian efforts with such force that they inflict unintended and astonishing injury to land they prize. But for the most part, despite their limited perspective, they effect an accommodation to the land that, in the short view at least, is reasonably productive and happy.

Against this constant interplay of people and land the writers unfold for us the procession of Indians, explorers, trappers and fur traders, missionaries, pioneers of the Oregon Trail, and the hordes who followed them. The Dickens show us not only the people but the use they made of the land and its resources: the beginnings of agriculture and primitive industry, the construction of the first passable (and sometimes impassable) roads, the building of ships and railroads and the development of transportation, the coming of the automobile and the highway system, the shock of two world wars and a depression, the enterprise of damming the rivers and electrifying a region, the growth of industry and the spawning of the giant machine and the technological society, and through it all, the never-ceasing in-migration of people. It is an engrossing tale, closing with a cloud on the horizon, a possible threat to Eden: the depletion of natural resources and the exhaustion of the potential energy supply.

Sam and Emily Dicken are the right people to tell the story. I have known them well and called them friends for the more than 30 years that they have lived in Oregon. They had scarcely crossed the border, en route to a new appointment at the University of Oregon, before they undertook an exploring trip into the Wallowas. They had, in that first sortie, plunged immediately into Oregon geography. In less than three years Sam, with Emily's assistance, had published his first manual, designed for the use of undergraduates, on the geography of Oregon.

The Dickens love the Oregon country for its own sake, and for what it does to the human spirit. And loving the land, they have come to know it intimately. They have driven its roads to the far corners, canoed its streams and lakes, hiked its trails, camped in its woods, flown over its mountain peaks, high plains, and Pacific shore. They have come to possess the land as one can possess only by knowing. They have photographed what they have seen, both for its beauty and, with the eyes of geographers, for the study of land forms — for the entertainment of their friends and the instruction of their students.

One might say that they are field geographers. But they are more. Like family physicians, they are generalists who bring together the insights of the specialists — the cultural, economic, and physical geographers, and the cartographers. They read a map the way a conductor reads a musical score, translating the symbols into a three-dimensional reality of a landscape. It is a legend at the University of Oregon that, before coming to Eugene, they chose the site of their hillside home by studying contour maps of the community. And those of us who visited the home Sam and Emily built on that site can never forget the great map they had mounted on the wall like a mural. It is no accident that Dr. Dicken gave much energy to the collection of a map library at the University that now contains more than 200,000 items. As one might expect, this volume on the historical geography of Oregon is richly illustrated with maps ranging from the imperfect and sometimes amusing representations of the first explorers to the mathematically calculated renderings from aerial photographs.

I have heard Sam Dicken argue that the library is as important a resource to the geographer as is the landscape — often a more important resource. He and Emily prove the point. They have pored over the accounts of the explorers and early settlers, the general histories, the census reports, guide books, gazetteers, the publications of the Oregon Historical Society, scholarly monographs, and the outpourings of governmental agencies, to distill from them the data that give body to their text. They have written a geographical source book in historical context that we shall turn to again and again.

Having read the text, we shall not soon forget the epilogue which, matching chapter 2, once again takes us on an imaginary flight over the state, this time to see what humankind has wrought of the land that is ours, and, indeed, to ponder the question whether we have wrought good or ill.

Robert D. Clark

President Emeritus
University of Oregon

PREFACE

In the two centuries, more or less, that the land we now call Oregon has been known to white men, great changes have been made in the landscape. From a few thousand Indians, the population has expanded a hundredfold. The grasslands, persistently maintained by Indian burning, are now in cultivated fields and pastures, interspersed with cities, houses, and the various other works of modern man. The forests have been cut over, burned over, and cut over again, and the new growth is different from the old; one burned-over pine forest may grow up in Douglas fir, another in brush. No part of Oregon is unchanged; few parts fail to show the effects of man's occupation and activities. Perhaps the most striking features in the landscape are the cities and houses, with a variety of shapes, styles, and materials, reflecting the various origins of the builders, the availability of materials, and the changing techniques of construction.

The transformation of the Oregon landscape from what it was two centuries ago to what it is today was a process of creation, destruction, and change, carried out by a group of people who, individually and collectively, were taking possession of the land. Thousands of decisions had to be made and are being made today, based many times on inadequate information or even misinformation. Each decision had to be made on the basis of one's perception of the particular part of Oregon under consideration. The early settlers were generally poorly informed—reliable information simply did not exist—but in later years when more information was available it was not always heeded. In the early 1900s many people bought or homesteaded land in southeastern Oregon, expecting to grow crops without irrigation. They were sadly mistaken. Even today people are building houses along the Oregon coast near the high-tide line, in spite of the well-known hazards of such locations. It is not always what Oregon is really like that influences decisions; it is man's perception of the landscape that counts.

Many of the early perceptions of the Oregon Country were derived from maps. Prior to the era of land exploration, initiated by Lewis and Clark (see chapter 4), the maps of the interior were sketchy and based mostly on imagination and rumor. The coast and the Columbia River were the first to be mapped; it was not until the late 1830s that the maps of the interior of Oregon began to show the major features of the land. In the chapters to follow, contemporary maps are shown to indicate the progress down to the present time. Today, maps, in great variety, are a very important part of our perception of the state.

The first chapter of this book is mainly concerned with the early perceptions of Oregon. What did people think of it, how did they evaluate it? The virtues and shortcomings, as they were seen in those days, were debated in the halls of Congress and around many a hot stove in the older settled parts of the United States, as well as by the first settlers after their arrival in Oregon. The second chapter gives a general overview of the state at present and a preview, designed for readers who may not be familiar with all parts of the state. The third chapter, concerned with the impact of the Indian occupation, is a geography of the period before white settlement. Chapters on the geography of the various settlement periods follow.

It will be obvious to the reader that this book could not have been written without the help of many people, more than can be mentioned. For 30 years we have traveled around Oregon, observing, photographing, and interviewing. In the last decade our interest has been extended and quickened by association with the staff and members of the Oregon Historical Society, especially with Executive Director Thomas Vaughan and with the editors, Bruce T. Hamilton and Priscilla Knuth. Our thanks are due to the University of Oregon for providing working space in the Department of Geography and for a small grant from the Graduate School for drafting expenses. Timothy Young drew several of the maps. Special thanks are due to William Loy and Stuart Allan and the staff of *The Atlas of Oregon* for making available materials collected in the course of its preparation. The late Martin Schmitt, as Curator of Special Collections, and Edward Thatcher and Susan Clark, Map Librarians, have been most helpful. Robert Frazier read the entire manuscript and offered valuable criticisms, encouragement, and suggestions. The following have either read parts of the manuscript or provided valuable source materials: Joel Berreman, Edwin Bingham, Max Brainerd, Philip Bredesen, Michael Donley, Gilbert Hulin, Deirdre Malarkey, Ralph Mason, Clyde Patton, Edward Price, Gary Searl, Carrie Singleton, Donald Smith, Everett Smith, Jr., James Tattersall, John Townsend, and Alvin Urquhart.

Finally, special thanks are due to Dr. Robert D. Clark, who read the manuscript with great care and wrote the Foreword.

PRO: *For richness of soil and other local advantages, I should not know where to find a spot in the Valley of the Mississippi superior to this* [Willamette Valley].
SAMUEL PARKER, 1838
CON: *Oregon Territory as a whole is, in its soil, the most cheerless and barren portion of the national domain.*
THOMAS J. FARNHAM, 1843

FACT AND FANCY—PRO AND CON

In the parable of the Blind Men and the Elephant one man grasped the elephant by the tail and said, "The elephant is like a rope"; another touched a leg and remarked, "The elephant is like a tree"; the third felt the side of the elephant, saying, "The elephant is like a wall." Since the time, nearly two centuries ago, when the western world first became aware of the existence of Oregon, opinions have varied almost as widely concerning the nature and quality of the land. The early observers were not blind but their perceptions were often based on limited observations, misinformation, and, in many cases, bias. Some early writers praised Oregon as a veritable utopia (some had ulterior reasons for doing so); others were highly critical. Some said Oregon was a desert; others remarked that it rained all the time. These varying opinions involved many aspects of the country—climate, terrain, vegetation, soil fertility, the nature of the Indians, the general healthfulness of the area, and, after settlement began, the quality of the settlers themselves.

Based on these contrasting and contradictory perceptions many important decisions were made. The United States government, after long debate, decided to acquire Oregon, to fix the boundaries, and to set up a local territorial government. Many thousands of people decided, on the basis of very little information, to migrate to Oregon. Perhaps many others, hearing only unfavorable reports, decided *not* to migrate. It is not surprising that there were vigorous disagreements about the geography of the area since so few firm facts were available. Communication was poor and the best information did not always reach interested parties. For example, before white settlement of Oregon, the files of the Hudson's Bay Company contained much detailed information collected by the fur traders that was not generally available to Americans.

POINTS OF VIEW

Early perceptions of Oregon depended on the point of view, as well as on the sources of information. Many of the mariners sailing along the coast were only mildly interested in Oregon per se. They were either looking for the Northwest Passage or seeking the sea otter, or both. The official explorers, Lewis and Clark, Charles Wilkes, Neil Howison, John Frémont, and others, were generally factual in their descriptions, but they did not cover all parts of the state. The fur traders and trappers of the Hudson's Bay Company, however, visited all regions of the state and kept daily records of their travels. Their chief interests were trapping and trading for beaver, but they described the country and had contacts with most of the Indian tribes. The missionaries, coming to Oregon in 1835, sent (or carried) back favorable reports to the eastern states. After immigration began (1842) settlers and visitors sent back reports to their friends and relatives in the East, generally favorable but not always reliable, causing much confusion as to the real character of the country. The reports were, indeed, a mixture of fact and fancy. During this period many immigrant pamphlets were printed and distributed, urging people to migrate to Oregon. Most of these publications described Oregon in glowing terms.

The first European observers to see Oregon approached by sea, and the first point they saw was Cape Blanco (**fig. 1.1**), its light-colored rocks mak-

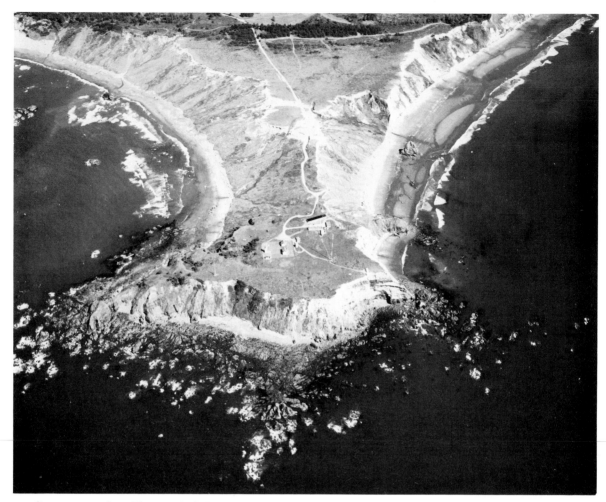

fig. 1.1   Cape Blanco. The light-colored cliffs make it the most visible point on the Oregon coast, all the more so because it is the westernmost point of the state. (Oregon Dept. of Transportation)

ing it visible for many miles. Early mariners usually kept a safe distance from the rocky, foggy shore (**fig. 1.2**), all the more dangerous because of unfavorable on-shore winds. A lee shore is risky for a sailing ship, especially in the fog, and many voyagers, for this reason, sailed past such significant points as the entrance to the Columbia River without recognizing them. Little wonder that the early maps of the Oregon coast were sketchy. Nevertheless, these early mariners provided the first descriptions of Oregon, poor as they were, since overland explorers and travelers did not reach Oregon until many years later.

The earliest voyagers, Juan Rodriguez Cabrillo (1542), Francis Drake (1579), and Sebastián Vizcaino (1602), did little more than name a few headlands and describe the bad weather. Drake's crew "did grievously complain thereof [the

weather], some of them feeling that their health was much impaired thereby.... there followed the most vile, thicke and stinking fogges."[1] In 1775 Bruno Hezeta must have enjoyed better weather, for he sighted the entrance to the Columbia River (**fig. 1.3**) and made an effort to enter it, but found the current too strong. Hezeta believed he had found the entrance to a great river. But the policy of the Spanish government was to conceal their discoveries, and the details of Hezeta's voyage were not generally known at the time. However, some subsequent maps showed Hezeta's Gateway (Entrada de Hezeta) in the latitude of the Columbia River.[2]

The early maps of Oregon,[3] based on the voyages and sometimes on the imagination, reflected the limited knowledge of the country. The coastline was mapped and a few prominent capes

2

fig. 1.2   The southern Oregon coast near Cape Ferrelo. Such a shoreline did not encourage
early mariners to venture near. (Oregon Dept. of Transportation)

named, but the interior was mostly blank. Sanson's map (1656) places the southern Oregon coast on the fictitious "Californie Isle"; capes Blanco and Sebastián are located on the "island" and the mainland interior is labeled "Nuevo Mexico." More than a century later Gerhard Müller's map (fig. 1.4) was published in St. Petersburg and reprinted in London in 1761. This was one of the first maps to show the "River of the West" with the notation that the entrance was discovered by Martin d'Aguilar in 1603. The area of Oregon and northern California is labeled "New Albion, discover'd by St. [sic] Francis Drake in 1578." The only place name on the Oregon coast is "C[ape] Blanco de St. Sebastion [sic]."

Jonathan Carver's "New Map of North America," published in 1778, resembles Müller's map so far as the Oregon area is concerned. Carver was the first to use the name "Origan" on a map, but he applied the name only to the headwaters of a river in what is now western Minnesota. In 1798 George Vancouver mapped the coast of Washington, British Columbia, and Alaska in considerable detail, but made little change in the Oregon map. The Lewis map of 1804 (fig. 1.5) shows how little was known of Oregon's interior prior to the expedition of Lewis and Clark. It was published in Philadelphia as a part of "A New and Elegant General Atlas."[4] Cape Blanco is the only name on the coast. A short river is located in the latitude of the Columbia River but not named. A single, irregular mountain range appears in the interior, probably intended to represent the Rocky Mountains, since the headwaters of the Missouri River appear immediately to the east.

The great overland explorations of Meriwether Lewis and William Clark, David Douglas, Charles Wilkes, Neil Howison, John C. Frémont, and

3

fig. 1.3   Astoria with the broad entrance to the Columbia River (upper right). Jetties at (a) and (b) now protect the entrance. Astoria is built on the north slope of Coxcomb Hill with very little land for the business district. The Columbia River Bridge (right) connects Astoria with the state of Washington. The Astor Column (lower left) depicts in a spiral mural the early history of Oregon. The northern end of the Clatsop Plains (c) is shown at upper left. (Oregon Dept. of Transportation)

others covered a span of many years. The results of these explorations are presented in chapter 4, but it is appropriate to mention a few of their perceptions here. Lewis and Clark encountered a very wet winter, living as they did at Fort Clatsop from November to April. Lewis noted in his journal of January 7, 1806: "This is the first day during which we have had no rain since we arrived at this place—nothing extraordinary happened today." William Clark noted in the same journal the effect of the rains on the steep slopes south of Tillamook Head: "The Coast . . . is slipping from the Sides of the high hills, in emence masses; fifty or a hundred acres at a time . . . into the Ocean . . . caused by the incessant rains."[5] David Douglas described the

country above the Falls of the Columbia as "hilly, destitute of timber, the soil sandy and barren."[6] John Frémont, traveling in eastern Oregon near Summer Lake, noted: "We are now in a country where the scarcity of water and grass make traveling dangerous."[7]

The fur traders, most of them employed by the Hudson's Bay Company, carried out extensive explorations in almost every major stream valley in Oregon. Some of the expeditions are described in chapter 4, but a few comments here will establish their point of view. The fur traders were interested most of all in finding streams where beaver could be trapped and in locating Indians who had furs to trade. For these reasons they tended to follow the

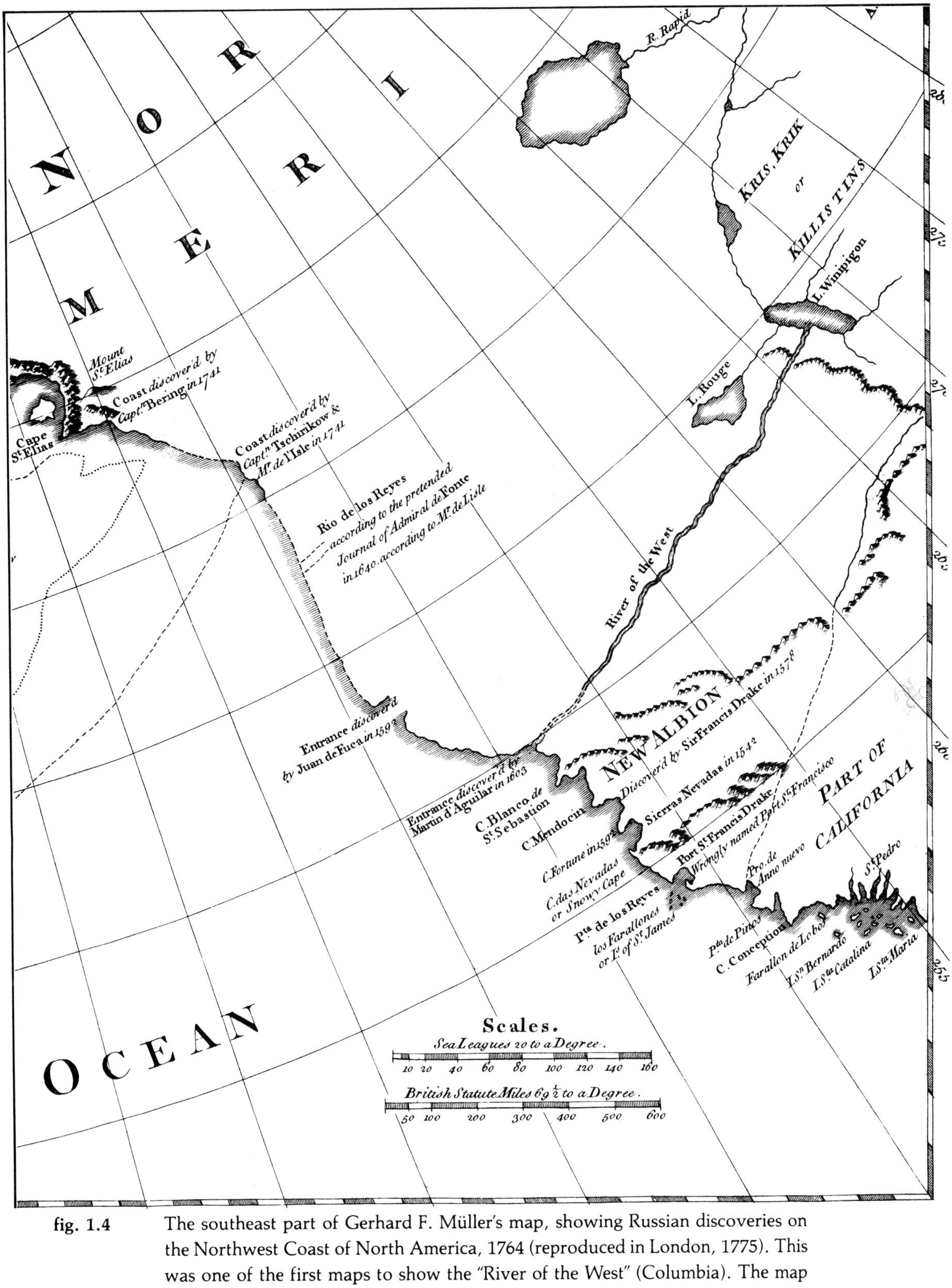
N O R
A M E R I
Mount St. Elias
Cape St. Elias
Coast discover'd by Captn. Bering in 1741
Coast discover'd by Captn. Tschirikow & Mr. de l'Isle in 1741
Rio de los Reyes according to the pretended Journal of Admiral de Fonte in 1640, according to Mr. de Lisle
R. Rapid
KRIS, KRIK or KILLISTINS
L. Winipigon
L. Rouge
River of the West
Entrance discover'd by Juan de Fuca in 1592
Entrance discover'd by Martin d'Aguilar in 1603
C. Blanco de St. Sebastion
C. Mendocin
NEW ALBION
Discover'd by Sir Francis Drake in 1578
Sierras Nevadas in 1542
C. Fortune in 1595
C. das Nevadas or Snowy Cape
Pta. de los Reyes
los Farallones or Is. of St. James
Port St. Francis Drake, Wrongly named Port St. Francisco
Pro. de Anno nuevo
PART OF CALIFORNIA
Pta. de Pinos
C. Conception
Farallon de Lobos
I. Sn. Bernardo
I. Sta. Catalina
I. Sta. Maria
St. Pedro
OCEAN
Scales.
Sea Leagues 20 to a Degree.
10 20 40 60 80 100 120 140 160
British Statute Miles 69 1/2 to a Degree.
50 100 200 300 400 500 600

fig. 1.4 The southeast part of Gerhard F. Müller's map, showing Russian discoveries on the Northwest Coast of North America, 1764 (reproduced in London, 1775). This was one of the first maps to show the "River of the West" (Columbia). The map states: "Entrance discovered by Martin d'Aguilar in 1603"; and "Port St. Francis Drake Wrongly named Port St. Francisco."

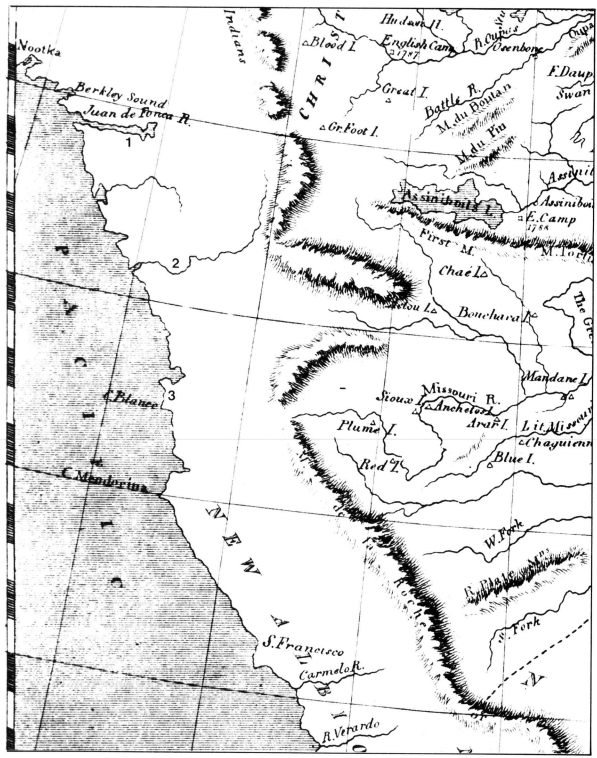

fig. 1.5   Part of the S. Lewis map of "Louisiana" (published in Philadelphia, 1804). This
map shows how little was known of the interior before the Lewis and Clark Expedition. On the coast the Strait of Juan de Fuca appears as a bay (1); also shown
are two rivers, one of which (2) could be the Columbia, and Cape Blanco (3). The
Rocky Mountains are represented by a single irregular ridge, east of which are the
headwaters of the Missouri River (4).

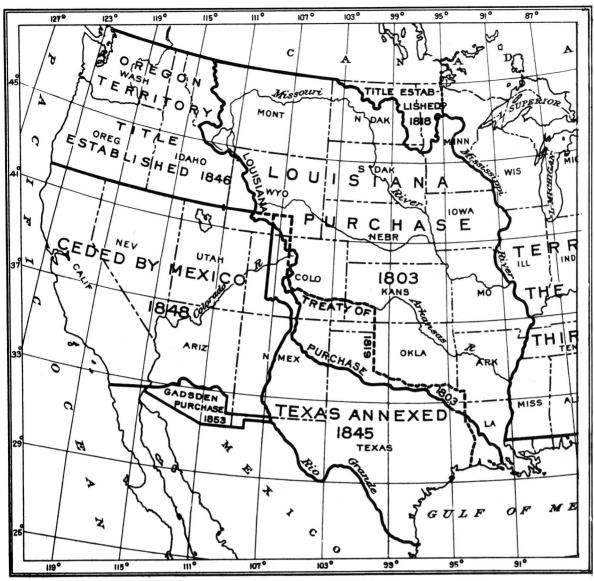

fig. 1.6   The Louisiana Purchase boundary of 1803 was modified by treaties with Great
Britain in 1818 and with Spain in 1819. The title to Oregon Territory was
established in 1846. Earlier the "Oregon Country" was considered to extend from
California to Alaska and eastward to the continental divide. (From *Geological
Survey Bulletin* 1212)

major stream courses, sending individual trappers
up the tributaries and along Indian trails wherever
possible, especially in western Oregon, often using
Indian guides. Observations were mostly concerned with beaver and the vegetation eaten by
them, especially willow, aspen, and poplar; game
for food; and grass for their horses. The weather
came in for many remarks. Peter Skene Ogden, in
the Rogue River Valley in February 1827, wrote:
"a fine Country and probably no Climate in any

Country equal to it." When, a few days later, there
was a heavy snowfall, he could only note:
"Strange weather."[8] In 1826, A. R. McLeod traveled south along the Oregon coast and up the Coquille River, looking for a good route from the interior to the coast. He followed "a well worn [In-
dian] trail leading from village to village.... It
was not a trail for horse travel."[9]

Among the earliest fur traders in Oregon was
Jedediah Smith[10] who entered from California in

7

1828, traveled along the coast to the Umpqua River, thence inland (after most of his party was massacred by Indians) and north to the Hudson's Bay Company's post of Fort Vancouver. Although Smith's interest was primarily in furs, he was a good observer, noting especially the many areas of grass near the coast suitable for stock farming (see chapter 4). About the same time American fur trappers, based in the Rocky Mountains, were beginning to trap and trade on the eastern fringe of the Oregon Country, competing with the Hudson's Bay men, who were trapping in the Snake River drainage. Some of the Americans carried descriptions of the lands they explored to St. Louis when they sold their furs, but apparently these descriptions had little effect on settlement. Later some of these trappers became guides for the immigrant trains on the Oregon Trail.

OREGON AS SEEN IN THE EAST

A number of events focused the attention of the people of the eastern seaboard on Oregon. The purchase of Louisiana in 1803 (**fig. 1.6**), the expedition of Lewis and Clark in 1804–1806 were merely highlights in a series of developments. The publication of William Cullen Bryant's poem, *Thanatopsis*, in 1817 did much to bring the name "Oregon" into popular usage. Previously the region had been known vaguely as the "American West." Bryant got the name, Oregon, from Jonathan Carver's *Travels*, published in London in 1778. Carver described this "Great River of the West" and showed the upper reaches on his map. In 1819 the treaty with Spain for the annexation of Florida fixed the southern boundary of Oregon, on paper, as the 42nd parallel. Five years later a treaty with Russia established the boundary with Alaska at latitude 54°40′ N, a line that at present forms part of the boundary between Canada and Alaska. These events, together with bits of information derived mainly from the fur traders, led to an active debate concerning the nature of the Oregon Country and the desirability of acquisition by the United States.

THE OREGON QUESTION IN CONGRESS

The United States acquired a claim to the Oregon Country in 1819 (Britain also claimed it), and almost immediately Congress began to debate the "Oregon Question." Congressmen, like most people, knew very little about the subject. After some years of debate they still knew very little; reliable information was not generally available. In 1828 Senator Edward Bates of Missouri noted: "As yet we know little of the geography of that country."[11] The major questions were whether to annex Oregon, which would involve contesting the British occupation, and if annexed, how the country could be settled and protected. The arguments raged for several years, pro and con.

PRO: Oregon would provide room for the expanding population. (The United States population in 1820 was less than 10 million.

It would have great strategic value. (Many did not like the idea of Britain or perhaps Russia establishing colonies on the Pacific Coast.)

Annexation would facilitate whaling and the fur trade.

CON: Oregon was too far away, too isolated, separated by broad deserts and lofty mountains. One "pro" senator answered this argument by saying, "We will build a canal to Oregon."

The coast of Oregon is rugged, "iron bound," and entrance to the Columbia River is hindered by a dangerous bar.

Annexation would result in the establishment of a colony on the Pacific Coast that would ultimately secede and form a rival nation.

In 1821, one of the "pro" congressmen, John Floyd of Virginia, prepared a report arguing the feasibility of a transcontinental water route to Oregon, essentially the same as that of Lewis and Clark, which would involve "a single portage of only 200 miles." He apparently did not know that in 1812 Robert Stuart had followed a much easier route which was to become the Oregon Trail. Floyd proposed the establishment of agricultural colonies at the mouth of the Columbia River, with a port, a customhouse, and an Indian agent. Floyd introduced a bill to implement his report but it was defeated.[12] However, the debate continued; in the period from 1823 to 1827 several other bills were introduced in Congress, intended to settle the Oregon Question, but all of them failed to pass. It was not until some thousands of settlers had moved into the area that action was taken to establish the northern boundary. The slogans "All of Oregon" and "Fifty-four forty or fight" were

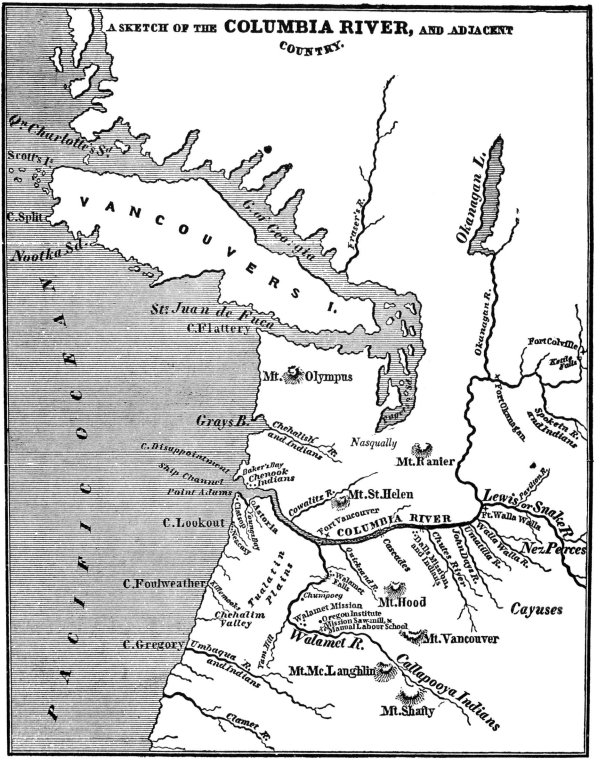

A SKETCH OF THE **COLUMBIA RIVER,** AND ADJACENT COUNTRY.

fig. 1.7   The Lee and Frost map of Oregon, 1844. The missionaries were evidently unfamiliar with much better maps of this time. "Mt. Shasty" is shown in Oregon
near the upper "Walamet River." Settlements are shown at Astoria, Fort Vancouver, and "Walamet Falls " (Oregon City), and missions on the Clatsop Plains,
on the middle Walamet River, and at "Dalls" (The Dalles).

9

heard until 1846 when the 49th parallel was established as the northern boundary.

MISSIONARIES AND INDIANS

The missionaries who came to Oregon in the 1830s were interested mainly in saving the Indians' souls and in establishing farms, in that order. They found fewer Indians than anticipated because of the ravages of diseases, and found the Indians less amenable to conversion. As a result, they gave more attention to farming and commerce and less to the Indians.

The missionaries disagreed amongst themselves about both the nature of the Indians and the quality of the land for farming. In 1835 the Reverend Samuel Parker visited Oregon as commissioner for the Methodist Missions (fig. 1.7). His task was to select sites for mission establishment and to make a reconnaissance of the region. "The Indians," he wrote, "are scrupulously honest in all their dealings, and lying is scarcely known. They say they fear to sin against the Great Spirit, and therefore they have but one heart, their tongue is straight and not forked."[13] Parker obviously had few direct dealings with the Indians. His fellow missionaries, as well as the explorers and fur traders, disagreed. Rev. D. Lee and Rev. J. H. Frost in *Ten Years in Oregon*[14] wrote: "They [the Indians] are both thieves and liars, and [as for their morals] in two instances 'attempts' were made on *white* ladies who resided among them."

The missionaries also differed as to the number of Indians in Oregon. The Reverend Mr. Parker estimated 50,000 between the California border and the 47th parallel. Perhaps he exaggerated a bit for the benefit of the mission headquarters in the East. Lee and Frost were inclined to agree with Wilkes (see chapter 3) in his estimate of 20,000. In contrast to Parker's view of the Indians was that of Rev. H. K. Hines and the Reverend Mr. Kone, assigned to set up a mission for the Umpquas. "The Indians," they wrote, "were few and scattered, degraded and cruel."[15] The plan to establish a mission was abandoned.

There were different opinions as to the quality of the land. Daniel Lee assessed correctly the difference in climate between the Willamette Valley and the Clatsop Plains, waxing eloquent about the latter: "In the month of May all nature puts on a smiling aspect and life and vigor pours through every vein of animated nature." But both Jason Lee and J. H. Frost, in separate articles, described the soil of the Plain as sandy, light, and poor (as indeed it was).

BOOKS AND GUIDES

After 1830 a number of books and reports on Oregon appeared, some of them based on firsthand observations. The principal firsthand contributors were the fur traders and missionaries. Paul J. Carey's *Geographical Sketch of the Part of the Country Called Oregon* appeared in 1830. John B. Wyeth's *Oregon* was published in 1833, and Washington Irving's *Astoria* in 1836. The voluminous reports of Charles Wilkes and John C. Frémont were published in 1845 and 1846. Both accounts were based on extensive travel in Oregon and included much new map information (see chapter 5).

In the 1840s immigrant guides and pamphlets were numerous but not always reliable; many were designed to lure immigrants to Oregon. One of the best-known guides was published by Lansford Hastings in 1845.[16] Hastings had come to Oregon with an immigrant train in 1842, left shortly for California, and then returned to the East. His description of the climate must have confused and discouraged some immigrants: "One day," he wrote of eastern Oregon, "you have the extreme heat of a southern summer, and the next, the excessive cold of a northern winter.... There are other portions of this section where, in the short space of 24 hours, you experience four distinct changes, corresponding in temperature, with a northern spring, summer, autumn and winter. The mercury in Fahrenheit's scale rising to 50° in the morning, to 120° at noon, and falling again to 50° in the evening, and to 12° below zero at night." Perhaps to lure prospective farmers, he wrote: "Having sowed your wheat, and having harvested it, a spontaneous growth will spring up the succeeding year, and you will receive a very good crop without a second sowing."

Some of the immigrant guides included fairly good maps of the Oregon Trail, the California Trail, and the bordering lands. The map in Horn's *Overland Guide to California and Oregon* was published by J. H. Colton in New York in 1852. The trails are clearly shown, with the major rivers and their tributaries. A few distances along the Oregon Trail from the Missouri River are shown in miles. The general locations of most of the major Indian tribes are indicated. Relief features are sketchy and inaccurate: the Blue Mountains extend as a single ridge into California to the east of Summer Lake; Mt. McLoughlin is located at the headwaters of the Willamette River; and Steens Mountain is not shown. Apparently most features were taken from Abert's map of 1838 but without benefit of Wilkes' map of 1841 (see chapters 4 and 5).

Many people, lacking specific information about Oregon, tended to extend the qualities of the Great Plains to Oregon, unlikely as that may seem today. At the same time that Lewis and Clark were crossing the Plains via the Missouri River, Zebulon Pike was crossing them further south. Of the Plains near the Rocky Mountains, Pike reported, "This region may become as celebrated as the sandy wastes of Africa.... [There are] tracts of many leagues where the wind has thrown up sand in all the fanciful forms of the ocean's wave, and on which not a speck of vegetable matter exists."[17] Others reported that the Great Plains were little better than a desert, uninhabitable, and would surely remain as a barrier to any sizable western expansion. Descriptions of the Great Plains, often exaggerated, were used as arguments against the annexation of Oregon.

Inevitably comparisons were made with California. Eugène Duflot de Mofras, sent to western North America by the French government in 1841, and having spent some time in California and several weeks in the Willamette Valley, compared them: "The Americans [in Oregon] are not unaware that the southern provinces [California] are much superior to the northern provinces of Oregon, and aside from a more agreeable climate and more fertile soil, they possess inexhaustible mineral wealth."[18] Duflot de Mofras found the French settlers in the Willamette Valley contented with their farms and their Indian wives. They were loyal to the Hudson's Bay Company, to the Pope, and to Queen Victoria, apparently in that order.

Comparisons, along with utopian ideas and flattering phrases, continued for many years after the state had been explored and settled. (In fact they are not unknown today.) In 1865 Samuel Bowles in *Across the Continent* wrote: "I was prepared for California. But Oregon is more of a revelation. It has rarer natural beauties, richer resources, a larger development, and a more promising future than I had learned of." Later he

wrote: "We were led down into this indeed paradisical [Willamette] valley.... The Californians call their northern neighbors the Web Feet; and from all accounts there is something too much of rain and mud during the winter season; but the fertility and perfection which its agriculture enjoys in consequence leave the practical side of the joke with the Oregonians."[19] Bowles would probably be surprised, were he alive today, to learn that California has ten times as many people as Oregon.

Some early descriptions of Oregon were intentionally and perhaps mischievously deceptive. James Neall and friends, traveling eastward from Oregon, met a party of immigrants heading for Oregon. He wrote in his diary:

It would be amusing if I could describe how one of our party would dilate upon the country we had left [Oregon], upon its hardships and worthlessness, to one group of anxious listeners, while another, like myself with exalted notions of its beauty, fertility and its great possibilities, would be extolling it without measure to another group within easy hearing. Missouri damned it and Maine considered it a Paradise.[20]

The settlers themselves came under the same keen scrutiny as the land, and opinion was divided. Lieutenant Neil M. Howison, in 1846, gave a professional opinion: "The population of the territory are honest, brave, and hardy."[21] Peter H. Burnett was more specific: "Among the men who went to Oregon the year I did [1843], some were idle, worthless young men, too lazy to work at home, and too genteel to steal.... But when they arrived in Oregon they were compelled to work or starve.... I never saw so fine a population, as a whole community, as I saw in Oregon most of the time while I was there."[22]

PLACE NAMES

Early perceptions of Oregon found expression in the place names given to various features by explorers and settlers.[23] In many instances the name derived from a single event but took on a descriptive meaning to those who were unaware of the specific incident, as time went on. The name "Malheur River" (later a county), given by French-speaking fur traders, was based on an "unfortunate" incident in which furs were stolen by the Indians. But some people read the name as "unhappy," in a descriptive sense. "Hardscrabble

Creek" (Linn County), a name repeated several times in the West, suggested the poor soil in this area. "Hungry Hill" in Josephine County indicated only a temporary lack of food but is nonetheless an unflattering name. "Oasis" in Gilliam County described a small area with a good spring, in an otherwise semiarid area. "Folly Farm" (Malheur County), a name applied humorously by the owner, must have suggested to some people that farming in the area was hazardous, as indeed it was.

Gradually some of the misconceptions and contradictions concerning the Oregon Country were resolved. But the tendency to apply descriptions of part of the region to the whole persisted. One of the first to recognize the need for regional subdivisions was Joshua Pilcher, who, in a long letter to the secretary of war in 1831, outlined three major regions in the Oregon Country:

The country must be viewed under three distinct regions —

1st. The mountain region, drained by the upper waters of the Multnomah [Willamette below the Falls], Lewis's [Snake] river, Clark's [Columbia] river, and McGilvray's [Kootenay?] river; all of which fall into the Columbia on its south side.

2d. The plains which lay between the foot of the mountains and the head of tide water.

3d. The tide water region, which extends from the foot of the plains to the sea.[24]

Pilcher was naturally a little vague concerning the boundaries of his regions but he described each, admitting that his personal observations were mostly in the first region. He was impressed by the numerous areas of level land in the mountain region:

Lewis's river, where I crossed it, affords some very extensive fertile low grounds [Snake River Plain], which appeared suitable for any kind of culture. The valleys were well covered with such grass; . . . white clover in great abundance, . . . blue grass, timothy, and clover were common in the country . . . .

The second region, consisting of the plains, is sandy, destitute of timber, quite unfit, in general, for cultivation, and famous only for the fine horses that are found among the Indians.

The third region is heavily timbered, and intermixed with considerable tracts of fertile soil, and, towards the sea, is bound in by mountains [the Coast Range] . . . through which all the waters of the valley of the Cumberland [Columbia] issue, by one channel, into the ocean.

Pilcher compared western Oregon to the Alleghenies. "To the question, how far a nation of people could subsist west of the Rocky mountains, it might be answered, comparatively, by referring to the east side of the Alleghanies [sic]. The resources of agriculture might be something inferior; for grazing and raising stock, superior; and for the salmon fishery, perhaps the very finest in the world."

Among the early settlers in Oregon, David Newsom was a keen and informed observer. He visited many parts of western Oregon, interviewed many settlers, and wrote critical and informative letters to Oregon and eastern newspapers.[25] He arrived in Oregon in 1851 and settled on a claim northeast of Salem, at the confluence of Abiqua Creek and Pudding River. He built a sawmill, planted an orchard, and engaged in general farming. On August 27, 1852, he wrote:

Editor Illinois Journal: I am well pleased with Oregon; and the exceedingly valuable claim which I own, and have proven up here, has made ample amends for all my losses and hardships on the plains. I have never regretted leaving Illinois, and had my success been far less than it has, I should still have been contented here . . . . Here we do not dread the approach of a long and dreary winter; no corn to cut up for stock; no shelters to build for them; no young stock to perish with cold; no wheat crops winter killed; no bank rags, nor empty "promises to pay," but gold and silver in abundance, and all the elements of great wealth and general prosperity with us here.

Although generally optimistic, he was very much aware of Oregon's shortcomings. In June 1854, Newsom wrote: "The dark cloud which has over-shadowed this country, is, to some extent, passing away, and a clearer sky is discernable [sic] in the distance. The vast amount of United States and Chili [sic] produce, which glutted the California and Oregon markets, and stagnated our own sales, is now either consumed or sent off to Europe and Asia, and a good demand has lately sprung up for Oregon produce." Later, in October of the same year (to the *Illinois Journal*) Newsom observed: "But as times are becoming worse and worse here, I may as well let you and your readers know how we are getting along in this far-off land. Well, as to money, we are not troubled with it. After the explosion of the State Bank of Illinois, you all thought that money was scarce; but it was pleasant compared with what is here now."

Thomas Vaughan sums up David Newsom's contribution in his foreword to *David Newsom: The Western Observer*: "David Newsom is unique. He was a keen and industrious observer, and he never quit. No other Western observer commented in quite such fashion or for so long upon so many matters of public and personal concern."

It is obvious from the "perceptions" of early Oregon cited above that knowledge of the country before settlement was sketchy and, in many cases, mistaken and misleading. This is not surprising considering its limited contact by Americans, many of whom were by no means trained observers. The very name of the region was in doubt. It was variously called "Columbia" (by the British), "The Territory of Oregon" (in Congressional Reports), "The Basin of the Columbia," "The American West," or just "Oregon." This must have been very confusing. Whatever term was used, it was customary at first to include all the country that is presently Oregon, Washington, and Idaho. But gradually, interest centered on the Willamette Valley, and by the time the first immigrant wagons began to roll, "Oregon" meant just one thing — the Willamette Valley. All the rest was just so much dry, rugged country to be endured in order to reach that goal. In the next chapter, an overview and preview, some present-day perceptions of Oregon are presented, as a background for the chapters to follow.

2 OREGON FROM THE AIR — OVERVIEW AND PREVIEW

A new scale in time and space has been added to our mental and material equipment.
E. A. GUTKIND

The early descriptions of Oregon, factual, flattering, or derogatory, did not do justice to the diversity of the land where settlement began nearly a century and a half ago. Today it is comparatively easy to see the variety of natural features on which the pioneers and their descendants built the Oregon of today. The quickest way to appreciate the variety of landscape and to introduce the study of historical geography is to view Oregon from the air. In so doing, we can locate and describe some of the important features that have played roles in the growth of the state.

Seen from a low-flying aircraft, the regional diversity of Oregon is apparent; the landscape can be observed as a whole and in great detail with the three-dimensional quality of a model. Mountains, plateaus, plains, and hills give the surface an irregular contour and pattern. Forests, grasslands, sagebrush, and cultivated fields give varying colors to the land—colors that change with the seasons. The vegetation gives a clue to the climate also, dense forests with undergrowth indicating the mild, humid climates; open pine forest outlining the districts of moderate rain; sagebrush suggesting the lands of little rain—the deserts and steppes. The most fascinating features of all are man and his works. The people themselves appear as tiny dots on the landscape, but man's work looms larger. Structures of all kinds, including factories, dams, and airports, stand out in the landscape. Lines of communication—roads, railroads, power lines, even pipelines—leave their mark on the land. On the ground one is too close to the local scene to comprehend the broader perspective of the region.

Sparing us the hazards or expense of air travel, aerial photographs make it possible to study the surface at leisure. Photographs taken from great heights tend to make even a mountain appear flat, but a stereoscope, used with overlapping photographs, brings out the third dimension.

Whether the land is seen directly from the air or in aerial photographs, the observer can see only what he is prepared to see; studies of books, maps, and the ground are necessary. Interpretation of aerial views is a highly sophisticated discipline. Even the most skilled technician cannot do without ground studies. From the air or from the photos, he can see field patterns but not farm or county boundaries, streets but not street names; in fact, from the air, most features are nameless.

The flight plan we shall follow (**fig. 2.1** and **fig. 2.2**) is designed to reach all the major regions of the state and to take us over or near many historic sites. From Portland we fly near U.S. Highway I-5 to Salem, Eugene, Roseburg, Grants Pass, Medford, and Jacksonville; thence almost due west to Gold Beach; then north, near U.S. Highway 101, to Coos Bay, Reedsport, Newport, Tillamook, and Astoria; then near U.S. Highway 30 to Portland. Next we go near U.S. Highway 26 to Barlow Pass and Madras; thence near U.S. Highway 97 to Bend—detour over Crater Lake—and Klamath Falls; then in a straight line to Burns—detour over Owyhee Reservoir—to Ontario; from there near U.S. Highway I-80N to Farewell Bend, Baker, La Grande, Pendleton, The Dalles, and Portland.

The following regions are described in order:
1. Willamette Valley
2. Klamath Mountains
3. Coast Range
4. Cascades
5. Basin-Range
6. High Lava Plains

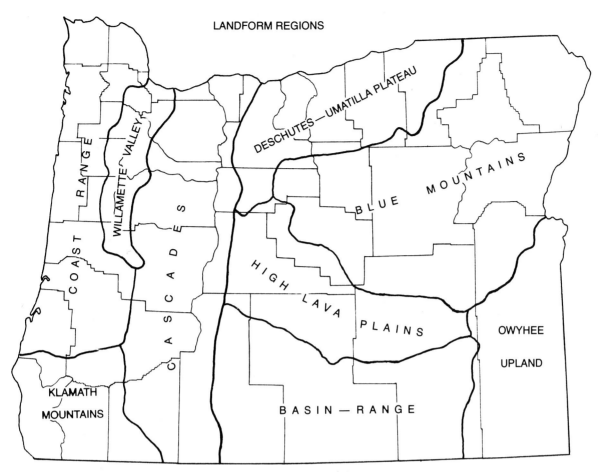

fig. 2.1   The landform regions of Oregon.

7. Owyhee Upland
8. Blue Mountains
9. Deschutes-Umatilla Plateau

WILLAMETTE VALLEY

It is most appropriate that a study of Oregon geography should begin at Portland (fig. 2.3), near the confluence of the Columbia and Willamette rivers (1).* This urban area, including the smaller cities in the vicinity (Oregon City was the goal of the first settlers, but Portland with its more favorable site soon outgrew it), is the hub of population, industry, and commerce of Oregon. It is the "focus on the rim."

As we take off from the Portland Airport, the Columbia River is below us and on its north bank is Vancouver, Washington, which played an important part in the history of Oregon. Here the im-

migrants, who had finished their journey by river, arrived, often broke and hungry, to be fed, supplied with seed, implements, and livestock, and sent on to the Willamette Valley by Dr. McLoughlin, the factor for the Hudson's Bay Company. Vancouver is still very much a part of the Portland urban area. To the west is the confluence of the Willamette and Columbia rivers, inconspicuous from a canoe and missed by Lewis and Clark as they canoed along the north shore of the Columbia on both their westward and eastward journeys. (Clark later turned back and explored the Willamette as far as Swan Island.)

Turning south we get a view of Willamette Falls and Oregon City, an early break point for waterborne traffic, later a source of power. Oregon City was the first capital of Oregon and for several years was the largest city, but its restricted site made it difficult for the city to grow.

The Willamette Valley is the storehouse of

* Boldface numbers correspond with those marked on flight lines in fig. 2.2.

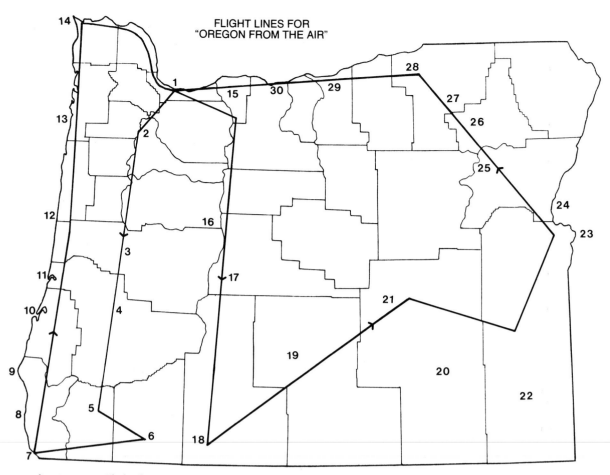

FLIGHT LINES FOR "OREGON FROM THE AIR"

fig. 2.2   Flight lines corresponding to the descriptions in this chapter (see bold face numbers). Numbers are keyed to the text. (Many readers will find it helpful to have a highway map of Oregon at hand as this chapter is being read.)

Oregon and reveals in its pattern of land use its dense population as compared with the other regions. Much of the land was originally prairie instead of forest, additional land has been cleared, and now the only extensive woodland is along the stream courses and on the crests of some of the hills. Grain farms, dairy farms, and orchards are the major features in the rural landscape. Cities are more closely spaced and larger than in the other regions of Oregon (fig. 2.4).

To the west are the rounded, wooded hills and cut-over slopes of the Coast Range, above which, here and there, rise grass-covered peaks, such as Saddle Mountain to the northwest and Marys Peak to the southwest. The Coast Range protects the Willamette Valley somewhat from the storms and heavy rains of the coast. To the east the Cascade Range with its snow-covered peaks, such as Mt. Hood and Mt. Jefferson, forms a barrier of

some consequence, especially in winter; but it also supplies great quantities of water for cities and for irrigation.

Continuing southward up the river, we approach French Prairie (2), a large area of nearly level land and just what the early settlers were looking for. It was originally settled by French Canadians (retired or unemployed fur trappers and traders). The field pattern is irregular, since the farms were laid out helter-skelter before the Donation Land Act was passed. Champoeg, now a state park, was the first real settlement in this area. It was also the meeting place in 1843 to consider a provisional government for the Oregon Country.

To the southwest of French Prairie is Mission Bottom, where the first missions were established, and beyond is Salem at a point where the Willamette River flows between the Eola and Salem hills

16

fig. 2.3   Portland, looking eastward toward Mt. Hood. The original nucleus of Portland
was in the foreground; later the city expanded to the east side of the Willamette
River. (Oregon Dept. of Transportation)

fig. 2.4   Willamette Valley near Wilsonville, looking east to Mt. Hood and showing alternating woodland and cropland. (Oregon Dept. of Transportation)

(fig. 2.5), making Salem a sort of "pass" city. Salem's central location in the Willamette Valley led to its selection as the capital.

Looking west and slightly north of Salem we see a fairly low section of the Coast Range, marked by the headwaters of the Yamhill River on the east side, and on the west side the headwaters of the Salmon and Nestucca rivers. This forms an easy pass route across the Coast Range and contributes to the importance of Salem as a trade center. On the east side of the Valley and slightly to the south is the Santiam River, which leads to a comparatively easy pass across the Cascade Range.

South of Salem the Willamette Valley opens up in the vicinity of Albany, Corvallis, and Eugene (3). In this area the river tends to hug the west side of the Valley because the streams coming in from the Cascades are so much larger than the Coast

Range streams. It will be noted that throughout the Valley the most important cities are on the Willamette River, in spite of the fact that nowadays river transportation is of little importance. Eugene and Springfield, the second-ranking urban area in Oregon, are at the focal point in the southern end of the Valley, between the confluences of the Coast Fork and the Middle Fork of the Willamette River and of the latter and the McKenzie River. To the east, Eugene has access to the McKenzie and Santiam passes across the Cascade Range. To the west, the Siuslaw River affords a route for rail and highway to the coast. Southward the main highway continues into the Klamath Mountain region, while another main highway goes up the Middle Fork of the Willamette River and crosses the Cascades at Pengra (Willamette) Pass.

18

fig. 2.5   Salem, looking northward, with the State Capitol and Willamette University in
the foreground. The Willamette River is to the left of this view. (Oregon Dept. of
Transportation)

KLAMATH MOUNTAINS

The southern part of the Willamette Valley had scarcely been settled when additional settlers trickled southward into the Umpqua country. From the plane, it is possible to see where they crossed the Calapooya Mountains (4), so named from the Indians who inhabited them, by following up the Coast Fork of the Willamette River, across a low divide to Elk Creek and down that stream to the Umpqua River, then up the looping meanders of the Umpqua River into the Klamath Mountain country. The settlers in the middle part of the Umpqua, in the vicinity of Roseburg, found many small areas of level land suitable for farming. They also found that the climate in summer was noticeably warmer and drier than in the Wil-

lamette Valley. The only trail down Elk Creek continued down the Umpqua River to the coast. This was the easiest way in the early days of traveling from the Willamette Valley to the vicinity of Reedsport and also to Coos Bay.

The Klamath Mountain region of southwestern Oregon extends into California. It is a rugged area, as rough as any part of Oregon, including the Cascades. South of Roseburg it is broken here and there by small basins or plains. One of these is in the vicinity of Grants Pass (5), another in the vicinity of Medford (6) — the Rogue River Valley (fig. 2.6) — and a third is in the upper Illinois Valley near the towns of Kerby and Cave Junction. Parts of the region have individual names, such as the Siskiyou Range on the border of California. The Oregon-California Trail, which led

fig. 2.6   Grants Pass, looking north, with the Rogue River in the foreground. The ridge in
the background is part of the Klamath Mountain region. (Oregon Dept. of
Transportation)

from the Willamette Valley to California, a route now followed by U.S. Highway I-5, was developed and used extensively during the California gold rush. This trail also brought settlers from California into southwestern Oregon after the gold-mining fever in California had begun to die down. At the same time, gold was discovered in a number of places in the Klamath Mountains, stimulating settlers to come into that region.

The broad Rogue River Valley is drained by Bear Creek and is surrounded by hills and mountains. To the east are the Cascades with the almost perfect cone of Mt. McLoughlin rising to an elevation of 9,495 feet. To the south and west are the steep granite ridges of the Siskiyou Mountains, culminating in Mt. Ashland at 7,523 feet. To the north two mesas called Table Rocks, the scene of

an Indian battle, mark the northern border of the basin.

The first settlement in the Rogue River Valley was at Jacksonville on the southwest margin of the basin. This followed the discovery of gold in the vicinity and at several other points in the Siskiyou area. Later on, when the railroad was built through the middle part of the valley, Medford became the most important city.

To the south of Medford and Ashland the Oregon-California Trail, U.S. Highway I-5, and the railroad cross Siskiyou Pass at an elevation of over 4,000 feet. There is also a pass eastward across the Cascades to Klamath Falls. Turning westward from the Rogue River Valley, we fly along the crest of the Siskiyou Mountains, over Mt. Ashland, the highest peak in the Oregon

20

fig. 2.7   Rogue River at Gold Beach. The jetties in the foreground were built to improve
navigation. The town of Gold Beach is to the right of this view. (Oregon Dept. of
Transportation)

Klamath Mountains, to Brookings (7), on the coast near the southwest corner of the state. Brookings has grown rapidly since 1950 and now has a new harbor for barges and fishing boats. Turning north, our flight passes over a very rugged section of the coast, over the highest highway bridge in Oregon and over a striking natural bridge. Passing Cape Sebastian, one of the first points on the Oregon coast to be sighted, we arrive at Gold Beach (8) on the Rogue River (fig. 2.7). This section of the coast has very little level land and, generally, short beaches, separated by steep headlands. To the north of Gold Beach the grassy hills are not so steep, while to the east we see the narrow canyon of the Rogue River, through which no road existed until a few years ago.

Gold Beach was settled largely because of mining activity. The beach sands of this section of the coast, in many cases, contain some finely-divided gold, very difficult to separate from the sands. Gold was also contained in the terrace deposits above the beaches and these proved more satisfactory for mining as long as the supply of gold lasted. Mining here stimulated many settlers to farm, in order to supply the miners with the necessities. And the gold mining in California provided a market for dairy products and other materials that could be shipped out by sea from this area, in spite of the scarcity of good harbors.

Heading north from Gold Beach, above U.S. Highway 101, we pass Humbug Mountain and come to Port Orford, the first settlement in this section of the coast. Port Orford is on a cove or open bay, protected from northwest storms but open to the west and south. It was originally settled for the purpose of landing supplies to the miners inland, and a number of trails were established leading in that direction. These were particularly aimed at the mining settlements along the Rogue River. To the north of Port Orford is a broad marine terrace where a few farmers settled and began to produce milk and butter for the miners and for shipment to San Francisco.

COAST RANGE

North of Cape Blanco (9), the first Oregon name to appear on a map, we pass from the Klamath Mountains to the Coast Range. Our flight goes over a broad terrace with an adjoining beach that leads to the Seven Devils area and Cape Arago. The early travelers used the beach from Bandon; arriving at the Seven Devils area, they took a trail eastward, over the ridges, to South Slough of Coos Bay; traveling by water north to the main part of the bay, they crossed the bay and reached the beach on the north. Jedediah Smith, traveling with horses in 1828, went along the coast over the Seven Devils area and Cape Arago with great difficulty.

The Oregon Coast Range extends from the Coquille River to the Columbia River, a distance of about 200 miles; it is about 70 miles wide in the south, thins down to about 30 miles in the middle part, and is about 50 miles wide at the north. The elevations are much lower than in the Klamath Mountains, but it is still a rugged region with most of the land in slope. Ridges seem to run in every direction, but, from the air, we can see a general tendency to north-south ridges. Most streams, however, tend to flow from the crest either westward to the sea or eastward to the Willamette Valley. Above the general level of the ridges a few peaks stand out. A repeating name is Bald Mountain, since many of the high peaks are not forested and have not been, at least for a long, long time. From the air, the pattern of the various forest types — old forests, cut-overs, burns — is clearly seen. Douglas fir, western hemlock, spruce, and cedar make up most of the timber. These forest areas appear as dark green carpets, completely hiding the surface of the land. Also visible are patches of cleared land, mostly along the narrow flood plains of the streams and around the larger estuaries and bays. The farm land is largely pasture but there are crops, including hay, fruits, cranberries, and various flowers.

On the western margin, the Coast Range breaks off to the sea in alternating headlands and low, narrow coastal terraces. In general the basaltic igneous rocks resist the ravages of the sea and form cliffs, making it difficult to travel along the coast or to construct a road. These are capes and heads — Cape Arago, Heceta Head, Cape Perpetua (fig. 2.8), Yaquina Head, Cascade Head, and Tillamook Head, to mention a few. These prominent features are, in the main, truncated ends of Coast Range ridges, eroded by the sea and yet resisting the waves more effectively than the adjacent areas. These headlands contribute to the character and scenic variety of the Oregon coast. The beaches and coastal terraces are of more direct use. Here the land is level enough for farming and the concentration of population along the terraces and the margins of the streams is notable.

No sooner had settlers moved into the Willamette Valley than a few of them decided to move to the coast. They faced some problems of travel: first, to cross the Coast Range; second, to travel along the coast; and, third, to use the harbors along the coast. A number of passes are available for crossing the Coast Range, easy so far as elevation is concerned but involving some steep slopes. Until roads were constructed there was great difficulty, especially in the winter during the heavy rains. Travel along the coast was also difficult in places, but the beaches did provide a good route, particularly at low tide. Trails across the headlands were more difficult and caused delays in travel. A number of small harbors along the coast were used from the earliest times, but all of them presented difficulties, particularly in crossing the bar at the harbors' mouths. Once one was inside a harbor, such as Coos Bay, Yaquina Bay, or Tillamook Bay, protection was available. But the bar was a constant threat to shipping.

Coos Bay (10) is an irregular estuary of a comparatively small river but it provides the best harbor on the coast of Oregon. In early days people were attracted to it by the level land around it, by the harbor itself, and by the coal beds in the vicinity. Coal was shipped out of Coos Bay in the early 1850s to San Francisco. The bar outside the entrance to the bay is a difficult one and many ships have been wrecked there, including the first coal barge to leave the bay.

North of Coos Bay our flight goes over a fine beach, which extends for 60 miles, broken only by

fig. 2.8   Looking south from Cape Perpetua. U.S. Highway 101 follows close to the rocky shoreline in this section of the Oregon coast. (Oregon Dept. of Transportation)

23

the streams that cross it. This route was traveled from the early days until 1920. It was used, not only by people on foot and on horseback, but by the stagecoach, with ferries provided at the rivers.

In the dune areas near the beach there are a number of fresh-water lakes—Tenmile, Clear, Tahkenitch, Siltcoos, Woahink, for example—most of which have been formed by the choking of stream outlets by dune sand. These lakes were convenient for the early travelers because they provided fresh water. The large streams, of course, are salt in their lower reaches. Today these lakes form an important part of the coast water supply for all the towns and cities and are also used widely for recreation.

The lower Umpqua River (11), with its broad, curving estuary, is now below us; the Umpqua River flows entirely through the Coast Range and provided a water route for early travelers. Its first settlement was at Gardiner on the north bank; Reedsport on the south bank was established later. A trail from the south end of the Willamette Valley reached the Umpqua in the vicinity of present Elkton (the fur post, Fort Umpqua) and continued down the river, which is navigable by small boats from Elkton to the sea.

North of the Umpqua River our flight crosses an extensive area of sand dunes, some active, some wooded, and some recently stabilized with grass. A large area, cut over many years ago, is just beginning to be reforested. This is a part of the Oregon Dunes National Recreation Area, extending from Coos Bay to the Siuslaw River. Florence is located on the north bank of the Siuslaw; jetties at the outlet make it a barge harbor.

The Siuslaw River also flows through the Coast Range, but it was little used for travel in the early days, partly because of the rugged nature of the route with its narrow gorges, but also because this area was a part of a large Indian reservation and was not open to settlement in the earliest years. Later a railroad was constructed, following the river valley, and a modern highway (State Highway 126) makes use of a tunnel to straighten out the route.

As we approach Heceta Head (12) the long beach comes to an end, and from this point northward there are alternate beaches and headlands all the way to the Columbia River. Most of the beaches are short. Sea Lion Caves headland and Heceta Head were the most difficult to cross in the early days because of the steep slopes and high cliffs along the sea. For many years it was not feasible to take horses across this particular area. North of Cape Perpetua our flight passes over an area of beaches, headlands, bays, and towns, including Waldport, Alsea Bay, Yaquina Bay, Newport, Yaquina Head, Cape Foulweather, Depoe Bay, Siletz Bay, and Cascade Head. Just south of Cascade Head the Salmon River flows into the Pacific.

North of Cascade Head is a stretch of beach, backed by low hills, through which U.S. Highway 101 meanders. Cape Lookout (13) points a slender finger to the sea. (It was to have had a lighthouse, but Cape Meares got it by mistake.) Beyond is Netarts Bay, separated from the ocean by a narrow spit; and further north is broad Cape Meares, flanking the south end of Tillamook Bay.

Tillamook Bay, called Quicksand Bay on the early maps, was one of the earliest settlements on the coast. Quicksand occurs at several places on the coast where fine sand and silt are washed into the margins of the estuaries; and it sometimes occurs on the beaches. It is neither deep nor dangerous, however. Tillamook Bay attracted people because of the harbor, in spite of the difficult bar outside the bay, because of the level land produced by the flood plains of five rivers that enter the bay, and because of the abundance of salmon. The early settlers reached Tillamook by going down the Columbia River by boat from Fort Vancouver to Astoria and then overland down the coast. North of Tillamook Bay only two large headlands extend out from the coast, Cape Falcon and Tillamook Head, the latter 40 miles to the north of the bay. Otherwise beaches were available for travel.

North of Tillamook Head are the Clatsop Plains, which were settled in the early 1840s, actually the first settlement along the coast. This is a broad, sandy area that has been built out with sand from the Columbia River, much of it within historic times. But it was not a favorable location for pioneer farming because the sandy soils were especially subject to drought in the long, dry summers. Many of the farmers who at first settled here decided to move to Tillamook after a few years of crop failure (fig. 2.9).

Astoria (14) was the first trading post in Oregon. The location is on the peninsula between the Columbia River and Youngs River and Bay on the south. Astoria is about eight miles from the Columbia Bar. At first glance this would seem to

fig. 2.9   Tillamook looking south and showing a portion of the Tillamook Plain. (Oregon
Dept. of Transportation)

be an ideal location for a big city and, in the early days, many people thought that Astoria would be the largest in the Northwest. They thought of it as having the whole Columbia River drainage as its hinterland. Astoria, however, has several disadvantages. The estuary of the Columbia here is so wide that bridge building is difficult and was delayed to very recent times, thus denying Astoria access to the country north of the Columbia River. The site of the city on the margins of Coxcomb Hill is not really suitable for a large city. Another factor of great importance is the fact that the immediate hinterland of Astoria is not very productive. In any event, Astoria grew in the early days and then settled down to periods of slow growth and even some losses.

From Astoria to Portland our route is never far from the Columbia River as it passes through the northern end of the Oregon Coast Range. The Columbia River is wide near Astoria (up to six miles wide) and widens again near Portland, but in between the river is comparatively narrow and is bordered in many places by high cliffs. This makes it a rather poor route for a road or railroad; when a railroad was constructed from Portland to Astoria it was necessary to provide tunnels at several locations to get through spurs of the Coast Range. (U.S. Highway 30 in many places leaves the river and goes over the hills to avoid the steep terrain.) The river has many islands and many side channels or sloughs. The wide parts of the river provide some hazards in times of high winds for small boat traffic. Lewis and Clark, arriving at the lower Columbia, were pinned down in a very small camp on the north side for several days, because the water was too rough for canoe travel. But, on the whole, the river affords such good water transportation that a trail was hardly necessary in the early days. Today, a channel deep enough for ocean-going ships is maintained by constant dredging, making Portland and Vancouver the most important ports on the lower Columbia.

CASCADE RANGE

Again over Portland, our route continues eastward over the Cascade Range south of Mt. Hood, near U.S. Highway 26, and then southward along the eastern margin of the Cascades, near U.S. Highway 97, to the Klamath Falls area. This route affords a view of the High Cascades and also of the western parts of the Deschutes-Umatilla Plateau, the High Lava Plains, and the Basin-Range regions (see fig. 2.1).

Approaching the Mt. Hood area (15), the barrier confronting the immigrants is apparent (fig. 2.10). In the Columbia Gorge steep cliffs made land travel impossible until a road and railroad were constructed. It was obviously necessary to find a route for wagons, and the best route was south of Mt. Hood at Barlow Pass, followed today by U.S. Highway 26. From the air, the difficulties are obvious, not only steep slopes but swampy areas. The route was explored in 1845 and 1846, a crude road was built for which toll was charged, and many thousands of immigrants used it. The alternative was to abandon the wagons and finish the journey below The Dalles by water, risking the hazards of the rapids.

The Cascade Range is the most important barrier in Oregon. From the Columbia River to the Klamath River in California no stream cuts across the range. All the crossings must be at high passes, many of them four or five thousand feet high. Below us we can see many gaps and passes but only a few are used. The next important pass south of Barlow Road is Santiam Pass (16), over which U.S. Highway 20 now climbs. South of that we can see McKenzie Pass (State Highway 242) which is closed in the winter. There is heavy traffic over Willamette Pass (Pengra Pass) followed by State Highway 58; this is also essentially the route followed by the Southern Pacific Railroad, the only railroad that crosses the Oregon Cascades south of the Columbia River. Two passes in the vicinity of Crater Lake are scarcely through highways. However, State Highway 138 by way of Diamond Lake and State Highway 62, which goes through Crater Lake National Park, do actually cross the Cascade Range. South of this area a new highway (State Highway 140) and an older one (State Highway 66) connect the Medford-Ashland area with Klamath Falls.

Looking north and south along the backbone of the Cascade Range, the most impressive points are the high peaks: Mt. Hood to the north, and Mt. Jefferson, Three Fingered Jack, Mt. Washington, and the Three Sisters further south. Below the peaks, the general level appears as a plateau area. It is obvious that the Cascade Range has two distinct parts. The western part is deeply dissected and has a large amount of local relief. The eastern part, sometimes called the High Cascades, is much smoother, although it is by no means flat. How-

fig. 2.10   Relief model of the Cascade Range in the vicinity of Mt. Hood and a part of the
Deschutes-Umatilla Plateau. Mt. Hood is lower left. Also shown are the Gorge of
the Columbia River and the canyons of the Deschutes and John Day rivers. (U.S.
Army Map Service)

ever, the eastern part can be described as a rough
plateau, above which rise the various peaks,
buttes, and mesas. Looking eastward we see the
Deschutes-Umatilla region, a fine example of a
plateau.

Our flight goes over the upper part of the Warm
Springs Indian Reservation, a large tract of land
now owned and operated by the Indians, who are
prosperous as the result of timber harvest and a
very attractive resort around the hot springs.

Looking eastward we see the Deschutes River
Canyon and its tributary canyons and, beyond
that, the John Day Canyon. Between the canyons
the land is comparatively level except for some
hills and mounds. Aside from the stream courses
and a few elevated areas, the land is cultivated,
much of it in wheat, and the individual field pat-

terns are discernible. This is the largest wheat-
producing area in Oregon.

Reaching the vicinity of Bend (17), a panorama
of regions, peaks, and other landmarks is spread
out before us. Bend has long been an important
crossroad in central Oregon; it is, among other
things, a "pass city." The route we are following,
along the east side of the Cascades, is an important north-south corridor and the nearby McKenzie and Santiam passes provide east-west routes.
State Highway 242 crosses the McKenzie Pass and
U.S. Highway 20 uses the Santiam Pass. The ap-
proaches to the passes from the east are comparatively easy; Santiam Pass is only about 1,200
feet above Bend. The descent on the western side
is steep and crooked. To the east, U.S. Highway
20 traverses the High Lava Plains to Burns, while

27

U.S. Highway 26 winds through the Blue Mountains. Here, as elsewhere, early trails became highways.

East of Bend are the wooded southern slopes of the Blue Mountains, with numerous east-west ridges and high prairies. To the southeast are the High Lava Plains, sometimes called, incorrectly, the Great Sandy Desert. For the most part, this is a smooth plain, above which rise isolated buttes and small mountains such as the Paulina Mountains to the south of Bend. Paulina Peak has a large crater similar to Crater Lake. The latter's six-mile-wide crater, or caldera, is the remnant of an old volcano that collapsed in glacial times, at the same time spewing out large quantities of pumice. The pumice spread over the surrounding country as far away as Bend. From numerous springs on the margin of the crater, it is evident that water seeps out of the lake; the level nonetheless remains very much the same. Crater Lake has rarely been frozen. It is almost 2,000 feet deep at the deepest place. The surface of the lake is 6,177 feet above sea level. Crater Lake was not discovered until 1853, and then almost by accident, as some prospectors were looking for gold in the area.

Further south, the north-south ridges of the Basin-Range appear, while, to the west of Bend, the Three Sisters peaks stand out above the general level of the High Cascades, along with several lesser peaks and buttes. Mt. Thielson and Mt. McLoughlin show up in the distance, and on a clear day Mt. Shasta can be seen. The Cascade Range continues into California.

BASIN-RANGE

Our flight continues southward along the boundary between the Cascade Range and the Basin-Range region to Klamath Falls at the southern end of Klamath Lake (fig. 2.11). Klamath Falls (18), which was called Linkville in the early days, lies in a trough or down-dropped block typical of the Basin-Range region. The city is flanked on both sides by steep, wall-like scarps that represent faults in the earth's crust and movement along the plane of the breaks. The nearby hills and mountains are in the form of tilted blocks with a steep slope on one side and a gentler slope on the other.

Throughout the Basin-Range region, between the blocks lie the basins, each usually several miles in width, many of them covered with pumice and occupied in part by lakes. Many of the lakes are dry most of the time. A series of these basins can be seen, indicated by Agency Lake, Upper Klamath Lake, the old bed of Lower Klamath Lake, and Tule Lake, part of which is in California. Formerly there were three lakes in the Klamath Falls area. The one to the north is now called Klamath Marsh. (This was mistakenly called Klamath Lake by John C. Frémont when he traveled through this country in 1843.) The present Upper Klamath Lake is the middle one and is the largest lake in Oregon. Because it is close to the mountains, it receives quite a bit of drainage from the Cascade Range. Further south, partly in California, is the original Lower Klamath Lake. This has been completely drained and much of the lake bed has been put under cultivation, using water from Upper Klamath Lake.

From the air, the eastern view presents a series of rims and basins as far as the eye can see. This is a part of a very large region that extends all the way from southern Oregon to Mexico City. It consists of alternating long ranges with basins in between. Many of the basins contain playa lakes—shallow lakes in glacial times, when the country was more humid. A few lakes still exist, like Summer Lake and Goose Lake; others are intermittent. Many of the ranges are wooded. Some of the rims are called mountains, some are called scarps; the basins are sometimes called flats.

From Klamath Falls we cross Modoc Scarp and then Swan Flat to the east of it. Soon another scarp appears, the Yawhee Plateau. Occasionally we see isolated buttes like Yainax Butte, elevation 7,200 feet. We cross the upper reaches of Sprague River, which empties into Upper Klamath Lake, and then come into the Coleman Rim area and the country south of Summer Lake (19), which is more rugged than most of the Basin-Range region. The highest peaks in this area are above 7,000 feet. We fly just south of Lake Abert, which occupies a trough between Abert Rim and Coglar Rim. In other words, it is in a down-dropped block or graben. East of Abert Rim there is a broad valley, part of which is called Warner Valley, with a few hills rising above the general level.

Farther east we see Hart Mountain, also called Poker Jim Ridge in the northern part. The steep slope is to the west, the gentle slope to the east. Part of Hart Mountain is reserved for an antelope refuge. Far beyond, visible on a clear day at the

fig. 2.11   Abert Rim in south-central Lake County is a typical Basin-Range feature. The steep-faulted face is surmounted by a gently sloping summit. Abert Lake occupies a part of the basin between Abert Rim and Coglar Rim on the west. Abert Rim rises approximately 2,000 feet above the lake. (Oregon Dept. of Transportation)

eastern margin of the Basin-Range region, is Steens Mountain (20) with gentle, almost plateau-like western slopes and a steep eastern scarp. This long, narrow ridge, typical of the Basin-Range country, reaches an elevation of 9,354 feet. This is the highest and the grandest of the region's ranges, high enough to have been modestly glaciated.

HIGH LAVA PLAINS

Continuing northeast, we enter the eastern part of the High Lava Plains, much more level than the Basin-Range. The transition line is difficult to mark exactly, but once we are over this transition zone, the difference in character is evident. The general level of the country is about 4,000 feet, above which rise a few isolated conical peaks.

Wagontire Mountain, for example, is 6,500 feet in elevation and Glass Buttes, composed of obsidian, reach 6,390 feet. As we approach Harney and Malheur lakes (21), the Blue Mountains to the north are very clear in the distance and the scarp or dividing line between the High Lava Plains and the Blue Mountains is clearly indicated. Malheur Lake gets most of its water from the Blue Mountains by way of the Silvies River, but also receives water from the west slope of Steens Mountain by way of the Donner und Blitzen River. Malheur Lake usually has an outlet into Harney Lake, which has no outlet and is sometimes completely dry. The waters of Malheur Lake are often fairly potable but the water in Harney Lake is salt and not drinkable. From this area, looking off to the southeast, we get a good view of Steens Mountain.

fig. 2.12   Owyhee Reservoir. The reservoir's water is used for irrigation further north in
both Oregon and Idaho. (Oregon Dept. of Transportation)

30

OWYHEE UPLAND

On an easterly course from Malheur Lake, our route takes us over the northern part of the Owyhee Upland (**22**). This is, in general, a dissected plateau. Parts of it are less dissected and fairly level at the upper elevations, but canyons of the Owyhee and Malheur rivers and their tributaries have made a rugged area of the northern part. To the south of our route, flat-topped Saddle Butte and many other mesas can be seen. As we come into view of the Owyhee River, one of its tributaries, Jordan Creek, and the town of Rome are visible. This is the central district for the Basque people who moved into eastern Oregon very early to herd sheep, often taking them to Steens Mountain in summer. Here the Owyhee River flows in a broad valley bordered by low cliffs. But, as we continue down the river, the Owyhee Canyon (**fig. 2.12**), which is occupied in part now by a reservoir, has very steep sides and high ground around it. Some of the high country above includes flats, often called meadows or basins. Unlike the basins of the Basin-Range region, these are at the higher elevations rather than at the lower. To the north of our course is the Malheur River, which drains the southern part of the Blue Mountains as well as part of the Owyhee Upland and joins the Snake River at Ontario. The confluence of the Owyhee River with the Snake marks the point at which the 117th meridian runs south from the Snake River to the 42nd parallel to form part of the boundary of eastern Oregon. Here, in the vicinity of Vale and Ontario (**23**), there is a fair amount of level land, which was passed over by the early immigrants because of the widespread growth of sagebrush. It is now cultivated with the aid of water from the Malheur River and the Owyhee Reservoir and with water pumped directly out of the Snake River, which is not deeply intrenched at this point. Just across the river in Idaho is the site of Fort Boise; here some of the immigrants crossed the Snake River on their way to the Willamette Valley.

BLUE MOUNTAINS

Our approach to the Blue Mountains region, from the Snake River Plain, is similar to that of the immigrants following the Oregon Trail, now marked out by U.S. Highway I-80N. Flying northwest, the course is over low, arid, dissected hills, only slightly used for grazing and with very little population. The Snake River lies ahead and to the right, following a northwesterly course. At Farewell Bend (**24**) near the town of Huntington, Oregon, the direction and character of the river change as it turns north and enters the gorge leading to Hells Canyon. The route followed by the immigrants, up Burnt River Canyon to the present site of Durkee, was by no means easy in the early days. This was one of the difficult points on a long and arduous trail. The canyon is narrow and the early trail was, in places, on the steep valley walls. Thanks to modern engineering, the route of U.S. Highway I-80N and the Union Pacific Railroad through the canyon is comparatively easy.

A tributary canyon leads up to Baker Basin (**25**), a comparatively level area 15 miles wide and nearly 20 miles in length at an elevation of about 3,500 feet. On the west, the rugged Elkhorn Mountains rise to nearly 9,000 feet; on the northeast are the higher Wallowa Mountains, their glaciated peaks and ridges covered with thin, non-commercial forest. Both of these mountain ranges furnish water to irrigate Baker Basin. The early immigrants ignored these areas as of little value, and it was not until the Willamette Valley was well settled that the discovery of gold brought about permanent settlement in Baker Basin. Gold production continued to be important until World War II.

Passing over a low divide to the north of Baker Basin, our course leads us, via the town of Union, over the Grande Ronde Basin (**26**) and into the drainage of the Grande Ronde River, so called because of the circular pattern of the basin. This landscape is similar to Baker Valley but at a lower elevation, about 2,700 feet. The land use is also clearly like that of Baker Basin with some additional emphasis on fruits. On the west side of the Grande Ronde Basin is the city of La Grande, located at the point where the river emerges from the rougher part of the Blue Mountains. To the east, compact, small, irrigated fields predominate, while on slightly higher ground that cannot be readily irrigated, the large light and dark pattern of wheat and fallow land is to be seen. Above the city to the west rises a steep escarpment of the Blue Mountains. Here the land is much more representative of the Blue Mountains region than are the areas previously seen. From the plane, the land appears as a well-dissected plateau (**fig. 2.13**), the crests of the ridges being of almost uniform eleva-

fig. 2.13   The Blue Mountains between La Grande and Pendleton. In the upper part of the picture is a smooth upland; below, the streams have cut deep valleys. Long, narrow belts of woodland (called shoestrings) are common, especially on north-facing slopes. (Oregon Dept. of Transportation)

32

tion and a network of narrow valleys separating one ridge from another. In some parts, often the highest, the ridge tops are flat, but more often they are gently rounded on top and rather narrow. Emigrant Hill, from which the pioneers obtained their first view of the Deschutes-Umatilla Plateau, can be seen below us. The vegetation pattern varies; the crest of the Blue Mountains is largely forest-covered in the vicinity of La Grande, but to the west more and more patches of grassland appear, until the area of grass seems equal to that of forest. Where the elevation is not too great, the grassy areas are cultivated; otherwise they are used for grazing. As we approach Pendleton, we can see that the Blue Mountains break off in an abrupt scarp to the lower Umatilla Plateau, and the forest and grassland give way to fields of wheat and peas alternating with fallow land.

DESCHUTES-UMATILLA PLATEAU

Our course now leads westward near U.S. Highway I-80N across the Deschutes-Umatilla Plateau, a roughly triangular region nearly 200 miles long and 100 miles wide at the western end. It lies south of the Columbia River, east of the Cascades, and north of the Blue Mountains. In contrast with the Blue Mountains, which it resembles in some respects, the plateau is lower, drier, and less dissected. The elevation varies from a few hundred feet near the Columbia River to nearly 3,000 feet near the Blue Mountains and along the lower slopes of the Cascades. The Deschutes, John Day, and Umatilla rivers, together with their tributaries, have intrenched themselves in this lava plateau to depths that, in some cases, reach several hundred feet. Between the streams are wide, undissected areas, gently rolling, sometimes almost flat. In this region most of Oregon's wheat crop is grown.

Pendleton (27) is the focal point in the eastern part of the region. It lies in and near the valley of the Umatilla River, at the confluence with Wildhorse Creek. The Umatilla here flows to the west and affords a route for the Union Pacific Railroad; this was one of the original routes for the Oregon Trail. U.S. Highway I-80N can be seen leaving the valley west of Pendleton and striking out across the low plateau.

In the vicinity of Pendleton, three routes were available to the immigrants on their way across the Deschutes-Umatilla Plateau. One led north to

Whitman Mission on the Walla Walla River where supplies could be obtained. Another led down the Umatilla River, taking advantage of the water supply, while a third took a shortcut across the plateaus, more or less in the same position as the present U.S. Highway I-80N. The three routes converged near the present town of Boardman.

To the north of Pendleton, the gently rolling plateau lies at an elevation of about 1,500 feet. This is "Palouse" country with rounded, parallel ridges, long, gentle slopes to the north and east, steeper slopes to the south and west. Here and there are shallow V-shaped stream valleys, trending northwest toward the Columbia River. This is excellent wheat country and the checkerboard pattern of cropland and fallow is especially striking in the summer. Near the Columbia River is a large irrigated area using sprinklers (28).

To the west of Pendleton, we can see the change in character of the plateau. The "Palouse" hills disappear and the canyons are deeper. The land between the streams is less rolling. Some valley floors are irrigated and the green fields stand out against the golden wheat lands above, but other valleys, like that of Juniper Creek, have little irrigation. Wheat fields dominate but some areas are too dry for wheat, probably because of the coarse texture of the soils. Still further west we fly over the canyons of the John Day and Deschutes rivers which are still deeply dissected. The John Day (29) enters the Columbia River at a low angle and the intervening ridge is high and steep. Arriving in late summer, the immigrants hurried across this hot, dusty region, not realizing that one day it would become good farming land.

At The Dalles (30) the immigrants faced a decision. Until the Barlow Road was opened, it was impossible to take wagons beyond this point. Some of the immigrants crossed the river to the Washington side and followed an Indian trail to Fort Vancouver. Others risked their lives and property on the Columbia River with its falls and rapids. Flying over the Columbia Gorge today (fig. 2.14) we can see no falls; they are flooded by the waters behind dams. In pioneer days they were a serious hazard, usually requiring portages. (Later highways and railroads were built on both sides of the river, but only after much blasting and tunneling.) Having passed these hazards and reached tidewater, it was easy for the immigrants to proceed by water to Fort Vancouver, Portland, and Oregon City. As we fly over the Columbia Gorge toward Portland and see the rail and high-

fig. 2.14   The Columbia Gorge at Crown Point, looking eastward. In many places the cliffs
bordering the river come down to the water's edge, calling for deep cuts and tunnels for the highways and railroads. (Oregon Dept. of Transportation)

way routes and the barge traffic on the placid reservoirs, it is difficult to appreciate what a barrier this was in pioneer days.

SUMMARY

Our overview and preview are now complete, involving about 1,500 miles and touching all the major regions of Oregon and many places of historic and geographic interest. It is evident that the historical geography of Oregon involves a variety of features, physical and human, some permanent, some ephemeral. Above all, this brief survey shows the importance of place; events do not happen just anywhere, they happen *somewhere*. It is suggested that the Oregon of today is the result of the interaction of peoples and the land over a period of many years. This is the theme of historical geography that the succeeding chapters attempt to portray.

THE IMPACT OF THE INDIANS
ON OREGON

3

Wherever men live they have operated to alter the aspect of the earth.
CARL SAUER

When white explorers, traders, and settlers first arrived in Oregon, Indians had already lived on the land for thousands of years. They had both adapted to the Oregon environment and changed it. The Indians came, explored, noted the resources they could use, and settled, usually near a stream. Undoubtedly they were skilled in fishing, hunting, and gathering before they arrived and needed only to modify their methods to conform to the new environment. They *changed* the environment in a number of ways, some of which were ephemeral; trails and clearings soon disappeared if abandoned, and Indian settlement was a shifting one. But widespread and long-continued burning of the natural vegetation, for which the evidence is clear, had a more lasting effect. With the decline of the Indian population and the advance of white settlement, Indian burning diminished and large areas that had been converted to grassland were gradually reforested. In many areas the dominant species of the new forest was Douglas fir, instead of the original pine and hemlock.[1] This was to be a great boon to the timber industry in the years to come.

The Indian occupation made settlement much easier for the pioneers than it would have been had they come to a virgin land. The burning of the forest, producing large areas of grassland, made it unnecessary for the first settlers to clear land. The Indians had accumulated a vast store of information about the Oregon environment, some of which they passed on to the pioneers—information concerning the plants, fish, game, trails, and rivers. They acted as guides as the whites explored what was to them an unknown land, in which it was easy to get lost. The Indians provided canoes for travel on and across the rivers until the whites could make boats of their own. On the negative side, however, the Indians' thievery and their violent reaction to encroachment on their lands undoubtedly delayed settlement in some parts of Oregon. The "Indian wars" were expensive in lives, time, and money.

HOW THE INDIANS CAME TO OREGON

Very likely the Indians came to Oregon as offshoots of a long-continued migration from eastern Asia to North and South America.[2] The route led northward and eastward along the coast of Siberia, crossing the land bridge at Bering Strait (**fig. 3.1**) which, at its maximum extent, was more than 200 miles wide. At this time, about 11,000 B.C., sea level stood about 300 feet below the present level, making it easy to cross from Asia to North America and to move, either afoot or by small boat, along the coastal margin of North America, where at present it is difficult for people to travel on foot because of steep, rugged headlands.

Perhaps the most important migration route led up the Yukon River Valley to the interior plains, and then south along the eastern front of the Rocky Mountains, but with branches to the Pacific Coast (see **fig. 3.1**). Eventually the Indians continued into Mexico and Central America, where they reached a high degree of cultural development. The Indians of Oregon were in peripheral locations and isolated from one another, and so they did not share in the cultural growth of tribes further east and south. Oregon Indians, for example, had no agriculture and did not work metals. They had no domestic animals except the dog.

If members of one tribe, on a hunting or gathering expedition, passed through the territory of

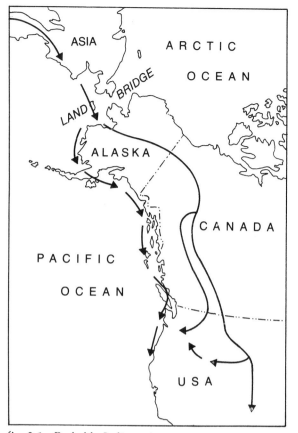

fig. 3.1 Probable Indian migration routes to Oregon across the land bridge between Asia and North America at Bering Strait. During the glacial advances sea level stood as much as 300 feet below the present level, forming the land bridge and making travel along the coast much easier.

another tribe, the contact must have been of minor importance. At the time of first contact with Europeans, the various Oregon tribes were distinct in languages, customs, and tribal organizations. This was especially true in western Oregon where mountains, hilly areas, and headlands provided natural barriers. With some exceptions, the Indian tribes were very restricted in their movements. On the Oregon coast few Indians traveled more than 25 miles from their homeland in a lifetime. The Indians along the Columbia River, however, often took part in trade between the coast and the interior. The Klamath tribes ranged north to the Columbia River. And some of the Indians of eastern Oregon became nomadic once they had acquired the horse (**fig. 3.2**); some

even traveled as far as the Great Plains to hunt bison.

INDIAN CONTRIBUTIONS

The Indians who came to Oregon had weapons, tools, and clothing, as well as techniques for hunting, fishing, and gathering the wild fruits and roots of the forests and plains. Most important of all, from the standpoint of the effect of the Indians on the landscape, was their possession of fire. Without fire they would not have been able to make the great migration from eastern Asia to North America. The Indians used fire extensively, as many early travelers testified.[3] Indirect evidence was provided by the numerous prairies in humid regions where trees grew rapidly once the Indian burning had declined; in western Oregon, any grassland left undisturbed will quickly revert to brush and then, more slowly, to forest. Fires were usually set by the Indians in late summer when the vegetation was driest, but any dry period enabled the Indians to burn the grass, the brush, and the forest. Burning did not kill all the trees; small clumps of oak, pine, and Douglas fir survived. The Indians burned the vegetation for several reasons: to drive the game; to concentrate the game by burning most of the grass; to insure that the prairies — so important to their way of life — would not revert to forest.

The Indians supplied the settlers with salmon and a variety of game, such as elk and venison, and with furs and skins, usually at very low prices. The Indians converted the furs and skins into useful articles of clothing — moccasins, leggings, and robes — all of which were helpful to the settlers, whose clothing was often in tatters when they arrived in Oregon. Sketches of the early pioneers showed them dressed in garments made of buckskin (**fig. 3.3**). The white settlers, busy with house construction, planting, and harvesting, were glad to be relieved, at least temporarily, of the necessity of hunting, fishing, and making their own clothing.

The Indians acted as guides to the explorers, trappers, and settlers. For example, Indians pointed out to Lewis and Clark an easy route across the continental divide (Lolo Pass); and William Clark had a guide when he crossed Tillamook Head to see a big whale that had washed up on the beach south of there. In fact, Lewis and

fig. 3.2   Artist's view of Indians catching a wild horse. (George Catlin, *North American Indian Portfolio*)

Clark were almost never without a native guide when traveling. To be sure, Indian guides were not always dependable once they were 25 or 30 miles from home, so the wise traveler changed guides when he passed into the territory of a different tribe. The missionary J. H. Frost, traveling with guides from the Clatsop Plains to the Willamette Valley in 1841, became temporarily lost on the upper Yamhill.[4] Warren Vaughan, traveling from the Willamette Valley toward Tillamook and guided by a Valley Indian, became lost and reached the coast at Siletz Bay, missing his target by 40 miles. Vaughan gave up then but tried again, successfully, the following year.[5]

Indian dugout canoes (**fig. 3.4**) were used extensively by the pioneers, sometimes with Indian paddlers, sometimes by "requisition." The canoes were of greatest use in crossing the rivers; there was usually an Indian village on the river along the routes of travel, from which a canoe could be obtained. Sometimes canoes were chartered to haul freight on the rivers and, rarely, along the coast. In eastern Oregon the Indians often sold

horses to the pioneers for the immigrant wagon trains and also for food.

On the negative side, the Indians were a threat to the settlers, ranging from petty thievery and grand larceny to murder. To the Indians theft was a way of life; their idea of personal property was quite different from that of the whites. They were even clever pickpockets, as soon as the whites provided them with pockets to pick. Punishment for minor theft often led to violent reprisals. When an ax was stolen from Jedediah Smith he seized a chief, placed a rope around his neck, and threatened to hang him if the ax was not returned. The ax, the only one the Smith party had, was returned, but most of Smith's party was killed shortly thereafter in reprisal.[6]

Many of the Indian raids on the wagon trains and on the settlements were motivated by the desire for booty, but much of the large-scale violence, particularly in the Indian wars, was the result of the settlers taking over the Indian lands, a subject to be discussed in a later chapter. The violence was progressively worse as more and

37

fig. 3.3   Stephen H. Meek dressed in buckskin.
(OHS)

more land was occupied by the whites. During the period of exploration and fur trapping, the Indians were generally friendly; the fur traders changed nothing and offered trade goods for furs. But when the settlers arrived and began to build houses and till the soil, the Indians immediately saw a threat to their way of life.

THE INDIAN POPULATION

The first white contact with Oregon Indians was in the lower Columbia River area but, before that time, indirect contacts had been made by way of Puget Sound. Several sea traders had visited the lower Columbia before the arrival of Lewis and Clark and had supplied the Indians with guns, knives, copper kettles, cloth, and various items of European clothing.

The number of Indians in Oregon at the time of white settlement is difficult to estimate for a number of reasons. There was, of course, no census, no real counting of the Indians in the early days, although some pioneers made estimates of

individual villages. The fur traders also made notes about the number of Indians; it was to their advantage to do so, since they were depending on the Indians for part of their furs. As a further obstacle to estimating the Indian population, the names of the various tribes were confused and the areas occupied were ill-defined and changing. Estimates were made, beginning with Lewis and Clark, who obtained most of their information from the Indians. Their own observations were limited to the vicinity of the Columbia River, and one wonders how well Indians living on the Columbia River could estimate the population of the Rogue Indians, for example, with whom they had little or no direct contact.

Lewis and Clark estimated the Indian population of the present area of Oregon at about 30,000.[7] In 1841 Charles Wilkes set the Indian population of the Oregon Country as a whole at 20,000, about half of whom lived within the present limits of the state of Oregon.[8] By Wilkes' time diseases had spread to many parts of the state and had reduced the Indian population. In his travels he found many villages completely abandoned because most of the people had died from disease.

Before 1800 the crews from trading ships, which visited the lower Columbia, probably introduced a number of diseases that almost wiped out some of the tribes by 1830. The western Oregon Indians suffered most but diseases were transmitted to eastern Oregon also. The depopulated areas provided a refuge for neighboring tribes who were under pressure from *their* neighbors. For example, Klikitat Indians from north of the Columbia River invaded the Willamette Valley after the Calapuya (Calapooya) population had been greatly reduced by diseases.

Thus, because of the isolation of many tribes, the changing boundaries, and the inroads of disease, early estimates may have been far afield. Estimates of some individual tribes at a particular time were probably more reliable. Lewis and Clark, who lived with the Clatsop branch of the Chinook Indians for several months, came up with a no doubt fairly accurate figure of 209. (Estimates of other tribes are given near the end of this chapter.) The United States Bureau of the Census finally began to count all of the Indians in 1900 (previously only the ones on reservations had been counted), but even today there are some difficulties. For example, the Oregon Indian population in 1960, according to the U.S. census, was 8,026; in 1970, 13,510, a phenomenal increase.

38

fig. 3.4   Indian with dugout canoe on the Columbia River. (OHS)

The problem was and is: Who is an Indian? Apparently in 1970 many persons who had previously been counted in some other category declared themselves as Indian.

INDIAN RESOURCE AREAS

Two distinct Indian resource areas existed in Oregon at the time of exploration and settlement:[9] the western Oregon and Columbia River regions, where salmon fishing was a major activity, and the eastern Oregon region, where hunting and gathering were more important.

In western Oregon, during the salmon run, even the small streams were full of fish. While some Indians were catching fish with hook and line, spears, nets (fig. 3.5), traps, and weirs, or simply raking them out of the water, others were cleaning, smoking, and drying the fish. Enough preserved salmon were needed to last through the year and for trading with the Indians of eastern Oregon. Other fish were caught, especially the candlefish, which complemented the salmon in the diet and also supplied oil. Occasionally a stranded whale provided a feast for hundreds of people.

Whales were rarely harpooned from canoes; considering the fragile nature of the craft and the inadequacy of the harpoons, this was a risky undertaking. Clams, mussels, and other shellfish were taken in large quantities, as is evidenced by the large shell heaps at various points along the coast.

The Indians, good botanists, shared their knowledge with the pioneers. The Indians gathered and ate a large variety of plants, some of which were acceptable to the whites at least on a temporary basis, such as salal berries, huckleberries, cranberries, barberries, and the wild crabapple. Roots were of great importance,[10] especially the camas, which grew and still grows in moist locations in various parts of the state. The wapato root grew along the margins of the Columbia River below the Sandy River. The bulb of this plant, about the size of a hen's egg, was harvested from canoes, the Indians wading into the shallow water to loosen the bulbs with their feet. The bulbs resemble potatoes in appearance and taste; some of the early explorers who saw only the bulbs assumed they were a form of white potato. The wapato was an important trade item along the coast and the Columbia River. A variety of other roots was harvested and eaten, but with

39

fig. 3.5   Indians dip-netting for salmon at Celilo Falls. (OHS)

the introduction of swine by the pioneers, this resource was seriously reduced—the hogs were better diggers than the Indians.

There were also berries growing in the coastal areas and along the lower Columbia, which were harvested in season and kept for winter food by making a sort of preserve and packing it in closely woven baskets. The hunting was mostly for small animals, but occasionally elk were obtained, usually by trapping. Elk were fairly abundant but were difficult for the Indians to kill with their primitive weapons. Their bows and arrows generally were not powerful enough to kill elk. Lewis and Clark, who killed many elk during their stay in Oregon, noted that in many cases the elk had old arrow wounds that had healed.[11]

In general, the Indians along the lower Columbia River and on the Oregon coast had well-established villages, some of them fairly large, including perhaps a few hundred people in one village. Even along the coast these villages were on a river and usually a short distance from the ocean.

Numerous shell heaps along the coast indicate that in earlier times the Indians lived on headlands and terraces very near the sea (**fig. 3.6**). The Indians had access to the large forest trees, especially cedar. With some hard work, cedar could be dug out to form canoes or could be split into boards. These Indians had houses of split cedar boards with gabled roofs covered with split shingles.[12] The canoes used by the Oregon Indians were smaller than those of British Columbia.[13] Occasionally these canoes were put to sea but more generally they were used on the rivers and in the protected bays.

The Indians' tools and implements included various kinds of fishhooks, nets, and traps for salmon fishing. They used wedges made from elk horns to split cedar logs. From reeds and other materials, including split bark, the Indians made baskets, woven closely enough to hold water. These baskets were used in cooking by placing a salmon, for example, in the basket, covering the salmon with water, and dropping hot stones into

40

fig. 3.6   Rocky benches like this one at Neptune State Park were the sites of many shell
heaps. (Oregon Dept. of Transportation)

41

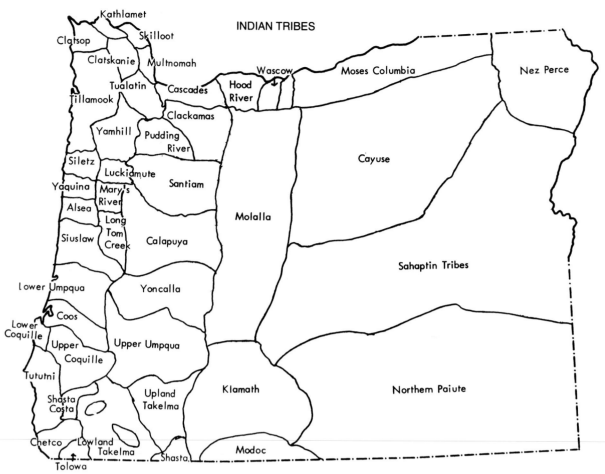

INDIAN TRIBES

fig. 3.7   A generalized map of Oregon Indian tribes about 1840-1850. Tribes, especially in eastern Oregon, were shifting their territories even before the coming of white men. Much of the area shown occupied by the Cayuse and Sahaptin tribes was at one time that of the Shoshone and Bannock tribes; the Umatilla and Tenino (Warm Springs) Indians lived south of the Columbia and west of the territory of the Nez Perce. (From maps by Joel V. Berreman and Claude Schaeffer)

the basket. Indian clothing was scanty and was made largely from skins and fiber. It usually included a large mantle or cape to ward off the heavy rains. Hats of basketry were common. Even before settlement the Indians had acquired white man's clothing from the traders and soon afterward the native costumes disappeared.

East of the Cascades, the Plateau Indians occupied a wide area stretching into the Rocky Mountains. These Indians depended on hunting, the digging of various roots (hence the name "digger Indians"), and the gathering of berries, seeds, and piñon nuts. Over 300 varieties of plants were used for food and medicine. In Oregon, at the time of white settlement, the Plateau Indians were represented mainly by the Shoshone Indians (see fig.

3.7). Included with them were the Paiute and Bannock tribes who occupied, respectively, southern and southeastern Oregon.

TRIBAL DISTRIBUTION, 1840[14]

The tribal distribution was apparently fairly stable before white contact. In some places it was related to natural barriers. The Cascade Range was the most important barrier; it was crossed by the Indians but only with difficulty. Coastal headlands also functioned as boundaries; Tillamook Head, for example, formed the boundary between the Chinook and Tillamook Indians.

At the time of first white contact, as early as 1740, the distribution of the tribes began to

42

change, especially in eastern Oregon. A number of factors was involved. The white settlement of eastern North America had a domino-like effect on the distribution of the tribes. For example, white settlement in New York pushed the Iroquois westward, the Iroquois pushed the Chippewa, who in turn pressured the Sioux. The Sioux pushed the Shoshone westward, causing them to expand into Oregon, and this pushed the Columbia River tribes northward and caused the Molalla to migrate westward across the Cascades.

Western Oregon and the Lower Columbia

The map of Indian tribes at the time of settlement (**fig. 3.7**) shows the significance of mountain barriers and drainage divides.[15] The crests of the Cascade Range and Coast Range were crossed from time to time but, nevertheless, they served to separate one tribe from another. In western Oregon a tribe was likely to be oriented to one or more rivers, although it might range over a wider area for hunting and gathering. The headlands along the coast also acted as barriers, even though some of them were easy to cross.

The Chinook group (see **fig. 3.7**) including, in order from west to east, the Clatsop, Kathlamet, Skilloot, Multnomah, Cascades, Clackamas, Hood River, and Wascow tribes, occupied both sides of the Columbia River from the ocean to The Dalles and south of the Columbia along the coast to Tillamook Head. They were fishers, hunters, and gatherers; they traded salmon, wapato root, and the pelts of sea otter with the tribes of eastern Oregon. Lewis and Clark estimated the population of the group on both sides of the Columbia as 16,000, noting that some tribes had been reduced by epidemics. The Chinook built permanent, wooden houses, large enough for three or four families. They flattened their heads and kept slaves.[16] They were more mobile than the other western tribes, using large canoes on the Columbia River and its tributaries. The Chinook were great traders and, perhaps as a result, their language, with the additions of English and French words, became the "Chinook jargon" used all the way from California to Alaska for communication between the traders and various Indian tribes.

The Calapuya Indians occupied all of the Willamette Valley above Willamette Falls and extended as far south as the Middle Umpqua. There were nine subgroups, named for their locality—

Tualatin, Yamhill, Pudding River, Luckiamute, Santiam, Marys River, Calapuya (in the Calapooya Mountains), Long Tom, and Yoncalla. These Indians were so devastated by disease before the settlers arrived that very little is known of them except that they lived along the streams, fished, hunted, and gathered, much like the Coast Indians; acorns and camas were staple foods. Lewis and Clark estimated the number of Calapuya at 3,000, Wilkes at 300.

Living on the west slope of the Cascades in the drainage of the upper Clackamas and upper Santiam rivers were the Molalla Indians, who had been driven westward across the Cascades by pressure from the Shoshone. Another group lived on the headwaters of the Rogue River. Lewis and Clark estimated the number of Molalla at 2,200, Wilkes at 400.

The Umpqua Indians lived along the middle and lower parts of the Umpqua River in houses made of boards and mats. They depended upon the river for most of their food and for transportation. The river was navigable for canoes with some difficulties at rapids. Wilkes estimated the number of Umpqua at 400.

South of the Umpqua Indians were the Takelma Indians, living in the Rogue River Valley and on the west slope of the Cascades. They lived much like the Umpqua, except they depended more on acorns for food, since oaks were very common in this area. They also ate manzanita and other seeds.

On the coast beginning at the north, the Tillamook (called "Killemooks" in the early days) ranged from Tillamook Head and Cannon Beach, where William Clark saw them in 1805, to Yaquina Head (**fig. 3.8**). Lewis and Clark and Wilkes estimated their number at 400, most of whom lived on the rivers tributary to Tillamook Bay. These Indians fished in the bay and the rivers and collected quantities of shellfish. After white settlers arrived in 1850 the two groups—Indian and white—lived in peace for the most part, even though one of the Indians was hanged for thievery. The Indians were responsible for clearing the Tillamook Plain by repeated burning, making it easy for the whites to establish farms. Individual Tillamook tribes were named according to the rivers where they lived—Nehalem, Tillamook, Nestucca, and Salmon. The Siuslaw Indians living to the south of the Tillamook Indians differed linguistically, but their way of life was similar.

fig. 3.8   Indians seated in front of plank house on the Oregon coast. (Burton Collection, Univ. of Oregon)

The Coos Indians lived around Coos Bay, on the lower Coos River, and on the lower Coquille River. They used canoes extensively on the bay and rivers and had two well-established portages, one from the south end of South Slough westward to the coast, the other from Isthmus Slough of Coos Bay to Beaver Creek, a tributary of the Coquille River.

The Tututni or Rogue Indians ranged from the Coquille River to Cape Ferrelo. They had eight bands on the coast and three on the Rogue River. When they were rounded up and placed on the Siletz Reservation in 1854 the population was 1,311. South of the territory of the Rogue Indians, the Chetco Indians lived along the Chetco River. One village with 42 houses was destroyed by the whites in 1853. In 1854 the population was 241.

Eastern Oregon

In the northern part of eastern Oregon, four tribes occupied the Deschutes-Umatilla Plateau and part of the Blue Mountain region. In order, from east to west, they were the Nez Percé, Cayuse, Umatilla, and Tenino (Warm Springs) tribes.

In Oregon the Nez Percé lived in what is now Wallowa County and parts of adjoining counties, but they also extended to the Bitterroot Mountains of Montana and the Salmon River country of Idaho. In Oregon the Nez Percé had been slightly displaced by the Shoshone Indians. Lewis and Clark estimated the population at 7,850. The Nez Percé depended on salmon, roots, and berries for food. They built large community houses but also had underground lodges.

The Cayuse, Umatilla, and Tenino Indians lived much like the Nez Percé but had been pushed northward by the Shoshone. In 1855 some of the Indians of these four tribes were placed on reservations—the Nez Percé in the Wallowas, later removed to Idaho, the Cayuse and Umatilla on the Umatilla Reservation, and the Tenino on the Warm Springs Reservation. All four tribes took

44

fig. 3.9   Modern Indian tepee at Tygh Valley, May 1968. (Francis Seufert photo, OHS)

prominent parts in the Indian wars of the 1850s. They also raided the immigrant trains along the Oregon Trail, since the trail led through or near their territories.

In Oregon the Shoshone and Paiute Indians lived in the Blue Mountains and the area to the south. They depended more upon plants and small game for food than did the Indians farther west. Important plant foods were bullrushes, tules, bitterroot, camas, and, from the higher altitudes, piñon nuts. The piñon harvest was very irregular, as it came late in the autumn and was often made difficult by early snows. Fish food included some salmon from the Snake River, trout and other small fish from the mountain streams. Almost anything that moved was considered edible by the Shoshone. They ate grasshoppers, crickets, bees, locusts, and ants. They were especially fond of grasshoppers and regretted that the great abundance of them occurred only once in seven years. What to the Mormons was a near disaster was a feast for the Shoshone.

Shortly before contact with the whites, the Shoshone and Paiute Indians had acquired three new culture traits, which had changed their way of life substantially. One was the horse. The horse was obtained from tribes further to the east, who in turn had obtained horses from southern tribes, especially from the Comanche Indians. The Comanche had acquired their horses by raids on the Spanish settlements in Mexico. The second Shoshone acquisition was the tepee (fig. 3.9). The tepee was used only in eastern Oregon. It was an ideal house type for Indians who, after acquiring the horse, became migratory. The third acquisition was the gun. Even without guns mounted Indians were able to hunt bison with bow and arrow, but with less success.

Apparently the American bison, which had been present in eastern Oregon at one time, had been eliminated from this area by the time the first white contact was made. The Shoshone, therefore, were either traveling into Idaho to hunt bison or they were depending upon the small game that remained. One might speculate that the acquisition of the horse by the Shoshone enabled them to hunt bison so effectively as to eliminate them from Oregon. Fur trappers in eastern Oregon in 1826 found bison bones but no bison (see chapter 4).

The Oregon Klamath and Modoc Indians lived in the southwestern part of the Basin-Range region in what is now Klamath and Lake counties (see fig.

3.7). The Klamath lived mainly on the shores of Klamath Lake and on the Williamson and Sprague rivers, while the Modoc were on the shores of Lower Klamath Lake (now dry), around Tule Lake in California, and as far east as Goose Lake. These Indians lived by hunting and fishing. The Klamath and Modoc Indians, like most of the Oregon tribes, had slaves, which they obtained by raids on neighboring tribes and by trading.[17] The hostility of the Klamath and Modoc Indians delayed white settlement in this area for many years, and bloody wars lasted until 1873. The Klamath often crossed the Cascades, raided settlements, and attacked travelers along the Oregon-California Trail.

SUMMARY

The Indian occupation of Oregon may be summarized in four phases:[18] (1) the pre-contact era to 1740, before the Indians felt any influence from Europe; (2) the period of traders and explorers, during which time there was extensive contact but almost no settlement; (3) the first period of settlement, 1840–1850, in which the Indian villages were only moderately disturbed; and (4) the 1850–1860 decade, the period of Indian wars, during which most of the Oregon Indians were removed from their homes and placed on reservations.

During the first period the Indians had only crude tools, but they did have fire and this was used to modify the ecosystem. The Indians were active agents in changing the face of the land, but, as compared to the changes made by the settlers, the alterations seem small indeed. It is well known that Indians periodically burned over forests and grasslands to improve the environment from their point of view.

During the second phase, traders visited all parts of Oregon, providing the Indians with a variety of things, including guns, knives, and alcohol. In the third phase, the settlers began to displace the Indians, at the same time taking advantage of the native knowledge of the environment. In the fourth phase, white settlement moved into most parts of the state, provoking the Indians to resistance, especially in northeastern and southern Oregon. During this period various tribes, which had been independent before, combined to wage war on the settlers. The last two periods will be discussed in following chapters.

Considering the great variety of resources in Oregon, it is surprising that the Indians had not developed an agricultural economy. They came in successive migrations from a cold, inhospitable land in northeast Asia—at least they came *through* northeast Asia, whatever their original home. They arrived in a cold part of North America but spread southward and eastward into warm lands. But, in spite of a long occupation, they did not learn to grow crops and they domesticated no animals. (The dog they brought with them.) To be sure, there were no native animals easy to domesticate. The Europeans have not been able really to domesticate the bison, the deer, or the elk.

Although the various Indian tribes were fairly well adapted to their Oregon environments, there were periods of famine and suffering. This was especially true of the hunting and gathering Indians. The fur traders on their winter expeditions reported Indians in a starving condition in eastern Oregon and even in the Rogue River Valley.[19] Game was scarce, much more so than today. White settlement made matters worse. The settlers were hunters also, thus putting more pressure on the land. The settlers' hogs destroyed the root plants on which the Indians depended for food. Afflicted by diseases and their way of life disturbed, the Indians suffered widespread want and hunger until they were placed on reservations.

4 EXPLORATION OF OREGON TO 1840

An intelligent officer, with ten or twelve chosen men, . . . might explore
the whole line, even to the Western Ocean.
Thomas Jefferson

The early exploration of Oregon was two-phased, by sea and by land. By sea the first explorations, dominated by Spaniards, were motivated by the search for new lands and for the fictional Northwest Passage through North America to Asia. Later the fur seal trade and the desire to claim the land were important motives. By 1529 Hernando Cortes had essentially completed the conquest of New Spain (Middle America). He then sent out expeditions by sea to explore the western coast, expeditions that went eventually as far as California and the Northwest Coast. Exploring parties were also sent out by land but none reached the Oregon Country. The early voyages of the Spaniards were not generally publicized, but enough information leaked out to stimulate exploration by other European countries. Exploration by sea, limited as it was to the shoreline, stimulated exploration by land, but it was not until the Louisiana Purchase (1803) that overland exploration of Oregon got under way with the expedition of Lewis and Clark in 1804–1806.

EXPLORATION BY SEA

The first ships to sail along the Oregon coast were probably Spanish Manila galleons, returning from the Philippines and the Moluccas. The Spaniards had learned that favorable winds and currents for the return voyage were near the 40th parallel. Evidence of such visits to the Oregon coast are to be found in the remains of wrecked ships, such as the famous "beeswax" ship, foundered on Nehalem Beach. John Hobson in 1848 saw at Nehalem Beach the remnants of a ship that has since been buried by the beach sands. Quantities of beeswax were recovered from the

sands over the years and dated by carbon 14, which indicated an age of about 280 years. It is known that a galleon, the *San Francisco Xavier*, left Manila in January 1707 laden with beeswax and was never heard from again.[1] This could very well be the "beeswax" ship. There may have been survivors; several examples of light-skinned individuals, some with red hair, were reported by early travelers. William Clark, in his journal for December 31, 1805, reported he saw "a man of much lighter Coloured than the natives are generaly, he was freckled with long duskey red hair . . . and must Certainly be half white at least."[2] These forgotten visits of the galleons provided little information to the outside world.

James Cook, in 1778, and George Vancouver, in 1792, sailed along the Oregon coast but added little to the knowledge of the coastline. Cook described the coast of "New Albion": "The land appeared to be of a moderate height, diversified with hill and Valley and almost every where covered with wood."[3] Vancouver sailed along the Oregon coast in April 1792 and described the vicinity of Cape Lookout: "The coast . . . is pleasingly diversified with eminences and small hills near the sea shore, in which are some shallow sandy bays, with a few detached rocks lying about a mile from the land. . . . the sandy beach that continued along the coast renders it a compact shore, now and then interrupted by perpendicular rocky cliffs, on which the surf violently breaks."[4] The major efforts of Cook and Vancouver were directed to the coast further north, and, between them, they proved that the Northwest Passage did not exist.

In May 1792, Captain Robert Gray discovered the Columbia River, entered it, and described and charted the lower reaches. An account of the event is given by one of the young officers aboard: "The

48

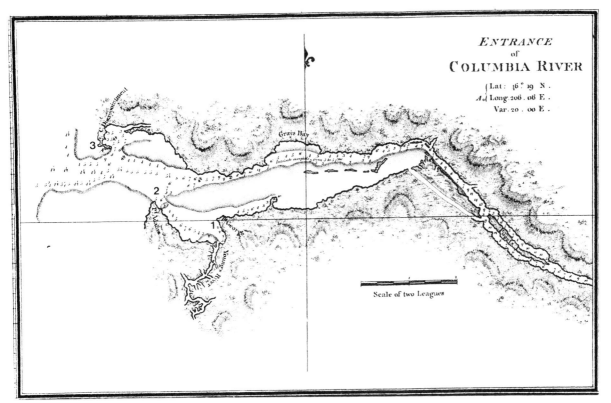

fig. 4.1   Part of William Broughton's chart of the lower Columbia River. Astoria (1) is
called Fort George. Point Adams (2) and Cape Disappointment (3) are shown, as
are the extensive sand bars. Soundings of three, four, five, and six fathoms follow
the main channel. (From George Vancouver, *Voyage of Discovery, Atlas,* 1789)

River extended to the NE as far as eye cou'd reach,
and water fit to drink as far down as the *Bars*....
We directed our course up this noble *River* in
search of a Village. The beach was lin'd with
Natives, who ran along shore following the
Ship.... above 20 Canoes came off, and brought
a good lot of Furs, and Salmon, which last they
sold two for a board Nail. The furs we likewise
bought cheap, for Copper and Cloth.... no
doubt we was the first civilized people that they
ever saw."[5] When Captain Gray and the *Columbia*
returned to Boston, interest in Oregon was excited
to new heights.

In the same year (October 1792) William
Broughton, under Captain George Vancouver's
command, explored and mapped the lower 100
miles of the river (**fig. 4.1**), as far as the present
site of Vancouver. He named Mt. Hood and
claimed the land for Great Britain. Broughton
noted deserted Indian villages along the banks of
the river, the first indication that many Indians
had recently died of disease.[6] The trading
schooner *Jenny* was anchored in the lower river,
probably having been informed of Gray's visit and
the favorable conditions for trade. In the following years, several trading ships entered the Columbia River, prior to the arrival of Lewis and Clark
in 1805.

As the nineteenth century began, the coast of
Oregon was fairly well known in a general way.
Many ships had sailed near the shore and a few
landings had been made and recorded. Several
new capes and bays had been located: "Quicksand" (Tillamook) Bay, Cape Lookout, and Cape
Meares. The last two named were confused down
to modern times and a lighthouse intended for
Cape Lookout was placed on Cape Meares. A few
inland points were identified, such as Saddle
Mountain (east of the present Seaside) and Table
Mountain (east of Cape Foulweather). The maps
of the period showed the above-mentioned points,
but aside from the Columbia no rivers were
shown. Before Lewis and Clark arrived, almost
nothing was known of Oregon's interior, but the
exploration by sea had aroused a keen interest that
led to land exploration.

49

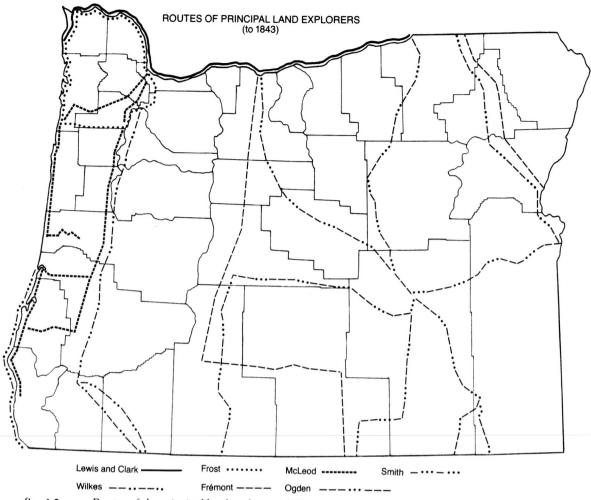

ROUTES OF PRINCIPAL LAND EXPLORERS
(to 1843)

Lewis and Clark ———	Frost ········	McLeod ---------	Smith — ··· — ···
Wilkes — — ·· — ··	Frémont — — — —	Ogden — — ··· — —	

fig. 4.2   Routes of the principal land explorers of Oregon to 1843. Most kept daily records and made sketch maps of the areas explored. The explorations of Wilkes and Frémont are described in chapter 5. The Wilkes expedition to California was led by George Emmons.

EXPLORATION BY LAND

It remained for the land travelers to describe the interior of Oregon (**fig. 4.2**). By far the greatest number were fur traders and trappers — Alexander Ross in 1810–1813, Gabriel Franchère in 1811–1814, Peter Skene Ogden in 1825–1827, A. R. McLeod in 1826–1827, Jedediah Smith in 1828, B. L. E. Bonneville in 1833, and Nathaniel Wyeth in 1833–1836. Meriwether Lewis and William Clark in 1805–1806, David Douglas in 1826, Charles Wilkes in 1841, and John C. Frémont in 1843 were primarily interested in exploration. Missionaries also made contributions, especially J. H. Frost in 1841. Early settlers, among whom was ex-trapper Ewing Young in 1834, also added

to the general knowledge. Bit by bit these men described the Indians, the flora and fauna, and the lay of the land. Much of the information recorded in their journals was derived from conversations with the Indians. Almost without exception these early explorers noted that the Indians had burned and were burning the natural vegetation at every opportunity. The explorers did not realize to what extent the Indians had altered the country, since they did not know what the land was like before the Indian occupation.

LEWIS AND CLARK

As early as 1782 Jefferson had suggested to

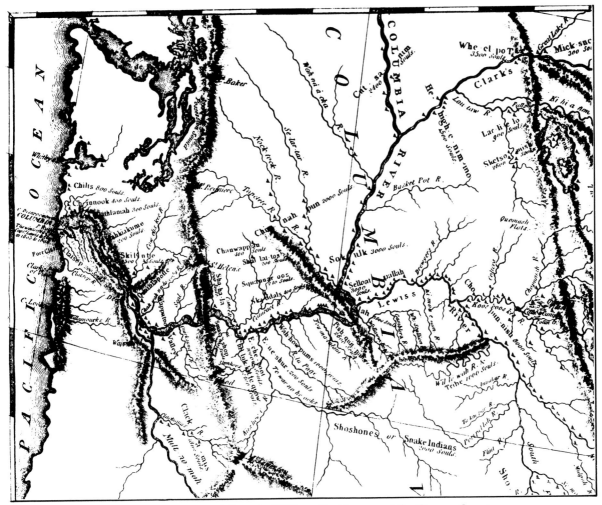

fig. 4.3   The western portion of Captain William Clark's map of the Oregon Country,
1810. In addition to the explorations of Lewis and Clark, use was made of Indian
maps and the surveys of Vancouver.

George Rogers Clark the possibility of an expedition to the Pacific Coast but nothing came of it.[7] In 1793 André Michaux, the French botanist, actually started a journey to the Pacific at Jefferson's request but was recalled, because of political intrigues, before he crossed the Mississippi.[8] Although the results of Lewis and Clark's expedition were many-faceted, Jefferson's instruction to Captain Lewis was very specific: "The object of your mission is single, [to find] the direct water communication from sea to sea formed by the bed of the Missouri, and perhaps the Oregon [river]."[9]

The Spaniards in Mexico were informed of the plan to send Lewis and Clark to the Pacific by Major-General James Wilkinson, who was secretly spying for Spain. As a result, four military expeditions were sent out from Santa Fe by the Spaniards to "arrest Captain Merry and his followers...and to seize their papers and instruments";[10] but each attempt failed. Spain was obviously anxious to keep the United States out of the Oregon Country. Lewis and Clark were apparently unaware that these expeditions were taking place.

With the expedition of Lewis and Clark,[11] knowledge of the interior of Oregon took a great leap forward. Their travels in Oregon, to be sure, were limited to the vicinity of the Columbia River, the Clatsop Plains, and a short section of the coastline as far south as the present Cannon Beach. But by judicious and frequent questioning of the Indians, they were able to collect much information concerning parts of Oregon they did not see, not only when they were in residence at

51

Fort Clatsop but while traveling along the Columbia River. This information included place geography, especially with respect to streams; the distribution, character, and numbers of the Indian tribes; and descriptions of the fauna and flora (fig. 4.3).[12]

Lewis and Clark were most interested in the mammals and birds they encountered, especially the game animals and the fur bearers. Some of the animals described were new to science. Although Lewis had some training in botany and zoology and knew the scientific names of many plants and animals, he did not assign scientific names to new species. Lewis is to be credited with the first descriptions of the mule deer (Lewis gave the name), the pronghorn antelope, the Columbian white-tailed deer, the black-tailed deer, the kit fox, the mountain beaver, the Oregon bobcat, the "Douglas" squirrel, and many others, some of which, like the grizzly bear, were described by Lewis and Clark before reaching Oregon.

Lewis wrote original descriptions of many birds, including the lesser Canadian goose, the whistling swan, the ring-necked duck, the Oregon ruffed grouse, the western grebe, the American magpie, Steller's jay, Clark's nutcracker, Lewis' woodpecker, Nuttall's poor-will, and the Pacific varied thrush. He decribed in detail the flounder, the eulachon (candlefish), and what he called the "common salmon" (King or chinook salmon). He also described two species of Northwest garter snakes, the hog-nosed snake, the horned lizard, and a "water lizard" (warty salamander).

Special attention was devoted to the sea otter, the beaver, and the salmon, and to the methods of capturing and trapping them. The sea otter, which ranged from Alaska to Baja California, was first reported at the extremities of its range in 1737 and 1741. Lewis and Clark first encountered them below Celilo Falls of the Columbia and described them as the size of a common "mastive" dog, with very small eyes and ears. Lewis and Clark obtained sea otter pelts from the Indians to replenish their clothing, which was badly worn and rotted from their long journey.

They valued the beaver for food as well as for fur. They found this animal all the way from Kansas to Fort Clatsop, usually in conjunction with willow and cottonwood trees. One of the secondary objectives of the journey was to explore the possibility of diverting some of the fur trade of the western Indians away from the British fur traders to the eastern United States. Certainly the reports of the widespread occurrence of the beaver encouraged the fur traders, both American and Canadian, to develop this virgin territory.

Lewis and Clark were amazed at the variety of unfamiliar plants on the Oregon coast and along the Columbia River. They described many of them in detail. The large trees especially attracted their attention and several measurements of height and circumference were made. Five species of "fir" were described, including the hemlock, spruce, and Douglas fir. Lewis described the white pine as differing little from the white pine of Virginia except the cone was longer. Also described were the black alder, broad-leaf maple, vine maple, cottonwood, ash, white oak, madrone, and various shrubs such as salal, ferns, and briars.

It is impossible, in a short space, to mention the variety of observations and maps (fig. 4.4) made by Lewis and Clark; both men were curious about everything they saw. Although unversed in geology, they often described the rock outcrops. The igneous rock along the Columbia River was noted: "the river became crowded with rough black rocks." Landforms were described in general terms such as "open plains." Soils were usually described by color and texture. Lewis kept a meteorological record, including wind direction at sunrise and at 4:00 P.M., and the aspect of the day; the usual entry was "cloudy and rainy."

After the party returned to the East the effect of the expedition was difficult to exaggerate. Although the official journal of the expedition was not published until 1814, detailed accounts were carried in the newspapers and magazines of the time. The net result was a quickened interest in the Oregon Country and the demand that it be annexed to the United States. Another effect was an increased interest in the fur trade on the part of Americans and Canadians. This, in turn, led to a more detailed exploration of the Oregon Country, so that a quarter century after Lewis and Clark's expedition all major parts of Oregon had been visited and described.

ASTORIA

For five years after Lewis and Clark left Oregon there is no record of a white man visiting the present area of the state. In March 1811, one of the parties sent out by John Jacob Astor arrived by ship at Astoria and built a fort and trading post. The scene and the subsequent events were de-

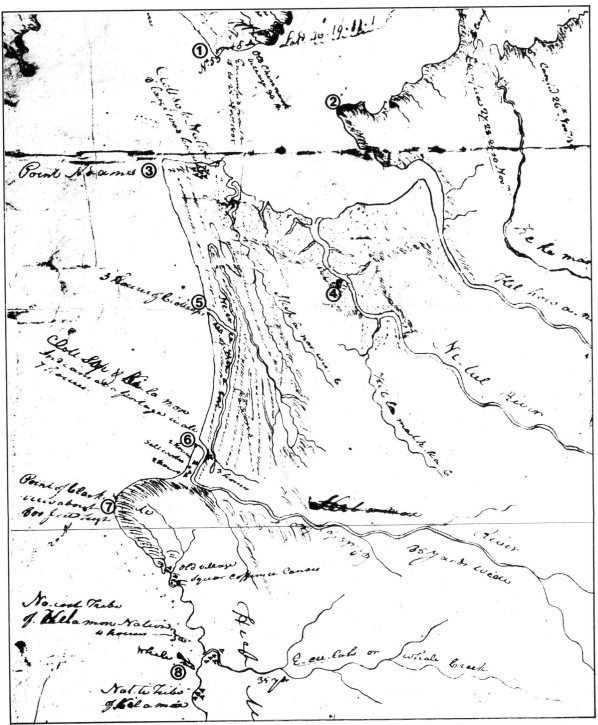

fig. 4.4   Part of William Clark's map of the Lower Columbia River, Clatsop Plains and Tillamook Head: (**1**) Point Ellice (Washington); (**2**) the site of Astoria; (**3**) Point Adams; (**4**) Camp Clatsop; (**5**) former mouth of Newauna Creek; (**6**) mouth of the Necanicum River (Seaside); (**7**) Tillamook Head; (**8**) the whale and the mouth of E-eu-col (Ecola) Creek (now Elk Creek) and the site of Cannon Beach. Clark noted a short portage from Necanicum River to Newauna Creek; the two streams are now confluent. (From Map 32 Part III, *Original Journals of the Lewis and Clark Expedition*, 1905)

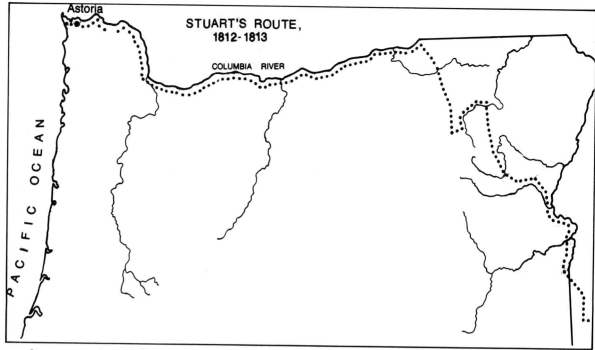

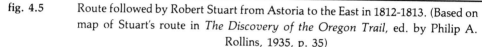

fig. 4.5   Route followed by Robert Stuart from Astoria to the East in 1812-1813. (Based on map of Stuart's route in *The Discovery of the Oregon Trail*, ed. by Philip A. Rollins, 1935, p. 35)

scribed and narrated by Gabriel Franchère.[13] Unlike Lewis and Clark, who arrived in November, Astor's party found the climate delightful. "The spring, usually so tardy in this latitude, was already far advanced; the foliage was budding, and the earth was clothing itself with verdure; the weather was superb, and all nature smiled. We imagined ourselves in the garden of Eden; the wild forests seemed to us delightful groves, and the leaves transformed to brilliant flowers. No doubt, the pleasure of finding ourselves at the end of our voyage, and liberated from the ship, made things appear to us a great deal more beautiful than they really were." For the first year the Astor party did little more than retrace the journeys of Lewis and Clark. Several parties traveled up the Columbia, renaming several of the features named by Lewis and Clark and trading with the Indians, who were more hostile than they had been with Lewis and Clark. The fur traders noted numerous prairies as they explored a few miles beyond the banks of the rivers. The ruins of Fort Clatsop were visited and described as "piles of unhewn logs overgrown with parasite creepers." At the falls of the Columbia Franchère talked to a blind old man called Soto, who said his father was a white man who had been shipwrecked on the Oregon coast and after living

with the Indians for some time had set off with three companions overland, in an attempt to reach the Spanish settlements in California.

Meanwhile, another Astor party was traveling overland to the Columbia, suffering many hardships and loss of life. To them we owe the first descriptions of the Snake River Plain of southern Idaho and the Snake River Canyon, scanty though these descriptions were. The effect, however, of their crossing the Snake Canyon and traveling along it was to make it clear to other trappers that this was not an easy place to travel. Near Farewell Bend, where the Snake River entered the canyon, they abandoned their remaining horses and set out on foot in two parties, one on each side of the canyon. Forced to leave the river and climb the cliffs of the canyon to avoid impassible spurs near the river, the parties were often out of touch with each other and without water, although they could see the river below them. The survivors eventually left the canyon and reached the Grande Ronde Basin, from which they found their way to Astoria. Unfortunately these travelers kept no journal and the best account is given by Gabriel Franchère, to whom the Astor party related their story.

The eastward journey of Robert Stuart from As-

54

toria to St. Louis in 1812–1813[14] led to the discovery of the easiest land route to Oregon, the Oregon Trail (**fig. 4.5**). Leaving Astoria on June 29, 1812, Stuart with six men traveled up the Columbia to the Walla Walla River, thence over the Blue Mountains to the Snake River, then up the Snake to the Portneuf River, near the site of Pocatello. Turning southeast, the party approached the Green River, skirted the Wind River Range, crossed the continental divide near South Pass, and reached the North Platte River. The party wintered on the Platte and reached St. Louis on April 30, 1813. This journey was given much publicity, the *Missouri Gazette* of May 15, 1813, stating: "It appears that a journey across the continent of North America might be performed with a wagon." But some years were to pass before many people realized that this route was the easiest land route to Oregon.

HUDSON'S BAY COMPANY EXPLORERS AND TRADERS

The American trading post at Astoria was short-lived. With the beginning of the War of 1812 and the threat of a British warship arriving at Astoria, the post was sold to the North West Company in 1814, in the person of David Thompson, who had previously established trading posts for his company on the upper Columbia. About the time the North West and Hudson's Bay companies were joined, the trading post was renamed Fort George.

The search for beaver led to the exploration of the Willamette Valley, the Oregon coast, and other parts of western Oregon, but not until the headquarters of the Hudson's Bay Company were moved to Fort Vancouver in 1824. In May 1826, Alexander R. McLeod left Vancouver with Donald Manson, an interpreter, five servants (two of whom were Hawaiians), three Indians, and a number of horses.[15] They traveled in a southwesterly direction from the confluence of the Willamette and Columbia rivers, crossed the headwaters of the North Fork of the Yamhill River, and followed "the Borders of the Mountain" because the valleys were so wet. It was common practice in Oregon in the early days to travel not along the floors of the valleys but in the edges of the hills, and the first roads were built in similar situations. As McLeod crossed the divide of the Coast Range he described areas of open country and brushy

country. He followed the Nestucca River to the coast, thinking it was the "Kellymoux" (Tillamook). Here he met another trapper, Laframboise, who with six men turned north while McLeod traveled south along the coast. The horses had some difficulty in the brushy areas and fell frequently on the steep, muddy trails over the headlands. McLeod was tempted to abandon the horses and travel by Indian canoes but the sea was rough and the local Indians advised strongly against it.

The party crossed the Salmon River and stopped at Devils Lake, finding very few beaver. They crossed the Yaquina River with little difficulty at low tide but had more trouble with the Alsea River. South of the Alsea, McLeod wrote: "Our progress with horses must terminate here," and so the horses were left with friendly Indians. Heceta Head and Sea Lion Point were very difficult places on the Oregon coast for horses. (Forty years later when Corporal Bensell traveled down the coast looking for runaway Indians there was still no good horse trail. Indians were engaged to take the baggage by sea when the weather permitted and the party continued by foot across these difficult points.) The lower Siuslaw and the North Fork were explored by canoes with some difficulty because the rivers were blocked by fallen trees. The Indians on the Siuslaw advised McLeod that a much easier return route to Fort Vancouver was by way of the Umpqua River and the Willamette Valley. Nevertheless, the party retraced their route, recovered their horses at Yachats, and arrived at Fort Vancouver on August 17. Throughout this journey the Indians were friendly and some furs were obtained by trading.

In September, McLeod, with 15 white men, 4 Indians, and 24 horses set out to explore the country south of the Umpqua River.[16] Taking advantage of the Indians' advice, he traveled up the Willamette River rather than along the coast. They had fine weather in the Willamette Valley but as they approached the coast the rains began. On arriving at the Umpqua River the party divided, some to explore the tributaries for beaver while McLeod traveled by canoe to the mouth of the Umpqua and then southward on foot along the beach. The Indians, who had not seen white men before, were very shy but friendly, in strong contrast to their reaction to the Smith party two years later (see below p. 57).

At Coos Bay canoes, paddled by local Indians, took the party southward to the head of South

Slough; thence they traveled on foot westward for six miles on a well-marked Indian trail to the beach at present Whiskey Run. Arriving at the Coquille River, they again used canoes to explore its reaches and to trade with some success for beaver pelts with Indians along the river, after which they returned to the Umpqua River. McLeod asked the Coquille Indians about "the great river" but they professed ignorance of it; in fact they could tell him little about the nature of the country except in the immediate neighborhood. The Hudson's Bay Company was seeking a large river in southern Oregon that might furnish a route into the interior and make it easier to transport furs from southern Oregon to Fort Vancouver. In this connection McLeod had two problems: to find the great river, and to locate a route overland suitable for horses. In pursuit of the latter he journeyed up the Coquille River, through Lookingglass Valley, and down the Umpqua River to Fort Umpqua at the junction with Elk Creek. This route he decided was not suitable for horses. He returned to the coast, then traveled south, crossed the Coquille River, followed the beach to the Sixes River, turned inland, and reached the Rogue River about four miles above the mouth. He was disappointed in the appearance of the stream. Obviously the Rogue with its narrow canyon was not suitable as a route to the interior, "its channel obstructed by shoals, . . . its entrance very narrow." In 1829 McLeod led a party over Siskiyou Pass, thus opening the Oregon-California Trail.

David Douglas, a professional botanist trained in Scotland, arrived in Oregon in March 1825 and spent nearly two years in and near the state.[17] Most of the time he spent on and near the Columbia River, where he added immeasurably to the knowledge of the flora and fauna. Douglas described and gave scientific names to hundreds of plants, many of them new to science. Among those he described was the Douglas fir, which now bears his name (it had been described before by Lewis and Clark). He called the Douglas fir *Pinus taxifolia*. It is interesting to note that Lewis and Clark classified Douglas fir under the firs, whereas Douglas included it under the pines. Douglas was the first well-trained scientist to explore Oregon but the full results of his studies were not immediately made known. His journal was not published until 1914, nearly a century after his exploration.

Douglas kept careful notes, including estimates of the mileage he traveled. In 1825 he traveled 2,100 miles, most of it in Oregon; the next year he covered nearly 4,000 miles, part by boat on the Columbia River and its tributaries, but much of it on horseback and on foot. He often loaded his horse so heavily with specimens that he was forced to walk.

In September 1826, Douglas traveled south in the Willamette Valley more or less along the route of the McLeod expedition. The course led up the "Multnomah River," as Douglas called it, on the west side of the valley in the edge of the foothills. Douglas described "the plains burned by the Indians to drive the game animals in certain parts for more convenient hunting." Not only the floor of the Willamette Valley was burned but the foothills as well. Douglas observed the Indians digging camas root in one of the low plains. A grizzly bear was observed but not shot. Later he shot grizzly bears and also purchased the skin of a very large bear to be used as a ground rug. The hills were covered with scattered oak and pine with grass between, the higher ground with Douglas fir. Much time was devoted to hunting, since game was scarce.

Joining forces with McLeod, the party traveled down Elk Creek, called "Red Deer River" at the time, to the confluence with the Umpqua River, where Douglas described the bed of the river, saying that the bottom was too rocky for large boats. He was particularly interested in finding a large pine, which had been described to him by an Indian. Seeking the pine, Douglas traveled with a single Indian guide in a southeasterly direction from his camp on the Umpqua. His first trip failed to find the pine, but on the second he found a number of specimens that he described as 150 to 200 feet high, 20 to 60 feet in circumference with cones 12 to 17 inches long. The cones were erect during the first year, pendulous the second. He named it *Pinus lambertiana*. The tree today is found in southwestern Oregon and in northern California, commonly called the sugar pine.

Peter Skene Ogden came to Oregon from Canada in 1825 and was assigned by the Hudson's Bay Company to the Snake River country (see below, p. 58).[18] Ogden was an experienced trapper and very good at managing men. Near the end of one of his journeys to eastern Oregon he traveled into California and entered southwestern Oregon by way of the Siskiyou Range. He reached the headwaters of the Applegate River, which he called the "Shastie," and followed it to the Rogue. His main purpose was to trap beaver and trade with the Indians, but like McLeod he was seeking "the big river," which he called the "Clammite." At this time it was thought that the Klamath River and the Rogue River were one and the same. Ogden noted the oak-madrone forest that was unlike anything he had seen in eastern Oregon. The party traveled along the Rogue for several miles below Grants Pass, but Ogden realized that any land route along that river to the coast would be very difficult. He was confirmed in this opinion by the local Indians. The party then retraced their route over the Siskiyous into California and back into eastern Oregon.

In June 1828, Jedediah Smith traveled along the southern Oregon coast with a dozen men and 150 horses loaded with furs that they had obtained by trapping and by trading in California.[19] He described the coast in southern Curry County as "pararie, covered with grass and brakes [brush]." The back country was "broken [hilly], and thickety, timbered with low scrubby pines and ceadars, the pararie hills covered with good grass and blue clover." Smith thought much of the coast was good country for raising cattle and hogs. He sometimes followed well-marked Indian trails; where possible he traveled along the beaches, but in many places he was forced to travel over rugged headlands, through dense brush, and over fallen trees. The last posed great difficulty for the horses. If he had been able to procure Indian guides, easier routes could have been found, but the Indians he saw were very shy and usually ran away. Crossing the Rogue River at the mouth a dozen horses were drowned but the furs had been ferried in canoes and were saved. His most difficult passage on land was in the Seven Devils section, south of Coos Bay. Here deep ravines and thick brush limited the day's travel sometimes to a mile and a half. But for the horses and the furs Smith could have followed McLeod's route to the southern end of South Slough of Coos Bay and thence by canoe to and across Coos Bay. When the Smith party reached the Umpqua River they made contact with the Indians and here most of his party were massacred (see above, p. 37). Smith and two of his men escaped and made their way on foot to Fort Vancouver. Later most of the horses and furs were recovered along with Smith's diary, with help from the Hudson's Bay Company men from Fort Vancouver.

By 1830 the main features of western Oregon were fairly well known except for the Cascades. The fictitious "Multnomah River" had been erased from the map and the courses and character of the major streams had been noted. The main relief features had been seen, even if they had not been adequately described. The major vegetational features had been noted, especially the occurrence of forest, brushland, and prairie. So widespread was Indian burning at that time that most of the Willamette Valley was prairie, and large areas of grassland were found in the Coast Range and Klamath Mountains. From the work of Lewis and Clark and David Douglas quite a bit was known about the species of trees, shrubs, mammals, and birds.

One of the results of the explorers' travels was the establishment of fairly definite routes of travel. The most important was the trail south from Fort Vancouver, along the foothills of the Coast Range, thence down Elk Creek and the Umpqua River to the coast, and along the beach to Coos Bay. Later the route was extended southward from Fort Umpqua, near the present site of Elkton, to California by way of Grants Pass. All this information, however, was known to only a few people. Many years were to pass before Douglas' journal and the journals of the Hudson's Bay Company were published.

EASTERN OREGON

Most of the exploring in eastern Oregon before 1840 was done by the fur traders of the Hudson's Bay Company and the North West Company. The two companies were keen rivals until their merger in 1821, when the Hudson's Bay Company took over the trading in Oregon. In eastern Oregon many trails were available in the open country, but in most parts it was not necessary to follow a trail and most explorers made use of them only here and there, and rarely noted their presence in their journals. As in western Oregon, the Indians burned the vegetation and for the same reasons, to drive game, to improve the grass, and to keep down the sagebrush. Even in the forested lands of the Blue Mountains burning had produced numerous prairies, described by Douglas and many of the fur traders. Eastern Oregon country was obviously much easier to burn than that in the west.

The Blue Mountains (see **fig. 4.7**) were crossed by the early explorers, beginning with the Astor (Hunt's) party in 1811. The region was and is a sort of bridge between the Snake River on the east and the Columbia River on the north. The most important route led from the Snake River in the vicinity of Ontario, up the Burnt River, then through the sites of Baker and La Grande, over the ridge to the vicinity of Pendleton, and thus to the Columbia River near Umatilla. There were many local divergences from this trail, which later became a part of the Oregon Trail. Another main route followed by the fur traders was established along the west side of the Deschutes River, north and south, and to Klamath Lake. Still another route led up the John Day Valley, crossed a ridge to Willow Creek, and reached the Malheur River.

Donald McKenzie of the Hudson's Bay Company crossed the Blue Mountains with a large party in 1818. He continued into Idaho and Wyoming and spent most of his time there. McKenzie did not keep a journal and we have only fragments of information about his journey across the Blue Mountains. It was apparently the intention of the Hudson's Bay Company to trap and trade so thoroughly in the Snake River country that it would be very difficult for American fur traders or for colonists to come in.

In the winter of 1825–1826 Peter Skene Ogden began his exploration of the Snake River country (**fig. 4.6**).[20] In the light of our present knowledge of places, it is interesting to have Ogden's definition of that area as "bounded on the North by the Columbia Waters, On the South by the Missourie, On the West by the Spanish Territories and the East by the Saskatchewan Tribes." As far as Oregon was concerned, Ogden thought that everything east of the Cascades and south of the Columbia was Snake country, perhaps because the Shoshone or Snake Indians roamed over most of this country at one time or another. Ogden's first trip into the country south of the Columbia River began in late 1825 and continued through the winter. The party left the Columbia near The Dalles and traveled in a southerly direction over the Deschutes Plateau more or less parallel to the Deschutes River and on the western side. Ogden described the country as overrun with fire. He crossed the Deschutes River and went upstream on the east side. He noted that there were trees along the streams, and he found evidence that Indians had visited the area recently but saw none. He did see various animals—beaver, deer, sheep, and wolves.

By November 1826, Ogden and his party had reached the Malheur and Harney lakes area. He found that the water in Malheur Lake was potable (in some years it is not), and the party remained there for several days, trapping for beaver on the Silvies River that comes down from the Blue Mountains. Ogden reported: "Some years since Buffalow visited this quarter as a number of heads and Carcases are still to be seen along the borders of the Lake at present however none are to be seen, nor anamals of any kind. Fowls in abundance but very shy, . . .Swans numerous." Game other than water fowl was scarce and the hunters were discouraged: "Day after day from morning to night are they in quest of animals but not one track do they see what a wretched Country." Ogden and his party then turned west and reached the Paulina Lake area and were delighted to be in the forest again. Obviously the Indians had camped and hunted here and many arrowheads were found. "A number of Bear tracks seen and all our rifle men in pursuit. . . . Our hunters retd. late in the evening without success." The party continued west to the Little Deschutes River and then turned south to the Williamson River, tributary to Klamath Lake. They were suffering from lack of food; they killed and ate some of their horses since they could not find game. Here they saw some Indians. Ogden wrote in his journal: "By their accounts in the month of January they have from five to six feet of snow and their Horses perish for want of Food. They subsist during the winter on Roots of an inferior quallity but in the Summer the Plain is covered with Antelopes and from Lakes not far distant from this we obtain Fish."

After a visit to the Rogue River country, described above (p. 56–57), Ogden and his party retraced their steps into California and then returned to eastern Oregon, reaching Goose Lake, which Ogden called "Pit Lake," in May 1827. He described the country as having fine streams and swamps. He estimated the size of Goose Lake as "not less than 20 miles [in length] and on an average not less than a mile and a half in width," probably a low estimate. (Goose Lake fluctuates over the years and has been dry at least twice since discovery.) Ogden saw many pelicans and he assumed from their presence that the lake had abundant fish; but much to his disappointment and hunger, the streams supplied almost no beaver. The Indians explained the scarcity of beaver. They had set a fire four years before in a very dry period with low water and it had burned the beaver houses. Game was very scarce and Ogden's party again had to kill some of their horses for food. From the north end of Goose Lake the party turned east and reached what is now

58

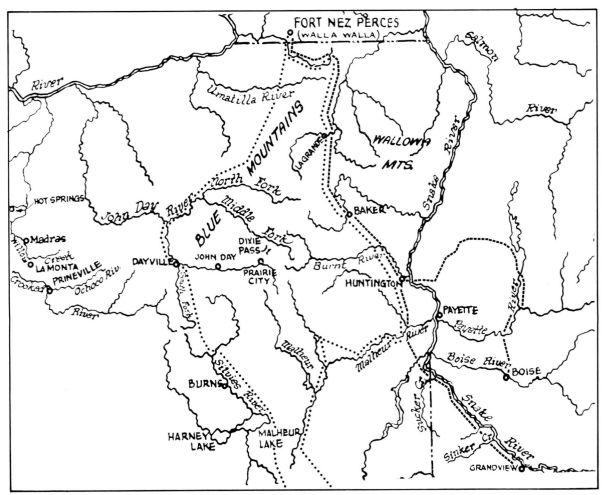

fig. 4.6   Part of Peter Skene Ogden's fur-trading expeditions to eastern Oregon in
1827-1828 (dashed line) and in 1828-1829 (dotted line). (From *Peter Skene
Ogden's Snake Country Journal*, 1950)

called Warner Valley. Here they killed a mountain
sheep and captured a lamb. It was the intention of
the party to send the lamb back to Fort Vancouver
alive, but it is doubtful if it ever arrived. Ogden
surmised that many of the small lakes they visited
would be dry in summer.

In later trips Ogden visited many other areas of
eastern Oregon; he traveled southward from Malheur Lake along the east side of Steens Mountain
and into Nevada by way of Denio. He also made
an excursion to Idaho along the Snake River
where he met with American trappers. He noted
that in southern Idaho, along the Snake River
Plain, there were still buffalo and Oregon Indians
went there to hunt them. Ogden crossed the Blue
Mountains in two places, one nearly along what
was later to be the Oregon Trail; the other crossing was farther west, bringing him out of the Blue

Mountains on the north, in the vicinity of Heppner. Much of Ogden's account is taken up with the
presence or absence of beaver and with the difficulties encountered. These included not only
hunger, when game and beaver were scarce, but
also difficulties with the men. His party was a
large one and it included a number of French
Canadians, some of whom deserted to the Americans who were offering higher prices for pelts.

Meanwhile, in June 1826, David Douglas visited
the Blue Mountains.[21] He traveled up the Columbia River from Fort Vancouver, his headquarters,
to the Walla Walla River and up the south fork of
that river with two Indian guides. His course lay
generally eastward, which must have brought him
to the summit of the Blue Mountains in the vicinity of Tollgate Pass. He traveled over a grassy
plain, some of it rolling (the Palouse Hills), before

59

he reached the Blue Mountains. This hilly area was broken by streams lined with willow and birch shrubs. By the third day he reached the middle of the mountains where the snow began. At the summit he estimated his elevation as 9,000 feet. (This is too high, since the highest point in the vicinity does not exceed 6,200 feet.) Douglas then turned back because of some difficulty with his Indian guides. Later in the month he tried again, reached the snow, but again failed to cross the range. His objective was the Grande Ronde Basin that had been described to him by some of the trappers. On these trips to the Blue Mountains Douglas collected more than 30 species of plants, including anemone, pentstemon, saxifrage, and willow, some of which he believed were new to science.

Benjamin Bonneville visited the Grande Ronde Valley in 1833 and saw it in terms of hunting and grazing.[22] Bonneville had crossed the Snake River Canyon from Idaho to reach the Grande Ronde. Though some descriptions of his crossing are available, they do not indicate the location very well. He described the Grande Ronde: "Its sheltered situation, embosomed in mountains, renders it good pasturing ground in the winter time, when the elk come down to it in great numbers, driven out of the mountains by snow. The Indians then resort to it to hunt. They likewise come to it in summer time to dig the camash root, of which it produces immense quantities. When this plant is in blossom the whole valley is tinted by its blue flowers, and looks like the ocean, when overcast."

At the close of the period of exploration, which we have arbitrarily fixed as 1840, eastern Oregon was fairly well known to a few, but much of the information collected was tied up in various records, especially those of the Hudson's Bay Company. These records were not generally available to the immigrants, whose interest, after all, was in getting across eastern Oregon as easily as possible and arriving at the Willamette Valley. For the people who settled eastern Oregon many years later, much of the exploration had to be done over again. But some of the fur traders and trappers were still around after the settlers arrived and passed on information to them.

THE OREGON MAP TO 1840

The map of the interior of Oregon, almost a complete blank in 1804, was slowly filled in.[23] But it was not until the 1850s that systematic instrumental surveys began, producing more accurate maps. The Clark map (see **fig. 4.3**), which was completed in 1810 and published in the journals in 1814, was an excellent beginning. It shows great detail along the Columbia and Snake rivers, on the basis of information obtained from the Indians, and extends the map far beyond the line of Lewis and Clark's travels. William Clark copied many of the Indian maps, which had been marked out on hides or other materials, and these were reproduced in the journals. Evidently the Indians had a good sense of direction and distance, for these maps are very good considering that the Indians had no instruments of any kind. Not only did Lewis and Clark supply a fairly good map of the Columbia River and the Oregon coast as far south as Cannon Beach, but they also depicted the Rocky Mountains as a series of ranges. Previous maps and some subsequent ones showed the Rocky Mountains as a single ridge. Clark's complete map extended from the Mississippi River to the Pacific Ocean; much of the map was derived from other maps, but the Oregon portion was almost completely original. The lower Columbia River is shown very well. In northeastern Washington, the Columbia and Okanogan rivers are confused. The source of the Willamette River (called the "Multnomah") is shown in the Rocky Mountains. The river flows entirely across the Cascade Range, which appears as two ridges, dividing at Mt. Jefferson. The Coast Range is shown as a single, short ridge southward from Tillamook Head. The text of the journal gave little attention to landforms; the Cascades and the Coast Range, as such, are scarcely mentioned, but this is not surprising considering that the expedition was in Oregon from November to April only, in what was apparently a very rainy, cloudy winter. The Blue Mountains are represented by a single, narrow ridge running southwest from "Lewis'" (Snake) River. From this ridge six rivers drain northward to the Columbia and the Snake. Although Indian names were given to these rivers, it is possible to identify the Deschutes, John Day, and Umatilla. The location of the lower courses of the rivers is fairly accurate but that of the upper reaches is less so. The upper part of the Snake is shown with many tributaries, among which the Grande Ronde, Imnaha, Salmon, Powder, Burnt, Malheur, and Owyhee rivers can be identified. On the eastern side of the Salmon River, the Weiser, Payette, and Boise rivers are shown. All were

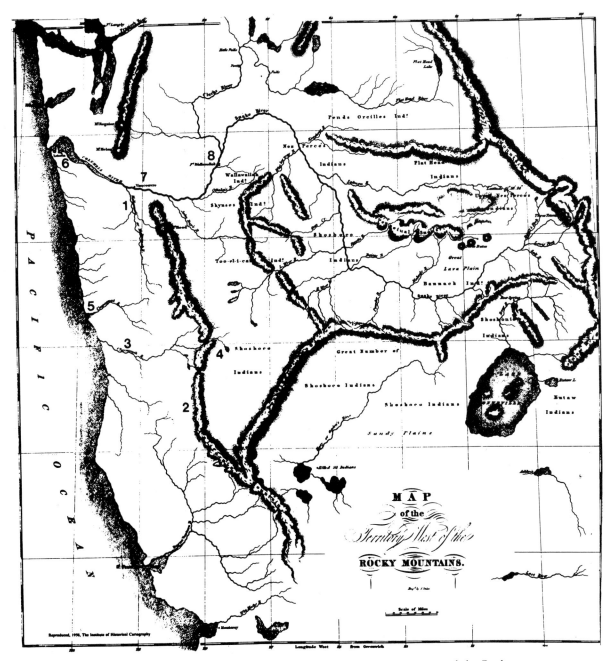

fig. 4.7   A part of Captain B.L.E. Bonneville's *Map of the Territory West of the Rocky Mountains*, published by Washington Irving in 1837. This represented an improvement in the delineation of the drainage as compared with previous maps. All of the "Wallamunt or Multnomah River" (1) is west of the Cascade Range (compare William Clark's map, (**Fig. 4.3**), which is labeled "California Mountains" (only partly shown) (2). A part of the long irregular ridge to the east later came to be called the Blue Mountains. The "Claymouth (Klamath) River" (3) is shown with a source east of the Cascades (Klamath Lake) (4). The "Umpaquah" (5) appears, but not the Rogue. The only settlements shown are Astoria (6) "Vancouvre" (7), and Fort "Wallawallah" (8).

61

MAP
of the
UNITED STATES
TERRITORY OF OREGON
West of the Rocky Mountains.

*Exhibiting the various Trading Depots or Forts
occupied by the British Hudson Bay Company connected with the Western and northwestern Fur Trade.*

*Compiled in the Bureau of Topographical
Engineers from the latest authorities under
the direction of Col. J.J. Abert by
Wash: Hood.*
1838.
M.H. Stansbury del.

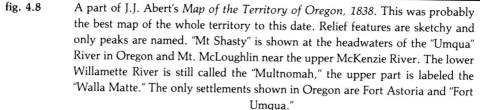

fig. 4.8   A part of J.J. Abert's *Map of the Territory of Oregon, 1838*. This was probably the best map of the whole territory to this date. Relief features are sketchy and only peaks are named. "Mt Shasty" is shown at the headwaters of the "Umqua" River in Oregon and Mt. McLoughlin near the upper McKenzie River. The lower Willamette River is still called the "Multnomah," the upper part is labeled the "Walla Matte." The only settlements shown in Oregon are Fort Astoria and "Fort Umqua."

given Indian names; of these only the name "Imnaha" remains. The others were renamed by the fur traders and early settlers.

In 1822 Henry S. Tanner published his *New American Atlas* with a much improved map of North America. In a revision (1829) Tanner included an inset map of the Oregon and Mandan districts and a sub-inset map showing the outlet of the "Oregon" (Columbia) River. The western, southern, and eastern boundaries of Oregon are heavily shaded; the northern border is not shown on the inset, since it was assumed at that time that Oregon extended to Alaska. The Rocky Mountains are represented by a single, main range, with

a few lesser bordering ranges. The only relief features shown in the present state of Oregon are Mt. Hood and Mt. Jefferson. The drainage features are similar to those of William Clark's map and many of the same names are used. As in previous maps, the only coastal stream shown is "Killemouk River" with its mouth south of Cape Lookout. The sub-inset map gives the depths in fathoms of the lower Columbia River and indicates the magnetic variation.

In 1837 Washington Irving, in his book *The Rocky Mountains*, published a map by Bonneville, entitled "Map of the Territory West of the Rocky Mountains" (**fig. 4.7**), based mostly on

Bonneville's travels from 1832 to 1835. The map shows many features not previously recorded, especially concerning the streams. The "Claymouth" (Klamath) is shown with its source in a lake to the east of the Cascade Range. The "Umpaquah" (Umpqua) is named and several other coastal streams are shown without names, but the Rogue River is missing. The Snake River and its tributaries are shown but the Columbia is labeled "Clarks River" above its confluence with the Snake. Great Salt Lake is called "Lake Bonneville," a term later applied to the much larger freshwater lake that existed in glacial times. In the southeastern part of the map "Ogden's River" (the Humboldt) is shown flowing into "Battle" (Pyramid) Lake. The Rocky Mountains are depicted as a single range with a branch extending westward to the north of the Salmon River. The Salmon River Range is called "The Perpetual Snows." The Cascade Range appears but is not named (except for Mt. Hood); further south the range is called the "California Mountains" (Sierra Nevada). Settlements are shown at Astoria, Vancouver, and Fort "Wallawallah."

One of the first maps made by an official surveyor was that of Colonel J. J. Abert, produced in 1838 (fig. 4.8). "The Territory of Oregon," as it is called on this map, is bordered on the south by the 42nd parallel and on the north by the 49th parallel, although the latter border did not become official until 1846. The eastern boundary of the Oregon Territory coincides with the crest of the Rocky Mountains, or "Stony Mountains," also called the "Oregon Mountains." On the coast, the "Killimoux River" is shown south of Cape Lookout and the name "Quicksand Bay," further north, probably refers to Tillamook Bay. Also shown are the Siuslaw and Umpqua rivers. Cape Blanco and Cape "Oxford" (Orford) are one and the same, and the river that reaches the sea immediately south of the cape is called the "Rouge," the "Clamet," or the "McCleods." Even the Indian name, "Too-to-nez," appears on the map. "Mt. Shasty" (Shasta) is located on this map in Oregon near the headwaters of the "Shasty River," which was actually the upper Rogue, while Mt. McLoughlin is near the headwaters of the McKenzie River. Mt. Jefferson is called "Mt. Vancouver," and Mt. Hood is located at the headwaters of the "Quicksand" (Sandy) River. The main river in the Willamette Valley is the "Multnomah," or the "Williamete," but the upper course of the river is the "Walla Matte." Unlike some previous maps, this shows the source of this river in Oregon and not in "Youta" (Utah) Lake. No roads or trails are indicated on the map and the only settlements are forts Astoria, Vancouver, and Umpqua. Although the missions were in existence at this time, on the Walla Walla River in northeastern Oregon and in the Willamette Valley, they are not shown on Abert's map.

SUMMARY

With the close of the period of exploration up to 1840, exploration, of course, did not cease. But with the beginning of settlement, the movement of people into Oregon took the spotlight away from the explorers. In the following chapter it will be seen that exploration was still going on. For example, Palmer and Barlow pioneered the road across the Cascades south of Mt. Hood in 1845 and 1846.

One of the most important changes on the landscape, during the exploration period, was due to the great diminution in the effect of the Indians. During this period thousands of Indians died of diseases presumably introduced by the fur traders. And many had their way of life completely altered by contact with the traders and the first settlers. Indian burning greatly declined and, in many areas, trees and shrubs began to grow up in what for many generations had been prairies. The only exceptions were the areas of cultivation occupied by the new settlers. In eastern Oregon, when burning declined bunch grass grew tall in the semi-arid lands, and not until they were overgrazed by the cattle and sheep of white settlers did the sagebrush invade some of these prairies.

5

EARLY SETTLEMENTS
1840–1850

Fly, scatter through the country to the Great West.
HORACE GREELEY

By 1840 the stage was set for the great migration to come. Oregon had been explored in a general way and a part of the story had trickled back to the East. Very few settlements had been established – the French settlement near Champoeg, missions on the Clatsop Plains, in the Willamette Valley, at The Dalles, and near Walla Walla. The focal point was the post of the Hudson's Bay Company at Fort Vancouver. The political status of the Oregon Country from California to Alaska (**fig. 5.1**) was in limbo; it was claimed by the United States and by Great Britain, although neither was taking a very active interest in governing. However, the Hudson's Bay Company and the missionaries, between them, provided limited restraints on the Indians and the few white residents.

In 1840 communications within Oregon were limited to waterways and trails. The Columbia River was the great highway for canoe traffic, in spite of its rapids and, in the broader stretches of the river, rough water. Other large rivers and bays were used for canoe travel, especially the Willamette and Umpqua rivers. Indians furnished the canoes and often the manpower to paddle them. The Oregon Trail had not been established, although some of the fur traders had traversed parts of it. The northern part of the Oregon-California Trail, via the Willamette Valley, was in frequent use but the southern part, over Siskiyou Pass, was used only rarely. Along the coast, the trail from the Columbia River to the California line had been used by the fur trappers, taking advantage of the beaches, but they found difficult stretches along the headlands.[1] Indian trails existed in many places, but some of them were overgrown with dense vegetation before the whites could make use of them.

Exploration had not ended; indeed, the period of official explorations had scarcely begun. Except for Lewis and Clark, most of the exploration up to 1840 had been done by the fur traders. In the decade 1840–1850, a number of official surveys or explorations were made, the most noteworthy of which were those of Lieutenant Charles Wilkes, Lieutenant Neil M. Howison, and Captain John C. Frémont. Wilkes and Howison came by ship; Frémont traveled overland and his explorations were limited to eastern Oregon.

LIEUTENANT CHARLES WILKES

Lieutenant Charles Wilkes, U.S. Navy, was commissioned to map and report on the rivers and harbors of the Oregon Country.[2] He arrived by ship at the Columbia River in April 1841, found the bar too rough for entrance, sailed instead to Puget Sound, and approached the Columbia overland. Wilkes and his crew surveyed the Columbia from Astoria to Fort Walla Walla, complaining that smoke from Indian fires interfered with instrumental work. He visited the old post at Astoria and found it in ruins but with good potatoes growing in the garden.

Wilkes produced an excellent map of the Columbia River and compiled a greatly improved map of the Oregon Country (**fig. 5.2**) and a part of northern California. The coast is well delineated and the "Rogues" and "Klamet" rivers are in their proper places. About half of western Oregon is mapped as woodland, with both coniferous and broad-leaved trees. The remainder is represented mostly as prairie, the majority of which lies in the valleys of the Willamette, Umpqua, and Rogue.

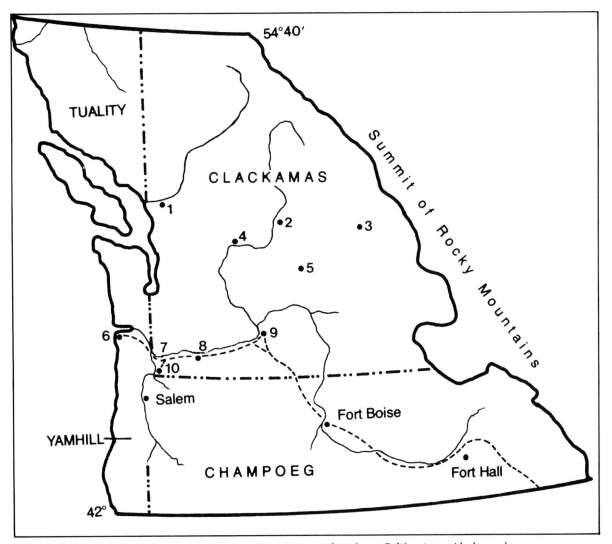

fig. 5.1   Map of the Oregon Country in 1843, extending from California to Alaska and
from the Rocky Mountains to the Pacific Ocean. The four original districts are:
Tuality, Yamhill, Clackamas, and Champoeg. Forts and trading posts: (1) Ft.
Langley; (2) Ft. Colville; (3) Ft. Kootenai; (4) Ft. Okanogan; (5) Spokane; (6)
Astoria; (7) Ft. Vancouver; (8) The Dalles; (9) Ft. Walla Walla; (10) Oregon City.
The Oregon Trail is shown by a dashed line. (From Gen. Forum of Portland,
Genealogical Material in Oregon Donation Land Claims, 1957)

The Cascade Range is shown as a sinuous ridge, with the major peaks in their proper positions. In eastern Oregon there are large blank spaces, but some grassland is shown and, surprisingly, no forest, in spite of earlier descriptions of the forests of the Blue Mountains by Ogden, Douglas, and others. The Blue Mountains are shown as a single ridge, trending southerly from the Grande Ronde Basin. The map has numerous notations on the margins, such as "The Cascade Range is the eastern boundary of the tillable land and the forest land." Wilkes saw only the Columbia River and the Willamette Valley. The rest of his map was compiled from the maps of Jedediah Smith, Aaron Arrowsmith, and Samuel Parker. But it was a great improvement over previous maps and superior to some that followed.

Wilkes estimated the white population living in Oregon in 1841 as between 700 and 800, of whom about 150 were Americans and the rest were largely Canadian fur trappers and traders. Most of these were living in the six settlements mentioned

65

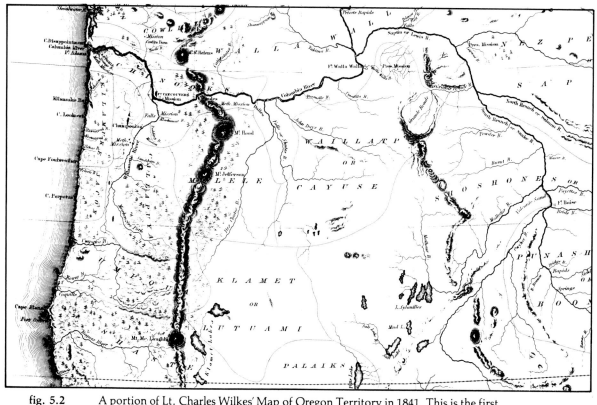

fig. 5.2   A portion of Lt. Charles Wilkes' Map of Oregon Territory in 1841. This is the first
map to show boundaries for the various Indian Tribes. The settlements shown in
the present area of Oregon are Astoria and the missions in the Clatsop Plains, at
the Falls of the Willamette, at The Dalles, and on the Willamette River below
Salem. (Recent print from original copper plate, OHS Map Collection)

earlier, with the largest number at Fort
Vancouver.

JOHN H. FROST

Although he was not the first to travel along the
northern coast of Oregon, the missionary John H.
Frost was the first to describe the country in
detail.[3] In 1841 Frost, with a companion, Brother
Sebastian Smith, and an Indian guide and horse,
traveled from the Clatsop Plains down the coast
by way of Tillamook, then up the Little Nestucca
River and across the Coast Range to the Willamette Valley. Although Indian trails were in existence in places, some were not suitable for horses.
For example, the trail that William Clark had followed across Tillamook Head was too steep for a
horse. Frost therefore had to take an inland route,
quite different, and great difficulties were encountered with brush. On the whole, however, Frost

followed the best possible route of the time, since
he had good advice from the local Indians as he
went along. The Indians were generally friendly,
often supplying him with food as well as directions. Frost's description of crossing Neahkahnie
Mountain (fig. 5.3) is a classic, taking up five
book pages in his published journal. The Indian
trail over the mountain was narrow, not much
wider than a man's two hands. Frost described
Neahkahnie Mountain as "prairie on the side next
the ocean." In bypassing Tillamook Bay on the
east, Frost crossed "the river four times." Actually
he crossed five rivers—the Miami, Kilchis, Wilson, Trask, and Tillamook—but it was foggy at
the time and his mistake is understandable. Frost
had difficulty in finding his way from the upper
Little Nestucca River across the Coast Range, but
eventually he reached the missions in the Willamette Valley and later returned to the Clatsop Plains
with cows and horses for the settlers. Altogether
this was a very remarkable journey by men who

NO.159 BRIDGE ON MT NEAH-KAH-NIE TRAIL SEASIDE TO NEHALEM ORE

fig. 5.3   Early road across Neahkahnie Mountain with a wooden trestle over the chasm.
(Wesley Andrews photo, OHS)

were not especially trained for the outdoor life. The entire round trip to the Willamette Valley had taken most of the summer.

CAPTAIN JOHN C. FRÉMONT

Captain Frémont with 20 men, a number of horses, and a small cannon entered Oregon by crossing the Snake River at Fort Boise in October 1843.[4] He followed the Oregon Trail, over which immigrants were passing, to the Grande Ronde Basin. Then he traveled northward past the site of Elgin and crossed the Blue Mountain crest at, or near, Tollgate Pass. He described the dense forest near the summit as including larches 12 feet in diameter and large spruces. Frémont summed up the Blue Mountains thus: "Hills and mountains here were rich in grass, the bottoms barren and sterile." He followed the Columbia River to The Dalles. Leaving his party at the mission, he traveled by canoe to Fort Vancouver. Returning to The Dalles in November, he turned southward, following nearly the same route Ogden had many years before, as far as Tygh Valley. Then Frémont continued along the western margin of the Deschutes River. He passed in turn through areas of sagebrush, prairie, and pine forest and reached Klamath Marsh, which he thought was Klamath Lake (Wilkes' map shows three lakes). Indians were camped in the middle of the "lake" but Frémont surmised this was not their permanent home. Turning eastward, Frémont encountered snow on the higher ranges. He crossed Winter Ridge and named it and Summer Lake. He judged from the white crust on the margin of Summer Lake that the water was not potable. Although the myth of "Multnomah River," which supposedly originated in the Rocky Mountains and flowed across the Cascades, had been exploded by Ogden and McLeod, Frémont was apparently not aware of this and expected to find such a river as he traveled southward along the eastern margin of the Cascades toward California.

LIEUTENANT NEIL M. HOWISON

Lieutenant Neil Howison, U.S. Navy, came to Oregon on July 1, 1846, in the schooner *Shark*, shortly after the treaty fixing the northern boundary of Oregon at the 49th parallel had been signed. He made a report to Congress[5] on trade, shipping, and the general development of the Oregon Country, based in part on a trip through the Willamette Valley. He surmised that the settlers came from the poorer classes, but praised their efforts to develop the country and to obey the laws.

He noted the poor condition of most of the towns but also some improvements. Of Astoria he said: "It may be considered in a state of transition, exhibiting the wretched remains of a bygone settlement and the uncouth germ of a new one." Astoria had 10 houses and a population of 30 whites. Oregon City had 70 buildings and a population of 500. At Portland, "eight or nine miles above Linton [Linnton is now a part of Portland] on the same side of the Wilhammette, we come to a more promising appearance of a town." Portland had a dozen new houses and a population of 70. A road had been laid out from there to the Tualatin Valley. Of Salem, Howison said, "too little exists to be worthy an attempt at description."

SOURCES OF IMMIGRANTS

When the migration to Oregon started, the upper Mississippi Valley had been slowly filling up with people for more than a half-century, but it was by no means full. The Middle Western states from which most of the Oregon immigrants came — Illinois, Indiana, Iowa, Kentucky, Missouri, Ohio, and Tennessee — had, in 1850, fewer than 4 million people, compared to 35 million in 1970. Obviously there was no great pressure to migrate due to crowding, unless one insisted on having his nearest neighbor more than a mile away.

Westward migration was a way of life for many of the Oregon immigrants. A common pattern of state-hopping was from North Carolina to Kentucky to Missouri. Daniel Boone made these moves and, had he been alive when the great movement to Oregon began, he would probably have joined one of the wagon trains. His grandson, Alphonso Boone, moved to Oregon in 1846 and *his* son, Jesse, operated a ferry across the Willamette River near Wilsonville. Although the 1850 census gave the state of immediate origin of the Oregon immigrants, it did not tell the whole story.[6] According to the census the origins and numbers were as follows (**fig. 5.4**): New England, 493; Middle Atlantic, 903; South Atlantic, 762; Gulf, 50; South Central, including Kentucky and

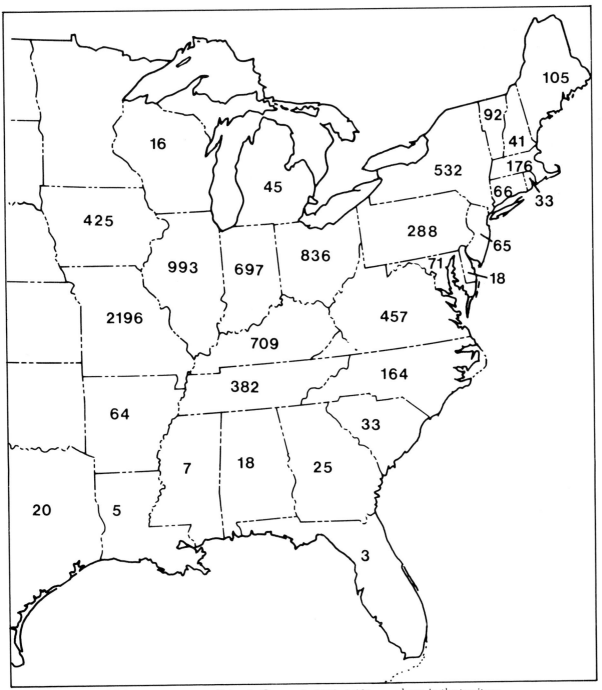

fig. 5.4   Of the 11,873 persons living in Oregon in 1850, 2,191 were born in the territory. Most of the remainder came from the eastern and middle western states. Twenty-five were born in California and a few more were foreign born. (Data from the U.S. Bureau of the Census)

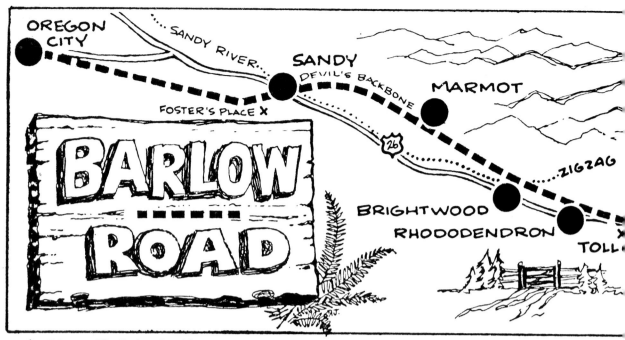

fig. 5.5   The Barlow Road between The Dalles and Oregon City. U.S. Highway 26 and
State Highway 35 are included for reference. The toll was five dollars per wagon
and the trip could be made in a week. Place names along the road included Faith,

Tennessee, 1,091; North Central, including Indiana, Illinois, Michigan, Ohio and Wisconsin,
2,587; Western Border, including Arkansas, Iowa,
and Missouri, 2,685. The Far West, including California, sent 2,249 to Oregon and Canada furnished 261. Other foreign countries supplied 449
immigrants and, of the 13,000 living in the Oregon
Country in 1850, 2,191 were native born.

WHY DID THE PEOPLE MIGRATE
TO OREGON?

In general, the migration to Oregon was due to
a "push-pull" effect. A number of circumstances
were tending to push people out of the Middle
West and the various descriptions of Oregon were
pulling them toward Oregon. The "push" was
mostly floods, diseases, and depression. During
and following the panic of 1837, crop prices and
land values fell and many mortgages contracted
during the previous period could not be paid. A
series of floods had damaged many farms and led
to crop failures. Diseases were prevalent in the upper Mississippi Valley. Malaria and ague were
common. Tuberculosis took more lives than any
other affliction. In the 1850 U.S. census mortality

figures, deaths from tuberculosis and cholera
totaled more than 30,000 each; dysentery more
than 26,000; fevers, 19,000; typhoid, 13,000;
pneumonia, 12,000; diphtheria, 10,000; scarlet
fever, 9,000; and a number of other diseases, such
as whooping cough, measles, erysipelas, and
smallpox accounted for lesser numbers.

Peter Burnett,[7] an Oregon pioneer of 1843, gave
his reasons for moving to Oregon: (1) to assist in
building up a great American community on the
Pacific Coast; (2) to restore the health of Mrs.
Burnett; (3) to be able to pay his debts. Many people moved to Oregon to improve their fortunes,
beginning with New England sea captains who
hunted sea otter and fur seals. Most of them, even
the missionaries who came to save the Indians,
succeeded. To a family in the Middle West, debt-
and disease-ridden, the prospect of a better
climate, at least a milder one, and free land must
have been very attractive.

THE WAY WEST

The immigrants moved to Oregon by three
main routes: across the Plains, following the
Oregon Trail; by sea around Cape Horn; and by

70

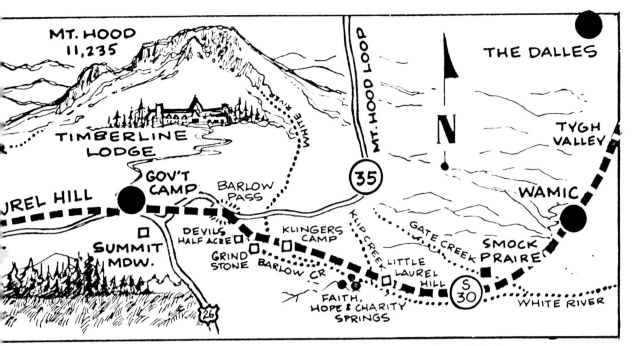

Hope and Charity Springs; Grindstone; Devil's Half Acre; and Devil's Backbone.
(Clackamas County Historical Society and the Wasco County Historical Society,
1975)

sea to Panama with a portage to the Pacific, then by sea again. By far the greatest number traveled overland along the Oregon Trail. All three routes were beset with difficulties and dangers. The Oregon Trail led over dusty plains, deserts, and mountains, and through hostile Indian country. The Panama route included two sea voyages and a difficult crossing of the Isthmus, with the added hazard of tropical diseases. The sea voyage around Cape Horn (or through the Straits of Magellan) was by no means an easy one in the small sailing ships of the day, and not least of the hazards was scurvy.

In a general way the Oregon Trail paralleled the present highways I-80 and I-80N, but there were many minor variations. The immigrants tended to travel near streams, mainly the Platte, Snake, and Columbia rivers, in order to assure themselves of a water supply, but they took several shortcuts. From Independence, Missouri, the route led northwest to the Platte River, thence up the North Platte, past the site of Casper, Wyoming, to South Pass on the continental divide. South Pass is merely a low gap in the Wyoming Basin and caused no difficulty. It was necessary to ford Green River, after which the route led northwestward into southeastern Idaho. Here there were

several variants of the trail. The Snake River was reached near the site of Pocatello and was followed, except for some shortcuts, to or near the area of present-day Ontario, Oregon, where the Snake is a gently flowing stream. The river could be crossed at several points, one of which was at Farewell Bend, below which the river plunges into the canyon. Leaving the Snake, the route led over the Blue Mountains, via the Grande Ronde Basin and Emigrant Pass, a steep, difficult scarp, descending to the Deschutes-Umatilla Plateau in the vicinity of present Pendleton. Frequently it was necessary to fasten felled trees to the wagons to slow their progress down the steep slopes. One variant of the trail followed the Umatilla River to the Columbia River; another turned northward to the Whitman Mission, where supplies and assistance could be obtained. By this time the wagons and draft animals were usually in poor condition. The route continued on the plateau near the Columbia River to The Dalles, where, until the Barlow Road (**fig. 5.5**) was marked out over the Cascade Range, the wagons had to be abandoned. Many immigrants descended the Columbia in boats or rafts; some used pack animals to cross the Cascades. The immediate goal for early immigrants was Fort Vancouver, where they could

71

supply their needs before moving south to Oregon City and the Willamette Valley.

The first settlers to come by sea, other than the fur traders, were the missionaries.[8] The Methodists were in frequent communication by land and sea with the eastern states; new recruits and supplies continued to arrive and generally enthusiastic descriptions of Oregon were carried east. As a result of the lectures given in the East by Missionary Jason Lee, the Peoria Party, consisting of 18 young men, set out for Oregon in May 1839 in search of health, wealth, and adventure, with the motto "Oregon or the Grave." Lack of experience and common purpose took their toll, and the party divided into quarrelsome cliques. They finally straggled into Fort Vancouver the following spring, almost a year after their departure from Peoria.

The year 1842 was a turning point in the migration to Oregon. Until then the movement was sporadic, often poorly organized, and with very few participants. In 1842 probably 150 white inhabitants were added to the population, most of them as members of the "first typical wagon train" to reach the Oregon Country.[9] The party included 112 persons with 52 men 18 years or older; for the first time women and children outnumbered the men. The party left Elm Grove, Kansas, on May 16, 1842, with 18 wagons, oxen, and a number of horses, mules, and cattle. They reached Fort Laramie on June 23. At the Green River crossing some of the wagons were cut up and made into packsaddles. The remainder of the wagons were disposed of at Fort Hall. Pack animals were driven along the Snake River and over the Blue Mountains to Fort Walla Walla. The party continued down the Columbia River, using Hudson's Bay Company river boats and Indian canoes. A few crossed the Columbia near The Dalles and followed an Indian trail for part of the journey, recrossing the river in the vicinity of Sandy River. Most of the party settled at Oregon City, and at the end of the winter of 1842-1843, this village at the Falls of the Willamette had 30 houses.

THE MIGRATION ACCELERATED

Early in 1843 wagons began converging on the Missouri frontier from Kentucky, Illinois, Tennessee, Indiana, Ohio, and a number of other states to form a huge wagon train (**fig. 5.6**) with over 500 persons (estimates vary), 120 wagons,

and 5,000 head of livestock—horses, mules, and cattle.[10] This was called "The Great Migration," although later ones were much larger. The party left Elm Grove, Kansas, on May 22, reached South Pass on August 5, and arrived at Fort Bridger on August 14. They completed the entire journey to Oregon City in a little over five and one-half months, a remarkably rapid passage. They had the advantage of fresh pastures and fairly abundant game, including bison, which later immigrants did not have. In succeeding years the Oregon Trail was in many places a broad overgrazed and overhunted belt. The party was divided into two parts, the fast and the slow. The slower group, led by Jesse Applegate and burdened with most of the livestock, came to be known as the "Cow Column."

At Whitman Mission near Walla Walla some of the migrants sold their cattle and traveled downriver by boat. Those who continued by wagon were temporarily halted at The Dalles. The season was too late to attempt a crossing of the Cascades and the party was too large to be accommodated by the available boats, and so hundreds of trees were cut and rafts constructed for the passage to Fort Vancouver.

Arriving at Oregon City, the party dispersed to various parts of the northern Willamette Valley. Daniel Waldo took his cattle to the hills, now known as the Waldo Hills, east of the site of Salem, and established a farm. The Applegates spent the winter at the Methodist Mission in the Willamette Valley, then moved to Salt Creek in Polk County in the spring. The Garrisons laid out a farm in the Tualatin Plain, where they were joined by Peter Burnett's family.

By early 1845 there were 2,100 white people living in the five counties of Oregon: Champoeg, Clackamas, Clatsop, Tualatin, and Yamhill. Champoeg was the most populous. Forty-eight percent of the inhabitants were less than 18 years of age and only seven percent were 45 years old or older.

In the migration of 1845,[11] which totaled perhaps 3,000 persons, one party of 200 families tried to find a shorter route across the semiarid regions of eastern Oregon and perhaps an easier route than Barlow Pass across the Cascades. They traveled up the Malheur River to Harney Lake, then over the divide to the Deschutes River. After much adversity and after failing to cross the Cascades, the party arrived at The Dalles.

The migration of 1846 was smaller; probably no

fig. 5.6   Artist's snowy scene of covered wagons on Barlow Road. (OHS)

more than 1,300 people entered Oregon, perhaps because more immigrants were going to California by that time. After the Barlow Road was opened over the Cascades, it became more difficult to estimate the number of immigrants, since some continued to travel down the Columbia by boat. Earlier most of the immigrants stopped at Whitman Mission and a count was kept there; later most of the immigrants bypassed the mission. In 1847 immigration picked up again, with about 5,000 reaching the Pacific Northwest, some of them settling to the north of the Columbia River.

Once they were in Oregon the new arrivals could choose from a variety of locations, according to religion, occupation, or some other preference. French Canadians tended to locate in or near Champoeg and St. Paul; Methodists near one of that church's missions. Most of the immigrants who came from the upper Mississippi Valley were farmers and continued to be so. Immigrants from New England and Canada were mostly town people – merchants, clerks, carpenters, and even ordinary laborers. These preferred to locate in the towns.

SCARCITY OF GAME AND WILD FRUITS

One of the unexpected conditions confronting the early settlers was the scarcity of game. This apparently was a phenomenon of long standing. Lewis and Clark reported the shortage of game along their route and in the Clatsop Plains, except for elk that were difficult for the Indians to kill. The fur traders, especially in eastern Oregon, noted the infrequent occurrence of game and that the Indians were often starving.

Peter Burnett pointed out the scarcity of wild game and fruits in the Willamette Valley: "The only wild fruits we found were a variety of berries, such as blackberries, raspberries, strawberries, blueberries, and cranberries, which were not only abundant but of excellent quality. We only found one nut in the country, and that was the hazelnut in small quantities. There were no wild grapes or plums, and no honey."[12]

Lieutenant Howison also reported poor hunting. "I was surprised," he said, "to find so great a scarcity of game in this country. I lugged a heavy gun more than a hundred and fifty miles through

73

the Wilhammette valley, and in all that ride saw but three deer. Wolves are numerous, and prey upon other animals, so that the plains are entirely in their possession. The little venison I saw in Oregon was poor and insipid; a fat buck is a great rarity. Elk are still numerous, but very wild, living in the depths of the forests, or near those openings which the white man has not yet approached."[13] The lack of game was probably related not so much to the hunting activities of the Indians as to the prevalence of predators, such as wolves, mountain lions, coyotes, and bobcats. The word went out that immigrants going to Oregon should be prepared to work and not to hunt.

DISEASES IN OREGON

The high incidence of disease among the Indians, noted in chapter 3, continued into the missionary period, affecting both Indians and whites. Malaria and a type of diphtheria were common. Both Daniel and Jason Lee were afflicted, as were John Frost and his wife on the Clatsop Plains. The first settlers blamed the cloudy, rainy winters for both their major and minor ailments. Undoubtedly the immigrants brought various infections with them from the disease-ridden Mississippi Valley and the numerous mosquitoes, especially near the streams, led to the spread of malaria, at least. Nevertheless, in a few years the incidence of disease declined substantially. Bancroft,[14] citing Dr. Elijah White, painted an optimistic picture of the late 1840s:

> The diseases which made such havoc during the early missionary occupation.... had disappeared as the natives died or were removed to a distance from the white race. Notwithstanding the crowded state of the settlers every winter after the arrival of another immigration, and notwithstanding insufficient food and clothing in many instances, there was little sickness and few deaths. Dr. White, after six years of practice, pronounced the country to be the healthiest and the climate one of the most salubrious in the world.

THE INDIAN PROBLEM IN THE 1840s

In chapter 3 the Indians were described at the time of first contact with the whites. Almost immediately after the first sea-borne fur traders visited the coast of the Oregon Country, the ways of the Indians changed radically. They acquired guns, ammunition, knives, and various other implements. They were also introduced to alcohol and various diseases. Many Indians felt that the whites deliberately introduced the diseases to kill off the Indians and take their land.[15]

In the earliest days of settlement the major conflict with the Indians was related to the immigrant trains, many of which were pillaged and some wiped out. In the Willamette Valley there was comparatively little trouble with Indians and they interfered very little with settlement, partly because so many had died of diseases before the settlers came. Also, the whites soon outnumbered the remaining Indians. In eastern and southern Oregon it was another story. In both areas settlements were scattered and small, making them especially vulnerable to attack.

The settlers mistreated the Indians by occupying their lands and by other wrongs or even killings, sometimes without specific provocation. The Hudson's Bay Company retaliated vigorously against many Indians who committed crimes. After the Smith party massacre in 1826 at the Umpqua, the Company sent a force to kill a few Indians, round up the horses, and recover the furs. When a ship was wrecked in the lower Columbia River and the crew disappeared, the Company sent a boat and fired a cannon into the nearest Indian village. From the whites' standpoint these killings were justified, but not from the Indians'. The stories of Indian atrocities were recounted, while the places and occasions where the Indians were peaceable and friendly were often forgotten.

As the 1840s drew to a close, new factors were introduced; the whites were expanding into southern Oregon and showing signs of moving into eastern Oregon as well. Also, many settlers and some soldiers left Oregon for the California gold mines, leaving some settlements with few defenders. And as an additional disturbing influence, gold was discovered in southern Oregon in 1852.

In the Willamette Valley treaties were made early with the few remaining Calapuya Indians. Large areas of land were taken over by the whites; some of these areas were already occupied before the treaties were signed. The Calapuya Indians were moved to reservations.

The real struggle with the Indians began with the Cayuse War of 1848. The immediate cause was the massacre at Whitman Mission in November

fig. 5.7   Sketch of Ft. Vancouver with Mt. Hood in the background and the Columbia
River at right. (OHS)

1847, but the settlers in the Willamette Valley also realized that some action had to be taken to protect the immigrant trains, especially in the area between the Blue Mountains and The Dalles. A force of several hundred soldiers was recruited and supplied with arms by private donations. The advance force reached The Dalles in January 1848, was reinforced, and moved to the site of the ruined mission. Efforts were made for a peaceful settlement; some of the Indians made peace, but others did not. An indecisive battle was fought on the Touchet River (Washington), west of the mission site. The chief result of the Cayuse War was to make the Oregon Trail in north-central Oregon safer for the immigrant trains. It was still Indian country and it looked like the Great Plains; few whites showed any intention of settling in the area until years later, when mining began and the Indians were placed on reservations.

AGRICULTURE

Most of the people who came to Oregon in the early days came to farm.[16] Ewing Young had established an independent farm in the Chehalem Valley in 1834 and, even earlier, several farms were established by the Hudson's Bay Company on Sauvie Island and elsewhere in the Willamette Valley by retired fur trappers. Many later immigrants brought seeds of wheat, corn, and various vegetables with them. Others had to depend on Dr. John McLoughlin of the Hudson's Bay Company (**fig. 5.7**), who furnished seeds, implements, and even clothing and livestock in exchange for a share of the crops.

Corn, a major crop in the Middle West, was tried but did not ripen well in the Willamette Valley; it failed as a staple crop. Later it succeeded in the drier, warmer areas in eastern Oregon and

fig. 5.8   The steamer *Annie Faxton* at Almota Landing on the Snake River. (OHS)

Washington with irrigation. In 1846, 160,000 bushels of wheat were produced in the Oregon Country. Before the California gold rush wheat sold for a dollar a bushel, an established price. Wheat was legal tender, although not always acceptable to all traders. During the gold rush the price rose to six dollars a bushel and ships came up the Columbia River to Portland to load wheat for California. In the 1850 census the total listed wheat production in Oregon was 208,000 bushels, mostly in the Willamette Valley; Clatsop County had a very small wheat acreage. Nineteen farmers were producing more than 1,000 bushels of wheat each. Nine market gardens, all but one in Clatsop County, produced more than $1,000 worth of produce each. Orchards were established in all eight Willamette Valley counties except Clatsop, but most of them had a very small production.

Livestock was, from the earliest stage, an essential part of the farm economy. In 1837 Ewing Young and others drove 600 head of cattle and horses from the Sacramento Valley of California to Oregon. He was acting as an agent for a number of settlers. In 1841 more cattle and horses, and also mules and sheep, were driven into Oregon from California over the same trail. Hogs and poultry were a part of the farm economy but hogs were only moderately successful because of the scarcity of corn. Sheep were first brought by ship to the Pacific Northwest by the Hudson's Bay Company. Later they came in with the immigrant wagon trains.

In January 1845, James Clyman[17] described a roundup in the Willamette Valley and the branding or slaughtering of 500 head of wild cattle. Apparently many of the cattle brought in by the pioneers became feral after a few years, since there were no fences or other means of restraining them. About 2,000 head of wild cattle were reportedly grazing in the Yamhill area. In 1850 at least 18 farmers had herds of milk cows larger than 40 animals. Most of these were producing both butter and cheese. Twelve farmers had horse herds of more than 30 animals; the largest herd was 125. Thirteen farmers had swine herds larger than 100 head; the largest was 300.

Many new crops were introduced by the immigrants—barley, potatoes, fruits, vegetables, and nuts. As it grew well in the cool summer climate, the potato was especially useful to those settlers who lived on the coast where neither wheat nor corn would grow well. In the early days the set-

76

tlers at Tillamook lived, at times, on potatoes and salmon, unable because of their isolation to obtain wheat or flour from the Willamette Valley. There was no road across the Coast Range and shipment by water to Tillamook was hazardous, especially at the Columbia Bar and at the entrance to Tillamook Bay.

The surplus production of wheat, beef, lumber, and other products obviously called for improved transportation, especially on land.

TRANSPORTATION: BOATS, TRAILS, AND ROADS

From the earliest times the people of Oregon, Indian and white, used water transportation wherever possible. When Lewis and Clark arrived, the Columbia River was the most important route, with hundreds of dugout canoes, some splendidly carved, plying the river. They could be portaged around the rapids. At first the whites merely appropriated Indian canoes, but soon they were building sturdy rowboats. It was not that rowboats were necessarily preferred; but they were easier to build. Construction of a dugout canoe required much patience as well as skill. Neither canoes nor rowboats, however, were safe on the broad reaches of the Columbia in stormy weather; larger, more seaworthy craft were needed. Sailing ships came into the river as far as Fort Vancouver but had difficulties with the currents and sandbars, and so it was inevitable that steamers would be introduced at the earliest possible moment (**fig. 5.8**).

The steamship had proved itself many years before it was introduced to the Columbia River. There was a steamboat in Scotland in 1802 and Robert Fulton's *Clermont*, with British-built engines, was paddling up and down the Hudson River in 1807. The *Savannah*, also a paddlewheel ship, crossed the Atlantic in 1819. (She had sails, as did many of the early steamers. Sails were hoisted and the engines stopped when the wind was favorable.)

The first steamer to enter the Columbia was the army transport *Massachusetts* from Honolulu in 1849, bringing troops (too late) to fight in the war with the Cayuses.[18] One of the earliest screw-propelled ships, she was much more seaworthy than the paddlewheelers. At Fort Vancouver the *Massachusetts* got a salute from Peter Skene Ogden, who was sharing the superintendency of the fort. The troops were disembarked and the ship immediately took on a cargo of lumber for the army posts in California.

In May 1850, the *Carolina*, a Pacific Mail Company steamer, arrived at the Columbia River, six days out of San Francisco. Two days later she was at Portland with mail, cargo, and passengers. From this date on, fairly regular steamer service was established between Portland and California, with a ship every month to six weeks. Steamers had arrived on the West Coast just in time for the gold rush and had more freight and passengers than they could carry. In July 1850, the first steamer to be built in the Columbia River, named the *Columbia*, slid down the ways at Astoria. Her engine had been assembled from parts obtained from San Francisco. She was 90 feet long, with a beam of 16 feet and a hold depth of 4 feet. There were no sleeping accommodations or galley, so the passengers had to fend for themselves on the two-day trip from Astoria to Portland (the ship usually tied up at night). The average speed was four miles per hour. The *Columbia* was a general workhorse; she would tow sailing ships and barges; she met immigrant parties at the Cascades and brought them to Portland. For a few months she had no rival on the river, until the *Lot Whitcomb* was launched at Milwaukie. The *Lot Whitcomb* was 160 feet long, had "luxurious" accommodations, and could do 12 miles per hour. Soon a number of other steamers were in service on the Columbia River.

Until 1846 water transport on the Willamette River was limited to canoes and rowboats. In the winter of 1846–1847 two keel boats, the *Mogul* and the *Ben Franklin*, equipped with sails and oars, were built for service above the Falls between Oregon City and Champoeg. The fare was one dollar in "orders" or fifty cents in cash. The owner announced in the *Oregon Spectator* of April 30, 1846, that he had "well calk'd. gumm'd and greas'd the light draft and fast running boats" and that the "passengers can board [eat] with the captain, by finding their own provisions." The expansion of steamer travel on the Willamette in the following decade is described in the next chapter.

Land transportation in the period 1840–1850 was limited largely to travel by horseback and transport of goods by ox-drawn wagons; prior to 1849, Bancroft states, there was not a single span of horses harnessed to a wagon in the territory.[19] Short roads or tracks led from the farms to the nearest river landing. In summer ox-drawn wagons were in use for longer distances, but in winter, mud, flooded lowlands, and swollen streams made wagon travel almost impossible.

The need for roads was acute, however, and many plans and schemes were in the air; several routes were laid out; a few roads were opened.[20] In 1844 the Provisional Government's Commission of Roads was directed to select the best route for a road from the Methodist Mission to Willamette Falls. In the same year a road was opened from Linnton to Tualatin. In 1846 Levi Scott and Jesse and Lindsay Applegate explored a route from the southern Willamette Valley to Fort Hall on the Oregon Trail that came to be known as the Southern Immigrant Road. Levi Scott and the Applegates met a party of immigrants at Fort Hall and persuaded them to follow the southern route, with disastrous results. Another road was authorized over Santiam Pass to Fort Boise with the provision that it be completed in 60 days. But the Indian trail over the pass had completely grown over and the pass could not be found. A proposal to lay out a road over Willamette Pass was turned down but one to improve the Barlow Road was approved, and Samuel Barlow was given permission to charge tolls.

In 1845 the legislature passed a law that led, in 1847, to the establishment of post offices at Astoria and Oregon City, but because of the lack of funds there were almost no mail facilities until 1848. It was customary to send mail by private individuals, sometimes with payment. It usually required at least five months for a letter from the Middle West to reach Oregon. In 1850 Congress passed an act to establish post roads: from Astoria to the mouth of the Umpqua River via Portland; from the mouth of the Umpqua River to Sacramento, California; from Oregon City to Albany; from Nisqually to the mouth of the Cowlitz River; from Portland to The Dalles; from Portland to Hillsboro; from Oregon City to Molalla; from Linn City to Hillsboro.[21] In spite of the act, mail service was not, in fact, established on all these routes. Ships carried mail to and from San Francisco at irregular intervals until monthly service was begun in 1851.

POLITICAL DIVISIONS

From the very beginning the settlers began to organize themselves for various purposes. They felt neglected by the U.S. Congress and chafed under the domination of the Hudson's Bay Company that, on the whole, had been very fair and helpful to them. Nevertheless the Company's interests conflicted with those of the settlers. Organization was also stimulated by Indian hostilities. In 1841 a meeting at the Methodist Mission elected a judge and other court officers. Lieutenant Wilkes, who was in the Oregon Country at the time, discouraged the organization of the settlers, but in 1843 a meeting at Champoeg adopted "articles of compact and laws."[22] These were confirmed in an election on July 25, 1845.

At a meeting of the Provisional Government in 1843, Oregon was divided into four districts (see **fig. 5.1**), Tuality, Clackamas, Yamhill, and Champoeg. In 1844 the districts were designated counties (**fig. 5.9**) with the addition of Clatsop in 1844 and Polk in 1845. Benton County was formed from Polk, and Linn from Champoeg in 1847; and in 1849 the legislature changed the names of Champoeg to Marion and Tuality to Washington.

Meanwhile the Oregon Country was being more narrowly defined. Originally it had extended from California to Alaska and eastward to the continental divide (see **fig. 5.1**). In 1846 a treaty with Great Britain ended the controversy over ownership and fixed the northern boundary of Oregon at the 49th parallel. The new boundary encouraged settlement, especially north of the Columbia River on land previously occupied by Hudson's Bay Company enterprises.

LAND OWNERSHIP

Most of the first settlers in Oregon were "squatters" in that they settled on vacant land with no title and with no provision for obtaining one. This was a common custom at the time, practiced in much of the territory west of the Appalachians. In 1820 Congress passed a land law designed to protect the rights of such settlers, providing for the purchase of land in the public domain at $1.25 per acre.[23] The Preemption Land Law of 1841, also called "Benton's Log-Cabin Bill," entitled male citizens over 21, widows, and certain aliens to settle on surveyed land and to purchase it at a minimum price. Although Oregon was not officially a part of the United States at this time, many Oregon settlers, lacking any other basis for a title, assumed (or hoped) that they came under the provisions of this law, or at least under some law. This condition was far from satisfactory and in

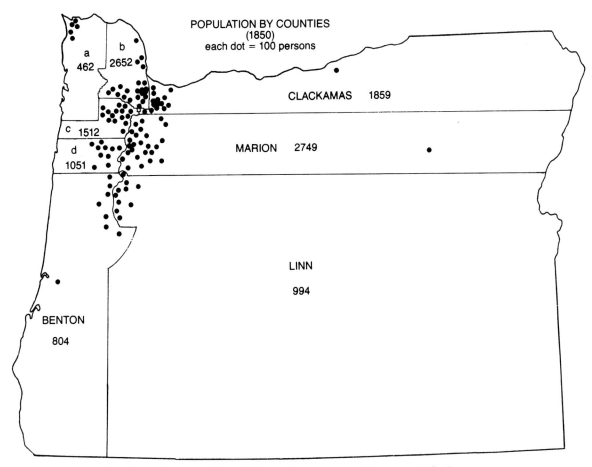

a
462

b
2652

CLACKAMAS   1859

c 1512

MARION   2749

d
1051

LINN

994

BENTON

804

fig. 5.9   Population by counties in 1850 (each dot represents 100 persons). The figures give
the total population for each county, (a) Clatsop; (b) Washington; (c) Yamhill;
(d) Polk. (Data from the U.S. Bureau of the Census, 1850)

1843 the Provisional Government adopted an organic code, including a land law that provided that an individual could claim 640 acres in a square or oblong form. This law, although it had limited authority, reassured the settlers and was in force until Congress passed on December 1, 1850, the Donation Land Claim Act, the provisions of which are discussed in chapter 6.

THE CALIFORNIA GOLD RUSH

The news of the California gold rush reached Oregon in July 1848.[24] It strongly affected the Oregon Territory in two ways. The exodus from Oregon left some communities almost completely deserted; crops were neglected for lack of manpower, newspapers closed down; even some of the missionaries joined the trek to the gold diggings. Soon, however, gold started to flow into Oregon

for the purchase of supplies, and so the farms, flour mills, and sawmills entered into a period of instant prosperity. Goods moved to California by sea and by wagons over the Oregon-California Trail, which prior to the gold rush was used only by pack animals. One of the effects generated by this prosperity was an increasing demand for the comforts of life; at the same time Oregon residents lost some of their sense of isolation. A few years later the gold rush in southern Oregon reversed the migration and brought thousands of miners to Oregon. This too had a stimulating effect on agriculture and manufacturing in Oregon, especially in the Willamette Valley (see chapter 6).

OREGON POPULATION IN 1850

By 1850 the population of the Oregon Territory was 13,294,[25] distributed in ten counties. Two of

79

POPULATION PYRAMID
(1850)

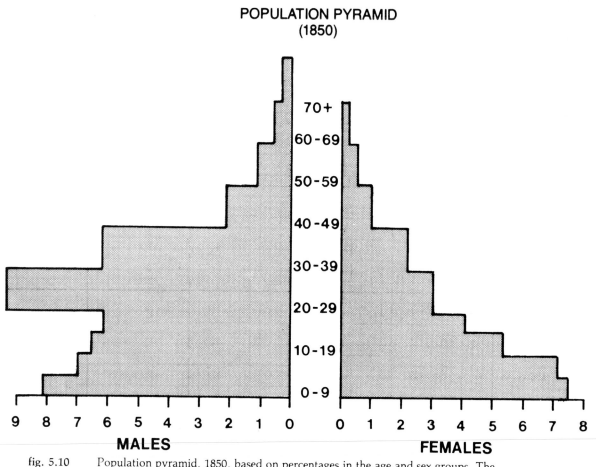

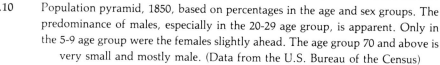

MALES   FEMALES

fig. 5.10   Population pyramid, 1850, based on percentages in the age and sex groups. The predominance of males, especially in the 20-29 age group, is apparent. Only in the 5-9 age group were the females slightly ahead. The age group 70 and above is very small and mostly male. (Data from the U.S. Bureau of the Census)

these counties, Lewis and Clark, are now in the State of Washington. In 1850 the total population of the eight counties in Oregon was 12,093, distributed as follows: Clatsop County, 462; Washington County, 2,652; Yamhill County, 1,512; Polk County, 1,051; Linn County, 994; Benton County, 814; Clackamas County, 1,859; and Marion County, 2,749. Marion County was the most populous, followed by Washington and Clackamas counties. Until 1860, some counties' eastern boundaries were not at the crest of the Cascades, but at the crest of the Rocky Mountains.

The 1850 census gave the place of birth of Oregon residents; only 18.8 percent were born in Oregon. Foreign-born totaled 1,144, most of them coming from Canada, England, Scotland, Ireland, and Germany. Many had come to Oregon after a residence in the eastern states. Most of the Oregon residents of 1850 were born in the Middle West, followed by New York and New England. Mis-

souri supplied 2,291; Illinois, 1,057; Ohio, 906; and Kentucky, 749. Virginia and North Carolina sent 485 and 169 respectively, probably via Kentucky and Tennessee. Indians were not counted unless married to white persons.

The population of Oregon in 1850 was young and predominantly male (**fig. 5.10**). The immigrants were mostly young single men and young married couples with children. The males in the 20–29 age group outnumbered the females three to one; in the 30–39 age group the ratio was two to one. Only in the 5–9 age group did the girls outnumber the boys and then only by a very small percentage. The over-70 age group was very small. This age and sex imbalance, plus the land ownership system that allowed more land for a married couple, led to early marriages. Many girls of 14 and younger became brides and single women or widows, arriving with an immigrant party, were soon married. However, because of the scarcity of white women many men took Indian wives; at the French settlement at Champoeg the majority of wives were Indian. At the time the colony was founded there were almost no white women in Oregon.

In the 1850 census it was apparent that most of the people of Oregon lived in the northern half of the Willamette Valley. A fair proportion of them lived in Portland, Linn City (West Linn), Oregon City, Lafayette, and Salem. The distribution of the 1850 population in the Willamette Valley has been mapped in detail by William A. Bowen.[26] The towns stand out on the map but the wide distribution of rural settlements is even more remarkable; in the short span of ten years settlers had moved into almost all parts of the valley. Of the rural clusters, "Tuality Valley" and French Prairie were the most populous. Many people lived on the margins of the valley or even in the small valleys of the Coast Range or Cascades. The Waldo Hills, east of Salem, were well populated, at least for a hilly area. The southern level plain between Eugene and Albany was almost completely unoccupied, the settlers clinging to the edge of the hills where wood and water were more readily available and avoiding the wet valley floor. Settlement extended south of the Willamette Valley and into the Umpqua Valley, in the vicinity of Elkton and Roseburg.

THE RIVAL TOWNS

With the continuing immigration and the increase in population, the towns of the Willamette Valley grew rapidly, leading to an intense rivalry.[27] Where would the major city be? Which town would become the great metropolis of the future? There were as many different opinions as towns and the 1850 census gave no clear indication of a leader. Oregon City, the oldest town, had 933 people; Portland, 805; Milwaukie, 103; Linn City, 124; Salem, 291; Lafayette, 125; and Astoria, 205.

Many people saw Oregon City as the future largest city of Oregon; today it is easy to see why they were wrong. It is, to be sure, located at a strategic point, the break-in-bulk point where goods moving into Oregon from the Columbia and Willamette rivers had to be portaged over Willamette Falls and transferred to smaller craft above the falls. (The break-in-bulk factor became of less significance after railroad construction.)

One disadvantage was Oregon City's inaccessibility to the shallow-draft ocean-going ships of the early days. But more important, Oregon City's site is unfavorable for a large city. The city grew up on a narrow terrace on the eastern side of the river, banked by steep bluffs, and its business district did not have enough room to grow. It is not feasible for a business district to expand up a steep cliff. In later years an outdoor elevator was constructed to facilitate movement of people from the constricted business district to the residential areas on the upland. A new elevator stands today as a symbol of the difficulty that restricted Oregon City's growth. Nevertheless in 1850 Oregon City appeared to be prosperous, blessed with what was for that time an abundance of water power. It had two flour mills and five sawmills, large hotels, and three dozen stores. There were two jewelry and watch establishments, eight or ten clothing stores, a drug store, a boot and shoe manufacturing plant, hardware and liquor stores, two bakeries, barber shops, a saddlery, a tinware factory, two cabinet shops, a blacksmith shop, a foundry, a brick kiln and yard, a dentist, half a dozen doctors, a score or more lawyers, four churches (Methodist, Baptist, Congregational, and Catholic), and a courthouse under construction.

The fact that the site of Portland was at or near the head of navigation played an important role in its growth. The original site was on the left (west) bank of the Willamette River on a gently sloping plain at the foot of the West Hills (or, as they are sometimes called, the Tualatin Hills). The plain provided room for the immediate growth, but eventually Portland joined the settlements on the opposite bank with the construction of several expensive bridges. (By hindsight it seems that a better original site would have been on the right bank, where there is plenty of room for expansion.) The West Hills present a barrier to the west, broken at one or two places but providing only slippery roads in winter (even with pavement) and somewhat hazardous sites for residences, subject to landslides. When railroads were built it was necessary to bridge the Willamette River both to the south and to the north, in the first instance to reach the Willamette Valley to the south and in the second to connect with the Puget Sound area.

Portland had several rivals other than Oregon City, some of them with deep water. Milwaukie claimed to be the "head of navigation," which was probably true for small ships at high water stage. A proponent of Portland replied that he had rid-

fig. 5.11   An early log cabin. (OHS)

den a horse over the bar at Ross Island (below Milwaukie). The argument raged back and forth but in the end Milwaukie lost. Downriver, Milton and St. Helens made bids to become the leading port, but they were too far from the main body of the Willamette Valley, which was and is the main hinterland. Curiously enough Vancouver on the Columbia River made no real bid to be the leading port, perhaps because it was British until 1846 and because it was not directly connected with the Willamette Valley.

In 1850 Salem was scarcely considered a rival by the towns below the Willamette Falls. Located on a broad terrace of the Willamette and flanked by the Eola, Waldo, and Salem hills, it is near the south end of French Prairie, which had attracted many early settlers. The "bottoms" in the vicin-

ity—Ankeny, American, and Keiser—attracted settlers from the Middle West who liked bottom land, in spite of the flood hazard. In 1850 Salem promised to be an important agricultural trading center and shipping point. Salem's growth was stimulated by its selection as the territorial capital in the early 1850s, and later, for many years, it was the second city in Oregon.

Astoria, near the entrance to the Columbia River, appeared to have the best strategic location of any of the rival Oregon towns. Was not the whole of the Columbia watershed in its hinterland? Some such thought must have been in mind when the fur trading post was established. But the tip-off came when the Hudson's Bay Company moved district trade headquarters to Fort Vancouver in 1824. It is well known that the best location for a trading post or a commercial city is near the head of navigation, rather than in an advanced position. Furthermore, Astoria has two other disadvantages: a hilly site and an immediate hinterland with limited productivity. Timber, fisheries, and transshipment functions have never been sufficient to support a large city.

The growth of all the cities on the lower Willamette was facilitated by the use of ships designed to operate between the settlements on the Willamette River and San Francisco. The ships were advertised as fast sailing vessels and, to insure against delays in the Columbia River, it was stated that they would be moved by steamer between the mouth of the Columbia River and Milwaukie. Soon sidewheel and sternwheel steamers were also in operation.

SUMMARY

In 1840 there were only a few missionaries and fur traders in Oregon, but by 1850 more than 11,000 settlers were established in the Willamette Valley and in a few outlying settlements, such as the Umpqua Valley and the Clatsop Plains. The arrival of white settlers in Oregon brought about a cultural revolution that soon had a profound effect on the land. The most obvious features were the towns, farms, houses, and roads. Scarcely noted at the time was the effect of diminished burning of the vegetation by the Indians. So many Indians died of disease, so many were killed or displaced, that many prairies of western Oregon, previously burned, began to grow up in brush and young trees. In eastern Oregon when burning ceased grass grew in abundance until overgrazing of sheep and cattle permitted the invasion of sagebrush.[28]

Thanks to the California market, stimulated by the gold rush, the Oregon Country was generally prosperous. The early land claims were large (one estimate gave 500 acres as an average), but the land under cultivation probably averaged less than 50 acres per farm. Wheat, beef, and lumber were the chief cash products. Wheat yielded well but there was little or no farm machinery for harvesting; the grain was cut with cradles or scythes and threshed by driving horses and cattle over the stalks. By 1850 "flouring" (grist) mills were well distributed throughout the northern part of the Willamette Valley. During that year mills consumed 319,000 bushels of wheat. Some flour was exported. Saw mills consumed 63,000 logs in 1850. Lumber mills were located at several points on the margins of the Willamette Valley and sawn timber was in good supply, but most of the houses on the farms were made of hewn logs (fig. 5.11). In the towns frame buildings were most common; some of the public ones were constructed of brick and stone.

Imported goods, especially tools, were in short supply and expensive. A cast-iron plow cost $45, nails brought 25¢ per pound, axes were very scarce and expensive. Coffee sold for 50¢ per pound, tea for $1.50 per pound, flour was $5.00 per barrel, potatoes were 50¢ per bushel. Coarse cotton cloth was 25¢ per yard and a single blanket sold for $5.00. (These prices seem moderate compared to today's but at the time they were considered quite high.) The lack of an established currency caused some difficulties; the common media of exchange were government scrip, orders on merchants, and wheat. (Imagine going to the store to buy a blanket with five bushels of wheat!) As this period came to an end, gold dust from the California mines was introduced as a medium of exchange (with some difficulties because of the variation in purity), as were Spanish doubloons and Mexican and Peruvian dollars.

The people had to become accustomed to the variations of the climate, to the cloudiness and heavy rainfall in winter, to the alternation of mild and severe winters. In December 1842, the Columbia River froze over at The Dalles and the temperatures in the Willamette Valley were very low. The next three winters were mild with heavy rains and some flooding, but the Columbia froze over at Vancouver in the winter of 1846–1847 (there was a curling match on the ice) and floating ice appeared in the river again in 1848–1849.

On the whole most Oregonians seemed to be satisfied with their new home: "Such was the country rescued from savagism by this virtuous and intelligent people; and such their general condition with regard to improvement, trade, education, morals, contentment, and health, at the period when, after having achieved so much without aid from congress, that body took the colony under its wing and assumed direction of its affairs."[29]

6 EXPANDING SETTLEMENT
1850–1870

Many who came to mine remained to farm.
ANONYMOUS

The period 1850–1870 was marked by a spectacular expansion of settlement into nearly all parts of Oregon. The population increased from 13,294 (Oregon Territory) in 1850, to 52,465 in 1860, and to 90,923 in 1870. Most of the increase was the result of immigration, even though Oregon had a high birth rate. The origin of the immigrants was much the same as that noted in chapter 5 — chiefly the Upper Mississippi Valley — but there was a substantial increase in the number of foreign-born, especially those from western Europe.

Immigration had declined in 1848 (700) and 1849 (500) as many migrants were diverted to the California gold rush, but the pace accelerated in 1850, estimated at 2,000 persons; 1,500 in 1851; 2,500 in 1852; and more than 6,000 in 1853.[1] During this period most of the immigrants arrived on the Oregon Trail, via The Dalles, Fort Vancouver, and Oregon City, and so the estimates are fairly reliable. After alternate routes such as the Barlow Road and the Applegate Trail were opened, it became more difficult to make estimates.

As more and more persons arrived, the newer ones were forced to locate their farms at greater distances from the original nucleus at Oregon City. The discovery of gold and other minerals, beginning in 1851, brought settlers to areas, especially the Klamath Mountains and in the 1860s the Blue Mountains, that otherwise would have been settled much later. The Indian wars, fought so bitterly during this period, were at first a hindrance to settlement, but once most of the Indians were placed on reservations, more land was opened for settlement.

Meanwhile Oregon became a territory in 1848 and a state in 1859. At the latter date the state acquired its present boundaries: the 42nd parallel on

the south, resulting from the treaty with Spain in 1819; the three-mile limit (one league at sea) on the west; the Columbia River and the 46th parallel on the north; and the Snake River and the 117th meridian (approximately) on the east. One index of the expansion in settlement during the period 1850–1870 was the formation of 15 new counties: Umpqua and Lane in 1851; Douglas and Jackson in 1852; Tillamook and Coos in 1853; Wasco, Columbia, and Multnomah in 1854; Curry in 1855; Josephine in 1856; Baker and Umatilla in 1862; and Grant and Union in 1864 (**fig. 6.1**).

THE OREGON GOLD RUSHES

The gold rushes, which had such a profound effect on Oregon settlement and development, were part of a great movement, over a period of many years, that reached from Mexico to Alaska. Gold fever brought people into parts of the state previously unexplored by whites. For example, it led to the discovery of Crater Lake by a party of prospectors in 1853. It encouraged the development of trails, roads, and water transport. If, as in many locations, the gold rush did not last more than a few months, it at least had the effect of bringing people into the area and of showing the potential of the area for farming, ranching, lumbering, and other activities.

Although there were many scattered placer operations (**fig. 6.2**), most of the mining was in two regions: in the Klamath Mountains and in a part of the Blue Mountains.[2] Both of these regions are rugged, massifs made up of a complex of igneous, sedimentary, and metamorphic rocks, folded and faulted with accompanying recrystallization—

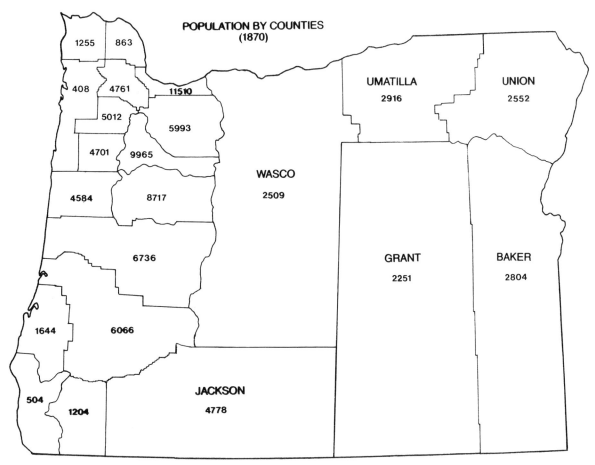

POPULATION BY COUNTIES
(1870)

1255   863

408   4761   11510

5012

5993

4701   9965

WASCO

2509

UMATILLA

2916

UNION

2552

4584   8717

6736

GRANT

2251

BAKER

2804

1644   6066

504

1204

JACKSON

4778

fig. 6.1   Population by counties, 1870. (Data from U.S. Bureau of the Census)

favorable conditions for mineralization. Streams eroded these rocks, washed out the heavy gold particles and deposited them in stream beds, on terraces, and even on the beaches. The Rogue River in southwestern Oregon and the John Day and Powder rivers in northeastern Oregon were especially productive. Tracing the gold deposits upstream led to the source of the gold, the "mother lode," which later was the basis of hardrock (lode) mining.

Gold was first found in Oregon by an immigrant party on the Meek Cutoff Trail, probably on a tributary of Crooked River. The party suffered many hardships and loss of life and was more interested in survival than gold. According to one story, members of the party found gold nuggets in a stream, pounded them out on wagon tires, and used them for sinkers on their fish lines; even with gold sinkers, the fish did not bite. In later years some of the party and then others tried to relocate the "find" but were unsuccessful, though their searches led to the 1861 discoveries in the Blue

Mountains.[3] The first effective discovery in southwestern Oregon was in 1850 and in northeastern Oregon in 1861. The discoveries were the outgrowth of the gold fever, engendered by the California gold rush a few years before, that had sent prospectors far and wide in the mountain streams of the West.

In Oregon, as elsewhere, many of the virgin placer deposits were rich, stimulating further prospecting. By 1865 placer mines were being worked in all the gold-producing areas of the state (fig. 6.2), and the total production had probably reached $19 million.[4] But the best placer deposits were soon worked out and production declined. Later placer mining was rejuvenated by the introduction of hydraulic mining and dredges, but it was the early placer mines that had such a profound influence on settlement in the period from 1850 to 1870. In the 1850s the movement of people was mostly to the Klamath Mountains; in the 1860s there was a substantial movement to eastern Oregon and across it to Idaho mines. The move-

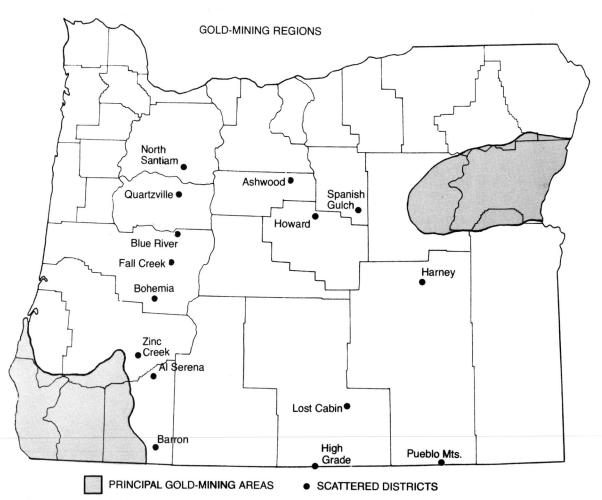

GOLD-MINING REGIONS

North
Santiam

Ashwood

Quartzville

Spanish
Gulch

Howard

Blue River

Fall Creek

Harney

Bohemia

Zinc
Creek

Al Serena

Lost Cabin

Barron

High
Grade

Pueblo Mts.

☐ PRINCIPAL GOLD-MINING AREAS   ● SCATTERED DISTRICTS

fig. 6.2   Gold mining regions. (From Brooks and Ramp, *Gold and Silver in Oregon*, 1968)

ment of settlers to the gold-mining areas continued after the mines declined and many of the miners became farmers after the placer deposits were exhausted.

The Klamath Mountains

In the summer of 1850 a few miners were working placer gold deposits on the Illinois River in the vicinity of Josephine Creek, but the Oregon gold rush did not get under way until the discovery of rich placers near Jacksonville in December 1851.[5] Thousands of miners poured into the area, and in 1852, Jackson County may have been the most populous in Oregon. When the county was formed in 1852 it included most of the Klamath Mountains; later the county was reduced in size by the formation of Josephine and Curry counties. The Jacksonville placers were near the Oregon-

California Trail, over which many Oregon miners had passed on their way to California, only to return and continue their mining operations in Oregon.

Soon prospecting and mining had spread to most parts of the Klamath Mountains (**fig. 6.3**), but the best deposits were found on the upper reaches of the Rogue River and its tributaries, especially the Illinois, Applegate, and Bear Creek. There was also some mining on the tributaries of the South Umpqua and Smith rivers. (Most of the Smith River is in California, but some of the tributaries reach into Oregon.) Attempts were made to work the gold-bearing beach sands along the coast, from the Coquille River south to the California line, but with little success. The gold on the beaches, finely divided by wave action, is difficult to recover by ordinary placer methods. The terrace deposits near the shore were more fruitful,

86

but most of these deposits were soon worked out.

The gold rush in the Klamath Mountains led to the establishment of towns, some temporary, some permanent. The names of some of the towns reflected the mining activity: Gold Beach (formerly Ellensberg), Gold Hill, and Placer. Galice, Jacksonville, Kerby, and Waldo owe their origin to placer mining; all declined in population after the peak of the gold rush. Central Point, although not directly related to a mining camp, was founded as a result of mining activity. It was at the crossing of the Oregon-California Trail and the road from Jacksonville to the Table Rock mining area and to the upper Rogue.

The location of some of the towns, convenient to the mines, did not fit in with the succeeding agricultural economy and the location of the new roads and waterways; some, like Randolph and Kerby, were moved to new locations; others declined or even disappeared. Only a few fragments — revealed after a little searching — mark the former sites of these towns. Empire, which owed its early importance to coal mining, was bypassed by the main coastal road and Marshfield (later named Coos Bay) and North Bend became the important towns. The tent town of Randolph on the coast north of Bandon boomed between 1853 and 1855, then was abandoned. The town, at least in name, was moved to the Coquille River, east of Bandon, with an entirely new function as a small agricultural center.

Getting supplies to the miners, such as food, clothing, picks, and shovels, was a major problem that led to the development of roads, trails, and waterways. Miners working close to the Oregon-California Trail were fortunate; they could obtain supplies from the Willamette Valley or from California, even though the road was a difficult one. Most of the foodstuffs, such as bacon, beans, and flour, came from the Willamette Valley; most of the implements came from California. The demand for goods and the high prices at the mining camps attracted a large number of traders, in spite of the difficulties of transportation.

Coastwise shipping brought goods to the southern Oregon coast in spite of poor harbors. One of the important ports in the early years of mining was Scottsburg, at the head of tide on the Umpqua River. From Scottsburg a trail (later a road) led to the Oregon-California Trail north of Roseburg. This route had been used by the fur traders as early as 1826. Later a road was laid out from

fig. 6.3 Panning for gold at Whisky Run, Coos County. (OHS)

Marshfield on Coos Bay to Roseburg. Port Orford was founded for the express purpose of supplying the mines of the middle Rogue and the south forks of the Coquille and Umpqua rivers, but difficulties of terrain and Indian hostilities limited the development and use of trails to these localities. Still later a road was built from the Grants Pass area to Crescent City, California, via the upper Illinois Valley and the Smith River, a route approximated today by U.S. Highway 199. Some of the trails supplying the miners could accommodate wagons with difficulty; others were usable only by pack animals. In some instances short sections of Indian trails were used.

Most of the placer gold produced in western Oregon came from the Klamath Mountains, but small placer deposits were worked in the Cascade Range also (fig. 6.4). Deposits in the Molalla, San-

fig. 6.4   Hydraulic gold mining near Medford. (OHS)

tiam, McKenzie, and Row rivers led to discovery of lode mines, which were not worked until the turn of the century. The chief lode mines associated with the placer deposits were North Santiam, Quartzville, Blue River, Fall Creek, Bohemia, Zinc Creek, Al Serena, and Barron.

The Blue Mountains

After the legendary "find" of gold by the immigrant party on the Meek Trail, many years elapsed before there was much mining activity in the Blue Mountains. A few prospectors worked in the John Day and Burnt river valleys in 1851,[6] but it was not until gold was discovered on a tributary of Powder River, near the site of Baker, in 1861 that placer mining really got under way. The first white settlement in the area was in 1862 at Auburn, a few miles south of Baker. Soon this mining camp had an estimated population between 5,000

and 6,000. Another center was at Canyon City, and from these two centers miners fanned out over a wide area from Canyon City to the Snake River. Most of the placers were in what is now Grant and Baker counties. Among the chief districts were Canyon City, Dixie Creek, Granite, and Susanville in Grant County; Sumpter, Auburn, Pocahontas, Mormon Basin, Rye Valley, and Connors Creek in Baker County.

Water for working the placers was scarce in the Blue Mountains, especially in summer, leading to the construction of long ditches. Many of the operations involved hydraulic mining, which required large quantities of water. The Auburn ditch was finished in 1863, that in Rye Valley in 1864, and the longest ditch, El Dorado, led more than 100 miles from the headwaters of Burnt River to the placers at Malheur, near Willow Creek. Pits and scars from these mining operations can still be seen in some localities. The peak of placer mining in the Blue Mountains was in the period from 1863 to 1866, after which there was a gradual decline in placer gold production.

Before placer mining began almost no white people lived in the Blue Mountains. Immigrants had passed through eastern Oregon by various routes but few had tarried, and to a considerable extent, eastern Oregon was settled from the west. Trading stations had been located at strategic points along the Oregon Trail, but these had very few permanent inhabitants. As mining began, towns sprang up in a number of places, some near the mines, others along the supply routes. La Grande, settled in 1851, became a source of food. It took the gold rush and the high prices for staple foodstuffs at the mines to reveal the mountain-fringed Grande Ronde Basin as the good farming and grazing area it is today. Auburn, John Day, Prairie City, Baker, Unity, Bridgeport, Granite, and many other towns were directly related to mining. Others were way stations on the supply routes, of which The Dalles was the most important.

It is difficult to evaluate the impact of gold production on Oregon's economy for the period 1852–1870, since adequate records were not kept. However, reliable records of the export of gold and silver (called "treasure") from Portland are available from 1864 to 1870,[7] during which time the value of gold and silver shipments declined from $6,200,000 in 1864 to $1,797,800 in 1870. This included bullion shipments from Washington, Idaho, Montana, and British Columbia. On the other hand, not all of the gold produced in Oregon was shipped through Portland. In spite of the indefinite record, it appears likely that gold and silver were the most valuable exports for this period. In 1867 flour exports were worth $727,000; wool, $132,000; wheat, $68,000.

While the prospecting and mining of gold and silver were going on, other mineral deposits were discovered, some of which became of commercial importance. Ores of copper, mercury, lead, zinc, chromium, and others were discovered. But during the period 1850–1870 coal was of the greatest value after gold and silver. Coal was discovered near Empire on Coos Bay in 1853 and mining began almost immediately. In 1854 coal was shipped to San Francisco and sold at a good profit, and for the next 16 years mining went on steadily. The mines are close to tidewater so that transportation was not a big factor, but the early methods of mining were expensive. Eventually, when rail transport reached Oregon, higher-quality coal was available and coal mining declined in this area. Also, Oregon was shipping wheat to Australia and the ships were returning with coal as ballast.

THE CIVIL WAR

Immigration, mining, and the expansion of settlement in Oregon did not stop with the Civil War. The promise of free land or at least cheap land, together with the excitement of the gold rush in the Blue Mountains, kept the immigrants coming. The effects of the Civil War on Oregon were mostly indirect. The state's principal contributions were to protect the frontier from hostile Indians and to guard against secessionists, of whom there were many in Oregon, including men in high places. Many Oregonians enlisted in the armies, Northern and Southern, but the draft was not applied to Oregon. The withdrawal of regular army troops from Oregon made it necessary to enlist volunteer cavalry and infantry companies to fight the Indians. The Indians, well aware that federal troops had been removed from Oregon, renewed their attacks on wagon trains and isolated settlements from British Columbia to northern California. There was a strong movement to unite the various tribes in their struggle against the whites.[8]

INDIAN WARS

The details of the Indian battles, massacres, and movements and the expeditions to subdue the Indians are beyond the scope of this book. It is relevant, however, to note the distribution of the conflicts and the effects on settlement. The whole story is a sort of merry-go-round, draped in black. The Indians were angered by encroachments on their lands and later by their mistreatment on and off the reservations. They reacted in the only way they knew, by killing. Some whites, such as Joel Palmer, tried to absorb or contain the Indians without punitive measures; others were quick to avenge hostile acts, sometimes by killing peaceful Indians, of whom there were many, for the misdeeds of others.

The gold rushes in the Klamath and Blue mountains served to intensify the struggles of the Indians to keep their land, and the resulting Indian battles delayed settlement in some areas. In the Willamette Valley the white settlers had tried, in some measure, to obtain land by signing treaties

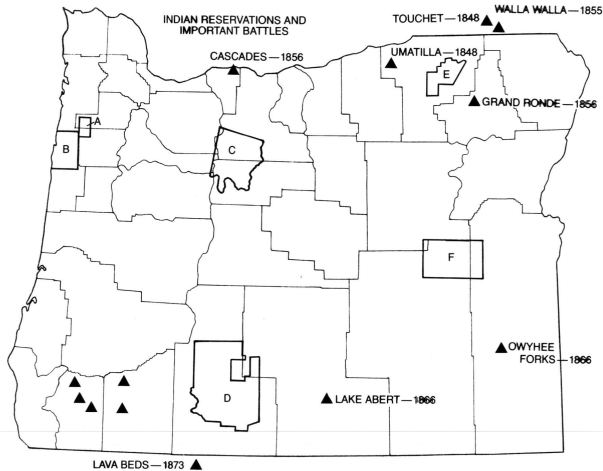

fig. 6.5   Indian Reservations and important battles. The reservations: (**A**) Grand Ronde; (**B**) Siletz; (**C**) Warm Springs; (**D**) Klamath; (**E**) Umatilla; (**F**) Malheur River. The five battles fought in southwestern Oregon were: Rogue River, 1851; Evans Creek, 1853; Graves Creek, 1855; Galice Creek, 1855; and The Meadows, 1856.

with the Indians. Peace (not ratified by Congress) was more readily accomplished because the Valley Indians, specifically the Calapuyas, were so reduced in numbers by diseases. But as the miners moved with great haste into the Klamath and Blue mountains, Indians' rights were disregarded. The miners were more aggressive than the agricultural settlers, and they were usually unencumbered by women and children and were willing to take greater risks.

The principal battles with the Indians were fought during or after the Oregon gold rushes, in the Klamath Mountains from 1853 to 1858 and in eastern Oregon from 1864 to 1867 (**fig. 6.5**). There were massacres of whites by Indians and of Indians by whites. All of this tended to discourage agricultural settlements but not gold mining. More

than a score of "forts" were established in strategic locations; some were garrisoned, others were mere blockhouses to which the settlers could rally in times of danger.

In eastern Oregon the Indians were semi-nomadic and often fled long distances after striking at settlements or wagon trains. When troops were sent to find them the soldiers suffered from sickness (from alkaline water), hunger, and cold. Army camps were established as bases from which expeditions could be mounted: Camp Henderson on Jordan Creek; Camp Maury and Camp Polk on the Deschutes River; Camp Colfax south of Baker City; Camp Logan near Canyon City; and Camp Warner in the Warner lakes area.

Efforts were made to arrange treaties with various Indian tribes in order to avoid further con-

90

flicts. The offered treaties involved placing the Indians on reservations, sometimes far from their
usual habitats. Reservations were established in
the Grand Ronde Valley of the Coast Range in
1856; at nearby Siletz in 1857; at Warm Springs in
Wasco County in 1859 (a part of it is now in Jefferson County); in Klamath County northeast of
Klamath Lake in 1864; and on the Umatilla River
in Umatilla County in 1855. A reservation was
established on the Malheur River in 1872 but was
soon absorbed into the public domain. Troops
were assigned to guard the reservation and to
retrieve the many Indians who ran away. Corporal Royal A. Bensell in his journal, *All Quiet on
the Yamhill*, paints a detailed and gloomy picture
of life on the Siletz Reservation in the Civil War
period:

> There is on this Agency, including Sub Agencies
> Alsea, Hill's, & Meckerson's [Megginson's], 800
> Indians, great and small. The Siletz Agent plants
> about 75 acres of Wheat and 5 of Potatoes. . . .
> This produce is supposed [to] supply all the
> demands for Subsistence. Meat, if they receive
> any, is obtained by hunting. Fish are plenty in the
> Spring only. . . . The poor Indians were to receive
> lumber for building comfortable houses, but a log
> or 'Shake' hut answers their purpose at pres-
> ent. . . . A Flouring Mill, built several years ago,
> stands unkempt, molding, and moss-covered. . . .
> Clothing: Of this necessary article each Indian is
> allowed so much, and on paper gets it, but in real-
> ity he obtains just such things as the Agent can
> not dispose off. . . . I do not wonder at the fre-
> quency of Indian out-breaks. . . . Indian Agencies
> are a curse to the Indians and likewise the
> country.[9]

Bensell indicated that the Indians were able to eke
out their miserable existence by prostitution; most
of the soldiers' pay went to the squaws.

POPULATION GROWTH AND
AREAL EXPANSION

In 1850 almost all of Oregon's 13,294 people
lived in the northern Willamette Valley (see **fig.
5.9**). The center of population was in the vicinity
of Champoeg and the only other clusters of significance were at Oregon City and Portland. By 1860
the population had almost quadrupled and had expanded to all parts of western Oregon; and by
1870 the increase was almost sevenfold (from

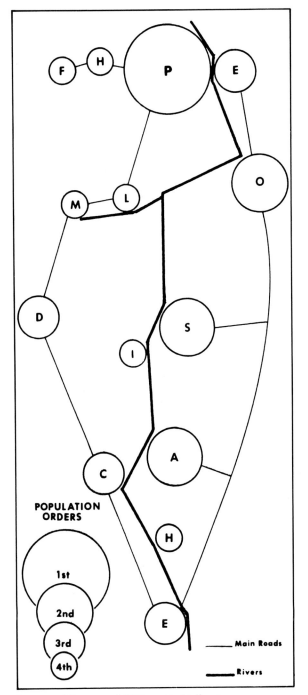

fig. 6.6 Diagram of Willamette Valley towns
and principal transportation routes in
1870. The size of the circles is proportional to the population. The heavy
line represents the Willamette River.
Compare with **Fig. 9.2.** (From Holtgrieve, "Historical Geography of
Transportation Routes and Town
Populations in Oregon's Willamette
Valley," 1973)

91

1850) and all the major regions of the state had been settled, although as yet parts of eastern Oregon were very sparsely populated.[10] By 1860 a number of people had moved to the coast, to Astoria, Tillamook, Coos Bay, and Gold Beach, but only in small numbers. The coastal settlements suffered from poor communications; their growth was slow and continues to be slow today. The gold rush did not help very much; good agricultural land was and is limited. Furthermore, the cool, rainy climate precluded the growth of many crops. In the Willamette Valley, Linn was the most populous county in 1860, followed by Lane, Marion, and Multnomah. Towns were growing along with the rural population. In 1860 Portland, Albany, and Oregon City were the largest; most of the towns were in the northern half of the Valley. The age-sex composition of the population in 1860 was more normal, but younger males still predominated. The foreign-born included 1,266 Irish, 1,078 Germans, 690 English, 663 Canadians, 425 Chinese (405 of whom were males), 217 Scottish, and a lesser number of other nationalities.

In the decade 1860–1870 population continued to grow in the Willamette Valley, and Multnomah became the most populous county with 11,510, followed by Marion, Linn, Lane, and Douglas. The coast counties were growing slowly. Clatsop had 1,255; Tillamook, 408; Coos, 1,644; and Curry, 524. Cities were growing more rapidly than the rural areas (**fig. 6.6**).[11] Portland reached 8,292 in 1870; Albany, 1,722; Oregon City, 1,382; Salem, 1,139; and Eugene, 861. It was in eastern Oregon that the highest percentage growth occurred. In 1870 there were only five counties east of the Cascades (see **fig. 6.1**): Wasco County, which stretched from the Columbia River to the California line, had 2,509 people; Umatilla, 2,916; Baker, 2,804; Union 2,552; and Grant, 2,251 — a total of 13,032. In view of the large area of these five counties, the density of population was very low. Aside from the mining camps, which for a short time had several thousand people, eastern Oregon had no towns with over 500 persons in 1870. Most of eastern Oregon's population was in the Blue Mountains gold-mining area. In the 1860s many post offices were established in eastern Oregon, most of them associated in some way with mining: Auburn in 1862 (discontinued in 1903); La Grande, Union, and Umatilla in 1863; Canyon City in 1864; John Day City in 1865; Baker in 1866; Wasco in 1868; Pendleton in 1869; and Prairie City in 1870. The proportion of the

Oregon population born in Oregon showed a substantial increase over 1860, reaching nearly 50 percent in Benton, Linn, Lane, Polk, and Yamhill counties. The percentage of foreign-born also increased, ranging from 2.1 percent in Lane County to 37.3 percent in Baker County, mostly Chinese.

AGRICULTURE

By 1850 settlers had learned that conditions in the Willamette Valley were quite different from those of the Middle West and had adapted their farm practices.[12] Asahel Bush wrote in the *Oregon Statesman* in 1853: "The experience and experiments of 'the [eastern] States' are of little or no service now. Our climate, seasons and soil differ from those of all of them, and agriculture and horticulture here must be conducted upon different systems. New experiments must be tried, and new modes adopted. In a great measure everything is to be learned anew." The average temperature in July of the Valley, 66°F., is almost ten degrees cooler than the Middle West. This makes it difficult to mature crops that require high temperatures. An additional difference is the cool nights in Oregon in contrast to the Middle West. The dry season of summer posed a serious problem until irrigation methods were learned and put into practice. Moreover, the farmers encountered such a variety of climate, soil, and slope that no single set of procedures would work for the whole state.

David Newsom, who came to Oregon in 1851, realized more than most people that new methods of farming were necessary. In 1857 he wrote:

What is strange, but yet true, apples and pears of superior size and flavor, are obtained here the third year from the graft or bud! Yet it is apparent to all close observers that the science of Pomology here, must be learned anew. And the same is true with respect to farming operations generally — all has to be learned anew! We must call to our aid here, practical chemistry for the purpose of analyzing our various soils — rich alluvial prairie bottoms — light, sandy, gravelly valleys, red clay buttes, or little hills, strongly impregnated with phosphate or iron — and black, rich, moist clay loam on the mountains. No man can successfully rear apples and pears here in consequence of what he may learn in any fruit book extant.[13]

As some of the settlers moved into the Umpqua and Rogue river valleys they found warmer summer weather, less rainfall, and less cloudiness than in the Willamette Valley. Roseburg has a July average of 68°F. and Medford 72°F.; the latter is the warmest place in summer west of the Cascades.[14] Settlers on the coast found *lower* summer temperatures than in the Willamette Valley; Coos Bay averages 59°F. for July and has more clouds and rain—too much rain for many crops. In eastern Oregon summer temperatures are generally higher, at low altitudes, than in the Willamette Valley, and although the winters are colder and the rainfall inadequate in many places, the conditions are in many respects more favorable for wheat and corn. The 40-inch rainfall in the Willamette Valley is actually too much for optimum yields of wheat. A 25-inch rainfall would be better considering the coolness of the climate in western Oregon. Since most of the crop is winter wheat, it receives most of the annual rainfall. It took the settlers in the Willamette Valley some time to realize that the area was more favorable for hay and other forage crops than for wheat and corn. But in 1870 wheat was still the most important crop in the Valley and only comparatively small amounts were grown in other regions. In 1850 Oregon had 211,000 acres of wheat; in 1870 the acreage had increased to 2,389,000. Benton, Lane, Linn, Douglas, Marion, and Polk were the leading counties.

Indian corn, the favorite crop in the Corn Belt from which most of Oregon's settlers came, does not fare well in the Willamette Valley. To be sure, it grows well as a green vegetable and became a favorite for canning and freezing, but in most years corn will not ripen. Transplanted by early settlers to the Umpqua and Rogue valleys and to some areas of eastern Oregon, it did better; in 1870, the leading counties for corn production were Douglas, Umatilla, and Wasco. In general, corn in Oregon requires irrigation and, perhaps for this reason, today it is a minor crop. One of the results of the failure of corn (for grain) is a low production of pork. (Besides, Oregonians prefer beef!)

On the coast neither corn nor wheat grows well; there is too much rain, too many clouds, and not enough sunshine. Wheat grows luxuriant thick stems but little grain, and that will not ripen. But potatoes and forage crops do well there, and the mild winter temperatures—January averages nearly 50°F.—permit year-round pasture. It seemed that dairy farming and cheese-making were almost inevitable choices for the settlers. The prairies cleared by Indian burning (see chapter 3) gave the dairy farms a good start, although the growth of shrubs was so rapid that many burned areas were grown up in brush before they could be utilized. The settlers, however, did not have to learn from the Indians how to use fire in clearing; they also burned whenever the weather allowed, which was not too often.

In all, Oregon was a great experimental farm, with a variety of climates, soils, slopes, and exposures. The farmers had to find out what would grow best in the various environments. The solutions of these many problems were facilitated by the organization of agricultural societies and later by the founding of Oregon Agricultural College at Corvallis.

The immigrants brought thousands of head of livestock with them—horses, oxen, milk cows, and beef cattle, lesser numbers of mules, sheep, and hogs. (Hogs are not good travelers.) In 1850 there were 8,000 horses in Oregon; in 1870, 51,000. In 1850 dairy cows numbered 9,000; in 1870, 48,000. Sheep got a slow start but increased rapidly from 15,000 in 1850 to 318,00 in 1870, mostly in the Willamette Valley. The emphasis on sheep shifted to eastern Oregon by 1900, only to return to western Oregon. Today most sheep are on irrigated pastures in the Willamette Valley and on year-round pasture near the coast.

MANUFACTURING

In the period from 1850 to 1870 manufactured goods in Oregon were in very short supply. Far removed from established industrial areas in the eastern United States and Europe, the people had to depend on the irregular arrival of ships carrying manufactured goods, and on their own skill and ingenuity. Some raw materials were in good supply. Timber of several kinds was more than abundant; there was wheat for flour milling, wool for weaving. But iron ore, coal, and limestone were scarce and of poor quality. Nevertheless, in this period a variety of industries were started or expanded: lumber mills, shipyards, flour mills, woolen mills, paper mills, and iron works.

The first lumber mill was in operation at Fort Vancouver in 1828. Hawaiians were employed to cut lumber for export to the Sandwich Islands, since there was a limited market in Oregon at that time. Later, a mill was built on Sauvie Island. After the settlers began to arrive, mills were constructed at Oregon City and in a number of other places along the Columbia and Willamette rivers. Lumber was in demand for home building as frame houses succeeded log structures, for shipbuilding, for furniture, for fencing, and for packing boxes (for the export of salmon).

The first sawmills were hand-powered, but soon water power was geared to circular saws. This put a premium on water-power sites, such as Oregon City, but shortly thereafter steam power was introduced, allowing for a wider distribution of the mills. By 1870 there were 173 mills operating in Oregon,[15] 41 of them with steam, 138 with water power; obviously a few had both steam and water power. A river location was necessary for the mills, since logs were usually floated down a stream. Furthermore, mills on the Columbia River loaded lumber on ships for export. Lumber mills were built in eastern Oregon in the 1860s, in or near La Grande, Canyon City, Union, and Elgin. These mills were cutting chiefly ponderosa pine.

Shipbuilding began with the fur traders and was accelerated after the settlers arrived. Small schooners were built at Fort Vancouver as early as 1826. Before the settlers arrived several small schooners were built on the lower Willamette River, many of them intended specifically for the lumber trade. Ships were built at various other points on the rivers — Astoria, Skipanon (Warrenton), St. Helens, Portland, Oregon City, and at Canemah above Willamette Falls for the Willamette Valley trade.[16] On the coast, shipyards produced small schooners at Tillamook Bay and Yaquina Bay, on the Siuslaw River near Florence, at Marshfield and North Bend on Coos Bay, at Coquille and Myrtle Point on the Coquille River, and at Port Orford and Brookings. As steam engines arrived from the East, they were installed in some of the sailing ships and soon steam engines took the place of sails. The average life of these ships was only a few years; many were wrecked on the bars of the rivers; others were merely outmoded as larger, faster ships with greater capacity were built.

Even wooden ships need iron, a metal in short supply in early Oregon. Iron ore was and is scarce in the state and much of it is of low quality. Coking coal is also scarce but this did not concern the early foundries, since they could use wood charcoal. The first iron foundry and blast furnace were built at Oswego in 1865 and began production in 1867.[17] Local iron ore was used with wood char-

coal until coal could be brought from Coos Bay. For many years these were the only blast furnace and foundry in the state. Others were planned in this period, including one at Linnton (now a part of Portland), but none of them was put into operation.

From the very beginning of agriculture in Oregon, the Willamette Valley was producing a surplus of wheat, some of which was being shipped out. But the residents and the miners needed flour; consequently mills were constructed in a number of places where water power was available. At first the mills were small, but by 1860 one mill in Milwaukie was turning out 250 barrels of flour per day, another in Oregon City 300 barrels. As more large mills were constructed, the small mills were converted to other purposes; but after 1900, when wheat production had declined in the Valley, most of the large mills were closed.

Sheep began to arrive with the immigrant trains of 1844 and 1845, forming the basis of a wool industry. Prior to this time a few sheep were brought to Fort Vancouver from the Sandwich Islands. Soon there was more wool in Oregon than could be spun and woven by hand, necessitating the building of woolen mills.[18] The first woolen mill on the Pacific Coast opened in Salem in 1857 with machinery from the eastern United States. Salem was selected as the site over the other competitors — Oregon City and Albany — simply because that city sold the most stock in the enterprise. The Salem site was improved by the construction of a canal tapping the Santiam River, which diverted additional water into Mill Creek. This task was made easy by the fact that in prehistoric times the Santiam flowed into the Willamette at Salem. The first products were blankets and cloth suitable for making clothing, and by 1859 some woolen cloth was being shipped out of Oregon. After mills were built at Oregon City, Albany, and Brownsville, the Oregon industry was able to supply Oregon's needs and additional amounts for shipment outside the state. By 1865 the number of sheep in Oregon and the supply of wool far exceeded the demand of the Oregon mills. As a result, two things happened; more wool was exported and large numbers of sheep were driven to California and to British Columbia.

In November 1861, a disastrous flood coursed through the Willamette Valley and other parts of western Oregon, causing heavy damage to the mills and farmhouses on and near the river banks.

This flood is described graphically by Bancroft:

Toward the last of November a deluge of rain began, which, being protracted for several days, inundated all the valleys west of the Sierra Nevada and Cascade ranges, from southern California to northern Washington, destroying the accumulations of years of industry. No flood approaching it in volume had been witnessed since the winter of 1844. All over the Willamette the country was covered with the wreckage of houses, barns, bridges, and fencing; while cattle, small stock, storehouses of grain, mills, and other property were washed away. A number of lives were lost, and many imperilled. In the streets of Salem the river ran in a current four feet deep for a quarter of a mile in breadth. At Oregon City all the mills, the breakwater, and hoisting works of the Milling and Transportation Company, the foundery [sic], the Oregon Hotel, and many more structures were destroyed and carried away. Linn City was swept clean of buildings, and Canemah laid waste. Champoeg had no houses left; and so on up the river, every where. The Umpqua River rose until it carried away the whole of lower Scottsburg, with all the mills and improvements on the main river, and the rains destroyed the military road on which had been expended fifty thousand dollars. The weather continued stormy, and toward christmas the rain turned to snow, the cold being unusual. On the 13th of January there had been no overland mail from California for more than six weeks, the Columbia was blocked with ice, which came down from its upper branches, and no steamers could reach Portland from the ocean, while there was no communication by land or water with eastern Oregon and Washington; which state of things lasted until the 20th, when the ice in the Willamette and elsewhere began breaking up, and the cold relaxed.[19]

TRANSPORT

As a result of the expanded mining and agricultural activity in the period 1850–1870, Oregonians were calling loudly for improved transportation by water and by land. On the Columbia and Willamette rivers steamships carried a variety of passengers and cargo, as did the ships between Portland and San Francisco. Water transport was all the more active because of the lack of roads, but road construction was beginning to get under way, which, together with the later advent of the railroads, was to cut heavily into the river transport. However, for this period from 1850 to 1870 the steamboat was king on the Columbia,[20] Willamette, Umpqua, Coos, and Coquille rivers, in spite of the many difficulties, such as shifting sandbars, treacherous rapids, and dangerous bars at the mouths of the bays. The Columbia River Bar, alone, accounted for a major wreck a year on the average.

To take care of the freight and passenger traffic generated by the Indian wars and the mining activity in eastern Oregon, a steamer, the *James P. Flint*, was put in service on the Columbia above Cascade Rapids in 1851. At first the venture was unsuccessful because the portages at Cascade Rapids and at Celilo Falls were bottlenecks, but by the early 1860s it was possible to take a steamer from Portland to Cascade Rapids, portage around the rapids on a tramway pulled by a mule, take another steamer to The Dalles, make another portage by rail around Celilo Falls, and continue upriver on a third steamer. The second mule-powered tramway proved inadequate and the first steam-powered railway in Oregon was constructed there with wooden rails capped with strips of iron. Another portage steam railway was constructed around Cascade Rapids. These were the precursors of the later railways, which finally drove the steamers off the rivers.

With a number of steamers carrying passengers and freight from Portland to Astoria and points between, and upriver to Umatilla City, it was obvious that steamers were needed also on the Willamette River. The difficulty was the shallowness of the river, especially at certain bars. Nevertheless, the *Multnomah* was assembled at Canemah above Willamette Falls with parts shipped from the East. Launched in 1851, she was unable to reach Salem on her first trip because of shallow water. Soon a number of shallow-draft steamers were navigating the Willamette, sometimes as far as Eugene during high water, otherwise to Corvallis or Harrisburg. The river steamers connected with a stage line from Champoeg to Salem, providing faster service for passengers.

The problem of providing shipping service to the settlements along the Oregon coast was a serious one, all the more so since there were only a few trails and no roads connecting the Willamette Valley with the coast. Harbors were available for small ships of the day at Tillamook, Newport,

Gardiner on the Umpqua River, and Empire on Coos Bay, once the ships had crossed the bars. But the bars were risky, except at the rare times when the seas and swells were very low and the tide was high. Passing the bars was particularly hazardous for sailing ships and many were wrecked. The first ship to enter Coos Bay to load coal for San Francisco was wrecked on the way out with loss of life. A sailing ship, built in Tillamook Bay for service to Portland, was little used because of the rough bar. This was prior to the construction of the Tillamook jetty (1914), which improved the entrance to Tillamook Bay but led to severe erosion of the shore to the south. The Columbia Bar was, of course, a big part of the hazard between Portland and Tillamook and other coast ports.

So difficult was coastwise navigation, especially in winter, that coastal communities often lacked necessities. Tillamook often lacked flour and the people lived on potatoes and fish. Gold Beach at times had no sugar, kerosene, or matches. Years later, when steamships arrived at the coastal harbors, conditions improved. The steamers could cross the bars with less difficulty, but they sometimes had to anchor outside and wait for favorable bar conditions. The principal traffic was with San Francisco; the ships brought various manufactured goods to the Oregon coast in exchange for lumber and foodstuffs, such as potatoes, fish, meat, and dairy products (after livestock had been established on the coast farms).

Inside the bars, on the bays and rivers, water transport played a very important role for the coastal communities. Indian canoes, rowboats, and in some cases steamers connected the lower harbors with the head of tide. The "rowboat pioneers" of Coos Bay could reach their farms on the various inlets only by water. The Yaquina River was navigable to Toledo, the Siuslaw to Mapleton, the Umpqua to Scottsburg, the Coos to Allegany, and the Coquille to Myrtle Point. These waterways promoted the growth of settlement and were the chief lines of travel until railroads were constructed.

Trails, marked out in turn by Indians, fur traders, and settlers, were the forerunners of Oregon roads. When roads were built the route selected was usually along an old trail, and many trails were obliterated by road construction. When the first settlers arrived in Oregon, a network of trails was in use; many continued in use, in some parts of the country, for many years.

Road building in western Oregon was especially difficult because of the terrain, the climate, and the vegetation.[21] On the prairies of the Willamette Valley, a wheeled vehicle could move in many places with little difficulty in summer. But in winter, mud, standing water, and swollen streams hampered travel. In hilly areas roads were washed out with the heavy rains almost as soon as they were graded, since modern paving materials and methods were not available. Some of the first roads were covered with planks or corduroy, but these were of only temporary value, since the soil washed from underneath the planks or poles.

The first long road in western Oregon was the Oregon-California Trail, suitable only for pack animals until the California gold rush. The route followed the west side of the Willamette Valley in the edge of the hills in order to avoid the wet lowlands and to find easier fords across the tributary streams. It connected Portland with Lafayette, Dallas, Corvallis (fig. 6.7), Elmira, Roseburg, and Grants Pass; it skirted to the east of Jacksonville and crossed Siskiyou Pass to California. The northern part of this road came to be called the Applegate Trail or the Immigrant Trail.

As more settlers arrived and settlement expanded, the demand for roads increased. But road building was expensive, even in those days, and methods of financing had to be worked out. Toll roads built by private individuals, usually on government land, was one solution.[22] "Military" roads were laid out and financed by appropriations from Congress, but improvements on most of them were minimal. The term "military" was used to make it easier to get the appropriation bills through Congress. In addition several land grants were made for road construction;[23] the land granted to the contractors was sold to settlers and speculators.

The builders of the toll roads charged a fee, often collected at several points along the way, to pay for construction and maintenance, and to provide a profit. Prices varied but an average charge was five dollars for a wagon and one dollar for each head of livestock. An important toll road was the Barlow Road (see fig. 5.5), across the Cascades to the south of Mt. Hood, a part of the wagon route from The Dalles to Oregon City. This road was marked out in 1846 and improved in the 1850s. "The construction of the Barlow road contributed more towards the prosperity of the Willamette Valley and the future State of Oregon than any other achievement prior to the building of the railways in 1870."[24] Other toll roads were the Canyon Toll Road between Portland and the

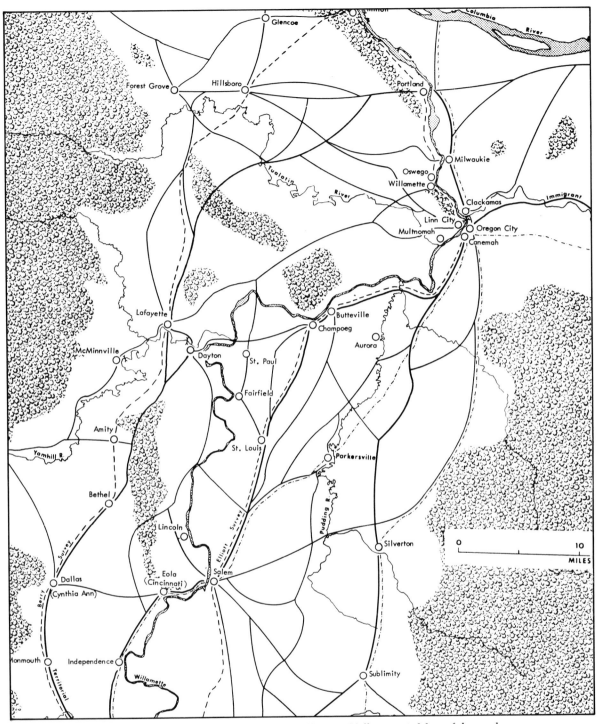

fig. 6.7   Roads and settlements of the northern Willamette Valley, 1860. Most of the roads
were unplanned and unimproved but surveys had been made (dashed lines) for
improved roads. (From Holtgrieve)

97

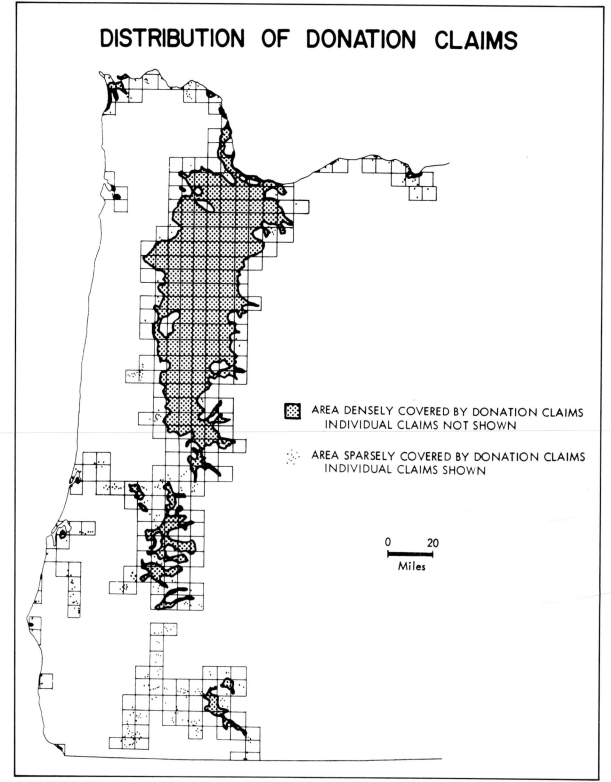

DISTRIBUTION OF DONATION CLAIMS

▦ AREA DENSELY COVERED BY DONATION CLAIMS
INDIVIDUAL CLAIMS NOT SHOWN

⋮ AREA SPARSELY COVERED BY DONATION CLAIMS
INDIVIDUAL CLAIMS SHOWN

0   20
Miles

fig. 6.8   The Donation Land Claims of western Oregon. (From Harlow Head, "The
Oregon Donation Land Claims and Their Patterns," 1971)

Tualatin Valley (1856); the Portland-Silverton Plank Road (1858); the Trask River Road (1871) from Tillamook to Yamhill; the Siskiyou Toll Road (1857–1858) over Siskiyou Pass, near the present route of U.S. Highway I-5; and in eastern Oregon, the Dooley Mountain Road, from Baker to the mines on Malheur River.

Roads financed by congressional appropriations and land grants, and at least partially constructed, included routes from Astoria to Salem; from Scottsburg to Myrtle Creek; from Yaquina Bay to Albany; from Coos Bay to Roseburg; and from The Dalles to Fort Boise. In 1864 the Oregon Central Military Road was authorized, reaching from Eugene across the Willamette Pass to the Idaho border. Later (1876) a road was planned from Corvallis across Santiam Pass, known as the Willamette Valley and Cascade Mountain Military Road. Many difficulties were encountered, some natural, some human. Workers often quit their jobs and took off for the gold mines. As a result, many of the roads were not finished until many years later. Many of the land grant military roads of the 1860s were inadequate; or they might incorporate sections of existing roads. For the so-called military roads of the 1860s, land speculation was usually a primary purpose. Eventually much of the land granted to road builders to finance the roads was revested by the government, just as the railroad lands were many years later. The problem of crossing the Cascade Range continued to cause concern; the Barlow Road was not entirely satisfactory and the crossing from Jacksonville to Klamath Lake was too far south.

Stage coaches were put into service as soon as the roads permitted, some in the early 1850s.[25] By 1857 one-day service was established between Salem and Portland via Oregon City. A weekly stage schedule was in force from Oregon City to Jacksonville by 1859, and a year later it had tied in with the stage to Sacramento, which in turn was connected with the overland stage to St. Joseph, Missouri. The trip from Sacramento to Portland required seven days if all went well; in the winter twelve days was a good average. Daily service was established, but the stage was rarely on time. The stages carried mail; in the absence of postage stamps, the fee was collected as the mail was delivered. The daily service from Sacramento to Portland required hundreds of horses, since they were usually changed every 12 miles. The first stage service over Siskiyou Pass was in 1856, the last in 1870, driven by the same man. The con-

struction of railroads meant the end of the stages.

The demand for telegraphic service to and from California led to the construction of a line from Portland to Oregon City in 1855 and to Corvallis in 1856.[26] The line was little used and was discontinued. In 1861 a line was completed from Marysville, California, on the transcontinental telegraph, to Yreka, California. This called for a new effort in Oregon and in 1864 a line was constructed from Portland to Yreka, thus connecting with San Francisco and New York. To celebrate, messages were exchanged between the mayors of Portland, Oregon, and Portland, Maine. In the same year a telegraph line was completed to Seattle, including an underwater crossing of the Columbia River. A line reached The Dalles by 1868, and Boise, Idaho, by 1869. The rate from Portland to eastern cities in 1869 was $7.50 for ten words.

LAND OWNERSHIP AND LAND SURVEYS

From the very beginning of white settlement in Oregon the question of land ownership was important to the new residents. Neither the Organic Code of 1843 nor the Territorial Act of 1848 specifically set up a land ownership system, but they did state that laws passed by the Provisional Government would be in force unless they were incompatible with the U.S. Constitution.

The Donation Land Claim Act was passed in 1850, setting up a system of land ownership and recognizing claims established under previous laws.[27] By the terms of the act each male white citizen, 18 years of age or older, was entitled to 320 acres of land if single; if married, his wife could hold an additional 320 acres in her own right. The claims were supposed to be square in shape, or if not square, then oblong. Later, a modification in the act required the boundaries of the claims to run north and south, east and west. This was the first large-scale disposition of land in the Pacific Northwest and its effects were far-reaching. Although the act was in effect for only five years, more than two and one-half million acres were granted to more than 7,000 claimants. It stimulated immigration and accelerated expansion into different parts of the state.

The distribution of donation land claims (fig 6.8 and fig. 6.9) reflected the extent of settlement in the early 1850s. By far the largest number were in the Willamette Valley; the entire floor of the Valley and the adjacent hills were practically

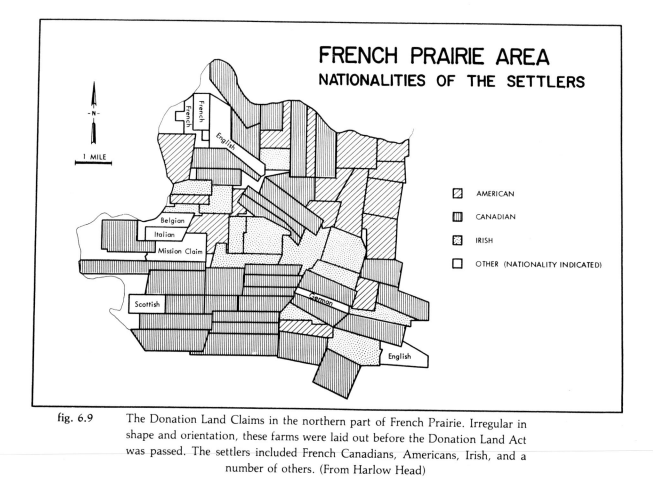

AMERICAN

CANADIAN

IRISH

OTHER (NATIONALITY INDICATED)

fig. 6.9   The Donation Land Claims in the northern part of French Prairie. Irregular in
shape and orientation, these farms were laid out before the Donation Land Act
was passed. The settlers included French Canadians, Americans, Irish, and a
number of others. (From Harlow Head)

covered with claims. Next in importance was the middle Umpqua Valley, followed by the Rogue River Valley. Smaller numbers of claimants were located along the Columbia River from The Dalles to Astoria; on the Clatsop Plains; around Tillamook Bay; on the lower Umpqua River; around Coos Bay, where some claims were staked out in the coalfields; on the South Fork of the Coquille River; at Port Orford; at Gold Beach; and at Brookings. Although the act was terminated in 1855, many years were to pass before all the claims were proved and legal title given to the holdings. The pattern of the claims impressed itself on the landscape, in the shape of the land holdings, in the arrangement of fences, and, more especially, in the road network.

Surveys and Maps

Obviously the implementation of the Donation Land Claim Act called for surveys on the ground to establish the boundaries of the claims in a legal fashion. In fact, the act called for the appointment of a surveyor general to carry out the surveys. It was stated that only lands fit for cultivation were to be surveyed, and these areas happened to correspond very nicely with the extent of the donation land claims.

Survey work began in 1851[28] with the establishment of a base line running east from Tillamook Bay through Portland to the Snake River, and a principal meridian south from the Columbia River, at the first outlet of the Willamette River, through the Rogue River Valley to the California line. A part of the meridian runs through the foothills of the Cascades, making it very difficult to survey. Work continued for many years before all the area of the claims was covered. Great difficulties were encountered—rugged terrain in some areas, dense vegetation, cloudy, rainy weather, and the temptation for the surveyors on the job to take off for the gold mines.

In many areas of western Oregon the surveys were made after settlement, and the boundaries of

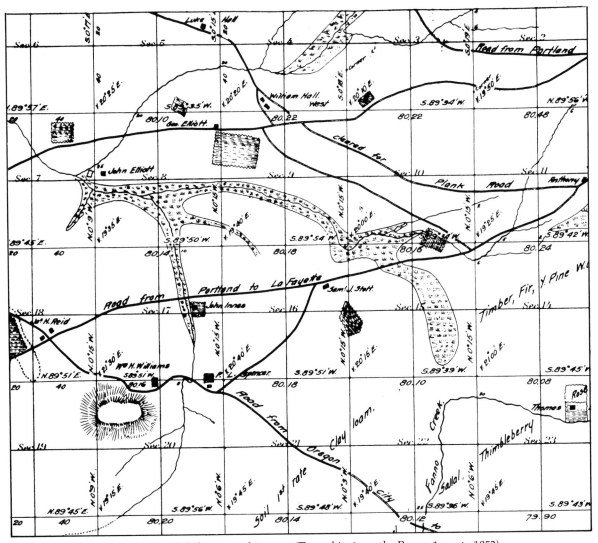

fig. 6.10   Part of a Land Office township map (Township 1 south, Range 1 west, 1852) divided in quarter sections. These maps, intended primarily for the location of property lines, usually show section lines, roads, hills, swamps, streams, cultivated land, and the names of settlers, with some notes on soils and vegetation. The city of Beaverton is located in the north-central part of this map.

the claims, laid out roughly by metes and bounds, had to be described in terms of townships, range, and section. Harlow Head gives the description of a donation land claim in the Molalla area provided by the survey:

> The southeast quarter of the southeast quarter (40 acres) of section 20; the south half of the south half (160 acres) of section 21; the southwest quarter of the southwest quarter (40 acres) of section 22; the west half of the northwest quarter (80 acres) and the northwest quarter of the southwest quarter (40 acres) of section 27; the northeast quarter (160 acres), the east half of the northwest

quarter (80 acres), lot 1 (33.60 acres), and lot 4 (13.10 acres) of section 28, Township 4 South, Range 2 East of the Willamette Meridian. Trullinger's claim has 646.70 acres which is 6.70 acres more than he was entitled to have.[29]

Individual maps were made of each township (fig. 6.10), showing the section corners and the subdivisions, with the type of terrain, vegetation, and cultural features, such as roads, trails, houses, and cultivated fields. The surveyors also made notes, all of which are valuable in understanding what Oregon was like at the time of settlement.

The surveyor general was charged with the

101

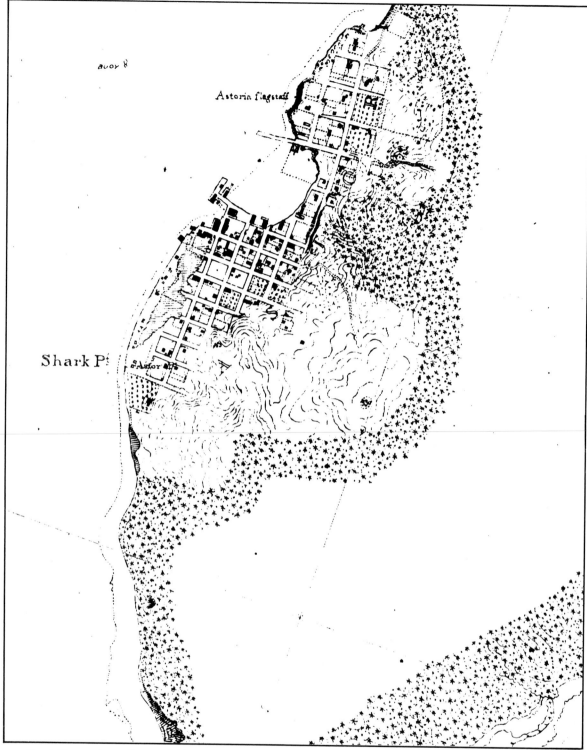

Buoy 8

Astoria flagstaff

Shark P:

Astor Ho

fig. 6.11   A small part of Cleveland Rockwell's 1868 U.S. Coast Survey map of the lower
Columbia River (Register No. 1123), including Astoria and vicinity. The maps of
the Coast Survey (later the Coast and Geodetic Survey) were large scale, detailed,
and accurate. At the time of this map much of Coxcomb Hill above Astoria was
treeless, probably the result of fires. (Map Coll. OHS)

preparation of maps of the whole area of Oregon, and new editions were issued from time to time. Gradually the errors made by the earlier cartographers were corrected and new material added. The content of these maps varied from year to year, depending on the current surveyor general. Some show the early county boundaries, others do not. The 1852 map shows the Smith River entirely in Oregon, but the Oregon-California Trail is well marked, as are other roads in the Willamette Valley. The gold-mining areas of the Rogue River are labeled. By 1863 the map of eastern Oregon was beginning to take shape, but with many errors and some fantastic topography. The Blue Mountains are shown as a "spidery" form, running from southeastern Washington Territory to the California boundary (actually the Nevada line), and including Steens Mountain. Gold mining is indicated in the upper John Day and Powder River areas. The Grande Ronde Valley is much too large, including most of the area of the Wallowa Mountains. On the map, the Snake River flows almost due north, with scarcely a bend; in fact it is quite crooked.

In 1851 the detailed survey of the Oregon coast, under the direction of George Davidson, began.[30] Previously only a few limited studies of certain harbors had been made. The United States Coast Survey (later called the Coast and Geodetic Survey) prepared two types of maps: the hydrographic maps, showing the shoreline, depths of the harbors, and the depths near the shore; and the topographic maps, showing the shoreline and the elevations of the land for a narrow strip, usually about one-half mile wide (fig. 6.11). The latter shows prominent landmarks, intended as an aid to navigators. George Davidson had the idea that a mariner, sailing the coast in foggy weather, might be able to recognize certain landmarks and thus fix his position. Davidson, in planning the survey, sailed along the coast at a safe distance of two or three miles, noting what he thought were extensive grassy slopes below the wooded ridges. Alas for his surveyors, these slopes were covered with heavy brush, eight to ten feet high, making the survey work very difficult.

The map scales are large, often six inches to the mile, making it possible to show the features in great detail. Few modern Oregon maps have equalled the detail and accuracy of the Coast Survey maps. (Only a few of these maps were published, but some originals and many copies are available in the library of the Oregon Historical Society.) Another result of the survey was the publication of a series of *Coast Pilots*, books with careful instructions for sailing along the hazardous Oregon coast. Both the maps and the *Coast Pilots* are of great historical value, revealing conditions as they were more than a century ago.

A number of other government agencies and some individuals contributed to the improvement of the Oregon map. The Pacific Railroad surveys, described in the following chapter, added a number of instrumental surveys along with descriptions of geographic features. Military maps, some of them made in connection with the Indian wars, were useful for other purposes. The General Land Office maps, usually revised every year as the surveys of the townships progressed, varied in content. Some show little more than the township, range, and section grid; others show county boundaries, streams, unsurveyed relief features, towns, and roads, as well as the progress of the surveys. In the map of 1866 the county boundaries are only approximately correct. For example, the south boundary of Columbia County is drawn to include most of Portland west of the Willamette River. The south boundary of Lane County follows the Siuslaw River instead of the drainage divide a few miles to the south. In eastern Oregon the Blue Mountains are represented by a narrow north-south band with a branch to the west. Relief is shown by hachures emphasizing the drainage divides of the major streams, with little attention to other parts of the mountains or plateaus. Indian reservations are shown with generalized boundaries, as are other reserves. Surveyed townships are indicated and also those about to be surveyed. (Federal lands in eastern Oregon had to be surveyed before they could be purchased or homesteaded.) Many place names were incorrect in both location and spelling. For example, "Le Grand" is located on the Powder River instead of on the Grande Ronde River. But the General Land Office maps together with the U.S. Army maps were the most up-to-date and useful maps available. After 1870 the construction of roads and railroads called for detailed surveys, thus adding to the accuracy of Oregon maps.

SUMMARY

The period 1850–1870 was one of phenomenal growth in population and areal expansion. It was a time of gold rushes, successful and otherwise, of

Indian battles, won and lost, of improved transportation by water and land; many new roads were laid out (but not many were improved) as a result of the gold rushes and the Indian wars. It was a time of expanding agriculture, some new crops and more of the old ones, and a veritable explosion of livestock—cattle, horses, and sheep. Thanks to continued immigration, a high birth rate, and a low death rate (a young population and little disease), the population doubled, redoubled, and almost doubled again, all in 20 years. Obviously immigration was the big factor, and as the fame of Oregon (gold and free land) spread to every corner of the United States and to many foreign lands the composition of the people changed. Before 1850, most of the immigrants came from the Middle West, but now increasing numbers came from the Old South, a part of the exodus from that region stricken by the Civil War. A small number of blacks was included. Foreign-born, never a large factor in the Oregon population, made up in variety what they lacked in numbers, with Canadians, Germans, English, Welsh, Irish, Scots, and Chinese, to mention the most numerous. In the decades to follow, transcontinental rail connections were to bring many more thousands of people from many states and many foreign lands to Oregon.

By 1870 man's impact on the Oregon land was evident in many parts of the state. Roads and trails were marked out in, near, and between the settlements. Some roads were surveyed and permanently located, but most were mere tracks used mostly in the dry season. A single wagon trip across the prairie left tracks in the soft soil that lasted a few seasons; a few trips over the same route left ruts that were preserved for many years.

In this period the land surveys began to affect the road patterns of the rural areas, as well as the street patterns of the towns. The first roads were in existence before the surveys were made and, therefore, were related more to terrain and drainage. Later roads conformed to the north-south, east-west lines of the townships, ranges, and sections, and to property lines.

Farmhouses, cultivated fields, orchards, and fences stood out in the prairies. Pasture lands that the Indians had maintained by burning were now grazed by thousands of head of livestock, thus preventing the return of the forest. Away from the settlements, the prairies were growing up in brush and small trees, so that later settlers had to clear land before they could cultivate.

Logging and mining were beginning to leave their marks on the land. By 1870 the demand for lumber to build houses for the settlers and for export led to the establishment of numerous sawmills in the towns and in other locations, particularly on the margins of the Willamette Valley. Moreover, wood was used widely for fuel, not only for domestic heating but to feed the boilers of the steamboats and the mills. And no one thought that Oregon's timber could be used up. Mining operations left their peculiar marks on the land. Placer mining converted the silt-covered flood plains and terraces to piles of gravel and cobbles. Hydraulic mining was the most destructive, washing down the sides of the valleys. In preparation for hydraulic mining miles of ditches were dug. The water from these ditches was used to wash down the sands and gravels from the terraces. Few miners thought that some of these flood plains and terraces would one day be laboriously reclaimed for agriculture.

7 THE RAILROAD-BUILDING ERA
1870–1900

*The Locomotive is a great centralizer. It kills little towns and builds up
great cities.*
HENRY GEORGE

The building of railroads was probably the most spectacular aspect of this period but it was by no means the only revolutionary change. Many new roads were laid out and some of them were surfaced; rivers and harbors were improved by dredging and the construction of jetties. Agriculture exploded into eastern Oregon with the aid of new machinery and irrigation. Mining generally declined but manufacturing, especially of wood products, increased substantially. Population expanded; after the first continental rail line was completed most of the immigrants came by rail. And the subjugation of hostile Indian tribes in the 1870s made it safe for settlers to move into all parts of Oregon.

POPULATION

In the period 1870 to 1900 the population of Oregon more than quadrupled from 90,704 in 1870 to 413,536 in 1900, thanks to continued immigration, high birthrate, and low death rate;[1] the population was young. But the growth rate was decreasing; never again would Oregon's population grow at such a rapid rate. From 1870 to 1880 the growth rate was 93 percent, or 84,000 persons; from 1880 to 1890 the growth rate was 84 percent, or 143,000 persons; and from 1890 to 1900 the growth rate was 32 percent, or 96,000 persons.

This period was also a time of settlement expansion into parts of Oregon previously settled only sparsely. The center of population was shifting southward and eastward. In 1870 the most populous counties were Multnomah, Linn, Marion, Douglas, Clackamas, and Yamhill. In 1900 they were Multnomah, Marion, Clackamas, Lane, Linn, Umatilla, Union, and Baker. In 1870 eastern Oregon had only 14 percent of the state's population, 13,000 persons; by 1900 it had 24 percent, 99,000 persons.

The composition of the population was changing also, in terms of origin. In 1870 from 15 to 50 percent were Oregon-born and from 2 to 37 percent were foreign-born depending on the location. Polk County had the highest percentage of Oregon-born, 50 percent, and Baker County had the lowest, 15 percent. Of the foreign-born, Chinese were the most numerous, 24 percent, located mostly in Baker, Grant, Umatilla, Multnomah, Josephine, and Jackson counties, all except Multnomah County in a mining region. Chinese led the other minorities in 10 of the 23 counties. The Chinese had been brought in to work in the mines, on the railroads, and in the canneries. When mining activity declined and the railroads were completed the Chinese moved to the cities, especially to Portland and Astoria, seeking employment. Some became farmhands and others domestic servants, but many were unemployed, leading to agitation against them. In 1886 an anti-Chinese "convention" was held in Portland that adopted a resolution asking the Chinese to kindly "remove themselves to San Francisco or some other suitable place where they are wanted by the people."[2] At the same time there was a large influx of Canadians, who contributed to the unemployment. Other minorities included Germans, English, Scandinavians, and Irish.

By 1900 the Oregon-born population had reached nearly 40 percent and the proportion of foreign-born had increased also. Clatsop County had the highest percentage of foreign-born, with Finns and Norwegians as the leaders. In most counties, however, Germans were the largest minority group, followed by English and Canadi-

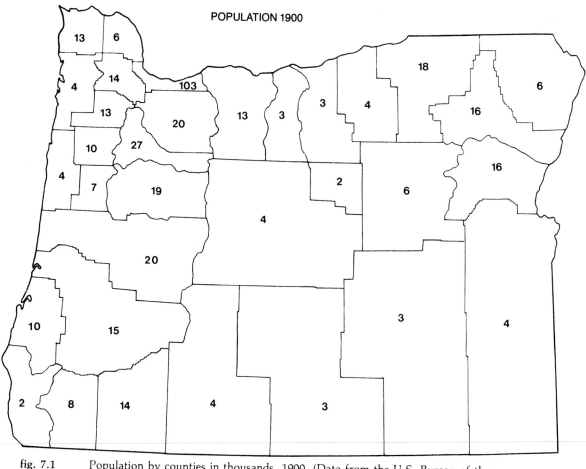

POPULATION 1900

fig. 7.1   Population by counties in thousands, 1900. (Data from the U.S. Bureau of the Census)

ans. The Chinese had declined in importance but still were the largest foreign group in Baker, Malheur, and Multnomah counties.

By 1900 the distribution of Oregon's population had taken on a pattern (fig. 7.1) from which it was not to vary substantially down to the present time. Growth continued, but the proportions in the different regions did not vary greatly: 59 percent in the Willamette Valley; 5 percent in the north coast counties; nearly 12 percent in the southwestern five counties; and 24 percent in eastern Oregon. It is difficult to keep track of population changes in the counties before 1900 because boundaries were changing, but after 1900 there were few boundary changes, except for the reduction of Crook County to form Deschutes and Jefferson counties, and the formation of Hood River County from part of Wasco County.

The one great agglomeration of population extended from Portland southward to central Doug-

las County in the form of a diminishing strip. This area stands out on the population map all the more since the interior parts of the Coast Range and the Cascade Range were almost completely uninhabited. Outside the Willamette Valley, the population was usually arranged in clusters with wide-open spaces in between. On the coast, these included Astoria (the largest), Tillamook, Newport, Florence, Gardiner, Coos Bay (Marshfield), North Bend, Empire, Bandon, and Gold Beach. Except for Astoria and the Coos Bay towns, the settlements were quite small. In the interior of southwestern Oregon the chief clusters were at Grants Pass, Jacksonville, Medford, and Ashland. In eastern Oregon the main clusters were at The Dalles, Prineville, Klamath Falls, Lakeview, and Pendleton. Later, significant clusters developed at Bend and Ontario. Some clusters, like Pendleton, increased in relative importance while others declined. As time went on some of the counties of

106

POPULATION PYRAMID
(1880)

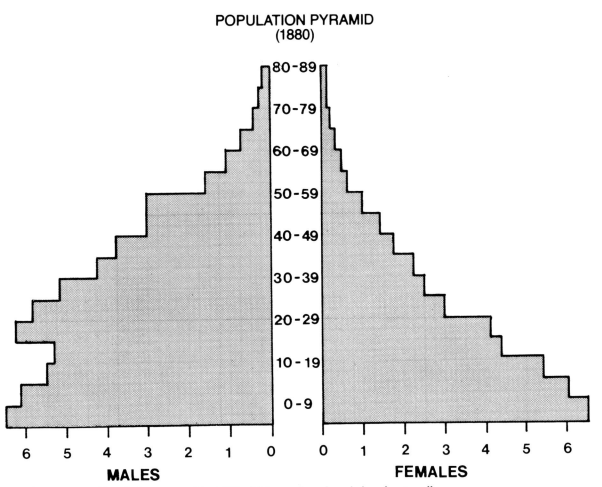

fig. 7.2   Population pyramid, 1880. Males outnumbered females in all age groups, especially those over 20. (Data from the U.S. Bureau of the Census)

eastern Oregon lost population, even while the state continued to gain, as the great migration from the rural areas to the cities and towns got underway.

By 1900 the age-sex composition of the population was approaching normalcy (**fig. 7.2**). The strong dominance of young males, especially in the 15–30 age group, was beginning to diminish and, in the younger ages, males and females were about equal. The slight majority of male children, ages 0–5, was a usual characteristic of the population and holds true today. The percentage of old people had increased.

Indians

The United States census of 1900 listed only 4,951 Indians in Oregon, which was probably a gross underestimate. Apparently few Indians not on reservations were counted; some lived in remote areas difficult for the census taker to reach, some were listed as white or Oriental. According to the census it appears that most of the Indians lived in counties with reservations: Klamath County had 1,037; Umatilla County, 995; Crook and Wasco counties together (Warm Springs Reservation), 951; Lincoln County (Coast Reservation), 465. The facts that not all Indians were living on reservations and that reservations were not total solutions in themselves were attested by the three Indian wars fought in the 1870s with the Modoc, Nez Percé, and Bannock tribes.

The hostility of the Modoc Indians[3] delayed settlement in the Klamath Lakes area for many years, but before 1870 settlers were beginning to move into the more favored areas, establishing cattle ranches along the Sprague River and near the military road (irrigation was to come later). Most of the decisive battles with the Modocs were fought in California but the Indians raided, pillaged, and murdered over a wide area. The rugged terrain of the lava beds was excellent for defensive purposes, providing natural rock forts and caves for shelter and concealment. Unlike the Klamath Indians, the Modocs did not accept life on the Klamath Reservation. The two tribes did not get along well together; the Modocs felt they were mistreated, and at every opportunity they ran away.

The Indian agent tried to conciliate the Modocs, feeding them well when they appeared at agency headquarters. The U.S. Army took a harder line but even it assumed a conciliatory attitude at times under orders from Washington, much to the disgust of the settlers whose lives were threatened. Frequent clashes with the Modocs brought the struggle to a head in 1872.

Before the war was over in 1873 the troops had suffered more casualties (from a very small number of opponents) than in any other Indian war in Oregon. After a series of battles the Modocs were driven from their rocky stronghold and dispersed. Most surrendered, their leader "Captain Jack" (Keintpoos) was hanged, and most of the remaining Modocs were sent to reservations in Wyoming, Nebraska, and Indian Territory.

The Nez Percé had been the most friendly of the eastern Oregon tribes prior to 1876. By the treaty of 1855 they had been given lands in the Grande Ronde, Wallowa, and Imnaha valleys, but a new treaty forced on them eight years later opened these lands to white settlement. As white settlers moved in, the Nez Percé in that area became hostile. At first raids by small bands were made on the white settlers; later a large group under Chief Joseph revolted. Most of the fighting was outside Oregon, in Idaho and Montana, as the Nez Percé tried to reach Canada. In the end the Indians were forced to surrender and were placed on reservations. Gradually more white settlers moved unmolested into the area that was to become Wallowa County.

In 1877 the Bannock Indians along with some Shoshones began to raid settlements near Fort Hall in Idaho, but soon moved to the Steens Mountain area of Oregon. They pillaged over a wide area of southeastern Oregon before sufficient forces could be sent to subdue them, and many settlers were forced to abandon their homes and ranches. When the U.S. Army arrived on the scene, the war was over in a month and all of eastern Oregon was safe from hostile Indians.

Long before any railroads were constructed in Oregon (other than the short portage roads), discussion of the topic was given a sharp impetus by the publication of *Reports and Explorations for Railroad Routes from the Mississippi River to the Pacific*, generally called the Pacific Railroad Reports. This ambitious undertaking, involving hundreds of men — surveyors, civil engineers, geologists, botanists, zoologists, agriculturists, artists, draftsmen, and various supporting personnel — in 1853–1857 surveyed various possible routes for transcontinental railroads. The project was sponsored by Secretary of War Jefferson Davis, and the result was eleven thick, quarto volumes, published as Senate Documents.[4]

Governor I. I. Stevens (Washington Territory) was in charge of the party of 67 persons that surveyed the northern route. A part of this route led through the Columbia Gorge, which was described by Governor Stevens in 1855: "The pass of the Columbia river . . . is remarkably favorable in its grades, which rarely exceed ten feet, in the ease with which debris from the ledges can be worked to form the embankments required to guard against freshets, and the great facility with which wood and stone, both of good quality, can be transported down the Columbia for purposes of construction."[5]

Although the proposed route did not enter Oregon, since it was planned for the north side of the river, it was of great interest to Oregonians. It was Oregon's best hope, at this time, for a transcontinental railroad. St. Paul, Minnesota, was the eastern terminus and some port on Puget Sound the western terminus. Puget Sound was chosen as a terminus in preference to the port of Astoria because of the good harbors on Puget Sound in contrast to the hazards of the Columbia River Bar, which were well known. Nevertheless, the Columbia Gorge was favored as the best route across the Cascade Range, even though it added about 180 miles to the route, as compared with a more direct line over the Cascades via Snoqualmie Pass. In 1883 the first transcontinental train to reach Oregon came to Pasco on the Northern Pacific Railway and then down the south bank of the Columbia River on the tracks of the Oregon Steam and Navigation Railroad. Many years later (1905) tracks were laid along the north side of the river (the Spokane, Portland, and Seattle Railroad).

Surveys were also made of possible railroad

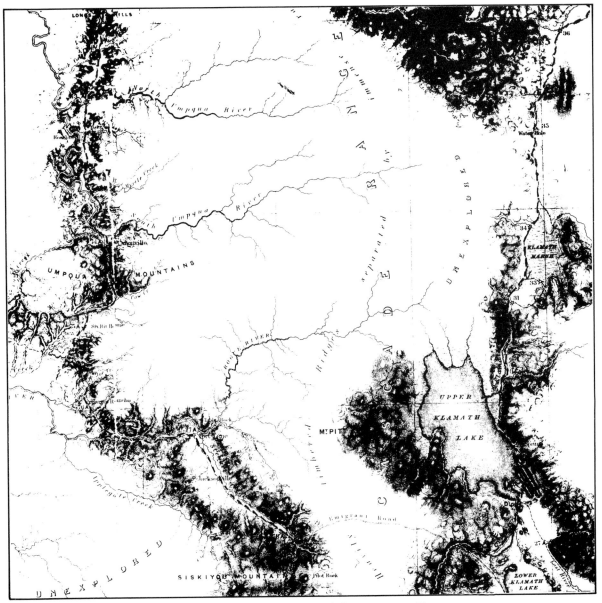

fig. 7.3   Part of a map from the Railroad Survey of Oregon, 1855. Two routes were
surveyed, one east of the Cascades and one to the west. Landforms are shown by
hachures along and near the projected routes. Later, the railroad construction
followed these routes with only minor modifications. The routes are shown by
dashed lines.

routes connecting California and Oregon, one
west of the Cascades via Siskiyou Pass, another
east of the Cascades via Pitt River, Klamath Lake
(fig. 7.3), and the Deschutes River. The work of
the surveyors was handicapped by the hostility of
the Indians, especially in the Umpqua and Rogue
River areas.

Thanks to the transcontinental surveys and the
success of railroads in the East, numerous schemes

and plans for railroads in Oregon were proposed,
none of which produced a single line of track until
1869. Many people thought that railroads were
needed in order to market lumber and agricultural
products more effectively. This meant, it was said,
north-south lines in the Willamette Valley and
beyond to carry goods to the Columbia River for
export. A transcontinental railroad was needed to
reach the eastern markets. Not everyone agreed

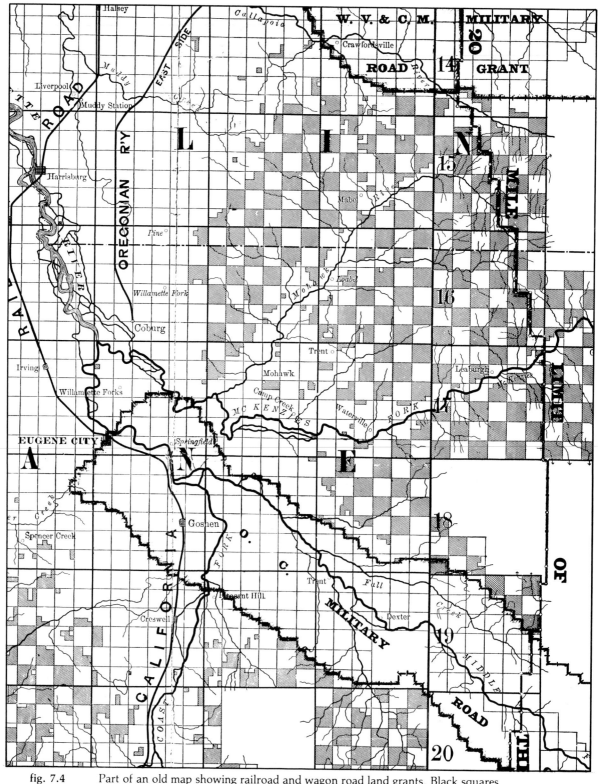

fig. 7.4   Part of an old map showing railroad and wagon road land grants. Black squares (one square mile) represent sections for sale by the Oregon and California Railroad Company. In the north is a part of the Willamette Valley and Cascade Military Road Grant; to the south is a part of the Oregon Central Military Road Grant. (Oregon and California Railroad Co.)

that railroads were needed. It was argued that Oregon's population was too sparse and freight too limited in amount to support railroads. One objector stated: "If one [railroad] should be built [in the Willamette Valley] the first train would carry all the freight in the country, the second all the passengers, and the third would pull up the track behind it and carry off the road itself."[6] In the light of the financial difficulties encountered by the early lines, the remarks were justified, but after a few years of hardship the railroads became a success, virtually driving out the steamers and most of the stagecoaches.

Two routes were proposed in the Willamette Valley, one south from Portland on the east side of the river and one on the west side. An argument followed and soon there were two opposing camps, the "East Siders" and the "West Siders." Capital was limited and it appeared that both roads could not be financed, at least not immediately. On the other hand, it was obvious that a single line would not serve the Valley effectively. As Jesse Applegate, a civil engineer, put it: "From the Calapooya mountains to Portland there should be two roads. A railroad cannot be made to wend its way through overflowed bottoms and cross and recross such a stream as the Willamette. . . . And if Congress will not aid both roads . . . let whatever can be obtained be equally divided between them."[7] Many difficulties were to be encountered, physical and financial; but the money problem was the greatest, money to buy rails and rolling stock and to pay hundreds of laborers.

On the physical side no great problems were encountered in the Willamette Valley proper. Grades were gentle with few exceptions, but bridging the tributary rivers was expensive and difficult where the banks were made of soft materials. Bridging the lower Willamette and the Columbia were more difficult and had to wait several years. The route from Portland to Puget Sound was also comparatively easy. Outside the Willamette Valley-Puget Sound area, difficulties were many. To the east, the Cascade Range imposed a formidable barrier, broken only by the Columbia Gorge that itself provided difficulties, with steep cliffs coming down to the river's edge in many places. What had been a barrier to the immigrants, forcing them to take to the water or to Barlow Road, was an even greater difficulty for the railroads. To the south, a series of ridges, called, in the early days, the Umpqua, the Calapooya, and the Siskiyou mountains,

required the railroad to cross several summits and also to take a circuitous route in many places. Another problem was to connect the Willamette Valley with the coast, not so much to serve the coastal communities as to provide additional outlets for the Valley products. A hazard common to all lines in hilly or mountainous terrain was, and is, the climate; the gentle but frequent rains cause landslides on the fills and in the cuts. Numerous tunnels were necessary in the rough terrain, an added expense in construction. These were some of the problems that the surveyors and planners had to face.

The railroads in Oregon could not have been constructed without government aid and the sale of bonds to eastern and foreign buyers. The financial manipulations are too involved to be recounted here but one phase of the financing, the land grants, deserves mention, since they left a permanent mark on the landscape. In 1869 the U.S. Congress granted 2,500,000 acres of land in Oregon and California for the Portland to California railroad, known today as the Oregon and California Revested Lands (O and C Land). Alternate sections of land in a checkerboard pattern were granted so that the railroad could sell the land at $2.50 per acre to prospective settlers and thus finance the railroad.[8] Large areas of land were sold, but the terms of the agreement were violated, and after many years of argument and litigation, part of the lands were "revested" and placed under the jurisdiction of the Bureau of Land Management. Much of this land is in forest, which is harvested in a checkerboard pattern (**fig. 7.4**). The proceeds of the sale of timber are shared by 18 Oregon counties.

RAILROAD CONSTRUCTION

Work really began on railroad construction in Oregon in 1868, but progress was slow because of financial difficulties and rivaly between the "East Siders" and the "West Siders." The east side road, the Oregon and California Railroad, reached Albany in 1871, Eugene in 1871, Roseburg in 1872 (**fig. 7.5**). At this point construction was halted for many years, but the line eventually reached Ashland in 1887 where it joined with construction from California to form the Southern Pacific Railroad. Meanwhile an alternate route, the "West Side Line," was progressing even more slowly, reaching Cornelius in the Tualatin Valley in 1871

fig. 7.5   Oregon and California Railroad passenger train between New Era and Canby,
Oregon, in 1870. (Southern Pacific Historical Coll., OHS)

and St. Joseph in 1872. This line eventually reached only to Corvallis.

The first railroad up the Columbia River from Portland, the Oregon Steam and Navigation Company Railroad (later reorganized by Henry Villard as the Oregon Railway and Navigation Company) was a narrow gauge, three feet, but it was converted to standard gauge in 1882 so as to connect with the Northern Pacific Railway in 1883. A branch of this line, the Oregon Short Line (a subsidiary company of the Union Pacific), was built across the Blue Mountains to connect with

the Union Pacific Railroad at Oregon's eastern border. The Oregon Short Line later became part of the Union Pacific.

By 1900, in addition to the two main lines in Oregon, the Southern Pacific Railroad to California and the Oregon Steam and Navigation Railroad (the Oregon Railway and Navigation Company), there were a number of short lines. Some were mere "feeders," such as the lines in Sherman and Morrow counties and line from Baker to the upper John Day Valley (fig. 7.6). The Astoria and Columbia Railroad was a little more ambitious

112

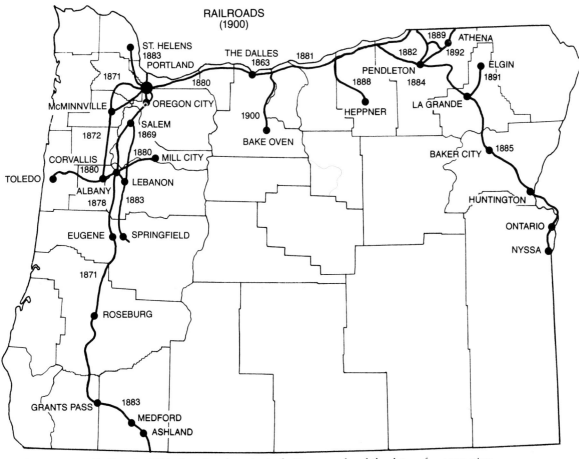

RAILROADS
(1900)

fig. 7.6   Railroads, 1900, showing the principal cities served and the dates of construction.
(From William Loy, *Preliminary Atlas of Oregon*, 1972)

and was, in effect, a part of the transcontinental system although not a main line. It reached Fort Stevens and Seaside and profited by holiday traffic. The narrow-gauge Oregonian Railroad was constructed from Dayton to Sheridan and Dallas in 1878. Another part of the line led from Ray's Landing through Woodburn, and south through Silverton and Brownsville to Springfield, but was not connected to the Dayton-Dallas line. This line was later (1892) purchased by the Southern Pacific and converted to standard gauge.

A line using various names in the course of its construction—Corvallis and Yaquina Bay, Willamette Valley and Coast, and Oregon Pacific—was planned with two purposes in mind: to provide a new outlet for Willamette Valley products, mainly wheat, via Yaquina Bay; and to form a link in a transcontinental line by constructing a railroad across the Cascade Range via the Santiam Pass, in order to connect with the Union Pacific Railroad in Idaho. Randall Mills called this the

"Frustration Route" because of the many difficulties.[9] Construction began on the Corvallis-Yaquina section in 1882 and was completed in 1884 after great difficulties, including collapsing trestles, fires in a tunnel (wood supports), and troubles with the Chinese laborers. The steamer *Yaquina*, one of several intended to carry freight and passengers, found it difficult to cross the bar of Yaquina Bay, and, for this and other reasons, the scheme was not a success. To the east, the line was completed to Idanha on the Santiam River near Detroit. In order to preempt Santiam Pass, a short section of track was built with materials brought in on ox carts and a railroad car was added to give further weight to the claim. Evidence of this track can be seen today to the north of U.S. Highway 20. East of the Cascades, the line was surveyed but never built. Later this line was taken over by the Southern Pacific Railroad and used to haul logs and lumber. The railroads did not bring prosperity to everyone. Cities and towns

113

fig. 7.7   Horse-car line at Grand and East Morrison, Portland, 1888. (D.H. Bates Coll., OHS)

along the right-of-way prospered, but many by-passed localities lost population.[10]

URBAN AND INTERURBAN LINES

The railroads did not solve all of Oregon's transportation problems; local transportation was needed within the cities and from the city centers to the suburbs and satellite towns. Construction of street railways began in 1871 but advanced very slowly in this period as compared to the railroads, perhaps because streetcars were not subsidized. The first line in Portland ran along First Street from Glisan Street to Caruthers Street; the total cost was only $10,000.[11] The motive power was one mule (fig. 7.7). Other lines followed, using mules or horses until steam was introduced in the mid-1880s. But steam was cumbersome for small units, such as streetcars, and construction was slow until the introduction of electricity in 1889, which gradually replaced steam. Even so, progress was slow until after 1900. The east side line in Portland, however, was extended to Mt. Tabor and Mt. Scott.

The first interurban lines were built in 1893, one from Portland to Vancouver, Washington (the cars were ferried across the Columbia River), and another to Oregon City, paralleling the Oregon and California Railroad. These were the first inter-urban lines in the United States. Most of the revenue was from passengers but mail, express, and light freight were also carried.

By 1900 the streetcar lines in the cities—Portland, Salem, Eugene, Medford, Corvallis, and Newport—and the interurban lines were beginning to change the character of the cities, the suburbs, and the satellite towns. These two forms of transportation were destined to play a very important role in Oregon's transportation after 1900 (see next chapter) and before the automobile became the chief means of movement.

ROADS

In December 1896, a "Good Roads" convention was held in Portland. One speaker defined a good road as one that is good in dry and wet weather. He further stated that there was no such road in existence in Oregon at that time. But progress was being made. In addition to the roads in the Willamette Valley, described in the previous chapter, a number of new roads were laid out and many trails were converted to roads in the period 1870–1900. Some roads surveyed were mere tracks, inadequate in the rainy season. A few roads were surfaced with gravel or well-rolled and oiled crushed rock.[12] (Many parts of Oregon have no good gravel for road building and must depend on crushed rock instead.)

Along the coast, parts of the Coast Trail were improved enough to be usable by wagons and stagecoaches, taking advantage of the many miles of beaches, especially good at low tide on the hard-packed sand. Obviously the stages had a

114

"flexible" schedule because of the tides. From the California border the route followed the old pioneer trail, which later became the old U.S. Highway 101, following along the terrace from the California line to Brookings, thence along the ridge crest through Carpenterville to Pistol River, then on or near the beaches to Bandon, with detours around Cape Sebastian and Humbug Mountain. From Bandon the road led up the Coquille River to the town of Coquille, thence via the banks of Isthmus Slough to Marshfield (now Coos Bay). This section has one long beach, from Port Orford to Bandon, but the beach was little used; instead the road followed the sandy terrace a few miles inland where the rivers were much easier to cross and where most of the settlements were located. The 100-foot terrace provided the best site for roads, wherever it occurred. The surface is nearly level and usually covered with a veneer of sand.

Coos Bay was crossed by ferry at Empire and the road continued northward along the beach, which was described as "a wonderful natural pavement," to Heceta Head. This is the longest beach in Oregon. Ferries were provided at the main river crossings, usually a few miles inland where crossing was easier; smaller streams were forded. North of Heceta Head the road continued over Cape Perpetua and along the terrace to Newport. Some sections of the coast, such as Cape Foulweather, had no road at this period. From Neskowin the route was inland, winding over the hills, much the same as U.S. Highway 101 does today, to Tillamook and thence near the coast to Nehalem. Neahkahnie Mountain did not have a road across it, only a pack trail. North of Neahkahnie Mountain and Cape Falcon travel was along the beach to Cannon Beach and thence over the hills to Seaside, then along the long, dune ridges to the Columbia River.

Roads across the Coast Range were few and far between. As noted in the previous chapter, roads had been authorized from Astoria to Salem, and from Tillamook via the Trask River to Yamhill.[13] Corvallis was connected to the coast via the Alsea River Valley. From Eugene and Junction City connecting roads led to the coast at Florence. Another road connected Roseburg, which for many years was the end of the railroad, to Coos Bay via Coquille. Scottsburg had a road to Drain to connect with the California Trail. The only through roads across the Klamath Mountains were the Oregon-California Trail, from north to south, and the road from Grants Pass to Crescent City, California, via Kerby and Waldo. In addition to the leading roads from the Oregon-California Trail across the Coast Range, many short, feeder roads led up the valleys on both sides of the range, especially on the eastern side, where many of the valleys tributary to the Willamette were settled at an early date.

In eastern Oregon the road problem was quite different; distances were greater but the drier climate and the large areas of smooth terrain made travel by wheeled vehicles much easier, even off the roads. Only a few well-defined routes were in general use by 1900. The old, reliable Oregon Trail had settled down to the La Grande-Pendleton route over the Blue Mountains, now Interstate Highway I-80N. The alternate route through Elgin and over Tollgate Pass via the Walla Walla River Valley was little used. Mining in the Blue Mountains stimulated road travel if it did not always mean road improvement. Roads were necessary to get the supplies in and the gold out. The principal road led from Ontario on the Snake River, up Willow Creek, and over several ridges to John Day and Mitchell (present U.S. Highway 26). From Mitchell the route led northwestward to The Dalles. This route was served for many years by stagecoaches that, as everyone knows, carried gold. From Mitchell a branch road led through Prineville and across Santiam Pass to Albany (U.S. Highway 20).

The military roads, noted in the previous chapter, continued in use but with little improvement. The Dalles Military Road was certified as completed when it was only an oxcart trail. All construction on the Willamette Valley and Cascade Mountains Road east of the Deschutes River was done by a small party on horseback, with a light wagon following. The party moved through the country at a rate of 10 or 15 miles per day, pushing down sagebrush, blazing trees (so the traveler would not wander off the road), doing a little construction on bad spots and locating fords for stream crossings. The Oregon Central Military Road, according to the Land Office maps of the time, apparently crossed directly over Steens Mountain, something no modern road builder has attempted. The route actually passed between Steens Mountain and the Pueblo Mountains. Further east the road followed approximately the old Applegate cutoff immigrant road.

If Oregon did not have very many miles of surfaced roads by 1900, it was not for lack of agita-

fig. 7.8   Jetties at the entrance of the Siuslaw River, Lane County. Since this photo was taken the south jetty has been repaired and extended. The low-lying land adjacent to the north jetty has been filled in since construction in 1892. Narrow strips of dune sand are in the background. (Oregon Dept. of Transportation)

tion. Numerous petitions by the counties to the state and federal governments indicated that roads had a high priority. Appropriations were made, but in small amounts, and road improvement was very slow, except for the Willamette Valley. Most parts of the state were sparsely populated with very limited tax monies available for roads.

RIVERS AND HARBORS

Along with the extension of railroads and wagon roads, the improvements of rivers, harbors, and dock facilities were of great significance

to transportation in Oregon in this period. Completion of the south jetty in 1885 and the north jetty in 1913 at the outlet of the Columbia River created a new, deeper channel on the south side of the river, replacing the old channel on the north side of the entrance that had fixed the boundary between Washington and Oregon. The natural depth of the river to Portland, about 15 feet at control points, was sufficient for the ships of this period; later the channel was dredged to 30 feet. Shifting sand bars were still a hazard, in spite of which most of the wheat produced in Washington and Oregon passed down the river to Astoria for export. There was also a heavy export of lumber.

Further south on the coast, jetties were built at the outlets of several rivers (**fig. 7.8**): on the Yaquina in 1881 and 1889; on the Siuslaw in 1892 and 1910; on Coos Bay in 1891 and 1924; and on the Coquille in 1881 and 1892. Later jetties were constructed on the Nehalem in 1910 and 1916; on Tillamook Bay in 1914 and 1974; on the Umpqua in 1917 and 1933; on the Rogue in 1959 and 1960; and on the Chetco in 1957. Not all these harbors were very usable; some jetties were damaged by storms, some subsided into the sands on which they were built. On the Oregon coast only the Coos Bay entrance was deep enough to accommodate large freighters. Others were suitable for small freighters, barges, fishing boats, and pleasure craft. The construction of the jetties caused the deposition of sand on their margins and, in some cases, accelerated erosion on the adjacent shores.

Locks in some of the rivers improved navigation for the river steamers, barges, and log rafts, especially at Oregon City. Portages were used around rapids and falls where locks had not been built and before 1900 goods were moving along the Columbia and Snake rivers as far up as Lewiston, Idaho, and also up the Willamette River to Corvallis. Occasionally, with high-water, shallow-draft boats reached Eugene. Log transport, for which there are no adequate records, probably accounted for the greatest tonnage on the Columbia, Willamette, and other rivers. During this period, steamers plied the Yaquina to Toledo, the Siuslaw to Mapleton, and the Umpqua to Scottsburg. In many places railroad and steamer were in competition, but in some places they were complementary.

AGRICULTURE

In the period from 1870 to 1900 agriculture expanded into areas of Oregon not previously cultivated and, at the same time, the farms and ranches became more commercial. After the Indian hostilities were over, the migration into eastern Oregon accelerated. Cropping in the semiarid areas called for new methods of cultivation—irrigation where water was available; dry farming where water was scarce; ranching where rainfall was too little for cropping. One effect of the railroads was to make outside markets more accessible so that the wheat, potatoes, fruits, meat animals, and other products could be shipped to other states or abroad.

Crops

The Willamette Valley was slowly losing its dominance in wheat-growing to eastern Oregon (as it was later to lose the dominance in potato production) and was turning more to forage crops and specialty crops, such as fruits, vegetables, flax, and hops. Oregon fruits were finding favor in eastern markets, thanks to their high quality and transcontinental railroads. At the Centennial Exposition at Philadelphia in 1876, people were impressed with the quality of Oregon fruits, all the more so since they had survived the long journey with so little deterioration. Medals were awarded Oregon growers for "'cherries of remarkable size and flavor,' 'pears, ten varieties of superior excellence and size, beauty and flavor,' 'apples, twelve varieties of remarkable excellence, flavor, color and size,' and 'prunes, four varieties, all superior, [all] illustrating how well the state of Oregon is adapted to their culture.'"[14] Marketing success was due in no small measure to new methods of packing and shipping.

In 1900 the apple was the most important fruit with plums and prunes, together, a close second. The chief apple-producing counties were Linn, Clackamas, Marion, Douglas, Lane, Yamhill, Wasco (in 1900 the area of Hood River County was in Wasco County), and Jackson. Pears had much the same distribution as apples but only one-seventh as many trees. The leading plum- and prune-producing counties were Marion, Douglas, Clackamas, and Linn. Jackson, Douglas, Wasco, and Josephine counties were the chief peach-growing counties and Marion, Clackamas, Lane, and Multnomah the principal cherry-growing counties.

Nut crops, especially the English walnut, became of commercial importance in this period. The black walnut, transplanted to Oregon by the early immigrants, did not achieve commercial importance because of its slow growth. Later, some farmers received good returns from the sale of the wood, since Oregon has so few native hardwoods of high quality. Cranberry bogs were constructed along the coast, where the abundant rainfall, sandy soils, and hardpan were especially favorable.

A variety of flax grows wild in Oregon and was used by the Indians. The cultivated variety was introduced as early as 1844, but for many years the crop was very small. Extensive cultivation had to wait until mills could be provided to process the

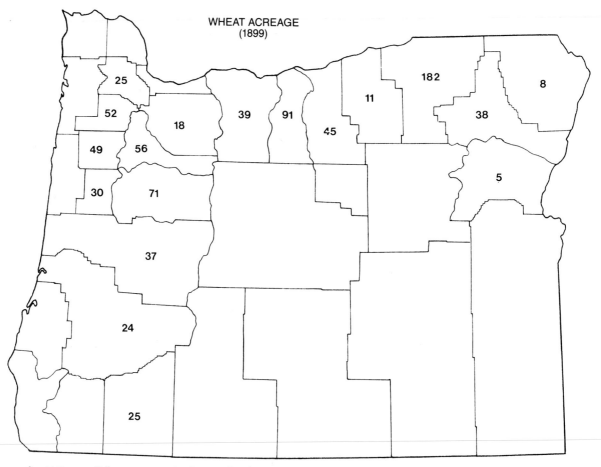

WHEAT ACREAGE
(1899)

fig. 7.9   Wheat acreage in thousands of acres, 1899. Counties with less than 5,000 acres
are not listed. (Data from the U.S. Bureau of the Census)

fiber and extract the oil from the seeds. Linn County became the chief producer of flax and a fiber mill was built in Albany in 1877. The main products were twine and thread; tow for upholstering was also manufactured. The seed produced, part of which was pressed in an oil mill at Salem, was worth about $45 per acre.

Potato acreage and production continued to expand. It was a first-rank crop in value in many parts of the state, and in others it was second only to wheat. In 1870 the production was only 481,000 bushels; by 1900 the production reached over three million bushels. The potato, so well adapted to the cool summers of the Willamette Valley and to the coastal areas, succeeded also in eastern Oregon with irrigation. Dairy products expanded in like manner, with emphasis on butter and, to a lesser degree, on cheese. In 1870 butter production was 1.4 million pounds; by 1900 it had reached 8.1 million pounds. Cheese production was 467,000 pounds in 1900. A large part of the butter and

cheese was exported and the Willamette Valley and some of the coastal areas, such as Tillamook and Coos Bay, were becoming known as "dairy belts."

Wheat was first grown in eastern Oregon on a commercial basis in 1866, but the big boom came in the 1870s. By 1900 six of the ten leading wheat counties were in eastern Oregon; Umatilla and Sherman counties were at the top of the list (fig. 7.9). Wheat farming had spread out along the northern margin of the Deschutes-Umatilla Plateau, from The Dalles to Pendleton and beyond, and into the basins of the Blue Mountains, such as the Grande Ronde. Most of the wheat was grown within 100 miles of rail and water transportation. The early immigrants had passed over these plateaus and basins, little dreaming that these lands would someday make some farmers rich. Produce they did, with special methods of cultivation known as "dry farming." (Dry farming can be defined as practices in a

118

fig. 7.10   Horse-drawn combine in eastern Oregon. (OHS)

semiarid region, designed to conserve moisture and get the maximum benefit from the light rains.) Two methods were in use. One was "fallowing," which involved cropping a field in alternate years; this meant that the farm must be large, at least two square miles on the average. A family would starve on a mere 160 acres in this country. The other practice was, and is, "mulching," in which the soil is cultivated after harvest, turning under the stubble and producing a fine "dust" (which sometimes blows), thus sealing the surface and helping to retain the moisture. In other words, one crop is obtained from two years', or even three years', rainfall. The dryland wheat farmers often spoke respectfully of "moisture" rather than "rainfall." ("If we can get a little moisture we will have a crop.") Sometimes the rains did not come and crop failure was the result, but a good year usually made up for the losses. When two or more dry years came in succession some farmers failed.

Agricultural Technology

Large farms called for large machines to cultivate, seed, harvest, and "thrash." In the last decades of the nineteenth century, new inventions in farm machinery — wide seeders and McCormack reapers, horse-powered and tractor-powered threshers, and finally the combine, which harvested and threshed at the same time — brought about a revolution in agricultural practices (fig. 7.10). At first the combines were horse- or mule-drawn, but the invention of the gasoline tractor put the horses out of business, except for riding.

In the 1880s, when wheat farming had exploded into north central Oregon (it had exploded into the Great Plains earlier), new types of farm machinery were being advertised in Oregon. *Willamette Farmer* advertisements extolled new headers, reapers, mowers, plows, seeders, and drills. Especially recommended was a "straw-burning traction

119

SKETCH MAP
OF
OREGON
SHOWING THE
IRRIGATED AREAS
ACCORDING TO THE CENSUS OF
1900.
Scale

Total Irrigated Area

387,095 Acres

fig. 7.11   Map of the irrigated areas, 1900. No irrigation is indicated for the Willamette
Valley but many small private projects were in operation. (From U.S. Bureau of
the Census, 1900)

engine" for use east of the Cascades where fuel was scarce. (It is ironical that in the 1970s great efforts were being made to develop a straw-burning "engine" in the Willamette Valley just to get rid of straw without polluting the atmosphere.) The advertisements also offered Studebaker wagons and an Ohio company advertised a new thresher, "built especially for the Pacific Coast trade." At the Oregon State Fair, farm machinery manufac-

turers competed for prizes. Most of the farm machinery was made in the Middle West; only a few of the smaller items were made in Oregon.

The steam traction engine was the basic machine. It could travel (slowly) from farm to farm on its own power, could pull heavy machinery, and could furnish power for stationary threshing machines. But it was expensive and noisy. (The owners of frightened horses often sued and laws

120

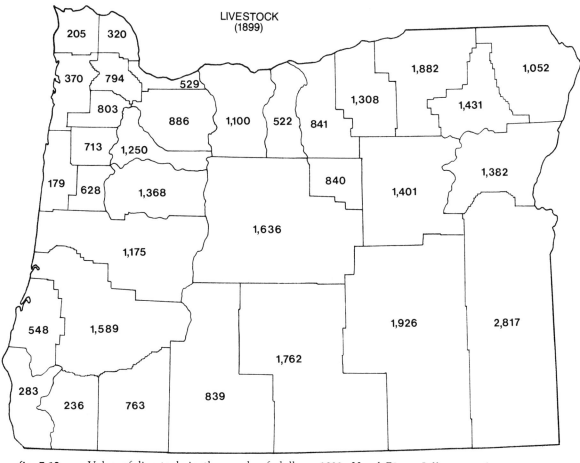

fig. 7.12   Value of livestock in thousands of dollars, 1899. Hood River, Jefferson and
Deschutes counties were not organized at this time. (Data from the U.S. Bureau
of the Census)

were enacted to restrict the transportation of the engines on the roads.) Fuel was scarce in the wheat-growing areas. Nevertheless, the traction engine was slowly replacing the horse. Henry Ford saw his first one in 1875 (he was 12 years old at the time), and later he said: "It was that first engine which took me into automotive transportation." Perhaps Henry Ford had a notion then that the horse was on the way out.

Mechanization of the farms meant that two men could work a farm two or more square miles in extent and have plenty of time for vacation. Some wheat farmers preferred to live in a nearby town and work the farm only at seeding, harvesting, and "mulching" times. On the other hand, some farms were diversified with livestock grazing on the unplowed areas and on the wheat stubble after harvest. Some farms even had small areas under irrigation.

Irrigation

Meanwhile irrigation was being introduced into eastern Oregon, in the few areas where water was readily available (fig. 7.11). The early immigrants were unfamiliar with irrigation practices, having come from the humid farming areas; some time elapsed before the possibilities of irrigation were realized. But once introduced it spread rapidly to all counties of eastern Oregon and to Josephine and Jackson counties as well. There was some small-scale irrigation in the Willamette Valley but not enough to be listed in the 1900 census. At first all irrigation was on a small scale; there were no high dams and huge aqueducts to provide large quantities of water. Most of the irrigation was from streams, parts of which were diverted to reach the low-lying fields. A common device was a low diversion dam that turned the water into

fig. 7.13   Early cattle ranch near Roseburg, Douglas County, Oregon. (OHS)

ditches; in some cases large water wheels, turned by the current, lifted small quantities of water to the fields. The chief irrigated crops were forage crops, especially alfalfa, clover, and millet, and fruits, vegetables, and potatoes.[15]

Livestock

Most of Oregon's livestock in this period was on farms in those areas too dry or too hilly to farm. The grazing of cattle and sheep, at least for a part of the year, was becoming more and more common. Western Oregon is especially suited to dairy farming and in the coastal region this is particularly true. The cool, often cloudy, summers and the rainy winters provide year-round pasture and ideal conditions for the production of hay and other forage crops. In 1850 the dairy cows of Oregon numbered only 9,000, but the number had grown to 48,000 in 1870 and to 122,000 in 1900. The growth of dairy farming was limited only by

the market. California was an early and continuous market for Oregon butter and cheese, and with better transportation these products were marketed also in the East. California became a market for surplus dairy cows too, since that state had its own dairies for its whole-milk requirements. Some areas, such as Tillamook on the coast, were highly specialized in dairying, while in the Willamette Valley the dairy farms were scattered among other types of farms. Much of the milk produced came from small herds on diversified farms.

Beef cattle numbered 24,000 in 1850, increased to 69,000 in 1870, and rose to 715,000 in 1900 (**figs. 7.12** and **7.13**). Obviously there was a great spurt in cattle raising once eastern Oregon was settled. There were 8,000 oxen in Oregon in 1850, many of them having pulled wagons across the plains, but they declined in numbers and almost disappeared. Although some mules pulled wagons along the Oregon Trail (and faster than the oxen),

122

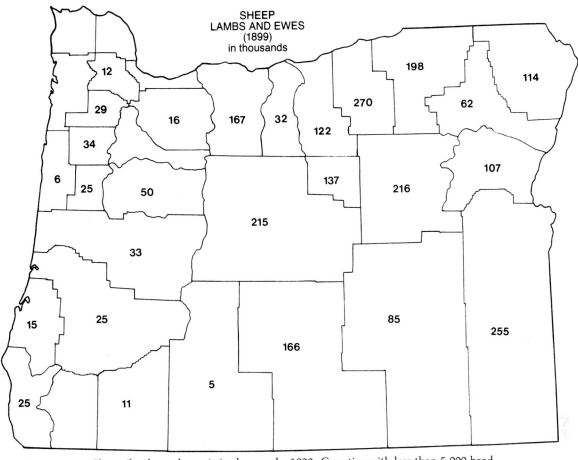

fig. 7.14   Sheep (lambs and ewes), in thousands, 1899. Counties with less than 5,000 head are not included. Hood River, Jefferson, and Deschutes counties were established later. (Data from the U.S. Bureau of the Census)

there were only 6,000 in Oregon in 1900. Horses were the chief riding and draft animals until tractors came into general use. They numbered 8,000 in 1850; 50,000 in 1870; and 280,000 in 1900.

By 1870 sheep had greatly increased in number and, as they spread into eastern Oregon, reached a total of 318,000. By 1900 there were 1,961,000 (fig. 7.14). High-quality wool sheep were imported from Europe, and Portland became the leading wool market for the Pacific Northwest. Since wool could be transported long distances by wagon because of its high value per pound, sheep ranches could succeed in remote parts of the state. High-altitude pastures were used in summer, especially in the vicinity of Steens Mountain and in the Wallowa Mountains but in other parts of the Blue Mountains as well. In fact, any elevated area would likely have better pasture than the lowlands. A lone sheepherder with his chuck wagon and a couple of dogs could take care of a flock of sheep on the range at minimum expense (fig. 7.15). It was a lonely job, however, and sheepherders had to be imported. The Irish herders tended to locate near Lakeview, while the Basques favored the Jordan Valley and Steens Mountain. (Later the Irish and Basques became sheep owners instead of sheepherders and it became difficult to find anyone to herd sheep.) Meanwhile sheep did not disappear from western Oregon; they became, for the time being, less important. Swine have never been as important as horses, sheep, and cattle in Oregon, even though the immigrants from the Middle West thought highly of them as farm animals. In 1870 there were 119,000 in Oregon and in 1900, 281,000.

The problem of transportation for livestock and livestock products was especially difficult for the more remote cattle and sheep ranches in eastern

fig. 7.15   Sheepherder and flock; the sheep belonged to Bartholomew Brothers, Heppner, Oregon. (OHS)

Oregon. The railroad along the Columbia River and across the Blue Mountains helped, but it was necessary for many ranchers to haul their wool or drive their cattle over long distances. Usually wool was hauled in wagons or carts to the nearest railroad, but cattle—and sometimes sheep—were driven over fairly well-marked trails[16] to the nearest rail point—The Dalles, Pendleton, La Grande, Huntington, or Winnemucca, Nevada (fig. 7.16).

The rapid expansion of wheat growing in the Deschutes-Umatilla Plateau, especially in Wasco, Gilliam, Sherman, and Umatilla counties, had the definite effect of reducing the number of cattle and sheep in that region. The smooth uplands between the streams had furnished good grazing prior to the wheat boom, but much of the good bunch grass was plowed under in order to plant wheat. In effect, this shifted the emphasis on beef cattle and sheep to the south and east where grazing conditions were inferior. Baker County had 29,000 beef cattle in 1900; Crook, Jefferson, and Deschutes counties combined also had 29,000 head. The shifting of sheep followed much the same pattern as that of the cattle. While the number of sheep in Oregon remained nearly constant, individual counties in eastern Oregon varied from year to year. Baker had 140,000 sheep in 1900, more than 177,000 in 1930. Harney County had 130,000 in 1900, more than 200,000 in 1930.

A number of factors in addition to wheat farming affected the numbers and distribution of the cattle and sheep. The railroads changed transportation from long drives to short drives and rail transport. During this period much of the range land was fenced, so that there was better control of the grazing conditions; even so, overgrazing was serious and the range was damaged. Later, grazing fees on the public domain served to protect the range, and the Taylor Grazing Act of 1934 (see chapter 9) put it on a sustained-yield basis.

124

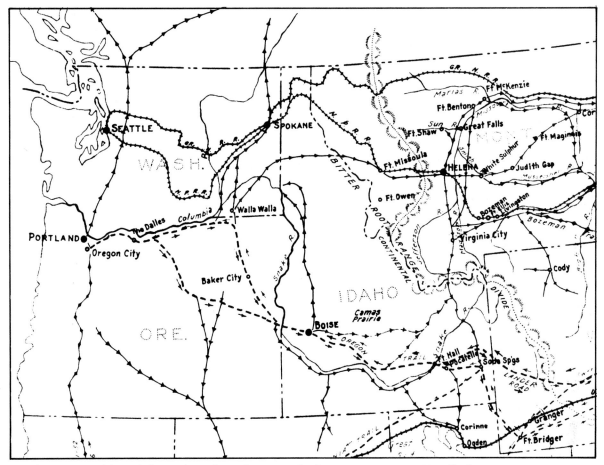

fig. 7.16   Map of the cattle trails in Oregon and adjacent states, 1865-1895. Cattle were driven south to California and north to Canada, southeast to the Central Pacific Railroad at Winnemucca, eastward to Boise on the Union Pacific Railroad, and also to Spokane, a city on the Great Northern and Northern Pacific railroads. (From *American Cattle Trails*, The Western Range Cattle Industry study in cooperation with the American Pioneer Trails Association, Denver, 1949.)

Finally, the ranchers began to feel the pressure from the homesteaders as more and more settlers came in.

THE GRUB LANDS

As noted previously (in chapter 3), the floor of the Willamette Valley was mostly prairie when the first settlers arrived, the result of continuous burning by the Indians. But by no means all of the grassland was immediately cultivated, and so half a century later much of it had grown up in brush and small trees. By 1880 some of these lands, known as "grub lands," were being cleared and put into cultivation. David Newsom in a letter to the

Oregonian, July 28, 1880, described the clearing of these lands and, with his characteristic thoroughness, estimated the acreage, the cost of clearing, and the expected return.

My means of finding out this matter have been ample. I therefore set down the aggregate acreage at 60,000 acres. These brush lands are exceedingly rich and productive. They are situated within and adjacent to the well settled parts of these counties, generally well watered and rolling. The Chinese have been paid about ten dollars per acre for grubbing and 85¢ per cord for cutting the grubs into cord wood. The farmers have generally burnt the limbs and roots. Multitudes of rails have been made from the fir saplings grubbed up. Nearly all the towns and a large number of the farm houses

125

in these counties have been half or more supplied with cordwood from these clearings for three or four years past. Part of the cordwood for the cars, steamers and furnaces of these counties has been of this sort. We will set down all these grub lands in their wild condition at five dollars per acre. This would be a cost of three hundred thousand dollars. The grubbing, fencing, and clearing up of them, we set down at nine hundred thousand dollars, which, added to the cost, foots up one million two hundred thousand dollars. We will credit only two crops of wheat from these sixty-thousand acres, placed at fifty bushels for these two years, 3,000,000 bushels. We will set down this bulk of wheat at 90¢ per bushel, and the sum of $2,700,000. Deduct one third for expenses and we have $1,800,000.[17]

FISHERIES

The Hudson's Bay Company introduced Columbia River salmon to the London market before American traders entered the business; but in 1829 Captain Dominis of the Boston brig *Owyhee* transported 50 hogsheads of salted salmon to that city, which were sold for 10 cents per pound.[18] The early settlers along the Columbia River and the coastal rivers depended on salmon for food and some of them sold a few barrels of salted fish. All the rivers and their tributaries had good runs of salmon in those days and if the settlers were too busy to fish they could buy from the Indians at a very low price. Salmon did not become of great commercial importance until canneries were built, beginning about 1866. Within a few years canneries were established at several points along the Columbia and in most of the coastal rivers and bays, including the Nehalem River, Tillamook Bay, the Nestucca, Siletz, Siuslaw, and Umpqua rivers, Coos Bay, and the Coquille and Rogue rivers. The preferred site for a cannery was on the shore near a good supply of fresh water. After a slow start the salmon pack zoomed from 10,000 cases in 1869 to 450,000 cases in 1878, making it the leading export after wheat and flour, which were listed as one item.

Salmon were caught by a variety of methods, of which the gillnet was most favored. Set nets, traps, purse seines, and drag seines, often pulled by horses in shallow water, were also common, as was trolling with baited hooks. A familiar sight on the Columbia River was the fish wheel (**fig. 7.17**), a device driven by the current of the stream that dipped the salmon and dumped them in a trough that led to the shore. (The fish wheel and the purse seine were later outlawed.) Most of the fishermen were Scandinavians and most of the cannery workers were Chinese. Even in the 1870s and 1880s the salmon run varied from year to year, causing some concern to the cannery owners. Two conservation measures were adopted, one to regulate the size of the gill nets so that the small salmon could escape, and the second to prohibit fishing from Saturday evening to Sunday evening.

Other varieties of fish were taken in the rivers and in the ocean in comparatively small quantities—tomcod, flounder, candlefish, smelt, and sturgeon, and shellfish, clams, crabs, shrimp, and mussels. Oysters were planted in several bays, with "seed" usually obtained from Japan (there are no native oysters in Oregon and the waters are too cold for spawning).

MINING

As mining continued in various parts of Oregon, mostly in the southwest in the Klamath Mountains and in the northeast in the Blue Mountains, it became apparent that Oregon possessed a great variety of minerals—gold, silver, copper, mercury, nickel, and chromium—as well as coal, building stone, and gravel. But it also was apparent that many of these deposits were scattered so widely and were of such low grade that mining was not feasible, at least in times of low prices.

Although placer mining for gold declined in the period 1870–1900, the hydraulic method, which sometimes required the construction of long ditches for water supply, continued to produce.[19] The emphasis in gold mining turned to lode mining or "quartz" mining, as it was commonly called, since it involved crushing hard rock, usually quartzite, to recover the gold. There were many quartz mines in this period, some very successful; others failed to yield enough gold to pay for the installation of the machinery. Some of the discoveries were fabulously rich. One lode yielded $10 to a pound of rock, but was soon exhausted. The lode gold was recovered by first crushing the hard rock with an *arrastra*, a crude stamp mill that broke the rock into small fragments; the gold could then be recovered by amalgamation with

fig. 7.17   Fish wheel on the Columbia River. (OHS)

mercury, after which the mercury was boiled off. The demand for mercury led to some mining of cinnabar, the red ore of Mercury. Some of the lode mines also yielded small quantities of silver, lead, zinc, and antimony, all from the same ore.

As noted earlier, coal mining began in the Coos Bay area in 1853. It continued for many years but faced keen competition from coals of other areas. No records of coal production were kept until 1880, when 40,000 tons were mined. The largest production was in 1904, over 111,000 tons. Some of the coal was used for locomotives, although most of them burned wood during this period; it was also used for domestic fuel. Eventually the advent of petroleum and the competition of better coals from outside the state brought production to an end, except during the two world wars when the mines were temporarily re-opened. The Coos Bay coal was described in the early days as a lignite, which it is not. It is a fairly low-grade bituminous coal with more than average amounts of ash and moisture.[20] The beds of coal are tilted and folded, making mining more expensive than in flat-lying coal beds. However, the mines are close to tidewater, favorable for export and for supplying other parts of Oregon.

MANUFACTURING

Manufacturing grew slowly in Oregon and there was great dependence on imported manufactured goods. Raw materials of some kinds were in short supply and so was machinery. The first manufactured or processed goods of importance were lumber and canned salmon. Otherwise there was a variety of local and handcraft industries, such as blacksmithing, carpentry, tanneries, and similar industries. By 1900 there were only 3,088 manufacturing establishments, employing 17,236 people, of which lumber mills accounted for 436 establishments, with 4,084 employees.[21]

127

The number of persons engaged in manufacturing increased slowly from 1870 to 1880 (20.4 percent), rapidly from 1880 to 1890 (382.6 percent), and very slowly from 1890 to 1900 (2.8 percent). At the same time the population was increasing 92.2 percent, 79.5 percent, and 30.6 percent, respectively. For the whole period the wage earners increased from 2,884 in 1870 to 17,296 in 1900, while total wages decreased slightly from 1890 to 1900. The last decade of the nineteenth century was a time of severe depression in Oregon and the country as a whole, when the price of wheat, Oregon's chief cash crop, was so low that it barely covered the cost of shipment. Many farms were mortgaged at interest rates as high as 20 percent.

Oregon was not by any means a "manufacturing" state (nor is it today); only 3.2 percent of the population was engaged in manufacturing in 1870; 2.0 percent in 1880; and 5.3 percent in 1900. Lumber was the leading industry in 1900 with 4,084 wage earners, followed by railway repair shops, with 751; woolen goods, with 672; fish canneries, with 636; printing, with 610; and flour milling with 413. Of the 3,088 manufacturing establishments in Oregon in 1900, 1,064 were in Portland; 88 in Salem; 81 in Astoria; 78 in Baker City; 64 in La Grande; and 37 in Oregon City. By value, lumber was first, followed by flour milling, fish canning, and printing.

Prior to 1900 the lumber industry of Oregon rated a poor third to that of Washington and California.[22] The main reason was inaccessibility of most of the Oregon forests to the kinds of transportation available at that time, as compared to Puget Sound with its hundreds of miles of shore. Most of the large mills were "cargo mills," located on tidewater where lumber from the mill could be loaded directly on ship for export. The chief mills were at Portland, Oregon City, Astoria, Florence, Gardiner, North Bend, Bandon, and Port Orford. Salem mills produced mostly for the domestic market. Transportation of logs from the woods to the mills was difficult, especially in winter.

But the stage was set for Oregon to go ahead with vastly increased production after the turn of the century. The timber supply in the upper Midwest was becoming exhausted, and large lumber companies were moving to the West Coast, bringing capital and new techniques with them. At the same time the demand for lumber in the eastern United States was growing rapidly.

The new technology also tended to remove the handicaps under which Oregon had been working. Advances ranged from improved axes and crosscut saws (longer ones for the larger trees of the West Coast) to the donkey engine and the winch with steel cable for yarding the logs and even dragging them to the mills. By 1900 there were 193 steam donkeys in Washington, 35 in Oregon, and 61 in California. Skid roads were improved, flumes constructed for both logs and lumber. Splash dams made it possible to use small streams. The mills were improved also with chain conveyors to lift the logs from the mill pond; with larger circular saws with replaceable teeth; and eventually with band saws that could handle the largest logs. As demand increased, improved planers and dry kilns were added, and molding machinery.

In this period most of the timber was cut on the lower eastern slopes of the Coast Range and the lower western slopes of the Cascades. The methods of logging, transportation, and milling varied little; the trees were felled, trimmed, and bucked into logs of convenient length, and skidded to the nearest stream, road, or logging railroad. Small streams were made usable by constructing a splash dam, forming a pond into which the logs were dumped. The dam was then knocked out, allowing the logs to move with the flood to a larger stream. In any event the logs were stored in a pond or river near the mill until hoisted by the conveyor to the big band saw, the "head rig," where the logs were sawed into various dimensions, two-by-fours, two-by-eights, and so on, and to one-inch thick boards of various widths. Most of the lumber was marketed "green"; some was shunted into dry kilns and then planed, while some varieties of wood, such as the pines, were shaped into moldings for interior finishing. Some logs never saw a sawmill in Oregon; they were loaded on ships or railroads or formed into rafts and exported.

Most of the lumber produced was exported from Oregon to San Francisco, southern California, Hawaii, and Hong Kong. (The local demand was still small.) This called for more ships that could reach the mills and carry a large payload. One solution was the single-decked schooner, which was easily loaded. Later steam schooners were used and four-masted barkentines for trans-Pacific traffic. But eventually the best solution for the coastwise trade was ships towed by tugs, the

128

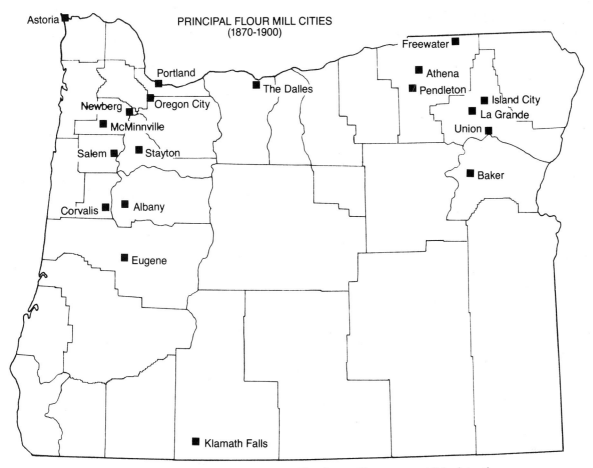

PRINCIPAL FLOUR MILL CITIES
(1870-1900)

fig. 7.18   Principal flour-mill cities, 1870-1900. The first mills were established in the
Willamette Valley where wheat was once the most important crop. Later, when
the Oregon Short Line Railroad was built, mills were established in northeastern
Oregon. Since the turn of the century the number of mills has declined.

forerunner of the present-day movement of lumber by tug and barge.

As noted in the preceding chapter, the shipyards were along the Columbia River and in the lower courses of the coastal rivers, usually near the lumber mills. With abundant lumber near at hand, the yards could compete with Bath, Maine, on the East Coast, which at that time was a great center of shipbuilding. Engines, however, had to be imported from the East, as were other hardware items. The ships built at Coos Bay enjoyed a very good reputation for durability and safety. The demand for ships was good, all the more because of the numerous wrecks on the bars at the entrances of the bays. By 1900 seventeen shipyards in Oregon, with 338 wage earners and a product value of $650,000, were turning out fishing boats for local use and ships for the coastwise and overseas trade.

The fishing boats were usually sloop-rigged unless motorized. The ships were schooner-rigged, many of them with decks designed to carry lumber.

Flour and grist mills continued to expand, not only in the Willamette Valley but in eastern Oregon, as the emphasis on wheat growing shifted. The 1900 census listed 153 flour mills in the state, employing 443 persons; obviously most of the mills were small (**fig. 7.18**). The largest mills were at Oregon City, Salem, Jefferson City, and Albany. The average annual wage in the flour mills was $548, compared to $388 for industry as a whole. For many industries, employment was seasonal and part-time.[23]

In addition to the major industries listed above, a great variety of smaller establishments were in operation. The most important, in terms of persons employed, were blacksmithing, boot and

129

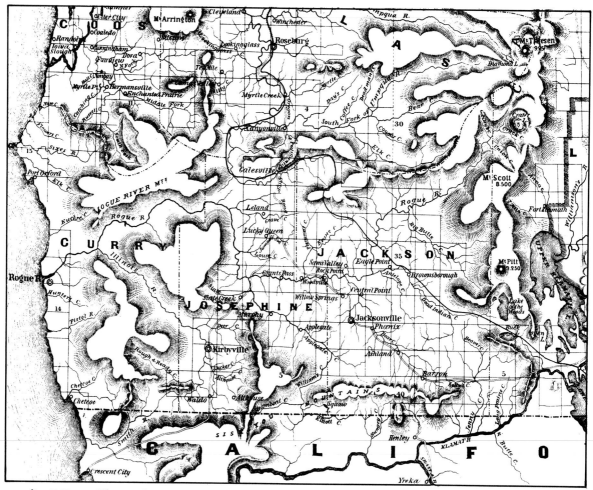

fig. 7.19   The southwestern part of the 1878 J.K. Gill map of Oregon. Mountains are
shown as blank spaces with hachure fringes, giving them the aspect of plateaus.
At this time the railroad ended at Roseburg, south of which the traveler could
follow the Oregon-Calfornia stage road via Canyonville, Grants Pass, Jacksonville, and Ashland. The solid line represents the projected continuation of the
railroad. Later the route was changed to follow the stage road. (From J.K. Gill
Co., the "Oregonter," 1878.)

shoe manufacturing, clothing, malt liquors, paint
shops, saddlery, and sheet-iron shops. There were
42 iron foundries, employing 388 hands.

EXPORTS AND IMPORTS

California provided a market for Oregon's surplus goods from the days of the gold rushes, and
in the period from 1870 to 1900 a flourishing trade
was in progress, for the most part by sea.[24] In 1880
the number of ships in service was more than 140,
most of them in the coastal trade. The exports to
San Francisco included canned salmon, wheat,
flour, oats, hops, butter, potatoes, lumber, hides,

gold, wool, and coal, at a total value of more than
$6 million. The foreign trade was mostly with
Great Britain and the Sandwich (Hawaiian)
Islands, involving a similar list of products, with
wheat, salmon, gold, and silver of the greatest
value. The first shipment of wheat to Great Britain
was condemned; the grains were so large that to
the English millers it appeared they were swollen
by excess moisture. The total foreign trade was
more than $14 million. Cattle were exported both
by sea and later by rail to the East.

Oregon's imports were chiefly manufactured
goods—liquors, glass, and railroad rails from
Great Britain, rice, sugar, and molasses from the
Sandwich Islands. Coal was imported from Aus-

130

tralia as ballast for the wheat vessels, even though Coos Bay coal was being exported to California. A variety of general merchandise came from China.

MAPPING

This period, 1870–1900, marked the substantial completion by the General Land Office of the township maps on which property lines were based, and the beginning of topographic mapping by the U.S. Geological Survey. The Land Office mapping program began in the late 1840s with the platting of the Willamette Valley and proceeded to the Rogue River Valley, and then to eastern Oregon. By 1884 most of the state had been mapped, or at least those areas that were likely to be settled. At one-year intervals a general map of the state was compiled showing the progress of the mapping.

During this period a number of commercial maps of Oregon were published by various companies and for different purposes; space will permit description of only two. In 1878 the J. K. Gill Company of Portland published a map called the "Oregonter" on a scale of 20 miles to the inch. The most conspicuous features are the broad, white areas representing mountains, giving the impression of broad plateaus (fig. 7.19). The Rogue River, Umpqua, "Calapooia," Cascade, and Blue mountains are so represented. The first three as names of relief features have not survived. Little was known of the summits of the mountains in this time, and so they were left blank! On the Gill map the Oregon and California Railroad ended at Roseburg; the projected continuation crossed the Cascades to Lower Klamath Lake and entered California to the east of Tule Lake. This was one of the alternate routes proposed in the Pacific Railroad Surveys, but a few years later the route across the Siskiyou Pass was completed instead. The Gill map does not show the wagon road across Siskiyou Pass, although it had been in use since 1849. This map outlines all the Indian reservations except the Siletz; the short-lived Malheur Reservation, then in Baker County, was the largest.

The George F. Cram map of Oregon (Chicago, 1900) was published with a gazetteer of about 1,500 place names, located by counties and by a grid of letters and numbers. Gone were the large, white areas of earlier maps showing mountains;

instead mountains were depicted as long, sinuous ridges or as isolated peaks; no elevations were given. The tendency to name mountains from the nearest river continued with Umpqua, Rogue River, and Powder River (Wallowa) mountains. The Siskiyou Mountains are not shown and rugged, southern Curry, Josephine, and Jackson counties show no relief features, not even isolated peaks. "Mt. Pitt" on the Cram map marks the southern end of the Cascades and Mt. McLoughlin is located northeast of Klamath Lake, probably at the present-day Saddle Mountain. All railroads are included with branch lines, but no roads. Misspellings are fairly common, like Mavry Mountains (for Maury) in Crook County and Steins (for Steens) in Harney County. This was probably the best commercial map of its time for showing drainage lines and the location of small towns and settlements. To get to these places, other than by railroad, one needed a road map, a very scarce item at this time.

But the modern period of map-making was beginning, based on primary triangulation by the Coast and Geodetic Survey and topographic mapping by the U.S. Geological Survey. The first quadrangle mapped was the Klamath Sheet (fig. 7.20), published in 1889 (surveyed in 1885, 1886, and 1887) on a scale of four miles to the inch and with a contour interval of 200 feet. This map covers an area of over 3,600 square miles. The map has three colors: cultural features in black; drainage in blue, including the few streams in this area and the major lakes; and contours in brown. Upper Klamath Lake, Lower Klamath Lake, and Little Klamath Lake were mislabeled. The correct names are Agency Lake, Upper Klamath Lake, and Lower Klamath Lake respectively (the last named has been drained). Very few settlements existed at that time because of Indian hostilities; some have had name changes—for example, Linkville became Klamath Falls—and some have disappeared. Many of the settlements, such as Olene, Bonanza, Bly, and Langell Valley, had only one house.

The Ashland Sheet, with the same scale and the same contour interval, was published in 1893. The area covered is mostly in the Cascade Range and the relief is somewhat greater and more complicated than on the Klamath Sheet. It was mapped in 1886–1887 by four topographers, each of whom surveyed a different part of the area. Elevations are quite accurate as compared with more modern maps; for example, Mt. McLoughlin, the highest

131

point on the map, is listed as 9,493 feet, whereas a recent map gives 9,495 feet. The map shows by contours the east scarp of the Cascade Range and the contrast between the High Cascades and the old Cascades on the west. The Rogue River Valley appears and also the upper Rogue and Crater Lake. The chief towns, Ashland, Phoenix, Medford, Jacksonville, and Central Point, appear with street patterns; all other settlements are shown as single houses. The Southern Pacific Railroad and the wagon toll road over the Siskiyou Mountains appear, as well as a number of other roads in the southern part of the sheet. These two maps, the Klamath and Ashland sheets, appear somewhat crude when compared to recent maps with larger scales and smaller contour intervals, but they represented a great step forward in mapping the state.

The other topographic maps surveyed before 1900 are at a larger scale, 1/125,000 or two miles to the inch, with a contour interval of 100 feet. They include the following quadrangles: Port Orford, Coos Bay, Roseburg, and Baker. The selection was probably based on mining with the prospect of geologic mapping to follow, but no mines are shown on the maps. Details of drainage and topography are much improved and, except for the larger towns, individual houses are shown. The shoreline on the Coos Bay and Port Orford quadrangles was obtained from the earlier Coast Survey. The logging railroad from Marshfield (Coos Bay) to Myrtle Point was not at this time connected to the Southern Pacific. A branch of this road led to the coal mines on Coalbank Slough. There were few bridges, none across Coos Bay. These early topographic maps have been superseded by modern, large-scale maps with much more detail, based on airphotos.

OREGON AT THE TURN OF THE CENTURY

By 1900 the hard times associated with the panic of 1893 had been forgotten, at least by many people writing about Oregon in books and periodicals. In the April 1900 issue of the *Overland Monthly*, W. A. Tenny wrote an article, "Evolution of the Northwest," in which he noted the shift of opinion as compared with the early days. He recalled Daniel Webster's (supposed) famous statement of 1843 (see chapter 1) indicating that the

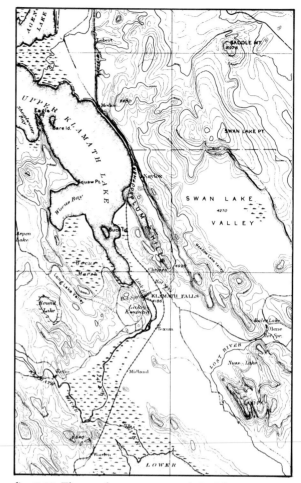

fig. 7.20 The southwestern part of the Klamath Sheet, U.S. Geological Survey, 1889 (revised edition). This is the first of the Survey's topographic maps produced for Oregon. The scale is 1:250,000, contour interval 200 feet.

Oregon Country was mostly a desert and not worth claiming and wrote:

> In 1897 the same State yielded in four metals — gold, silver, copper, and lead — $14,000,000....
> Here is the largest belt of continuous forest on the globe [the U.S.S.R. would argue];...the yellow [Douglas] fir excels any other known lumber....
> The water-power [potential] in the Northwest is unlimited [today we know better].... The time will come when the timber on high and precipitous mountains will be in demand. Neither teams nor steam-engines can reach it, but electric force can climb the wires, and saw the lumber where it grows.

Mr. Tenny's vision did not come true, but logging by balloon and helicopter did make it possible to harvest timber "on high and precipitous mountains."

Some writers of this period extolled specific parts of Oregon. R. L. Fulton in the May 1897 issue of the *Overland Monthly* wrote about Yamhill County:

> Its soil was impounded by the beavers in dams that concentrated thousands of acres of fertile alluvium from the uplands, and assisted by a climate as genial as that of any country on the globe, will produce fabulous crops, . . . Wheat . . . as high as 60 bushels [to the acre] . . . Indian corn—no, table corn, yes. . . . Oregon cider rivals the most popular beverages for private tables as well as for public bars.

Imagine asking for cider in an Oregon bar today.

Even the staid United States Bureau of the Census[25] was inclined to be optimistic, sometimes even contradicting the data in the tables: "The natural resources of the state are extensive, furnishing material for its various manufacturing enterprises. . . . the mines are producing a continually increasing supply of coal for fuel."

IMPACT ON THE LAND

As the nineteenth century came to a close, the 413,000 Oregonians were using more of the state's resources and making a greater impact on the land. Thanks to the growth of export crops and the expansion of the lumber industry, the Willamette Valley was prosperous. In eastern Oregon, with mining, expanding wheat farming, and irrigation, the population had increased in most occupied areas, but it was still sparse. Most of the counties had acquired their present boundaries, except that Hood River County had not yet been separated from Wasco County and Jefferson and Deschutes counties were still part of Crook County. The maps, military, Land Office, and commercial, were greatly improved. The Land Office maps were accurate enough as far as the surveyed townships, sections, and ranges were concerned but many parts of the state were unmapped. Many maps showed roads but did not distinguish planked, graveled, or unimproved dirt roads.

The major change in the Oregon landscape was brought about by the very expansion of settlement. Dry farming and irrigation were introduced where only cattle and sheep ranches had existed before. New farms, towns, and settlements grew up in all parts of the state. Large areas of cut-over, burnt-over land appeared on the margins of the Willamette Valley. The construction of railroads, railroad stations, warehouses, and grain elevators gave a new look to many towns. Where new towns grew up along the railroad, the direction of the tracks often determined the street pattern. The railroad land grants (the O and C Land) set the pattern for land ownership for large areas in western Oregon and the military road land grants had a similar effect on the homesteads of eastern Oregon. The interurban lines in the northern Willamette Valley were beginning to bring about a dispersion of urban settlement, contributing to the growth of suburbs and satellite towns and affecting the character of rural life as well. General farms became dairy farms or truck farms to supply the needs of the growing cities. With improved transportation the rural general store was beginning to show the first signs of decline. By 1900 a thin film of humanity had spread over a large part of Oregon—a film that was constantly changing.

8 AUTOMOBILES, HOMESTEADS AND LUMBER BOOMS
1900–1930

We will give you a farm. Uncle Sam has a farm for every one of us.
ABRAHAM LINCOLN

The boom in lumber production, the explosive advent of the automobile, World War I, together with the increase of population and the occupation of homesteads in eastern Oregon, brought about a cultural revolution in the state of Oregon in the first three decades of the twentieth century. These factors were interrelated. The war excited the economy in a number of ways: it boosted lumber production, which had been growing rapidly before; it brought about an expansion of agriculture and the food-processing industries, including fisheries; it stimulated various other industries, especially shipbuilding, bringing many new workers to Oregon.

Immigration continued, including a good percentage of foreign-born, some of whom settled temporarily on homesteads in eastern Oregon in areas that previously had not been settled. Three new counties—Hood River, which was separated from Wasco County, and Deschutes and Jefferson counties, which were separated from Crook County—were added to the state list in this period. This completed the formation of Oregon counties, after which only small boundary changes were made down to the present time. The first decade, 1900–1910, was fairly prosperous. In the early part of the second decade, 1910–1914, the economy slowed down; then prosperity, produced by war industries, increased sharply, continuing at a slightly lower level to the end of the period—that is, to the beginning of the Great Depression in 1929.

The effects of World War I were felt in Oregon before the United States entered the conflict. The lumber industry, shipbuilding, food production and processing, including fisheries, boomed. At the beginning of the war in 1914, England and France purchased large quantities of lumber from Oregon for general purposes, and for airplane manufacturing. Sitka spruce from the Coast Range was especially desired for airplane framing, for a few years, until aluminum planes came into general use. From 1914 to 1917 spruce production in Oregon increased from 65 to 120 million board feet, and when the United States entered the war, the demand for timber doubled again; army barracks and housing for industrial workers were being constructed in many parts of the country. Sawmills and logging operations were greatly expanded and were busy until the end of the war. The expansion swelled the tide of immigration and brought to Oregon for the last time a flood of farmers and for the first time more than a few black people.

Prior to 1905, when 218 passenger cars were registered,[1] Oregon had almost no motor vehicles. The increase was very slow until after 1910, when 2,493 were registered. In 1920, 103,790 passenger cars were counted along with 3,517 motorcycles. By 1930 the Model "T" had given way to the Model "A" (each was a favorite in its day) and 235,351 passenger vehicles and 10,657 trucks were registered in Oregon. The effects of this rapid increase in automobile transportation were far-reaching: living habits changed; city people began to move to the suburbs and the number of railway passengers began to decline; and everyone who owned an automobile or even a bicycle was clamoring for improved roads.

By 1900 most of the good farming land in western Oregon had been occupied through donation land claims or purchase. Therefore, as immigration continued and even accelerated, prospective farmers and land investors turned to eastern Oregon, which earlier immigrants, accustomed to humid regions, had scorned as unfit for agricul-

134

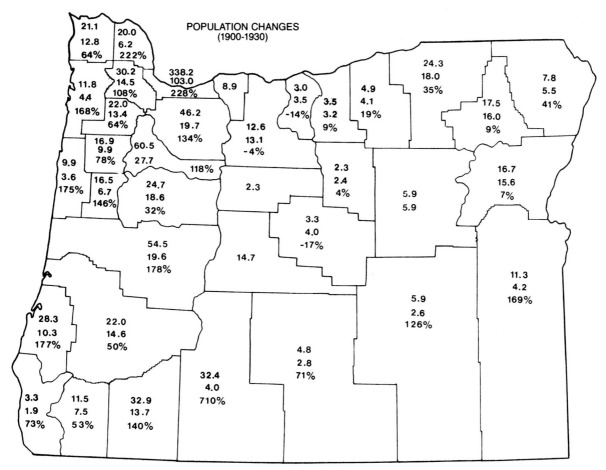

fig. 8.1   Population changes by counties from 1900 to 1930. The first figure in each county
represents the 1930 population; the second is the 1900 population; the third, the
percentage change. Four counties lost population during this period, mostly as a
result of boundary changes. (Data from the U.S. Bureau of the Census)

ture. To be sure, wheat farming had spread to the Deschutes-Umatilla Plateau in the 1870s and it had been demonstrated that dry farming could be successful with two or more square miles to the farm. But now southeastern Oregon was opened to homesteading, mostly in 160 acre lots, too small for success in this semiarid land. Thousands of farms were obtained by homesteading or by purchase, and many thousands of absentee, innocent, uninformed people acquired land as an investment. Alas, most of the farmers failed and the land reverted to grazing, for which it was better adapted.

POPULATION

The population of Oregon (**fig. 8.1**) increased from 413,000 in 1900 to 953,000 in 1930, a gain of

131 percent in 30 years.[2] During this time the United States as a whole was gaining only 60 percent. The greatest gain in Oregon, in numbers and percentage, was in the Willamette Valley. Multnomah County gained 225 percent; Lane County, 176 percent; Clackamas County, 135 percent; and Marion County, 90 percent.

The coast counties, thanks to the expansion of the lumber industry and fisheries, showed substantial gains. The construction of a large spruce lumber mill at Toledo to supply airplane factories was a factor in increasing the population of Lincoln County by 190 percent. In southwestern Oregon all counties were growing, especially Coos County with its lumber industries and Jackson County with lumber and expanding irrigation. Isolated Curry County, with few roads, no through railroad, and almost no harbors, grew the least.

135

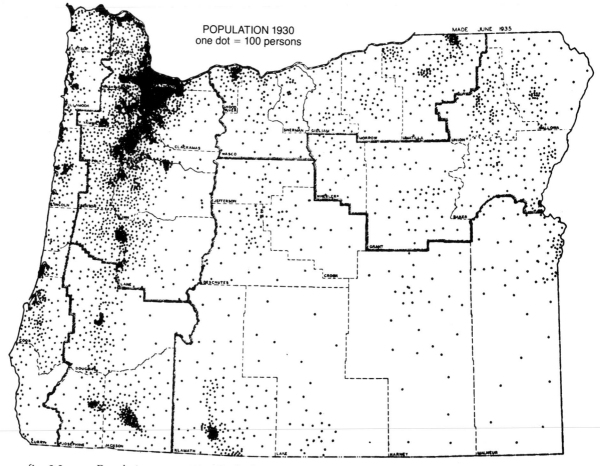

POPULATION 1930
one dot = 100 persons

fig. 8.2   Population map, 1930. Each dot represents 100 persons. (From W.D. Smith, *Physical and Economic Geography of Oregon*, p. 138)

In eastern Oregon, in spite of the general prosperity, the rate of growth was slowing down. Baker, Grant, and Wheeler counties were almost static in this period; this suggests a net out-migration, since otherwise the natural increase would produce a gain. Wasco, Gilliam, and Crook counties lost population because of boundary changes; these counties lost territory to Hood River, Deschutes, and Jefferson counties. On the other hand, some counties showed remarkable percentage gains: Klamath County, 710 percent; Malheur County, 169 percent; Harney County 126 percent; and Lake County, 71 percent. These gains were mostly related to more intensive settlement that, in turn, was related to irrigation and homesteading (**fig. 8.2**).

The various minority groups — Indians, Japanese, Chinese, and Europeans — were much in evidence in the 1930 Oregon census. The numbers of minorities were static in some places, in other places they were declining or were gaining. Most of the minority peoples tended to be segregated in a few areas. The Indians, 4,700 in number (they were probably the most difficult group to count), were mostly on the reservations in Lincoln, Jefferson, Wasco, Umatilla, and Klamath counties. Other Indians, not on reservations, were living in Coos, Curry, Douglas, Marion, Multnomah, Yamhill, and Harney counties; only two counties, Crook and Wallowa, counted no Indians in the 1930 census.

Most of the Japanese, numbering more than 5,000, lived in Clatsop, Clackamas, Multnomah, Marion, and Hood River counties. Chinese, of whom there were more than 2,000, were decreasing in number; they lived mainly in Clatsop County as cannery workers, and in Marion and Multnomah counties, specifically in Portland. Mexicans, 1,500 in number, lived in Douglas, Gilliam, Klamath, Lane, Linn, and Multnomah counties; it can be presumed that most of them were agricultural workers. Blacks, more than

136

2,000 in number, came to Oregon to work in the shipbuilding industry; some remained in Portland after the industry declined. Canadians and Germans led the list of foreign-born Caucasians; both groups were widely dispersed. Finns and Swedes were located mostly in Clatsop, Columbia, Lincoln, and Coos counties, most of them employed in the lumber industry and fisheries. Lake County had the largest number of Irish, many of whom were recruited in Ireland; they spoke only Gaelic, and, as the story goes, they had been shipped to Oregon with a tag around their necks that said simply, "Lakeview, USA." Other nationalities represented in Oregon at this time were English, Scottish, Russian, Norwegian, and Basque, the last named working as sheepherders in Malheur County.

The cities were growing faster than the rural areas, partly by immigration and natural increase and partly by annexation of suburban areas. Portland had 90,000 people in 1900 and 301,000 in 1930. Salem grew from 4,000 to 26,000 in this period; Eugene from 3,000 to 18,000; Medford from 1,700 to 11,000; Klamath Falls from 447 to 16,000. Astoria was an exception to the general pattern of urban growth. From 8,000 in 1900 it grew to 14,000 in 1920, then declined to 10,000 in 1930. And there Astoria's population stabilized, except for a small increase in the late 1950s. Astoria's population in 1975 was 10,680. This departure from the norm is sometimes blamed on the great fire that destroyed Astoria's business district and many residences on December 9, 1922. But other cities have had devastating fires and have risen again. Other factors are more fundamental. Astoria has an unfavorable site for a large city, on the steep slopes of the margins of Coxcomb Hill, and is subject to severe landslides. Also, the limited production in the immediate hinterland and the lack of a bridge across the Columbia River, until very recently, were drawbacks. The growth of cities, like that of the counties, was uneven during this period: rapid growth from 1900 to 1910, slow growth to 1917, and then more rapid growth again until 1930.

HOMESTEADING

The period 1900–1929 was one of massive land transfers and land frauds on land derived from the public domain. At the beginning of settlement, as noted before, the federal government owned nearly all of the land in Oregon. As time went on some was transferred to private ownership and some to the state of Oregon. (The federal government retains today, 1979, about 50 percent of Oregon's land.) The method of transfer from the public domain to private ownership varied. In previous chapters the O and C lands and the donation land claims are discussed. In the period under consideration now, homesteads were the most important method of transferring land in Oregon, and to see it in perspective a list of land categories is given, together with their acreage:

homesteads, 11,000,000 acres
donation land claims, 2,600,000 acres
military wagon road grants, 2,490,000 acres
railroad grants, 1,588,000 acres
sales, 6,455,000 acres
given to the state of Oregon, 4,329,000 acres

All these were transfers of land from the public domain.

A very large part of the homesteads were obtained in the period from 1900 to 1929.[3] The original Homestead Act of 1862 provided that qualified persons could file on 160 acres for a fee of $10. Residence or cultivation for five years was required before a clear title could be obtained. From 1900 to 1909, 1,700,000 acres were entered originally, of which 1,676,000 acres had final entries. From 1910 to 1919, 5,380,000 acres were original entries, 1,873,000 acres were final entries. From 1920 to 1929 there were 3,700,000 acres claimed originally, 2,517,000 of which were final. The discrepancies between the original entries and the final entries give us a clue as to the number of failures on the homesteads, but only a partial clue. Many of the homesteads that were given final entry papers nevertheless turned out to be failures.

Since most of the good land in western Oregon was already occupied by farmers, ranchers, and owners of timber land by 1900, the bulk of the homesteaders turned to eastern Oregon where, for the most part, the land was not suitable for small farms of 160 acres. H. L. Davis, the Oregon novelist, describes homesteading in eastern Oregon as he saw it: "And they were not much to look at. They were coming to take up farms, which the Government was willing to give away; and everybody in the country knew that there were no farms worth having as a gift." A ranch foreman in the area explained the homesteaders rush to Davis: "It's one of the things we figger on about every 10 years. It ain't anything a man can help.

fig. 8.3   An automobile on a muddy road; steam tractor shown was used to grade roads.
(OHS)

They don't run to sense, like ordinary home-steadin'. They can't because there ain't any sense to them.... Any of them tell you how the rush started? They seen an advertisement. You know what kind of people answer advertisement, don't you?"[4]

Settlers could not legally move onto their homestead lands until the vacant public lands had been surveyed, but the rush was so great that many of them did move onto lands and occupied them as squatters, that is, by the preemption claim right. This was legal, but most settlers did not feel secure until they had a title that had been patented by the United States.

In 1909 the Enlarged Homestead Act allotted 320 acres to each individual. This greatly stimulated interest in homesteads in eastern Oregon. At the same time, the area opened to homesteading was marked out on the map, including large areas in Lake, Harney, Umatilla, and Morrow counties. There were scattered areas in other counties. In successive years the area open to homesteading was increased until, in 1918, nearly all of eastern Oregon not previously occupied by farms or in national forest or Indian reservations was opened up to settlement.

Some of the lands already occupied by ranchers were offered for sale, and these lands were adver-tised in glowing terms. For example, a pamphlet issued in 1898, advertising lands in Lake, Harney, and Malheur counties, had the following statement about Lake County:

> Here is a county with a total area of land surface of 5,049,300 acres,...the area unappropriated, unreserved, surveyed and unsurveyed, 4,215,855. Thirty years ago this section had among its population not more than 10 white persons, and now its white population can be safely estimated at 4,000. The county is prosperous, and never more so than at the present time.... All varieties of fruit, such as apples, pears, prunes, plums, cherries and all kinds of berries grow hardy and abundantly.... Lake County does not fear to place her apple, for comparison, beside that fruit grown in any other section of the world.[5]

Of Harney County it was said that the county could easily support a population of 350,000!

Many thousands of acres of this land were settled in homesteads between 1906 and 1911. A large part, however, was abandoned by 1914, and most of it was vacated by 1920. Only the large-size holdings in the better locations, which permitted farm-ranching combinations, were able to survive. Nor was this a time of exceptionally low rainfall. In fact, in the period from 1912 to 1917 the precipitation was above normal for most

138

years. This demonstrated that crop production without irrigation was not feasible in this region.

When homesteaders failed and abandoned their holdings, the titles to their lands reverted to the counties and then to the state. This transfer of title took place through legal proceedings as foreclosures for their delinquent taxes. The greatest amount of tax-foreclosed land was acquired by the counties in the period between 1920 and 1940.

The military wagon road grants deserve special mention. As noted in the previous chapter, large grants of land from the public domain, totaling nearly 2,500,000 acres, were made to finance the military wagon roads in Oregon. The lands thus obtained were, in many cases, sold by the original construction contractors to "land companies" who held them until the market was favorable. Then the lands were advertised widely, with a variety of sales promotions including lotteries. "Farms" were sold in units of varying sizes, either for occupancy or for investment. The result was a double swindle; the roads were not finished and most of the land sold was not suitable for farms,[6] nor did it soon appreciate in value.

The thousands of people who bought military wagon road grant land and hoped to sell at a profit, like most of the homesteaders, were disappointed. A typical case was recounted in a letter from an Oregon attorney to a lady in Massachusetts, who had asked him to sell her land:

> Your letter of recent date [1914] in regard to Sec. 29. T. 33s, R. 39 EWM in Malheur County has been received. . . . You ask me if I can dispose of your land. I cannot and do not think I could give it away. . . . I have never known a lawyer who has been guilty of selling such land as yours, even to an enemy. . . . I assume that you got this in a lottery scheme conducted by the old Southern Oregon Military Wagon Road Company [Oregon Central Military Road], . . . if so, it is one of the penalties of gambling. . . . it would have been better that you drew five acres than 640. . . . I can only salute you as being a fellow free-holder of the County of Malheur and express my sorrow that you have so much of it.[7]

Many areas passed through a sort of cycle before the best form of land use could be found. Isaiah Bowman describes such a cycle for central Oregon:

> There were four steps in the occupation of the Central Oregon region. The first was pre-railroad. The farming-ranching combination succeeded then in spite of the great distances from ranch to railroad because the land was cheap and the price of grain or of livestock sufficiently high. Cattle and sheep could be grazed widely and walked to railway shipping points. The second period was marked by the spread of dry farming just before and just after the railway came to Bend in 1911. The third stage was marked by the failure of dry farming except in the best locations and the best years and by the rather exact adaptation of farming and ranching to the local possibilities of soil, irrigation, and accessible mountain pastures. When the two big lumber companies arrived in 1915, with production in 1916, they inaugurated a fourth stage, in which the lumber industry offset the losses of the homesteaders, steadied the industrial and business life of the town of Bend, and greatly enlarged the extent of tributary industries.[8]

The stimulation of large-scale irrigation and recreational activities was yet to come to central Oregon.

AUTOMOBILES AND ROADS

The year was 1910. One of the first automobiles in Oregon was on its way from Portland to Tillamook (**fig. 8.3**). The driver had made elaborate preparations for his trip. He had two spare tires with covers strapped on the rear; a tool box on the running board with the usual set of mechanic tools; a tire pump; extra spark plugs; a fan belt; rim lugs and valves; an extra spring. He had a sheet of cork and shellac for repairing gaskets and a box of assorted bolts, nuts, cotter pins, and so forth. The driver had all this and more, but he did not have a road—only a muddy track. When, inevitably, the car became stuck in a mudhole, the driver was fortunate enough to be near a farm where horses were available to pull the car out and send him on his way to the next mudhole. Little did the driver realize the explosive impact the advent of the automobile would have. It set off a period of intensive road building; it changed the way of life of the people profoundly; and it created a number of problems, many of which are still with us today.

The national good roads movement was launched officially in 1902 by the Good Roads Association, but there was some agitation for roads in the 1890s, especially by cyclists. After 1902 the good roads program received wide support; even the railroads contributed, their officials not realizing that passenger automobiles and trucks would soon take away some of their revenue. It began to be obvious by 1916 that although the roads acted as "feeders" to some extent, they were also competing directly for passengers and freight.

Until 1917 nearly all expenses and efforts at road building in Oregon were the responsibility of the counties. This involved mostly grading and draining roads and only a small amount of surfacing. During this time the state contributed only $696,000, while the counties $53 million. Most of the state's contribution was derived from a half-mill tax on properties levied in 1914.

In 1914 a survey[9] was made of existing roads in Oregon, showing a total of 37,000 miles classed as follows: paved, 25 miles; plank, 232 miles; unoiled rock, 962 miles; gravel, 3,700 miles; and unimproved, 32,000 miles. After 1920 the tabulation by the State Highway System was limited to the state and federal roads. In 1930 the total mileage was only 4,300, of which 223 miles were concrete; bituminous, 684 miles; macadam, 324 miles; oil, 1,371 miles; unoiled crushed rock, 1,009 miles; gravel, 408 miles; and only 340 miles unimproved. It was not until 1970 that the unimproved classification for the state and federal highways could be dropped from the list.

In 1916 the U.S. Congress passed the Federal Aid Act, providing funds to the states for road construction on a matching basis, dollar for dollar. This resulted in a great surge of road building and the reorganization of the State Highway Commission. A number of bond issues were levied, a tax of one cent a gallon was placed on gasoline, and a one-mill property tax yielded about $10 million annually. Automobile license fees were added. All this was necessary to provide matching funds in order to get the federal appropriations. These monies did not go very far, considering the expenses of the right-of-way, grading, surfacing, and bridge building involved.

The construction and maintenance of highways in Oregon can only be described as a struggle against distance, terrain, and the elements. Conditions vary in different parts of the state, but no through road is without slopes steep enough to be subject to landsliding and slumping. Slides may come down from above, or they may appear below the road, in which case they are called slips. The (usually) gentle, long-continued rains of western Oregon saturate the thick mantle of weathered material and make the area especially susceptible to landslides, which are a normal part of the erosion process, but are greatly accelerated by road construction. The Columbia Gorge is particularly troublesome in this respect. And it was entirely possible for a traveler on the Coast Highway during this period to come upon a landslide that had recently covered the road completely, then to turn around, seeking a different route, only to find that another slide had appeared behind him. And in 1917 Oregon had few modern roads. By 1927, the expenditure for repair after landslides and other expenses of maintenance had reached more than $3 million. Today annual maintenance expense for U.S. Highway 101 alone, which includes landslide repair, snow removal, resurfacing, and other items, amounts to more than $4 million.

When the first comprehensive plan for the Oregon State Highway System was announced in 1917 it was necessary to make a selection of roads to be improved.[10] This selection was based upon existing roads, trails, and tracks, and the routes outlined became the basis of the present system of federal and state highways in Oregon. The number system, 1 to 36, introduced in 1917 survived only a short time. There were no U.S. highway numbers at this time. Only minor modifications were made in these routes down to the present. Seven of the thirty-six routes are listed below with their names and the modern equivalents:

1. Pacific Highway, now U.S. Highway 99 and Interstate 5.
2. The Columbia River Highway, now U.S. Highway 30 and Interstate 80N.
3. The Coast Highway, now U.S. Highway 101.
4. The California-Banff Beeline Highway, also called The Dalles-California Highway, now U.S. Highway 97.
5. The John Day Highway, now U.S. Highway 26.
6. The Oregon Trail from Umatilla to Ontario, now U.S. Highway 30 and Interstate 80N.
7. The Central Oregon Highway, now U.S. Highway 20. (Many years were to pass before U.S. Highway 20 got a number.)

These together with 29 shorter routes, appeared on maps at this time.[11]

By 1930 great progress had been made in road construction but much more remained to be done (**fig. 8.4**). The system of numbering had been almost completely changed, distinguishing federal from state highways. There were three classes of roads so far as surface was concerned: paved; improved, which usually meant oiled gravel or oiled crushed rock; and unimproved. By 1930 there

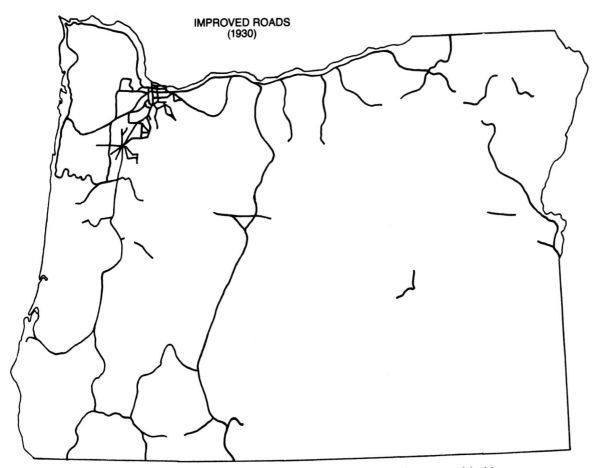

IMPROVED ROADS
(1930)

fig. 8.4   Improved roads, 1930. (From the Official Highway Map of 1930, modified by
William G. Loy, *Preliminary Atlas of Oregon,* 1972)

were 2,600 miles of hard surface and 1,700 miles of gravel in the state highway system alone.

Old Highway 1 became U.S. Highway 99 and was all paved. The alternate route, later called U.S. Highway 99W, was also paved. Old Highway 2 had become U.S. Highway 30, extending from Astoria by way of Portland to Ontario. It was paved from Astoria to The Dalles, otherwise graveled and oiled. Highway 3 became U.S. Highway 101, paved from Astoria to Seaside, improved to Newport, unimproved and mostly very poor from Newport to Coos Bay, and then improved again to the California line. The beaches were used extensively for travel along the coast in the early days. This was especially true of the area from Coos Bay to Heceta Head. Almost all of Highway 4, now U.S. Highway 97, was "improved" but there was no pavement. Old Highway 5 became U.S. Highway 28, later changed to U.S. Highway 26. It started at Florence, was mostly unimproved to Eugene, then improved over McKen-

zie Pass and through Redmond to Baker, where it joined U.S. Highway 30. Old Highway 6 became U.S. Highway 20, later U.S. Highway 30 and Interstate 80N. It was paved from Astoria through Portland to The Dalles; the remainder, except for short stretches, was gravel. Old Highway 7, later (in 1941) to become U.S. Highway 20, had no number in 1930 and was mostly unimproved.

In addition to these main roads there were a number of shorter sections of improved state roads, including the old Barlow Road from Oregon City to The Dalles; a road from Corvallis to Newport; one from Roseburg to North Bend on Coos Bay; and an open network of county roads, many of them unimproved.

Road Maps

With the advent of the automobile and accelerated road construction, a good road map became a necessity and a series of annual maps by the Ore-

141

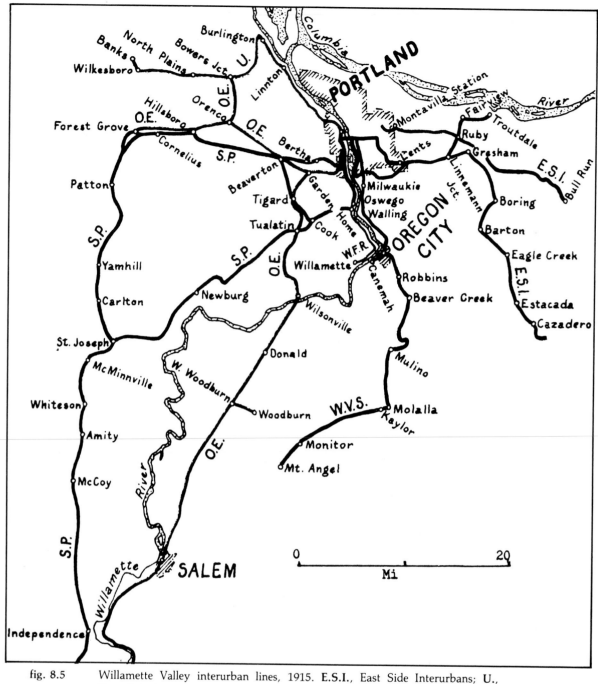

fig. 8.5   Willamette Valley interurban lines, 1915. **E.S.I.**, East Side Interurbans; **U.**,
United Railways; **O.E.**, Oregon Electric; **S.P.**, Southern Pacific Red Electric;
W.V.S., Willamette Valley Southern. The Oregon Electric extended south to
Eugene and the Southern Pacific Red Electric to Corvallis. (From Throckmorton,
'The Interurbans of Portland, Oregon")

gon Highway Commission became the most-used
maps in the state. One of the first maps, 1918,
shows the main all-weather roads in heavy black
lines and seasonal roads in lighter lines.[12] There

are no highway numbers on the map and only the
Columbia River Highway is named. Roads corresponding to present-day highways — U.S. Highway 101 from Astoria to Hebo, U.S. Highway

99W and U.S. Highway 99E, U.S. Highway 30 and Interstate 80N, U.S. Highway 97, and U.S. Highway 20 — are marked as all-weather roads, as is the present State Highway 18 west of McMinnville. No road is shown along the coast from Coos Bay north to Neskowin; on much of this section the beaches were used. The Cascade Range crossings correspond to modern U.S. Highway 26, State Highway 242 (the McKenzie Pass Highway), State Highway 62 via Crater Lake, and State Highway 66 from Ashland to Klamath Falls. Very few ferries are indicated on the map, but at Coos Bay, which is approached from the north via Scottsburg and Allegany, is the terse instruction: "Take the Boat."

By 1930 the state highway map[13] was printed in three colors — red for paved roads, yellow for oiled roads, and black for graveled or crushed rock roads. There was still only a track from Coos Bay to Newport, but this was on sandy surfaces, making it possible to travel above the beach in the rainy season, but with the risk of becoming stuck in the sand. However, seven improved roads connected U.S. Highway 99 with the coast and ferries are shown at Newport, Waldport, Florence, and North Bend. It therefore can be assumed that some travelers were using the highway, at least in stormy weather or at high tide. As usual on the maps of this period, relief features are sketchy. Mountains are shown as narrow bands that appear easy to cross — a few simple hachures for the Klamath Mountains, nothing for the Coast Range. The narrow Cascade Range seems to end near Crater Lake. East of the Cascades the 1930 map shows a broad network of roads, mostly unimproved except for the California-Banff Beeline Highway (present U.S. Highway 97) and the Oregon Trail (present Interstate 80N). The Oregon Highway Commission's road maps were widely copied and auto road atlases of the United States began to appear.

RAILROADS AND INTERURBANS

In the period 1900 to 1930 several additions were made to Oregon's railway system, including one important alternate route, the Natron Cut-off of the Southern Pacific Railway.[14] At the same time interurban lines expanded rapidly in the Willamette Valley. Many of the short rail lines were designed to serve agricultural areas such as the wheat belt or to transport logs and lumber from the forests. Most of the lines were branches of the Union Pacific and Southern Pacific main lines. Some were ill conceived and few of them yielded a profit to the original investors. Nevertheless, they served their purposes well until the automobile and truck took over a part of their function. Some of their names were as imaginative as any applied to the earlier, longer routes.

In eastern Oregon a number of short lines and one long one were constructed southward from the Columbia River and the Union Pacific line. In 1904–1905 the Great Southern Railway was built from The Dalles to Dufur in Wasco County. In 1909–1910 James J. Hill's Oregon Trunk Railway and E. H. Harriman's Deschutes Railway were involved in a construction race south from the Columbia River toward Bend. The two roads followed parallel routes, along and near the Deschutes River, as far as Madras, after which they were combined in one line and continued south to Bend and Chemult, and to a junction with the Southern Pacific's Natron Cut-off from Eugene across the Cascade Range to Klamath Falls. In 1900 E. E. Lytle built a railroad from Biggs in Sherman County to Shaniko in Wasco County. Another line reached from Arlington to Condon and (later) to Kinzua in Wheeler County.

In 1908 a line was built from La Grande in Union County to Joseph in Wallowa County via Elgin, to transport passengers, lumber, grain, and livestock. A branch line from Ontario to Burns required 18 years to complete, from 1906 to 1924. For a time this route was part of an earlier scheme to build a railroad across middle Oregon from Yaquina Bay to Boise, Idaho, with a branch line to Winnemucca, Nevada. Before the line reached Prineville, the trans-Oregon project was abandoned.

In western Oregon branch lines were built from the main line of the Southern Pacific Railway in the Willamette Valley into the foothills of the Cascades and through the Coast Range to the coast. All were intended primarily to transport logs and lumber, but they also carried general freight and passengers. These lines were a boon to the coastal towns, where there were neither good roads nor harbors. In 1911 E. E. Lytle built a line from Hillsboro to Tillamook, via the Nehalem River. In 1908–1909 a line reached Fall City from Salem and other short lines were built to Willamina and Valsetz. In 1914–1915 the Southern Pacific Railway completed a line from Eugene via the Siuslaw River to Gardiner (near Florence) and south to Reedsport and Marshfield (Coos Bay), which tied into a previously constructed line to Myrtle Point and Powers in southern Coos County. On the east side of the Willamette Valley short lines reached Boring, Molalla, Mill City, Sweet Home, and Marcola. In later years many of the short lines were abandoned, as were the lumber towns at their terminals. At the peak of railroad development every county in Oregon had at least a few miles of track, if only a short logging road. The extension of the rail lines led to the occupation and exploitation of areas previously unsettled. New land was put under the plow; forests were cut over and burned over as a result of railroad building.

After 1900 renewed interest in interurban transportation led to the construction of lines throughout the Willamette Valley (**fig. 8.5**).[15] The first and strongest demand came from the area east of Portland, known as the East Side, where settlement was expanding most rapidly. In 1902 the Oregon City Line was extended to Canemah above Willamette Falls, making it unnecessary to portage goods around the falls. This line was a major source of revenue, thanks also to the fact that it passed by the golf course of the 1,000-member Waverly Country Club. Later this line was extended to Molalla and Mt. Angel as the Willamette Valley System (W.V.S.). In 1903 service began on the 36-mile line from Portland to Cazadero via Gresham, Boring, and Estacada. Branches of this line reached Troutdale and Bull Run. These lines served agricultural, logging, and recreational areas.

In 1905 construction began on the Oregon Electric Interurban Line.[16] The route ran from Portland through Tigard, Tualatin, Wilsonville, Salem, and Albany to Eugene. Construction of the main line began at Salem, because of the difficulty of construction through the Tualatin (West) Hills where a serious problem of grade was encountered. (The Southern Pacific Railroad had preempted the best route.) Other problems included bridging the Willamette River at Wilsonville and at Harrisburg. The line reached Eugene in 1912, 122 miles from Portland. Meanwhile another line of the Oregon Electric was built west of Portland to Hillsboro and Forest Grove. Passenger traffic reached a peak about 1915 when more than 100 trains moved over the system; 20 trains per day between Portland and Salem, 7 between Portland and Eugene. The *Limited* required a little over five hours from Portland to Eugene. The *Owl*, running nightly each way, had sleeping cars.

In 1912 the Southern Pacific Railway Company decided to electrify their West Side steam lines and to run interurban trains in the Willamette Valley. This route came to be known as the S.P. Red Electric line west of Portland. Two routes were used: one through Beaverton, Forest Grove, and Yamhill; the other through Tigard, Tualatin, and Newberg. These routes joined at St. Joseph and the line continued through McMinnville, Amity, and Independence to Corvallis. Steam trains continued to use the same tracks. The S.P. Red Electric was less successful than the Oregon Electric, which had better equipment and more frequent schedules.

The United Railway Interurbans began as a freight line along Front Street in Portland. Construction continued along the Willamette River to Linnton and Burlington (these towns are now a part of Portland) and turned southwest through the West Hills via Cornelius Pass, later through the long Cornelius tunnel to North Plains and Banks. The promoters were ambitious; it was hoped that the line could be extended to Tillamook and that another line could be built via the Willamette Valley to San Francisco. However, the line was not profitable and there was no construction west of Banks. The line began to decline in 1914 and ceased operation in 1923.

The Willamette Valley interurbans had a short life, excepting only the east side lines. After World War I the number of automobiles and trucks increased rapidly and roads were being improved also. The interurbans first lost the weekend excursionists; it was cheaper to pile the family into a Model "T" and take off for places, some of which the interurbans did not serve. The first regular customers to desert the interurbans were the traveling salesmen, followed by the casual traveler, and finally by the commuters. The Great Depression was a serious blow too. The Red Electric line ceased operation in 1929; the Oregon Electric quit in 1933; the last parts of the east side lines hung on until 1958.

The combined effect of better roads, more rail lines, and more automobiles stimulated recreational travel and tourism in Oregon. Horse and buggy resorts were expanded to take care of more visitors. The coast resorts were the most popular, especially Seaside, Cannon Beach, Bayocean on Tillamook Bay (**fig. 8.6**), and Newport. Hot springs, lakes, and rushing rivers in the Cascades attracted many visitors. This was just the early stage of Oregon's recreational activity; later, with

fig. 8.6   Artist's view of Bayocean resort and Tillamook Bay, about 1912. All the buildings on the peninsula — hotels, natatorium, and 25 cottages — were destroyed by erosion, beginning about 1925. (Special Collections, Univ. of Oregon)

more and better roads and automobiles, a greater boom in tourism occurred (see chapter 9).

TOPOGRAPHIC MAPPING

After the turn of the century topographic mapping of Oregon[17] was slightly accelerated and mapping has continued down to the present time with few interruptions. (World War II interrupted the work, but publication was resumed afterward.) The progress of this important project depends on several factors. Surveying and publication are expensive and the number of skilled topographers is limited; also both state and federal governments support the work. For several years after 1900 not more than one quadrangle was published each year. The common scales used during this period were two miles to the inch and one mile to the inch. For special areas, such as rivers and scenic areas, larger scales were used. The contour interval varies from 5 feet to 100 feet, depending on the scale and the steepness of the terrain.

The chief priorities for selecting the areas to be mapped were mining, irrigation, and the improvements in rivers and harbors. The U.S. Army Corps of Engineers mapped most of the Willamette Valley and parts of the Oregon coast; most of these maps were later revised and republished by the U.S. Geological Survey. The newly-formed National Forests called for topographic mapping, as did Crater Lake National Park; the latter map appeared in 1909 with accompanying text and diagrams.

AGRICULTURE

By the turn of the century, even though most of the best farming land of Oregon was occupied, much of it was still not intensively cultivated. The period from 1900 to 1930 was one of continued change, continued growth of agricultural production, but with many fluctuations in yield of certain crops. There were also shifts in the areal distribution of crops, with large-scale production in eastern Oregon of crops that had previously only been cultivated in the Willamette Valley (fig. 8.7). Many factors were involved. One was the increase of population, which was both a cause and an effect. Urban growth had its effect upon the distribution of certain agricultural products, particularly dairying (see fig. 8.11) because of the large demand in cities for whole milk and other dairy

145

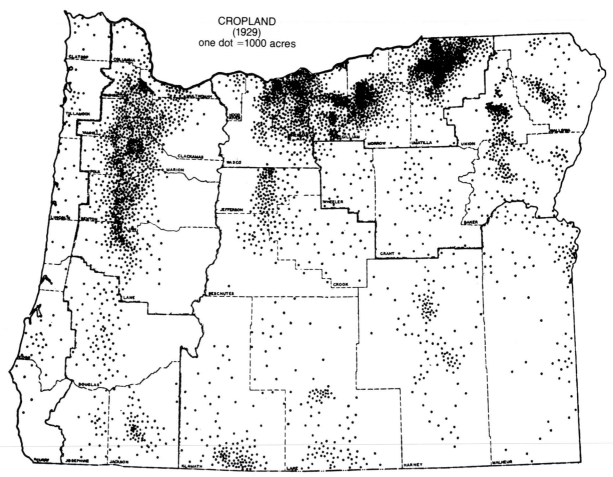

CROPLAND
(1929)
one dot =1000 acres

fig. 8.7   Cropland, 1929. Each dot represents 1,000 acres. By this time the Deschutes-
Umatilla Plateau had 25 percent of Oregon's cropland and the Willamette Valley
had 12 percent. Of all the cropland, 50 percent was in grain and 39 percent in hay.
(From W. D. Smith, p. 158)

products. Improvements in transportation also contributed. New techniques of production, including improved seed and methods of cultivation, were positive factors. The increase in irrigated acreage was also significant. At the end of the war, however, the markets declined and so did the acreage in crops.

Agricultural Technology

The traction engine had helped to bring about a revolution in large-scale farming in the 1880s; the gasoline tractor brought about another revolution in the first quarter of the twentieth century, especially during and after World War I.[18] The gasoline tractor was introduced in the closing years of the nineteenth century, but the early models were unsatisfactory, difficult to start and to keep in repair (repairs might cost as much as $1,500 in one

season). But by 1907 improvements had been made and at least 600 tractors of various sizes and shapes were sold in the United States. Some of the early models looked very much like the traction engine and weighed as much as 11 tons. By the beginning of World War I there were 14,000 gasoline tractors on United States farms, and with the wartime boom, the number skyrocketed.

Improvement of the combine (**fig. 8.8**) was another great leap forward in agricultural technology. Basically a mobile threshing machine with a harvester attached, the combine headed, threshed, and cleaned the wheat. At first combines were pulled by 10 or more horses, later by steam traction engines, and finally by large gasoline tractors. The combines were expensive and slow to gain acceptance until it was demonstrated that they could cut the cost of harvesting in half and they could be moved from farm to farm. The war boosted the

fig. 8.8 Combines harvesting wheat near Condon, Gilliam County. Small combines are used where some of the slopes are fairly steep. In the distance the skyline shows a nearly level part of the Deschutes-Umatilla Plateau. (Oregon Dept. of Transportation)

use of tractors and combines in two ways: by the increased demand for food crops, especially wheat, as the United States shipped large quantities of food to Europe; and by the decrease in manpower on the farms, as many of the young men entered military service. With fewer men on the farms, labor-saving machinery became a necessity. Furthermore, the farmers were prosperous and could afford to buy tractors and combines.

Cropland and Crops

Irrigation was slow to develop in eastern Oregon;[19] the early immigrants thought of eastern Oregon as very dry, since they crossed it at the end of the dry season. However, conditions were favorable for irrigation in many places, especially on the margins of the Blue Mountains and on the east side of the Cascade Range. The mountains had rain in greater quantities than the lowlands and the snow on the mountains melted slowly in the spring, insuring a good supply of water in the immediate vicinity. In some localities it was comparatively easy for a farmer to divert a stream by a low dam and lead the water to his fields. By 1902 Oregon had 440,000 acres under irrigation, most of it in eastern Oregon and nearly all of it under private enterprise (for later irrigation distribution, see **fig. 8.9**). During this period, however, two large federal irrigation projects were introduced, one in the Umatilla Valley and the other in the Klamath Lake area. In the federal projects land holdings were limited to 160 acres per farm.

Land prices doubled and, in some cases, tripled in the period from 1900 to 1930; in some areas during the first decade wheat land that sold for $10 an acre in 1900 cost $30 an acre in 1910. Homesteaders continued to move into the free

147

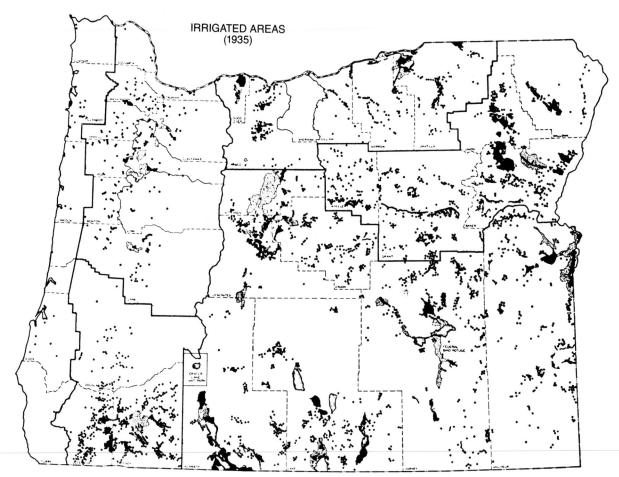

IRRIGATED AREAS
(1935)

fig. 8.9   Irrigated areas, 1935. Black areas were irrigated with water rights, shaded areas
had water rights but were not irrigated at this time. Each small dot represents 100
acres of irrigated land. (Compiled from various sources and published by W.D.
Smith, p. 168)

marginal land, many of them to their sorrow. Dry years brought crop failures to thousands of acres in eastern Oregon, in contrast to the Willamette Valley where crop failures were comparatively rare. The wheat farmers with their large acreages were prepared for a crop failure because of drought now and then, but on the small homesteads one dry year could be disastrous.

In 1929 the total land area of Oregon, 61 million acres, included 26 percent in farms, 6 percent in crops, and only 4 percent in harvested crops.[20] Fallow land accounted for 27 percent of cropland and crop failure accounted for 2.7 percent. There were 55,000 farms in 1929, averaging 300 acres each; farm size ranged from 6,600 farms with less than 10 acres each, many of them part-time farms, to 2,900 farms of over 1,000 acres each, and 350 farms (or ranches) of over 5,000 acres each. The largest farms were in the Deschutes-Umatilla wheat belt and the largest ranches were in southeastern Oregon.

During this period, 1900-1930, few new crops of importance were introduced into Oregon, but new varieties and hybrids did bring about changes in cultivation. Hay and wheat continued to have the largest acreage with oats a poor third. Barley, corn, rye, hops, and potatoes made up most of the remainder. Plums, prunes, apples, and pears accounted for most of the tree fruits and English walnuts dominated the nut crop. In small fruits, strawberries, raspberries, loganberries, and blackberries were the most important.

From 1900 to 1929 wheat production not only varied with the world market conditions and the weather, but showed some definite shifts in areal distribution.[21] From 873,000 acres in 1900 Oregon

148

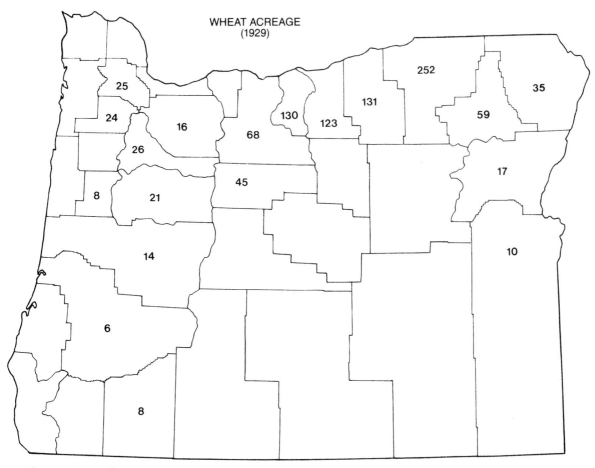

WHEAT ACREAGE
(1929)

252

131

35

25

130

59

24

16

123

68

17

26

45

8

21

10

14

6

8

fig. 8.10   Wheat acreage, in thousands, 1929. Counties with less than 5,000 acres are not shown. (From the U.S. Bureau of the Census)

wheat acreage reached a million acres in 1919, at the end of the war, declined to 859,000 acres in 1924, and peaked again at over a million acres in 1929 (**fig. 8.10**). Meanwhile, the increasing dominance in wheat acreage of eastern Oregon, especially the Deschutes-Umatilla Plateau, was even more noticeable. Comparing production in bushels in 1919 with that of 1929, which were almost the same for the state as a whole, it can be seen that wheat declined in the Willamette Valley substantially by 1929. On the other hand, the leading counties in eastern Oregon—Umatilla, Morrow, and Gilliam—showed an increased wheat acreage during this period. Because of Oregon's peculiar position with respect to the world wheat market, it was necessary for Oregon to put emphasis on wheat. Oregon wheat found little or no market in the eastern United States; that market was supplied by the Winter Wheat Belt and Spring Wheat Belt in the interior of the continent. Therefore,

Oregon had to send its wheat over long distances, either to the Orient or to western Europe, in addition to selling it in California. The high keeping and shipping qualities of wheat made it the ideal crop for this purpose.

Oats was the second grain crop in this period, totaling 213,000 acres, most of it grown in the Willamette Valley. Oats were used mostly as a feed grain for horses, dairy cattle, and poultry. As horses declined in numbers, so did oat acreage in some places. The leading oat counties at this time were Clackamas, Benton, Lane, Linn, Marion, Polk, Washington, and Yamhill—in other words, most of the agricultural counties of the Willamette Valley.

Barley was also used as a feed for horses, but most of it was grown for the production of beverages. The total acreage in 1929 was 78,000 and much of the crop was exported. Baker, Linn, Marion, Union, and Malheur counties produced

149

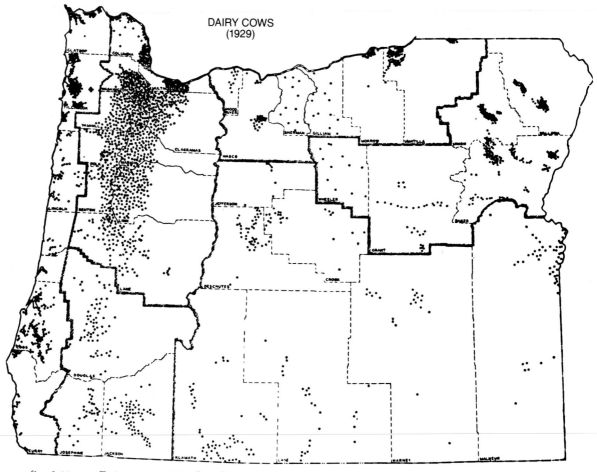

DAIRY COWS
(1929)

fig. 8.11   Dairy cows, 1929. One dot represents 100 cows. (Data from the U.S. Bureau of
the Census, published by W.D. Smith, p. 193)

the bulk of the crop, showing that barley was grown in both eastern and western Oregon. Corn has always been limited as a feed crop in Oregon because of the cool summer season. Corn needs hot weather, not only by day but by night, to give good yields. The total corn acreage in 1929 was 58,000; the most favorable places for corn-growing were in the Willamette Valley, chiefly in Marion, Benton, Clackamas, Lane, and Linn counties, the Umpqua Valley, and in the Ontario region of eastern Oregon.

Alfalfa acreage increased in eastern Oregon as irrigation was expanded and by 1929 there were 249,000 acres under cultivation. Most of the irrigated alfalfa was grown in Baker, Crook, Klamath, Malheur, Umatilla, and Union counties; the only county in western Oregon that grew large quantities of alfalfa was Jackson. In addition to alfalfa, other feed crops, mainly clovers and legumes, were grown in the irrigated areas. Grass

seed was becoming an important crop during this period in Clackamas, Deschutes, Lane, Marion, Linn, Umatilla, Washington, and Klamath counties. The potato crop declined in the Willamette Valley, reaching only 33,000 acres for the whole state in 1929, but it was increasing in the irrigated areas. Clackamas, Deschutes, Marion, Umatilla, Washington, and Klamath counties had the highest yields. Sugar beets had been tried but with little success except in the Ontario and Umatilla areas of eastern Oregon.

Livestock

Dairying continued to expand in the irrigated areas and became the greatest single source of farm income in this period.[22] There was no great increase in the number of dairy farms but there was in the number of cows milked, from 122,000 to 224,000; 21,000 of these cows were purebreds,

150

mostly Jerseys (**fig. 8.11**). The greatest expansion was in the Willamette Valley but the Tillamook, Coos Bay, Grande Ronde, Enterprise (in the Wallowa Mountains), and Ontario areas showed growth also. The leading dairy counties, in order, were: Marion, Washington, Linn, Clackamas, Coos, Lane, Tillamook, Baker, Yamhill, and Umatilla.

Beef cattle expanded from 531,000 head in 1900 to 805,000 head in 1929. Of this number 40 percent were in southeastern Oregon on ranches, 25 percent in the Blue Mountains, 14 percent in the Willamette Valley, 10 percent in the wheat belt of the Deschutes-Umatilla Plateau, and the remainder in other regions. A variety of beef cattle were fattened on farms, mostly in the Willamette Valley. In eastern Oregon many ranchers drove their cattle to higher elevations in summer with use permits for grazing on public lands, particularly in the Blue Mountains and in the Cascades, and wintered them on the home ranch using alfalfa and other hay crops grown on the irrigated land of the home ranch or nearby areas. Beef cattle were shipped on the hoof by rail to California and to the Corn Belt for finishing.

Sheep increased in this period from a little under two million to 3,319,000. As noted earlier, sheep got their start in the Willamette Valley, expanded to eastern Oregon, and then in recent times increased in the Willamette Valley. Between 1900 and 1929 most of the sheep were on the range in eastern Oregon. The distribution there was fairly even but there was concentration on the north slope of the Blue Mountains. Wool and lambs were shipped outside the state. Swine have never been important in Oregon because of the difficulty of growing corn, but during this period hogs began to appear in some numbers in the irrigated oases. They also were concentrated to a certain extent near dairy farms, where they could be fed on skimmed milk.

By 1920 the horse in Oregon was beginning to be technologically unemployed, as buggies gave way to automobiles, wagons to trucks, and plow horses to tractors. The number of horses had steadily increased until 1900; at the peak there were more than 300,000 horses in Oregon; by 1930 there were only 178,000. Most of Oregon's horses were in eastern Oregon, in Harney, Malheur, Umatilla, Wallowa, Wasco, and Lake counties; Marion, Linn, and Lane counties had the most horses in western Oregon, while the coast

counties had very few, fewer than 1,000 each. Horses, largely for recreational purposes, have been increasing rapidly in recent years and it is estimated that by 1980 Oregon's horse population will equal that of 1900.

FISHERIES

All along the Columbia River on both sides, fishing gear was being improved and expanded.[23] Near Astoria horses were used in shallow water to haul in the long seines; pound nets and traps were set and the gillnetters were busy. The two methods were often in conflict; numerous fixed nets and traps forced the gillnetters to operate farther out, sometimes in rough water. In some parts of the river nets overlapped and extended almost from shore to shore, interfering with navigation. Fish wheels, either attached to a scow or to the shore, were, until they were outlawed, an efficient method of lifting fish from the water.

At Celilo Falls, near The Dalles, Indians with exclusive fishing rights balanced precariously on their slippery wooden platforms and lifted large quantities of chinook salmon with their long-handled dip nets. The Indians often offered to sell fish to passers-by. The construction of The Dalles Dam put an end to this kind of fishing at that location.

Chinook salmon continued to dominate the market in Oregon, with silver salmon a close second in value although first in tonnage. Chum salmon, steelhead, halibut, and pilchards (sardines) accounted for substantial values. Smaller catches of sockeye salmon, shad, tuna, flounder, and rock fish were taken. The catch of the different species varied widely from year to year, as did the value of the catch. Generally speaking, Oregon's fishery was valued at about $2,000,000 per annum; the state of Washington, with Puget Sound as well as the Columbia River in which to fish, had a much higher catch. The conflict between the states made it difficult to enact and enforce conservation measures, but in this period the purse seine and the fish wheel were outlawed and shorter seasons for commercial fishing were established. Conflict was beginning also between commercial fishermen and the sportsman; the chambers of commerce felt that a salmon on a sports fisherman's line was worth more to the local communities than one in a gillnet! The commercial

fig. 8.12   A gold dredge, Sumpter, Oregon. (OHS)

fishermen thought otherwise, especially when they began to be excluded from some waters. The construction of numerous dams on the Columbia River and its tributaries, which were to limit severely the salmon fishery, was yet to come. Bonneville, the first of the big dams, was completed in 1937.

MINING

In the period from 1900 to 1930 mining began to fade as a source of Oregon income, as compared to agriculture and manufacturing. In 1900 gold production was valued at $1,727,000; by 1930 it had declined to $297,000.[24] Silver had also dropped drastically from $81,000 to $3,400. This decline was temporary, however; silver production increased sharply in the middle 1930s, only to decline again (see next chapter). Most of the gold was produced in five counties, Baker, Grant, Union, Jackson, and Josephine, by the use of bucketline dredges (**fig. 8.12**). However, gold lost its rank as the leading mineral in value, replaced by lowly sand, gravel, and stone. By 1929 the order of value was stone, sand and gravel, clay for brick and tile, mercury, gold, and copper. Minerals of lesser value were lime, cement, pumice, and diatomaceous earth.[25]

Several factors accelerated the mining of all kinds of building materials, not the least of which was the road-building program. As noted above, this was a period in which many of the roads of the state got a coating of gravel or crushed rock to form, with oil or asphalt, an all-weather surface. Although gravel was in good supply along the upper courses of some streams and sand along the lower courses, these were not available in all parts

152

of the state. The abundant sand of the dunes and beaches is not generally suitable for building purposes. Rock for crushing, such as basalt and sandstone, was widespread in most parts of the state and hundreds of quarries were worked. Rock that occurs in large masses and is resistant to crumbling and fracture is particularly desirable for jetty construction. During this period jetties were constructed on the Columbia (north jetty), Nehalem, Tillamook, Siuslaw (south jetty), and Umpqua rivers and also at the entrance of Coos Bay (south jetty). Jetty rock was also beginning to be used as riprap and for stone walls to protect shorelines, river banks, and steep slopes in residential areas.

Although the list of minerals produced in Oregon is impressive, some are notable by their virtual absence, such as coal, iron ore, and petroleum; it was and is necessary to import them. Except during World War I very little coal was mined in Oregon during this period. In 1929 Oregon imported nearly four million tons of minerals, valued at about $75,000,000. Of these, coal and petroleum were the largest items and they continue to be up to the present.

MANUFACTURING

In this period, 1900–1930, it became possible to evaluate Oregon's potential for manufacturing. Surveys and descriptions had revealed the extent of the natural advantages, as well as the shortcomings, in raw materials and energy. The abundant potential water power, as yet little developed, together with an excellent water supply, favored many industries, such as paper and food processing. The forest resource of softwood timber, the best in the nation, with a limited amount of hardwoods, favored a variety of industries. Agricultural resources, including large areas of level land with water for irrigation of the semiarid regions, made it possible to produce large surpluses of grains, fruits, and livestock, most of which had to be processed. Some efforts were being made to preserve the salmon resource, but other varieties of fish were not being exploited.

On the other hand, some of Oregon's deficiencies were recognized: the absence of good coal, high-grade iron ore, petroleum, and natural gas. The location and extent of a variety of metallic minerals were known but most of the deposits were too low-grade to be profitably mined after the "cream" had been skimmed. Oregon's strengths and weaknesses can be summarized by the "balance of payments" for 1929, expressed in millions of dollars:[26]

	Exports	Imports
Agricultural products	44	22
Forest products	120	0.3
Minerals	0.2	7.5
Manufactured goods	23	163
Totals	187.2	192.8

It was evident that Oregon's strength in manufacturing at this time was in the processing of forest and agricultural materials.

Lumbering

In the closing years of the nineteenth century, the lumber industry of Oregon was beginning to get into high gear. Previously Oregon was a poor third in production with respect to the states of Washington and California because of limited transportation facilities, especially in the interior of Oregon. Several factors contributed to the change: (1) the exhaustion of timberlands in the Great Lakes states and the migration of lumber companies to the Pacific Northwest; (2) the increasing demand for lumber for housing construction in the eastern United States; (3) the new technology described in chapter 7; (4) the extension of railroad lines requiring ties and trestle timber and the construction of roads with many wooden bridges.

The timber resource of Oregon had scarcely been touched by previous logging, which had been going on since settlement. The Douglas fir region, including most of the Coast Range, part of the Klamath Mountains, and the west slope of the Cascades, had enormous reserves of timber.[27] Most of the acreage was in Douglas, Lane, Clackamas, Linn, and Coos counties. In Clatsop, Columbia, Washington, Multnomah, and Polk counties the stands were smaller; particularly in Clatsop and Columbia counties the timber had been extensively cut over because it was close to water transportation. In eastern Oregon the great reserves were chiefly ponderosa pine with some Douglas fir. They were on the eastern flank of the Cascade Range and in the Blue Mountain region, mostly in Klamath, Grant, Lake, Deschutes, and Wasco counties. Only Gilliam, Sherman, and Malheur counties lacked significant reserves of timber.

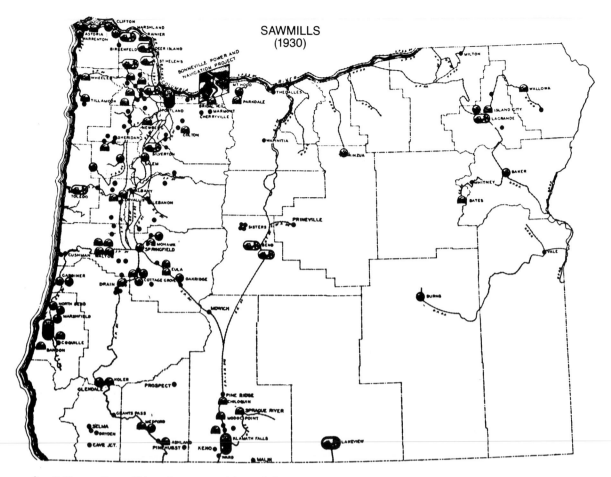

SAWMILLS
(1930)

fig. 8.13   Sawmill locations, 1930. Most of the mills were in the Willamette Valley, along
the lower Columbia River, and in Coos County. Small mills are not shown.
(From W.D. Smith, p. 229)

The increased production of timber in this period was accompanied by wild speculation and as much as a tenfold increase in prices for timberland. The Weyerhaeuser Company and other large companies bought large areas of timberland, and by 1913 Weyerhaeuser and the Southern Pacific Railroad combined owned 22.4 percent of the standing timber in western Oregon.[28]

In the previous chapter mention was made of the large grants of timberland and range land to provide funds for road and railroad construction. The companies involved were supposed to sell the land to individual settlers in 160-acre lots at $2.50 an acre.[29] As early as 1894 the Southern Pacific Railroad Company began to sell large tracts of 1,000 acres or more each, contrary to the law setting up the system. By 1906 they had sold 820,000 acres at from $5.00 to $40 per acre. According to the original agreement, the Southern Pacific Company, originally the Oregon and California Rail-

road Company, was entitled to more than four million acres of timberland. Seeing the rapid rise in prices for timberland, the Southern Pacific Company decided to close the sales for a while, giving as an excuse that they wished to preserve timber for railroad ties. This caused a considerable uproar in Oregon and later in the U.S. Congress. People who wished to buy land from the railroad company could no longer do so. The Portland *Oregonian* expressed the opinion that these lands might be rented out as feudal estates. All of this brought the matter to the attention of Congress. A resolution was introduced in Congress to recover the lands that had been illegally sold, and after a long controversy, the Supreme Court decided in favor of the government in 1915; by another resolution, lands were revested by the United States in 1916 and came to be known as the Oregon and California Revested Lands, O and C for short. This brought a new deal in the disposition of the

fig. 8.14   Early lumber mill with oxen used to transport logs. (OHS)

lands, which were open to homesteading now only after timber was cut off. The price was still $2.50 an acre, but there were almost no takers because the land was too rough for cultivation. And once the timber was cut, the land was not worth the taxes. Altogether, almost three million acres of timberland were forfeited by the railroad and revested by the United States and put under jurisdiction of the Bureau of Land Management. The income from the sale of timber from these lands was divided as follows: 25 percent to the state of Oregon; 25 percent to the individual counties; 40 percent to the Bureau of Land Management; and 10 percent to the general fund of the United States Treasury. It was not until 1937 that the O and C Lands were brought under sustained yield management. (The allocations have been changed from time to time. The O and C Act of 1937 gave 75 percent to the counties and 25 percent to the U.S. Treasury. In 1974 the counties received $57 million of a total income of $115 million.)

By 1929 there were 608 lumber mills in Oregon (**fig. 8.13**), 5 paper mills, 47 furniture factories,

and 64 planing mills.[30] Planing mills were usually associated with lumber mills. There were factories also for wood preserving and for the production of wooden boxes, especially for the packing of fruits, and three establishments were engaged in cooperage. Altogether there were 760 establishments engaged in the forest industries, with a wage-earner list of over 40,000.

The distribution of lumber mills had changed substantially as compared to the previous period. There were still a number of large mills along the Columbia River from Portland to Astoria and along the shores of Tillamook, Yaquina, and Coos bays. By far the largest number of mills were in or on the margins of the Willamette Valley, drawing logs from both the Cascade Range and the east side of the Coast Range. There were large mills at Bend, Klamath Falls, Lakeview, and La Grande in eastern Oregon, smaller mills in Wallowa County, and some in Baker and Burns. A few small mills (**fig. 8.14**) were located in other sections.

In addition to lumber—planed, dried, green or in various other forms—the wood industries turned out a variety of products. Smaller trees were marketed as poles, pilings, or fuel wood; a million cords of fuel wood were cut in 1929. Large quantities of fence posts, pulpwood, railroad ties and timbers, shingles, excelsior bolts, mine timbers, and cascara bark were listed among the forest products. By 1929 lumber industries in Oregon accounted for 62 percent of the wage earners, 64 percent of the wages earned, and 44 percent of the value of products. The forest industries were of greatest importance to the economy of the state, but it is evident from the statistics of employment that most of the lumber was marketed in the rough form. Lumber mills employed 35,000 persons in 1929; planing mills, 1,400; furniture factories, 2,000; wooden box factories, 27; cooperage, 16; and paper and pulp industries, 1,800.

SUMMARY

In the period from 1900 to 1930, the 540,000 new people added to Oregon's population, the impact of World War I, the end of free land, and the introduction of the automobile were the chief factors of change. The major effects of the war were temporary but it brought to Oregon many workers, skilled and unskilled, many of whom remained to become permanent settlers. The decline of homesteading and the rise of land prices had long-range effects, but some of the effects were noticeable in this period. In the first part of the period, rural population increased in eastern Oregon, but in the decade 1920–1930 it decreased, nine counties losing population. The losses were not great, but considering the continuing high birth rate, it was obvious that a substantial migration from the counties was occurring.

One of the effects of widespread settlement in eastern Oregon was a more precise knowledge of specific area. The settlers learned that some selected areas could be farmed successfully without irrigation with a risk of occasional crop failures, and that irrigation could be extended on the margins of the Cascades and the Blue Mountains.

The expansion of irrigation in Klamath County, for example, was accompanied by an increase of population of 184 percent between 1920 and 1930.

Meanwhile in western Oregon most of the counties continued to grow, stimulated largely by the lumber boom. Clatsop was the only county in western Oregon to lose population, though Curry County showed only a slight gain. Irrigation was increasing in the Willamette Valley and in the Rogue River Valley.

By 1930 Oregon's agricultural products sold were worth $63 million and the manufactured products twice that;[31] the various industries, such as canning, meat packing, milk processing, and flour and woolen milling, employed 3,841 persons. In agricultural industries location near the raw materials is necessary and most of the plants were in the Willamette Valley, but fruit and vegetable canneries were also located in the Rogue River Valley and at Hood River. In addition to the Willamette Valley, flour mills were located at Astoria, The Dalles, Klamath Falls, and in northeastern Oregon. The milk-processing plants turned out quantities of butter, condensed milk, ice cream, cheddar cheese, dried milk, and cottage cheese. About 1921 Oregon began to export butter to California and cheese to a wider market.

Woolen mills, which had flourished with the growth of sheepherding (see chapter 6), had begun to decline by 1930; only nine were left in Oregon, eight of them in western Oregon, one in Pendleton. With the growth of synthetic fabrics they were to decline even further.

The 235,000 automobiles in Oregon by 1930 brought about changes in life styles; some people moved out to the fringes of the cities and thus added a new group to the census reports, "rural non-farm." The national road system, although by no means completed, began to bring large numbers of tourists to Oregon. Crater Lake National Park, the Oregon coast, and sports fishing were the main attractions. The tourist industry was well on the way to become Oregon's third-ranking source of income.

156

9 DEPRESSION AND RECOVERY
1930–1950

*The onset of the great depression of the 1930's saw the second major
period of creative thinking in the resource and conservation field.*
Marion Clawson

The period of Oregon's rapid growth, described in the previous chapter, ended with the stock market crash of October 1929. There were both immediate and long-term repercussions. The population gain for the decade 1930–1940 was only 14 percent, the lowest ever recorded.[1] Many thousands of people were forced to go on welfare; others, too proud to accept welfare or unable to obtain it, lived in dire poverty in tarpaper shacks in such places as Sullivan Gulch in Portland, called "Hooverville." Although immigration to Oregon declined, a new wave of migrants from the Dust Bowl of the midcontinent, where several years of drought added to the woes of the depression, invaded Washington, Oregon, and California. Called "Okies," regardless of their state of origin, these people came in old jalopies with little money and few worldly possessions, and their condition was worse than that of the resident poor.[2]

Oregon adjusted to the depression with the help of various governmental agencies and appropriations, such as the WPA (Works Progress Administration) and CCC (Civilian Conservation Corps), but it took the preparations for World War II and the war itself to pull the state out of the slump. Hundreds of new factories were established to produce the materials of war, and thousands of new workers came from other states to satisfy the job market. The most spectacular boom was in shipbuilding,[3] but lumber mills, flour mills, canneries, and other food-processing establishments were busy. Wheat, flour, and dairy products, including canned milk, were exported in large quantities to western Europe and to Russia via Siberia. The new prosperity was reflected in the increased population growth rate for Oregon from 1940 to 1950, 39 percent.

Changes related to the war affected many aspects of Oregon's way of life. Families were disrupted when the fathers left for military service and juvenile delinquency increased. Teachers, both male and female, entered military or government service or sought more lucrative employment; as a result, the quality of the schools declined. Colleges and universities lost many students and some of their faculty, a loss partly compensated by military training programs established in the institutions. The farms changed also; the demand for farm products was accelerated and manpower was short. One answer was larger machines, such as tractors and combines. After the war the "big machine" trend continued. One of the most important changes during this period, only partly due to the war, was the accelerated internal migration of the people, especially the movement from rural areas to towns and cities, reversing the temporary trend in the depression years. Commuting increased rapidly, especially in the Portland area.

Effects of the war, including economic recovery, continued after its conclusion. Thousands of soldiers who trained in Oregon and thousands who came to work in the factories became permanent residents. The housing pattern changed; temporary buildings of various kinds, hastily built for wartime purposes, were converted to civilian use. At Vanport, on the outskirts of Portland, 9,942 housing units were constructed, some of which were destroyed in the great flood of 1948. Altogether Portland had over 17,000 such units.[4] Similar temporary prefabricated houses were constructed in various parts of the state and many were moved to other locations after the war. Some of them, alas, are still in use.

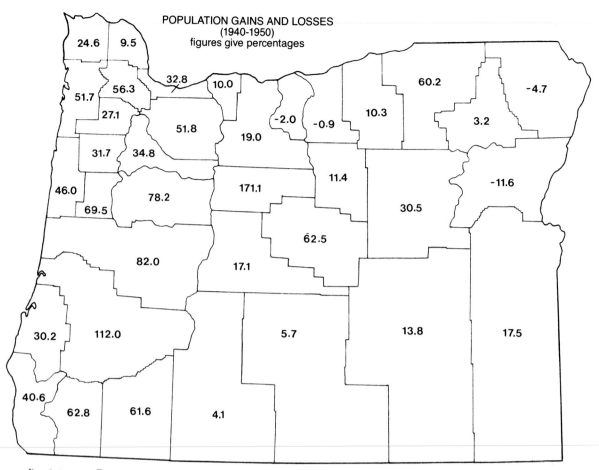

POPULATION GAINS AND LOSSES
(1940-1950)
figures give percentages

24.6 9.5
32.8 10.0   60.2   -4.7
51.7 56.3
27.1   -2.0 -0.9 10.3   3.2
      51.8   19.0
31.7 34.8   11.4   -11.6
             171.1
46.0   30.5
69.5 78.2
                    62.5
      82.0   17.1
30.2 112.0   5.7   13.8   17.5

40.6
      62.8   61.6   4.1

fig. 9.1   Percentage gains and losses in population, 1940-1950. In this period Oregon as a
whole gained 39.6 percent in population. (In the previous decade, 1930-1940, the
gain was only 14 percent.) Jefferson County had the greatest percentage gain.
Four counties – Sherman, Gilliam, Baker, and Wallowa – lost population. (Data
from U.S. Bureau of the Census)

POPULATION

The comparatively slow growth of population in Oregon between 1930 and 1940[5] was related to the Great Depression; it was a time of slightly lower birth rate and diminished in-migration. A slightly higher death rate was also a factor. In 1930 the natural increase rate was 3.1 per thousand inhabitants; by 1935, when the effects of the depression began to show up, the rate was 1.7 per thousand. The distribution of the growth was uneven; the growth rates of 13 counties were well below the Oregon average of 14 percent; and 7 counties in eastern Oregon actually lost population. All the counties in eastern Oregon were below average except Crook, Deschutes, Klamath, Lake, and Malheur. Expanding irrigation was a factor in the growth of these counties.

In western Oregon no county lost population and most gained more than the average; Clackamas, Curry, Hood River, Josephine, Lane, Lincoln, Linn, Marion, Washington, and Yamhill showed the greatest percentage gains. Multnomah County showed only a five percent gain but at the same time the suburbs of Portland in Washington and Clackamas counties showed substantial gains.

A slight but significant change in the urban-rural components of the population occurred during this period. The urban population had grown consistently from zero in 1850 to 51.3 percent in 1930. By 1940 for the first and only time the trend was reversed with only 48.8 percent of the population classed as urban. There was a definite but short-lived "back to the farm" movement as unemployed city people moved to the rural areas. The growth of cities was mixed. Portland, for example, gained 16.9 percent from 1920 to 1930, but only 1.2 percent from 1930 to 1940. Some cities, however, showed substantial gains from 1930 to 1940—West Salem, Salem, Pendleton, Springfield (the highest percentage gain), Grants Pass, and Hillsboro.

In 1937 during the depths of the Great Depression, a well-known population expert predicted that Oregon's population would stabilize at about one million. The 1940 census seemed to confirm his prediction, when 1,089,000 people were counted. But the 1950 census confounded him with a count of 1,521,000, a gain of 39 percent (fig. 9.1). The overall percentage gain from 1930 to 1950 was 59 percent. The gain was fairly equally distributed between rural and urban areas. But the general distribution of the gains was quite uneven. Four counties in eastern Oregon—Baker, Gilliam, Sherman, and Wallowa—actually lost population from 1940 to 1950, and five counties had a growth rate of less than five percent. On the other hand, some counties showed phenomenal growth. Jefferson County led all the rest with 171 percent, thanks to a new irrigation project by which water was brought from the Deschutes River to the plateau, which previously had been dry farmed. Douglas County gained 112 percent and Benton, Clackamas, Crook, Curry, Deschutes, Lane, Lincoln, Tillamook, Umatilla, and Washington counties all gained more than the average for the state. Growth of most cities was also spectacular. Portland gained 22 percent; Eugene, 72 percent; Salem (with the annexation of West Salem), 39 percent; Albany, 78 percent; Corvallis, 93 percent; and Medford, 53 percent. A part of the gain in many cities was the result of annexation of suburbs and fringe areas (fig. 9.2).

The population pattern of 1940 (fig. 9.3), showing the effect of the low birth rate of the 1930s, was altered by the rapid increase in the birth rate from 16.0 per 1,000 in 1940 to 23.7 in 1950, the "baby boom," and the in-migration of thousands of young people, many of them with young children; also the death rate declined from 11.3 to 9.1. These changes show up in the population data for 1950 and in the decline of the median age, but the two most significant changes are the increase of the 0–14 age group and of those over 65. The former had serious repercussions for the public schools in the late 1950s and in the 1960s, and later for the colleges and universities as the "boom babies" grew to college age.

The age composition of Oregon's population in

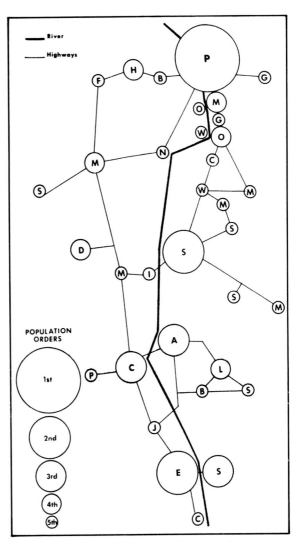

fig. 9.2 Size order of towns and cities in the Willamette Valley, 1950. The heavy line represents the Willamette River, the light lines, the main roads. Compare with Fig. 6.6. (From Holtgrieve)

1950 varied in different parts of the state. Counties with declining or static populations had a low percentage of young people in the 0–14 age group and a relatively high proportion of old people (65 or older), but there were exceptions. The averages for the state were 26.5 percent in the 0–14 age group and 8.7 percent in the over-65 age group. Benton County had the highest percentage in the 15–24 age group because of the residence of several thousand university students. Benton also had the lowest percentage of the 65 and older group. On the other hand, Multnomah County was near the top in the 65 and older group with 10.3 percent. Many older people were migrating to the

POPULATION PYRAMID
(1940)

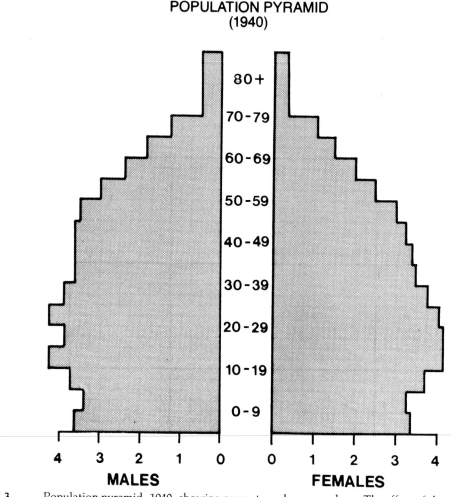

80+
70-79
60-69
50-59
40-49
30-39
20-29
10-19
0-9

4   3   2   1   0   0   1   2   3   4
MALES   **FEMALES**

fig. 9.3   Population pyramid, 1940, showing percentages by age and sex. The effect of the low birth rate in the 1930s is seen in the 0-9 age group. The male majority had shrunk and the percentage of persons over 65 had increased. (Data from U.S. Bureau of the Census)

cities, as a survey in the lobbies of the older hotels would clearly show.

The distribution of minority groups had shifted by 1950. Many Indians still lived on reservations but some had moved to the cities (Portland counted 174 Indians in 1930 and 592 in 1950); it is probable that some of them lost their identity as Indians, as far as the census is concerned. Most of the Chinese were living in Astoria (cannery workers) and in Portland. The Japanese were concentrated in Hood River County, where they had been established as horticulturists for many years, and in Malheur County, to which they had been forced to migrate during World War II. The foreign-born whites, mostly Germans, Canadians, and British, were fairly evenly distributed, many of them in the cities. The Irish continued as a

sizable minority in Harney, Lake, and Wheeler counties, as did the Finns in Clatsop and Columbia counties. Russians have always had a low profile as a minority group in Oregon but thousands entered the state over the years; some of them changed their names (perhaps so that people could pronounce the names) and lost their identity as Russians.

TRANSPORTATION

By 1930 Oregon's rail lines were complete, substantially as they are today; however, large areas remained without rail service and one county, Curry, had no railroad except for a logging railroad. Improvements continued in trackage, freight yards, and other facilities. Freight loadings continued to rise in this period but passenger traffic declined as the automobile, the bus, and later the airplane took over. Actually this period and the years following saw the abandonment of about 300 miles (10 percent) of Oregon's rail lines,[6] mostly short branch lines outside the Willamette Valley: also from Colton to Tillamook; from Dallas to Monmouth; from Yaquina to Idanha; from Portland to Dundee; from Tallman to Crabtree (narrow gauge); and from Monroe to Eugene. With the increased use of trucks for log hauling, hundreds of miles of logging railroads were abandoned, their rails pulled out, and their rights-of-way all but lost in tangles of vegetation.

Oregon highways, state and federal, continued to be improved by additional paving, widening, regrading, and the construction of new bridges. In 1931 the State Highway Commission was authorized to plan a system of secondary county roads coordinated with the existing system. Construction continued during the Great Depression, and by 1940 Oregon had more than 7,000 miles of primary and secondary roads, including 350 miles paved with concrete, 1,800 miles with bituminous surface, and 1,500 miles with crushed rock or gravel.[7] With the expansion of the highway system problems of maintenance were multiplied. Heavy rains, flooding, washouts, slides and slips, snow, and drifting sand were some of the natural hazards. Overloaded trucks damaged even the best of the pavements and high speeds rippled the gravel roads into a chattering "washboard" condition. In 1949 highway maintenance costs were over $11 million.[8]

The economic and social effects of the automobile and the expanded road system were far-reaching. One result was a movement to the suburbs and greater mobility of the people. Though some remained independent, many of the suburbs were absorbed into nearby cities. The more remote crossroad stores and small trade centers declined in importance as the automobile allowed people to trade in the larger centers. But new and improved roads contributed to the growth of many places as more resources, especially timber, were made available. Sweet Home, Lebanon, Molalla, Springfield, Creswell, and Willamina grew rapidly in this period.[9]

The automobile gave a boost to tourism not only for out-of-staters but for Oregonians, who had formerly depended on rail and horse-and-buggy transportation. In 1937, a depression year,

600,000 out-of-state tourists, most of them from California, Washington, and Canada, visited Oregon and spent $20 million.[10] Large numbers of Oregonians also visited the resorts and scenic wonders of the state. To accommodate the visitors, numerous tent cities, cottages, resort hotels, marinas, and other facilities were constructed (**fig. 9.4**). Additional camping facilities were provided in state parks, in the national forests, and on privately-owned land. Guest (dude) ranches and spas were additional attractions.[11] Trails for hiking and horseback riding were extended and improved. Skiing was becoming a popular sport, and in 1937 Timberline Lodge on the slopes of Mt. Hood was designed for skiers, as well as for hikers, climbers, and other visitors.

The airplane brought a new dimension to mail, passenger, and freight transportation in Oregon.[12] Preliminary steps included, in 1926, the inauguration of airmail service between Seattle, Portland, and California, and in 1929 direct airmail service was established to the East. In 1934 United Airlines absorbed two local airlines and began coast-to-coast service, using 21-passenger planes. During this time "barnstorming" pilots were flying around the state, taking passengers on short flights and whetting their appetites for air travel. By 1940 United Airlines was flying planes to California, the Midwest, and the East on regular schedules (16 hours and 40 minutes from Portland to New York), and Northwest Airlines was flying from Portland to Yakima, Spokane, the Twin Cities, and Chicago.

World War II gave an enormous boost to airplane design and construction, and, although civilian travel was limited, the commercial airlines were busy transporting military personnel and high-priority freight. After the war, surplus airplanes, available at bargain prices, were adapted to various civilian uses. The most common plane was the DC-3, some of which are still in use on "feeder" lines. Increased air traffic called for more and larger airfields and landing fields, not only near the cities but as emergency fields along the lines of flight. Many of the airports were subsidized by the federal government, as were the airmail contracts.

A BREAKTHROUGH IN MAPPING

One of the unexpected results of the widespread use of the airplane was a revolutionary method of

fig. 9.4   Early resort hotel, Gearhart. (Pacific Northwest Electric Railway Association photo, OHS)

mapping, perhaps the most valuable mapping technique ever invented. The airplane, capable of long, continuous flight in a straight line and at nearly uniform altitudes, made it possible to take overlapping, vertical photographs that, with the aid of a stereoscope, provided a three-dimensional view. With a minimum of ground surveys and with suitable instruments, these photographs can be converted by skilled operators into detailed maps of various kinds, such as contour maps, cadastral maps, and forest-type maps. The process is faster, cheaper, and more accurate than the old method, using plane table, alidade, and rodman.

Although vertical airphotos were in use in a limited way in the late 1920s, very few were available in Oregon until the late 1930s when Howard Brubaker set up a business in Eugene and began to take photos in a systematic manner for various purposes (fig. 9.5). In the period 1930–1950 more than a score of new topographic maps were completed by this method in western Oregon. The vertical photographs have a variety of uses other than map making, such as road planning, urban planning, mapping vegetation (using infrared film), timber cruising, and land-use studies. With special films, soils and geologic formations can be mapped.

Other types of mapping continued in this period: the U.S. Army Corps of Engineers mapped and remapped the rivers and harbors; the U.S. Geological Survey, in cooperation with the Oregon State Department of Geology and Mineral Industries, made detailed maps of selected areas and continued a long-time project of a comprehensive geologic map of the whole state.

In 1936 the U.S. Forest Service published a large-scale (1:250,000) map showing types of forests, stages of growth, and burned-over areas. Even more detailed maps of forest types were prepared on a scale of one mile to one inch, based on airphotos. These maps were not published but are available as blueprints. During this period the Forest Service continued to revise and publish maps of individual forests, showing the boundaries of the forests, townships and section lines, roads, trails, ranger stations, lakes, and streams. The Oregon Highway Commission compiled and published detailed county maps with roads, railroads, towns, cities, section lines, and streams. The General Land Office continued to revise the

162

fig. 9.5   Vertical airphoto of an area north of Tillamook along the Wilson River. Taken in 1939, this was one of the first overlapping vertical photographs made in Oregon, designed to portray elements of the landscape in three dimensions. Different types of woodland, cutover land, pasture and cultivated land are clearly shown. Most topographic maps are made from a series of photos such as this. (Top of the photo is to the east.) (Howard Brubaker photo)

163

township maps and the Metsker Map Company published their revised plat book, showing the location and ownership of all properties in the state. As the cities continued to grow, new streets were surveyed and mapped. Airphotos played an important role in the making of most of these maps, especially in the revisions. The books and periodicals published in this period contained hundreds of maps of various aspects of the Oregon scene.

In addition to the various state and local maps, hundreds of national maps were published during this period, portraying Oregon along with the other 47 states. The Department of Agriculture and its various subdepartments, such as the Soil Conservation Service, produced maps of land use, soil erosion, and land capability, among others. Efforts to improve the low farm income of depression years led to new organizations and many new maps. A succession of agencies, the Agricultural Adjustment Administration, the Commodity Stabilization Service, the Production and Marketing Administration, and the Agricultural Stabilization Service, produced maps during this period, many of them based on airphotos. The limitation of crop acreage, in order to improve farm prices, called for airphotos of every farm involved, so that crop acreage could be measured quickly and accurately. In brief, as a result of new techniques of map making and greatly increased interest in the distribution of resources and production, in the period 1930–1950, a great step forward was made in the number and quality of maps.

rapidly and so did the prices. The depression was world-wide and many of Oregon's markets were in foreign lands. The extent of the slump is shown by the decline of farm prices in the period from 1929 to 1932.[13]

The lasting effect of the slump is evident in the price of sugar beets, which sold for $8.12 a ton in 1927 and in 1939 brought only $4.07 a ton.

Prices continued low throughout the 1930s and crop acreages were reduced also, but by 1939 with the beginning of the war in Europe, demand and prices soared and Oregon agriculture was profitable again. The peak of production was in 1944 (the war ended in 1945), but after the war the decline was less than expected. By 1949 the wheat acreage in Oregon was over the million mark with a production of 21 million bushels. The leading producers were Gilliam, Sherman, Morrow, and Umatilla counties. Wheat was still grown in the Willamette Valley, but with sharply reduced acreages, even though the yields in bushels per acre in the Valley were higher than in eastern Oregon.

The number of farms increased from 55,000 in 1929 to 59,000 in 1949, the average farm size from 300 to 340 acres.[14] Farm size varied from 34 acres in Multnomah County, where there were many part-time farms, to 3,800 acres in Harney County. For the state as a whole, 33 percent of Oregon's 61 million acres was in farms but only a small proportion was harvested land. The highest percentage of land in farms was in the "wheat counties," Gilliam, Morrow, Sherman, Umatilla, and

TABLE 9:1

	1929	1931	1932
Wheat	$1.10/bu.	$.38/bu.	
Oats	$.53/bu.	$.27/bu.	
Barley	$.75/bu.		$.34/bu.
Corn	$1.05/bu.		$.55/bu.
Hay	$13.80/ton		$7.10/ton
Potatoes	$1.78/cwt.		$.50/cwt.
Apples	$1.30/bu.		$.52/bu.
Wool	$.30/lb.		$.09/lb.

AGRICULTURE

After the stock market crash of 1929 the demand for Oregon's agricultural products fell off

Wasco. In the Willamette Valley, Benton County was high with 53 percent, Lane County was low with 16 percent of the land in farms. By 1949 harvested crop land had expanded in Oregon to

164

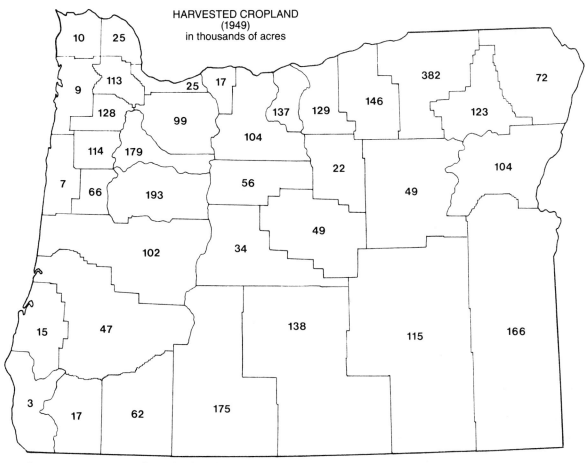

HARVESTED CROPLAND
(1949)
in thousands of acres

fig. 9.6   Harvested cropland in thousands of acres, 1949. Comparison with earlier maps
shows a continuing shift of harvested cropland to eastern Oregon as irrigation
and dry farming expanded. The state total of harvested cropland for 1949 was
3,218,000 acres. (Data from the U.S. Bureau of the Census)

3,218,000 acres (**fig. 9.6**); fifteen counties had more than 100,000 acres each, nine of them in eastern Oregon. The distribution of cropland was by this time well established. A few changes were yet to come, due mostly to irrigation, which was on the increase in the Willamette Valley. Some counties had a very large proportion of their cropland under irrigation: Hood River, 91 percent; Baker, 85 percent; Klamath, 76 percent (**fig. 9.7**).

Although beef cattle increased to 507,000 head by 1949, the meat supply did not keep up with demand in the period 1940–1950, when population was increasing rapidly, and Oregon became a substantial importer of beef. Dairy cows increased to 203,000 in 1949 and the distribution was very similar to that of the population, except for some concentration in the Willamette Valley and on the coast at Tillamook and Coos Bay. Horses declined

to 72,000 and sheep to 913,000. The shift of sheep from eastern Oregon to the Willamette Valley was well under way; several factors were involved, including the increase of beef cattle in eastern Oregon, the inroads of predators, and the difficulty of hiring sheepherders.

The passage of the Taylor Grazing Act in 1934, regulating the use of federal range lands, also had the effect of reducing the number of livestock in eastern Oregon. Prior to this time grazing on the public domain had been free and unregulated. As a result, the semiarid pastures had suffered severe and in some cases permanent damage. Overgrazing by sheep was especially damaging, leading to the encroachment of sagebrush and thus preventing the natural reseeding of the range. The Taylor Grazing Act provided for the organization of grazing districts, the payment of rents, and the limita-

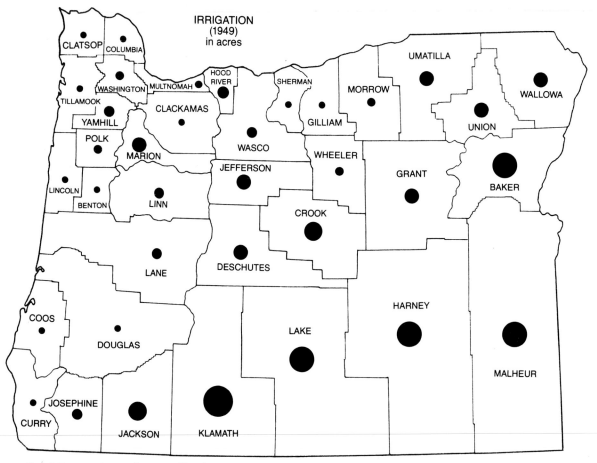

fig. 9.7   Acres of irrigated land, 1949. The small circles represent less than 5,000 acres, the largest more than 200,000 acres. By this time every county had some irrigated land. (From U.S. Bureau of the Census)

tion of the numbers of livestock grazed, as well as the season of grazing.

FISHERIES

Oregon's fisheries continued to fluctuate in tonnage from year to year, but a general advance in prices led to a substantial increase in value. In 1935 the value of all Oregon fisheries was a little over $2 million, with salmon accounting for 75 percent, pilchard, halibut, clams, and crabs making up most of the remainder. By 1948 the value had increased five-fold, distributed as follows (in thousands of dollars):[15]

Salmon	3,910
Halibut	101
Albacore	3,583

Crabs	1,047
Flounder	683
Oysters	10
Lingcod	128
Sablefish	107
Shark	413
Total	9,982

The most significant changes in the relative importance of species include the great increase of the albacore and shark catches and the decline of halibut. Albacore were formerly caught only in warmer waters, but in 1937 they appeared in large numbers off the Oregon coast. Halibut declined largely because of overfishing in Oregon waters but the banks off British Columbia and Alaska continued to produce well. Sharks brought a high price during this period for the liver oil and, to a lesser extent, for the meat and skins. It should be noted that Oregon's commercial fishermen were not limited to Oregon waters; many of them ranged over thousands of miles from Alaska to Peru.

The Columbia River fishery, of greatest importance to Oregon and Washington, was threatened during this period, as it is today, by the dams and by pollution. Although the provision of fish ladders and elevators at some of the dams allowed upstream migration of salmon, the problem of the fingerlings, passing downstream through the power turbines, remained. And high dams, such as Grand Coulee, completed in 1942 and 550 feet high, completely blocked the upstream migration. The decline of salmon fishing in the Columbia and its tributaries brought about a series of regulations, including a closed season, limits on the kinds of gear used, and limits on catches. At the same time artificial propagation was expanded and salmon were, in effect, transplanted to lower tributaries, below the higher dams. A research program was begun, sponsored jointly by the U.S. Fish and Wildlife Service and by the fishery departments of Oregon and Washington.

MINING

Metal mining, gold, silver, copper, lead, and zinc, had its ups and downs in the period 1930–1950. In the early years of the depression its value was less than $500,000; in 1940, stimulated by the war, the value soared to the four-million-dollar mark, after which there was a sharp decline. During this period 32 lode mines and 40 placers were in operation; some of the lode mines, however, were forced to stop operations because of the lack of machinery, which had a low wartime priority. Most of the active mines were in Baker, Grant, and Lane counties.[16] Gold mining declined sharply, almost to zero, after 1940. An acute shortage of nickel in the United States in 1950 pushed Oregon primary production to 913 tons, most of it in the form of nickel-iron ingots. The single smelter operated near Riddle at the foot of Nickel Mountain in Douglas County.

The value of sand, gravel, stone, and cement far surpassed that of the metals except during their peak period. These raw materials are present in great quantities in the state and production can be expanded to meet the demand. In 1950 the value of sand and gravel alone, more than $8 million, ac-counted for more than half of the total mineral production. In 1950 Oregon produced 2,600,000 barrels of Portland cement, at Lime in Baker County and at Lake Oswego in Clackamas County.

MANUFACTURING

During the period from 1930 to 1950 wood products continued to dominate the Oregon industrial scene, with over half of the employees and half of the value added. Moreover, this industry had the greatest impact on the land, as large areas of forest were cut over with a limited amount of reforestation. The other major industries, in order of number of employees in 1947, were food processing, metals (primary and fabricated), printing, textiles, machinery, and transport equipment, such as bus and truck bodies, ships, and boats. During the war shipbuilding was a major industry.

The industrial demands for power during World War I had stimulated plans for extensive hydroelectric development in Oregon. Abundant precipitation, snow storage in the mountains, and high relief make the state a potential leader in this field. The first large unit, Bonneville Dam and power plant, was begun in 1933 and put into operation in 1938 in time to supply power to some of the industries of World War II. The dam, with a static head of 66 feet, backed up water to The Dalles and, when all the generators were installed, supplied 564,000 kilowatts of energy.[17] This was the first in a series of dams that were to make slack water of most of the Columbia River, thus improving navigation and providing flood control. The expansion of hydroelectric energy production, the improvement of power transmission, and the organization of the Northwest Power Pool made relatively cheap power available in most parts of the state. The availability of cheap power had a special impact on the aluminum refining industry. During World War II aluminum ore from the Guianas and elsewhere was processed (calcined) in the eastern United States, shipped to Oregon and Washington, and refined, and the aluminum metal in the form of sheets, rods, and tubes was shipped back to the East for fabrication; some of the finished products were then shipped again to the Northwest.

The map of value added by manufacturing for 1947 shows the general distribution of manufacturing in Oregon (**fig. 9.8**). The counties on the

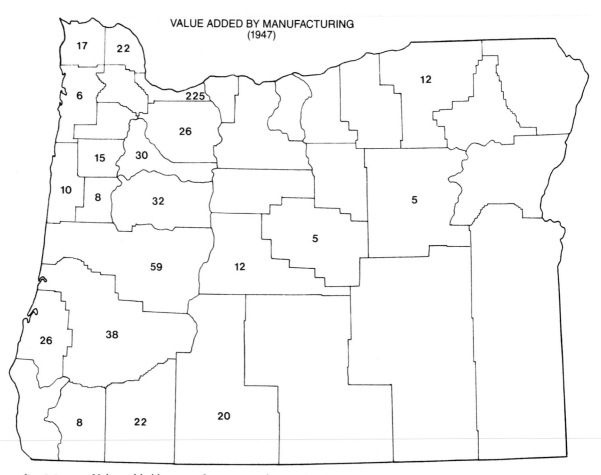

fig. 9.8   Value added by manufacturing in thousands of dollars, 1947. Counties with less than $5,000 added value not included. (Data from the U.S. Bureau of the Census)

east side of the Willamette Valley, especially Clackamas, Marion, and Linn, included most of the wood-products establishments, as well as other kinds of manufacturing. Lane and Douglas counties were growing rapidly, as the figures show, indicating the growth in millions of dollars from 1939 to 1947. Curry and Josephine counties were low in manufacturing for this period, but a few years later production boomed. In eastern Oregon the chief centers were in and near Bend, Klamath Falls, and Pendleton.

The forest industries grew continuously during the period 1930–1950, except during the depression years. Forty thousand people were employed in 760 establishments in 1929, but only 25,000 people in 361 establishments in 1933.[18] World War II brought the industry out of its slump and by 1947 more than 51,000 workers were employed in 3,000 mills. Plywood, millwork, furniture, and paper grew in importance as greater values were added to the raw materials. In addition, large

quantities of poles, pilings, fence posts, mine timbers, fuel wood, and cascara bark added to the economy.

The distribution of the forest industries was quite uneven in relation to the known resources. Accessibility was being improved by road construction, thus opening up new areas for logging. Some areas in the Northwest were almost completely cut over, causing a shift of production southward. In a time of greatly increased production for the state as a whole, log production declined in Columbia, Multnomah, and Washington counties and increased many times over in Coos, Lane, Douglas, and Curry counties. This shift in production was soon observable in the landscape, as more and more forest land was cut over in the south while in the north the abandoned land was growing up in brush or was being reseeded.

Food processing, including freezing, canning, and drying of vegetables, fruits, and fish, meat packing, and milk processing (butter, cheese,

168

dried milk, condensed milk, and ice cream), although a poor second to wood processing, was growing rapidly, except for flour milling and fish canning. In 1947 more than 16,000 persons were employed in all Oregon food-processing plants, with an added value of $100 million. Employment was distributed as follows: meat products, 1,926; dairy products, 1,242; fish, 1,296; flour, 895; canned fruits and vegetables, 4,581; frozen food, 2,031.

Other industries included textiles and apparel with 4,949 employees; printing and publishing, 4,493; primary metals, 3,000; clay and glass, 1,172; machinery, 3,817; and transportation equipment (truck and bus bodies, ships, and boats), 2,804. Shipbuilding was important in Oregon for only a short period.

IMPACT

The period 1930 to 1950 was a time of alternating depression and prosperity, of slow growth and rapid growth, of war and post-war adjustment. What did all this do to the Oregon landscape? In the first place, the growth and redistribution of the population was noteworthy, because it reflected changes in the economy. Population expanded in some parts of the state and was static in others. The migration of the lumber industry southward, as the northern forests were cut over or burned over, was a factor. Huge fires, mostly man-made, such as the Tillamook Burn in 1933 and later years, along with many smaller ones, hastened the migration. It also resulted in the harvesting of timber in more remote areas, which in turn called for more access roads. Clatsop and Columbia counties lost many lumber mills and some population, although a high birth rate prevented a net loss. At the same time people were moving from the rural areas to the cities and suburbs. The building of dams on the Columbia River and its tributaries contributed to the power resource and the aluminum industry, to flood control and navigation, but interfered with the salmon migrations. Food processing advanced relative to other forms of industry with substantial increases in canning and freezing. In general, all phases of Oregon's economy advanced during this period, except mining.

10

URBANIZATION
AND SUBURBANIZATION
1950–1978

Electric power and the internal combustion engine have made it possible for urban land use and urban ways of life to expand widely into the countryside.
ROBERT E. DICKINSON

The third quarter of this century brought forth no earth-shaking event in Oregon, such as the coming of the railroads in the 1880s, the two World Wars, or the Great Depression. Two comparatively small wars, in Korea and Vietnam, created only moderate ripples in Oregon's life and economy. The construction of a nuclear power-plant on the Columbia River may turn out to be a very significant advance, but so far it has contributed little to the economy; it has, however, initiated bitter arguments. The impact of the automobile, so striking when it first became popular, was dampened temporarily by the Great Depression and World War II, and then revived in full force. Automobiles increased in numbers faster than the population. By 1975 it was possible for all the people of Oregon to ride in automobiles at the same time with only one and one-half persons per car. One difficulty: not enough qualified drivers were available.

The rapid increase in the number of automobiles had far-reaching effects on Oregon, especially on the cities (**fig. 10.1**), creating a number of problems.[1] The urban "sprawl," with its slow out-migration of stores, industries, schools, and people from the inner cities, made it difficult and expensive to furnish these new areas with water, electricity, telephones, roads, streets, and adequate sewage disposal. The inner cities were left with empty stores, factories, and houses; and this situation was only partially rectified by urban renewal. Not all of the blame, perhaps not the major blame, can be placed on the automobile. High taxes, congestion, and obsolescence tended to push people out of the inner cities. However, at the same time people were moving from the small towns and rural areas to the cities, either to the

suburbs or to the inner city, as a partial replacement for those who had left.

This was a period of increasing conflicts, some brought about by the growing population, by the depletion of resources, and by attempts in planning. In general the conflicts revolved around various aspects of land use and public policy, especially with respect to communications, energy, forest management, pollution, and recreational facilities. Plans for the construction of new freeways met with increasing resistance and there was a rising demand for more public transportation, especially in the light of expected shortages and higher prices of gasoline. A related phenomenon was the great increase in the use of bicycles, both for commuting and for recreation. As Oregon approached the limit of hydroelectric development and as there were increasing demands for energy per capita, questions concerning nuclear, solar, and geothermal energy were hotly debated. Pollution and problems of waste disposal, including sewage, industrial wastes, effluents from paper mills, and smoke from field burning, were some of the bases of conflict.

Growing demand for more recreational facilities, such as parks, camping areas, and bicycle, horse, and hiking trails, came into conflict with agricultural land uses and private property. Inflated land values made it difficult for government agencies to acquire more land to meet the increased demand for recreation. High interest rates and high cost of land and building materials slowed down residential and other construction, not only in Oregon but throughout the nation, strongly affecting Oregon's economy, based as it is so heavily on wood products. Some progress has been made on these problems, but the 1970s

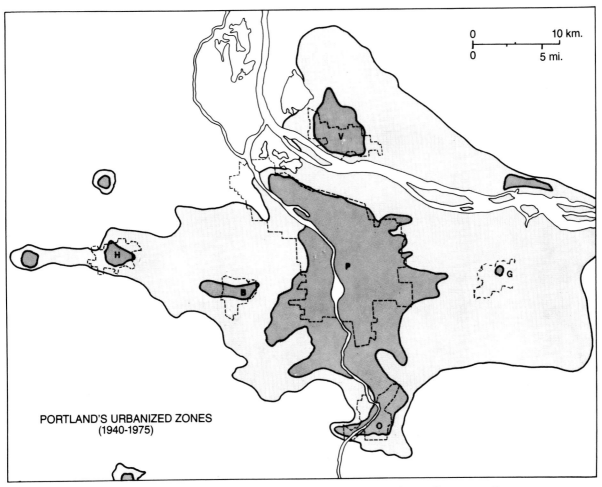

fig. 10.1   Portland urbanized zones 1940 and 1975, and some of the satellite cities. **P.** original site of Portland; **V.** Vancouver, Washington, the largest satellite; **G.** Gresham; **O.** Oregon City; **B.** Beaverton; **H.** Hillsboro. The broken lines indicate the 1975 city boundaries. (From *The Atlas of Oregon*)

brought no clear and final solutions. It is an over-simplification to state that these problems are *caused* by the increase in population. Perhaps it is more reasonable to say that population gains have aggravated these conditions and will continue to do so as the dots on the population map continue to multiply.

POPULATION

The increase in Oregon's population in this period, from 1,521,000 in 1950 to 2,472,000 in 1978, was fairly even in time but uneven in areal distribution. From 1950 to 1960 the increase was 248,000,[2] 16 percent; from 1960 to 1970 it was 322,000 or 18 percent; and from 1970 to 1978, an eight-year period, the increase was 380,000 or 18.2 percent. (The population data since 1970 are based on estimates by the Center for Population Research and Census at Portland State University.) Most of the gains were in or near Oregon's three Standard Metropolitan Statistical Areas, Portland, Eugene, and Salem. Six counties showed substantial gains from 1950 to 1978: Clackamas, 124,000; Jackson, 66,000; Lane, 137,000; Marion, 86,000; Multnomah, 75,000; and Washington, 154,000. Eleven counties showed either slight losses or insignificant gains—Baker, Clatsop, Gilliam, Grant, Lake, Malheur, Morrow, Sherman, Tillamook, Wallowa, and Wheeler. All but two of these counties are east of the Cascades. All the regions shown in **figure 10.2** gained. The Willamette Valley showed the greatest increase in

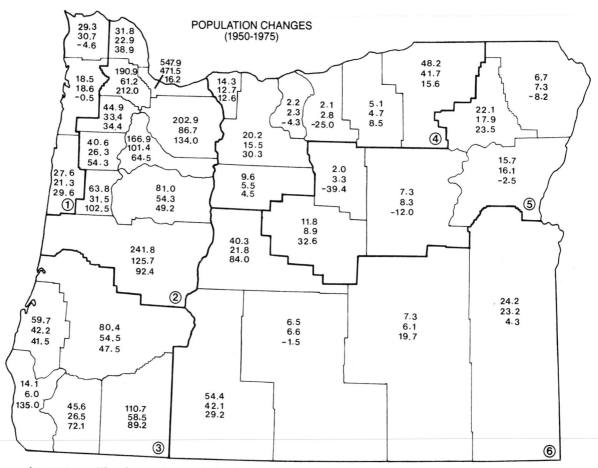

fig. 10.2   The changes in population from 1950 to 1975, by counties (in thousands). The first number represents the population for 1975 (estimated); the second gives the 1950 population; and the third, the percentage gain. The regions are: **1.** Northwest Coast; **2.** Willamette Basin; **3.** Southwestern Oregon; **4.** Deschutes-Umatilla Plateau; **5.** Blue Mountains; **6.** Southeastern Oregon. (Data from U.S. Bureau of the Census)

numbers; southwestern Oregon had the highest percentage growth rate. The table (**10:1**) below gives the gains in numbers and percentages for the period 1950 to 1978 and also the percentage gains for 1974 to 1978.

The gains and losses of individual counties and cities were irregular. A change in the local economy, such as the addition of a new industry, the closing of an old one, or the completion of a new irrigation project, can lead to a sharp change in population. For example, the population of Curry County grew rapidly in the early 1950s as additional lumber mills were moved in from the cut-over lands in northwestern Oregon and western Washington. The county showed the highest percentage gain in the period 1950 to 1960. In the following decade, the county lost some popula-

tion, only to gain again in recent years, 1974–1978. In Wasco County the construction of The Dalles Dam and the establishment of related industries led to a gain of 29 percent from 1950 to 1960. A new irrigation project in Jefferson County produced a gain of 26.8 percent in the same period.

The annual growth rate in the state in recent years is of special interest, showing a sharp acceleration. In 1975 the growth rate was 1.45 percent; in 1976, 1.84 percent; in 1977, 2.32 percent; in 1978, 3.17 percent. The last mentioned was the highest annual growth in the state in many years and undoubtedly reflects a substantial increase in net in-migration. About one-fourth is caused by natural increase and about three-fourths by net immigration. During the year 1977–1978 no coun-

172

TABLE 10:1

Region	Gain 1950–1978 (in thousands)	Percentage gain 1950–1978	Percentage gain 1974–1978
Northwest Oregon Coast	11.0	13.6	6.4
Willamette Valley	707.1	68.8	8.0
Southwestern Oregon	153.8	81.9	12.2
Deschutes-Umatilla Plateau	23.6	53.1	16.7
Blue Mountains	1.6	2.6	7.1
Southeastern Oregon	49.1	49.3	7.5
State	946.2	62.5	9.0

ties and only one city, Portland, lost population.

SUBURBANIZATION

In recent years the pattern of population within the cities has been changing; people are moving out of the inner cities to smaller satellite cities and to the suburbs. Recent growth in Oregon, as in other states, has been in and outside the city limits. Although the limits of some cities have been extended slightly by annexation, some of the growth has occurred in areas that have been inside the city limits for several years, as new subdivisions are developed. Oregon's cities have not generally lost population because of their natural increase, but in December 1976 an Oregon newspaper headlined, "Population dips in 7 of state's largest cities."[3] These cities were Astoria, Lake Oswego, Milwaukie, Coos Bay, Bend, Salem, and Klamath Falls. The losses were slight and in most cases temporary, but they were significant in that they suggest the reversal of a trend.

The table (10:2) below shows the growth of Oregon's largest cities for one year, 1977 to 1978. In 1978, 59 percent (1,465,918) of Oregon's people lived in incorporated places and 41 percent (1,006,082) in unincorporated areas.

For many years some people have preferred to live on the fringes, commuting to their jobs in the city, in spite of some inconveniences. The movement from the inner city, involving residential, commercial, and industrial elements, has been stimulated by the demand for more space, cheaper land, and lower taxes. In the suburban areas the home owner can have more land at a lower cost, enough for a large garden or even a part-time farm, with a horse or two. A quarter of a century ago, some people found this sort of life unsatisfactory and moved back to the city. But in recent

TABLE 10:2

	Population 1977	Population 1978	Population Increase Numbers	Population Increase Percent	
Portland	384,500	366,650	−17,850	−4.6	(loss)
Eugene	100,450	103,500	3,050	3.0	
Salem	83,170	90,000	6,830	8.2	
Springfield	37,500	42,000	4,500	12.0	
Medford	37,100	39,500	2,400	6.5	
Corvallis	38,538	40,500	1,962	5.1	
Gresham	26,000	30,280	4,280	16.5	
Beaverton	23,800	26,600	2,800	11.8	
Albany	24,030	26,150	2,120	8.8	
Hillsboro	22,000	25,750	3,750	17.0	
Lake Oswego	21,100	21,700	600	2.8	

years the realtors and subdividers have brought all the comforts of the city—sewers, power lines, water supply, and shopping centers—to rural locations. In effect many suburban dwellers are city people who resist the efforts of the city to extend its limits because of its higher taxes.

The large shopping centers outside the cities or on the fringes are in part a response to this suburbanization of population, in part a movement away from the congestion of the central business district. The central cities have reacted by providing more free parking lots and multi-story parking structures, but they have not been able to stop the outward movement. Once a new outlying shopping district is established, most of the downtown businesses either move to the new location or establish branches.

Suburbanization initiates a number of problems and conflicts. Where agricultural land is occupied, the new residents and the farmers come into conflict; the city people demand more schools and other services and a higher assessed valuation of property to pay for them, thus adding to the farm costs. They object to farm operations, such as spraying and burning. Pollution of groundwater, streams, and lakes by excessive use of septic tanks is common. In the more dispersed communities more busing of school children is necessary. Suburban residents often have poor access to the central core of the city and to parks. The greatly increased use of gasoline in commuting poses a serious problem in the light of expected energy shortages.

Suburbanization has created problems for the central city also and the commercial cores of Oregon cities have changed markedly in this period, 1950–1978. Losing some of the stores to the suburban shopping centers and some of the light industries also, the cities have continued to construct more high-rise buildings, such as banks, office buildings, hotels, and various government structures. The skylines of Portland and Eugene have changed in recent years. Multi-story building has replaced the low profile of previous years. Under the Urban Renewal Program, a federal agency purchased older, run-down buildings, removed them, then sold the land, often at bargain prices, to a builder. This gave some much-needed face-lifting to Portland, Salem, and Eugene. In spite of the out-migration of people and businesses, the central cores of most of Oregon's cities still retain their main functions—

banking, management, wholesaling, and a good part of the retailing, as well as government, education, and other social services.

HOUSING

From 1950 to 1978 the construction of new housing units, including single dwellings, apartments, condominiums, mobile homes, and trailers, did not keep up with the increase of population. The number of occupied housing units increased from 524,000 in 1950 to 735,000 in 1970 (42 percent), while the population increased 52 percent.[4] By counties, the housing increases or decreases were roughly proportional to population gains and losses; Curry, Jackson, Lane, Marion, and Washington counties had the highest percentage gains, while Baker, Gilliam, Grant, Wallowa, and Wheeler counties had fewer occupied housing units in 1970 than in 1960. The greatest increase in housing was in Portland's suburbs or satellite cities—Beaverton, Gresham, Canby, Hillsboro, Lake Oswego, Tigard, and West Linn. Springfield, Oakridge, and Woodburn also showed substantial increases. As of 1970, 62 percent of Oregon's housing units were owner-occupied, 32 percent were rented, and the remainder were vacant.

During this period the structure and appearance of the new houses changed dramatically.[5] New sites were being occupied and life styles were changing, as were house types all over the United States. Space is available here for only a brief mention of these changes. Even before the beginning of this period a few "modern" residence types had appeared in Oregon. They were also called "functional" or "California" houses and featured low roof angles and wide "view" windows (often on the street side). A variation was the "ranch" house, long and narrow, suitable for building on hillsides and requiring a wide lot. Apartment houses became larger and taller, especially on the margins of the business districts, often replacing the older types of residences, such as Cape Cod and colonial or the even older "L"- or "T"-gabled types, some of which had been converted into duplexes. A variant of the apartment, the condominium, became very popular during the last part of the period in resort areas; the residents usually owned the units, often renting them out for short periods.

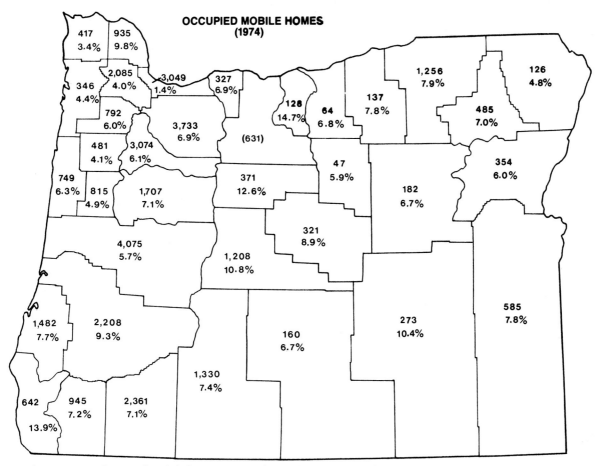

OCCUPIED MOBILE HOMES
(1974)

417 3.4%
935 9.8%
2,085 4.0%
346 4.4%
3,049 1.4%
327 6.9%
792 6.0%
128 14.7%
64 6.8%
137 7.8%
1,256 7.9%
126 4.8%
485 7.0%
481 4.1%
3,074 6.1%
3,733 6.9%
(631)
47 5.9%
354 6.0%
749 6.3%
815 4.9%
1,707 7.1%
371 12.6%
182 6.7%
4,075 5.7%
321 8.9%
1,208 10.8%
273 10.4%
585 7.8%
1,482 7.7%
2,208 9.3%
160 6.7%
1,330 7.4%
642 13.9%
945 7.2%
2,361 7.1%

fig. 10.3   Occupied mobile homes, 1974. The number of occupied units is shown by the upper figure; the lower figure gives the percentage of mobile homes compared to
total housing units. (Data for Wasco County is missing; however, the county had
631 mobile home spaces in 1974.) (Data from Steven W. Belcher)

One of the most striking innovations in housing in recent years is the mobile home (**fig. 10.3**). Although some Oregonians were living in travel trailers as a substitute for conventional housing many years ago, the mobile home did not become popular until about 1960, when Oregon had 14,000 units.[6] The number jumped to 37,000 in 1970 and to about 72,000 (estimated) in 1974. This house type has the advantage of low cost and the speed with which the units can be moved to a site and set up for occupancy. But mobile homes do not always meet the standards of local building codes and are, therefore, restricted to the less desirable parts of the cities and to rural locations. A large proporation are located in mobile home parks, which average about 25 units per park.

The distribution of mobile homes is uneven in Oregon. In 1970, Multnomah County had the lowest percentage as compared with conventional housing, Wheeler and Curry counties the highest. In numbers, Lane County had the most units, 4,075, followed by Clackamas, 3,700; Marion, 3,074; and Multnomah, 3,049. Wheeler County had the fewest, 47, and was the only county to show a loss of mobile homes from 1960 to 1970. In 1974 most of the mobile home parks were in western Oregon with a total of 28,000 spaces. Lane County had the most parks, 114, followed by Clackamas, Douglas, Jackson, and Multnomah. About 65 percent of all mobile homes in Oregon are in rural areas, many in parks, some as singles.

ENERGY

The period 1950 to 1978 marked a great surge in

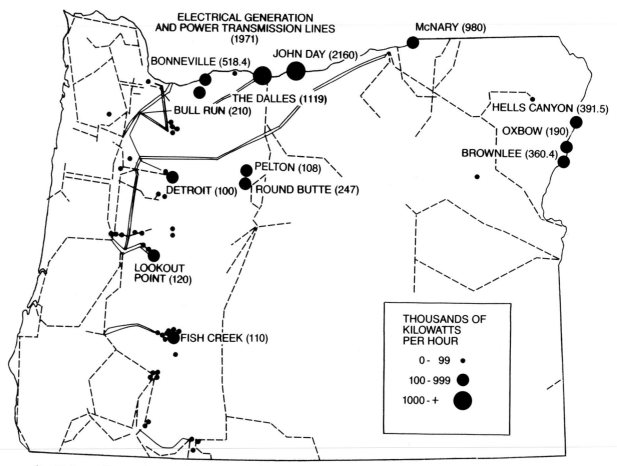

ELECTRICAL GENERATION
AND POWER TRANSMISSION LINES
(1971)

McNARY (980)

BONNEVILLE (518.4)   JOHN DAY (2160)

THE DALLES (1119)

BULL RUN (210)

HELLS CANYON (391.5)

OXBOW (190)

BROWNLEE (360.4)

PELTON (108)

DETROIT (100) ROUND BUTTE (247)

LOOKOUT
POINT (120)

THOUSANDS OF
KILOWATTS
PER HOUR

0 - 99   •
100 - 999   ●
1000 - +   ⬤

FISH CREEK (110)

fig. 10.4   Power plants and transmission lines, 1971. Most plants are hydroelectric, either
federal or private. The solid lines carry 150,000 or more volts, the dashed lines
less than 150,000. The capacity of the power plants is shown by solid circles in
thousands of kilowatts per hour. There are a few thermal plants in Portland,
Salem, and Eugene. (Data from Bonneville Power Administration)

the production and use of electricity in Oregon, both hydro and thermal.[7] Hydroelectric production increased almost seven-fold and production of thermal plants, using coal, wood waste, petroleum, and natural gas, more than tripled. Hydro still accounted for about 90 percent of the power. Most of the thermal installations were supplemental, designed for emergencies or to supplement hydro at peak periods, but some, as at Astoria, Tillamook, and North Bend, were in areas remote from hydroelectric power plants.

Most of the hydroelectric power plants in Oregon are on the large rivers, the Columbia, Snake, and Willamette, and on the smaller streams on the slopes of the Cascade Range (fig. 10.4), where heavy precipitation and high stream gradients are favorable. Half of the power is generated by publicly-owned plants, half by privately-owned

plants. The large dams on the Columbia—Bonneville, The Dalles, John Day, and McNary—and also Detroit Dam on the Santiam and Lookout Point Dam on the Willamette are publicly owned; the large ones on the Snake—Brownlee and Hells Canyon—are privately owned. Dozens of privately-owned plants are located on the west slope of the Cascade Range and on the Deschutes River east of the Cascades. Fuel plants, using mostly petroleum, are located in Portland, Salem, Eugene, and a few other localities.

Nearly all the power plants in Oregon and the Pacific Northwest are connected in a "power pool" and this pool is tied in with the California system. Surplus power from some areas can be fed into the system at the time of high reservoir levels, which comes at different times in various regions, and taken out at times of low water or at peak de-

176

fig. 10.5 Bonneville Power Administration power relay station, The Dalles. (Francis Seufert photo, OHS)

mand. The development of new high-voltage, direct-current power lines has added to the efficiency of long-distance transmissions. The major transmission system connects Grand Coulee Dam, Spokane, Seattle, Portland, and Eugene with lines leading into California (see **fig. 10.5**). Eastern Oregon is powered by plants on the Deschutes and Snake rivers and by branch lines. Both public and private utilities are included in the intertie. Fuel for Oregon's thermal power plants is imported, mostly as petroleum, natural gas, and coal.

As late as 1946 private utilities were reporting a surplus of power in Oregon, as well as in other parts of the Pacific Northwest,[8] but since 1950 it has appeared certain that a serious shortage would develop. With no oil or gas in the state, a limited amount of low-grade coal, and an unknown amount of geothermal energy, the state is faced with an increase in demand for energy from 12 million kilowatts to 32 million in the next 20 years.

One proposal is to increase the production of hydroelectric energy by building more dams, regardless of the loss of scenic and recreational values. The lower canyon of the Snake River (Hells Canyon) is a case in point. Three dams in existence on the Snake River adjacent to Oregon, the Brownlee, Oxbow, and Hells Canyon, are highly productive. But a strong effort is being made to preserve the lower Snake Canyon in something like its original state; however, the demand for additional power is very insistent. Another case is the McKenzie River in Lane County, which has no power dams on the main stem, only one diversion dam. The McKenzie Valley is widely used for recreation and agriculture, and the residents are opposed to dams. Many other small rivers, including those in the Coast Range, provide possible sites for small dams but regulations and restrictions are in the way. Unless there are marked changes in public policy, it appears that Oregon is now generating almost all of the hydroelectric energy available that does not jeopardize the fishery and scenic values.

Another proposal is to develop geothermal energy (**fig. 10.6**). Parts of Oregon are underlain by hot rocks of igneous origin, as is attested by numerous hot springs. Preliminary tests, including some drilling, indicate a large potential.[9] Several leases have been granted on federal land in eastern

177

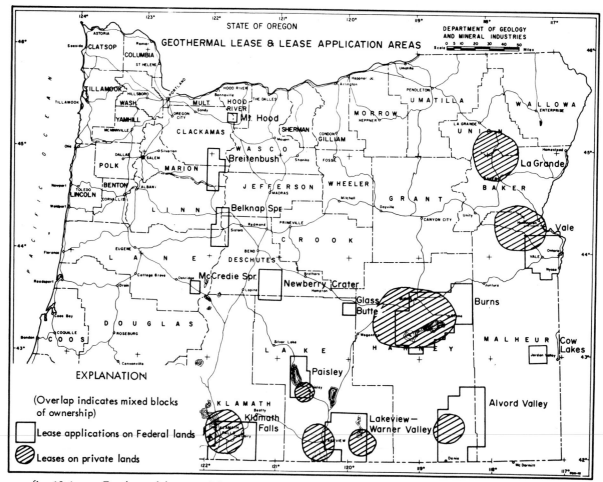

fig. 10.6   Geothermal lease and lease application areas. Areas in black outline are on
federal lands, those diagonally ruled on private land. (From *The Ore Bin*, 1975)

Oregon, in Klamath, Lake, Harney, Union, and Baker counties. Further exploration was planned for the "Hot Springs Belt" along the west slope of the Cascades near Mt. Hood, Breitenbush, Belknap Springs, and McCredie Springs. Geothermal energy has been in use for several years on a small scale in the Klamath Falls area and in California for heating purposes, but the water is not hot enough (only about 200°F.) for steam power plants.

It has been suggested that the low-grade coal of the Coos Bay area could be burned at the mine to furnish steam and generate electricity, which could be transmitted to other parts of the state. Coal is abundant in the Rocky Mountain states; more and more is being mined and some of it comes to Oregon. Both the mining, especially by the strip method, and the burning have unfavorable effects on the environment. Nevertheless,

coal probably has a larger place in future power development because of its abundance.

Nuclear power is the most controversial of all the sources of energy, partly because it is new and partly because of the potential danger of harmful radiation. The potential is large. The Trojan nuclear power plant, constructed in Oregon on the Columbia River near St. Helens, is capable of generating as much power as Bonneville Dam. Cost of construction has been high and the unit cost of power will be high. One of the greatest concerns is the disposal of the radioactive wastes. Criticism has been widespread and legislation has been considered to prohibit the building of additional nuclear plants. A number of nuclear plants are in successful operation in other states and in other countries and, aside from the serious risk of radioactive contamination, the plants are "clean."

A source of energy that has attracted very little

178

attention in terms of research and development is the sun.[10] It has been demonstrated on a small scale that solar energy can heat water, form steam, and generate electricity; it can heat houses and water for domestic use and supply energy in a number of different ways. In Oregon the sun shines up to sixteen hours per day in summer, but not on cloudy days, and only eight hours per day in winter. Many problems remain to be solved before solar energy can play an important role, but in the future it could supplement other forms of energy. It seems likely that Oregon will have to be reoriented in its uses of energy; sharp curtailment of the scarce items, such as oil and gas, will occur and greater use of the abundant ones, such as coal and solar heat, will be necessary.

Petroleum supplies most of the energy that drives automobiles, buses, trucks, tractors, trains, and other forms of power machinery. Petroleum in the form of crude oil and its various products, such as gasoline and diesel oil, move from many oil fields to Oregon by pipeline, barge, tanker, and railroad tank car. Three main pipelines serve Oregon, one from Utah, one from Montana, and one from Canada (Alberta). With the construction of natural gas pipelines (the first in 1953) from Canada and the mid-continent, gas consumption increased rapidly in Oregon, for heating residences and commercial buildings and for industrial uses. In many cases natural gas replaced petroleum.

TRANSPORTATION

In the period 1950–1978 the various forms of transportation in Oregon were extended and improved. Demands for the extension or construction of mass transit systems have had little effect. During most of this period, passenger train traffic dropped sharply while freight traffic increased; the new, nationally subsidized rail network, Amtrak, has been well received in Oregon but it has not noticeably reduced automobile traffic. Bus traffic also decreased;[11] passenger buses declined in number from 3,357 in 1951 to fewer than 800 in 1973, most of which were in city service. In 1973 Portland had 422 buses; Eugene, 60; and Salem, 25. Truck registration, on the other hand, climbed from 83,000 in 1950 to 164,000 in 1973.

People were traveling more than ever by their favorite method, the private automobile. As a result, new freeways and belt lines were constructed and many of the main roads were widened, straightened, and repaved, designed for speeds up to 70 miles per hour. When the national speed limit was reduced to 55 miles per hour in 1974 to conserve energy, only a few drivers slowed down. At the same time antipollution devices on the newer cars lowered the miles-per-gallon performance.

Perhaps because of the energy crunch and the high price of automobiles, this period has seen a tremendous increase in the use of bicycles. It is estimated that Oregon in 1975 had 500,000, used for commuting and for recreation. In spite of the construction of many paths and trails exclusively for bicycles, the cyclist still has to compete with the automobile for the right-of-way on city streets and on highways.

Navigation was improved on the Columbia and Snake rivers by the construction of dams and locks and by dredging. On the coast, new jetties were constructed at Tillamook Bay and at the outlets of the Rogue and Chetco rivers. Some of the old jetties were repaired.

Nine cities in Oregon are served by scheduled commercial air carriers, transporting passengers and freight. Airline operations reached a peak in 1968 and then declined slightly. With the use of larger planes in recent years, more passengers and freight were handled per operation. During this period many of the airports were improved and extended and many small airports were constructed in various parts of the state, suitable for private and charter planes and usable for emergency landings. Seventy-seven airports were listed for the state at the end of 1975 and most counties had at least one.

FORESTS

In 1951 two loaded logging trucks were observed on U.S. Highway 99, going in opposite directions, a not unusual sight. The size of the logs was impressive, three feet in diameter or larger. In 1975 similar trucks were loaded with much smaller logs, which one might measure in inches rather than in feet. And a glance at the "cold decks" adjacent to the mills gives the same impression—the logs are definitely much smaller. As a result of the increasing cut of small-diameter trees, numerous "small-log" sawmills sprang up in recent years,

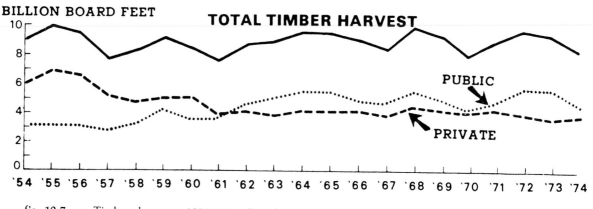

fig. 10.7   Timber harvest, 1954-1974. For the period the total timber harvest was remarkably uniform, but with many variations from county to county. (USDA Forest Service Resource Bull. PNW-63, 1976)

usually adjacent to larger mills. Tables, maps, and graphs of log production, including those in this chapter, do not show the size of logs; they show that log production goes on fairly steadily, up a little one year and down a little the next. Obviously not enough large logs are available, and so smaller ones are being harvested. This is visual evidence of Oregon's shrinking timber supply. During this period, from 1950 to 1978, Oregon's forests continued to yield large quantities of logs that were converted into lumber, plywood, veneer, pulp, and other products, with only moderate variations in volume from year to year. The harvest ranged from 7,890 million board feet to 9,800 million board feet. Peak years were 1955, 1964, 1967, and 1972. Low years were 1961 and 1970 (fig. 10.7). During the first part of the period most of the cut was on privately-owned timber land (i.e., industry-owned); at the end it was mostly on public land, administered by the U.S. Forest Service and the Bureau of Land Management. State forest and Indian lands accounted for a small part of the timber harvest.[12]

The areal distribution of logging operations changed over the period with a general increase in eastern Oregon and a slight decline in the west. In 1951 western Oregon had 85 percent of the cut, eastern Oregon 15 percent. In 1976 western Oregon had 76 percent and eastern Oregon had 24 percent. Ten counties in the west showed a marked decline in logging; only Lane and Douglas counties showed an increase and, as usual, these two counties led all the others and, together, accounted for about one-third of the logs produced in the state. The fact that these two counties are the only ones with large forest areas in both the Coast Range and the Cascade Range is significant. Clatsop and Columbia counties, after having been cut over in years past, began to make a comeback in log production. The cut in Washington and Clackamas counties declined sharply. In eastern Oregon, the leading counties in log production were Klamath, Lake, and Grant, and only Jefferson showed a decline. The record of some counties shows a great variation from year to year. Local factors, such as large forest fires or a severe storm with heavy blowdown, as in the Columbus Day Storm of 1962, can affect production temporarily.

The map showing changes in log production (fig. 10.8) also shows that most of the timber came from the Douglas fir regions of western Oregon. The high rainfall and mild temperatures of most of this region are favorable for the growth of large trees. The long-continued forest fires, man-set and lightning-set, together with clear cutting have helped maintain this Douglas fir forest. Otherwise it is likely that the climax forest would have been mostly western hemlock. As it is, the forest has many mixed-in species, including Sitka spruce, western hemlock, western red cedar, and ponderosa pine. Hardwoods—oak, maple, and alder—have been harvested in small quantities for many years. The second-ranking source of timber for the period was the ponderosa pine forest on the eastern slope of the Cascades and in the Blue Mountains. The open stands of these trees made logging comparatively easy. (Some areas of this forest have been grazed in summer.) Other forest types—lodgepole pine, larch, and true firs—have been harvested in smaller quantities, since they produce lumber of poorer quality than that of Douglas fir and ponderosa pine.

180

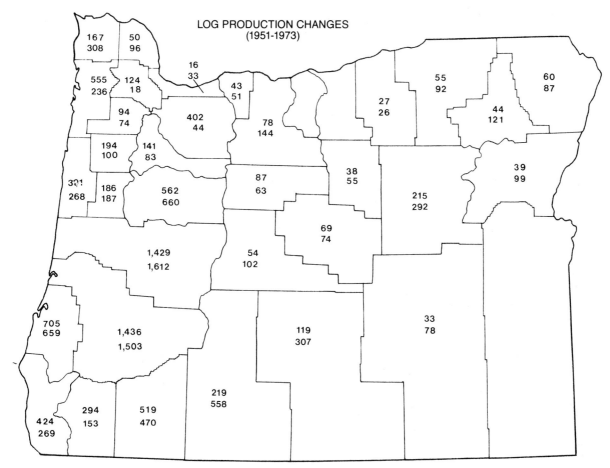

LOG PRODUCTION CHANGES
(1951-1973)

fig. 10.8   Changes in log production, 1951-1973. The upper figure gives the average production for 1951-1953 and the lower figure the average production for 1971-1973
in billions of board feet. Eleven counties in western Oregon show declining log
harvests, while all but two counties of eastern Oregon show gains. Three counties
produce no logs. (From U.S. Forest Service Resource Bull. PNW-55, 1974)

In recent years the harvest of timber in Oregon has exceeded the growth by ever-increasing
amounts. This is especially true in western Oregon, where most of the reserves and most of the
production are located. By 1975 it became apparent that the situation had become critical in some
parts of the state. It is estimated that on industry
lands, in 1975, the growth rate was 175 billion
board feet per year and the harvest 890 billion
board feet.[13] If this ratio continues, saw timber on
industry lands will have vanished in about 17
years. In the national forests the timber supply,
assuming the present harvest rate, will last only 60
years. Because of the heavy lumber production in
recent years many of the present stands on industry lands are young and immature and will not be
ready for harvest for a half-century. It is a fiction

to assume that any large area of timber in Oregon
is worked on a sustained-yield basis.

The ratio of timber harvest to available timber
supply varies widely in different regions. Lane and
Douglas counties, which in recent years have accounted for 40 percent of western Oregon's production, face a serious deficit of timber in the coming decade. On industry lands in Lane County the
present rate of harvest can only be maintained
until 1985. To ease the situation somewhat in
western Oregon, it is suggested that log exports be
prohibited and that special methods be used to
speed up regrowth. Herbicides are being used to
defoliate broad-leaved trees and shrubs so that the
young timber trees can get an early start. This
practice presents a hazard to animal life and
pollutes the streams.

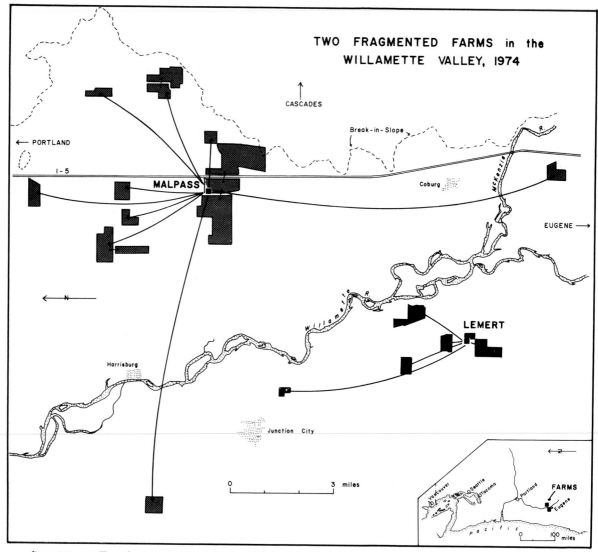

TWO FRAGMENTED FARMS in the
WILLAMETTE VALLEY, 1974

CASCADES

Break-in-Slope

← PORTLAND

I - 5

MALPASS

Coburg

McKenzie R.

EUGENE →

← N

Willamette R.

LEMERT

Harrisburg

Junction City

0   3   miles

Vancouver Seattle Tacoma Portland FARMS
                                      Eugene

pacific   0   100
                        miles

fig. 10.9   Two fragmented farms in the Willamette Valley north of Eugene, 1974. (The top
of this map is to the east.) (From Everett G. Smith, Jr., in *Annals of the Association of American Geographers* 65, 1975, p. 59)

AGRICULTURE

The character of the agricultural landscape in Oregon changed less in the period from 1950 to 1978, perhaps, than in any other period, but there were still some significant alterations. The maps of crop and livestock distribution for 1972 look much like those of 1949, except that wheat acreage had expanded. The number of farms declined from 59,000 in 1950 to 26,000 in 1974,[14] but the total farm acreage changed little, while the value of the farms and their produce nearly quadrupled.

The average farm size increased from 340 to 620 acres as individual farmers acquired additional parcels of land. Many of the larger farms are fragmented,[15] requiring the farmer to "commute" with his tractors and implements from one tract to another. Two such farms in the Willamette Valley are located to the north of Eugene (**fig. 10.9**). The Malpass farm (grass seed) includes ten separate tracts, totaling more than 3,000 acres. The Lemert farm (fruits, nuts, and beans) has six separate tracts with over 600 acres. Fragmentation would be unsatisfactory for a dairy farm; it seems to work very well for field crops and orchards.

In 1974 wheat, hay, and barley together occupied 77 percent of Oregon's cropland, followed by potatoes, dry peas, snap beans, mint, fruit, nuts, and grass seed. Livestock numbers changed a little; beef cattle increased and became the most important farm product; dairy cows and sheep declined. In 1949 there were 203,000 dairy cows in Oregon; in 1974 there were only 87,000.[16] In the ten-year period 1965–1975, the prices of Oregon farm products increased substantially but farm expenses climbed also, so that net farm income advanced little, accounting perhaps for the decline in the number of farms.

Eight counties accounted for a large share of Oregon's farm products in 1974, five in western Oregon (Marion, Clackamas, Washington, Linn, and Lane) and three in eastern Oregon (Klamath, Malheur, and Umatilla). The value of farm products in each of the eight counties was over $38 million. Irrigation is of paramount importance in Klamath and Malheur counties; only a small part of the cropland in the other counties is irrigated. Wheat and barley are concentrated in Wasco, Sherman, Gilliam, Morrow, and Umatilla counties with lesser acreages in Union and Jefferson counties and in the Willamette Valley. In the last years of the period, high prices for wheat, following heavy foreign sales, led to a substantial increase in wheat acreage and the cultivation of foothill and upland areas not usually cropped. Where slopes are steep this calls for smaller machinery for seeding and harvesting and, in some cases, introduces a serious erosion hazard. The hay crop is widely distributed, being most important on irrigated land.

The most significant advance in agriculture in this period was in irrigation, which expanded in all parts of the state. Especially important was the increase of sprinkler irrigation, which functions on rolling, or even low, hilly land without expensive leveling. Some new, large-scale irrigation projects were added in connection with new dams, as at The Dalles, but most of the expansion was in existing systems.

Various methods of irrigation are used in different parts of the state, depending on the terrain and the nature of the water supply. Much of the water supply comes from streams, which are diverted by dams and the water led by gravity to the fields. Pumping from streams and wells is also common. In the "wild" flood method, used on very level land or on a slight slope, the entire surface is flooded. In furrow irrigation, water is brought to the fields by a canal and diverted into furrows or small ditches, often with the aid of plastic siphons. If the slopes are too steep for furrow irrigation, closely spaced contour ditches can be used or, if suitable equipment is available, sprinklers. Sprinkler irrigation requires the use of pipes and sprinklers must be supplied with water under pressure, which usually involves pumping water from streams or wells. The sprinklers have rotating heads and, in some systems, are mounted on wheels that automatically advance across the field.

In eastern Oregon irrigation has been developed in areas where most crops would not grow well without it. Hay leads in irrigated acreage, with 539,000 acres, followed by pasture, 309,000; grains, 153,000 (most grain in eastern Oregon is not irrigated); and field crops, 85,000 acres.[17] Field seeds are grown in the irrigated areas of Jefferson, Malheur, and Umatilla counties, sugar beets in Malheur and Umatilla counties. Only small amounts of field corn, sweet corn, fruits, berries, and melons are grown in eastern Oregon.

FISHERIES

From 1950 to 1975 the tonnage of fish landed at Oregon ports almost doubled, from 58 to 98 million pounds, and the value more than quadrupled, from $7 million to $34 million. The catch varied in amount from year to year and also in the relative importance of the various species. Chinook and coho salmon, crabs, shrimp, tuna, and bottom fish accounted for most of the value. Less important were sturgeon, shad, striped bass, smelt, clams, and oysters. The chief ports for Oregon fish landings were Astoria, Tillamook (Garibaldi), Pacific City, Depoe Bay, Newport, Winchester Bay, Coos Bay, Port Orford, and Brookings. All these ports, except Depoe Bay and Port Orford, have bars at the entrances of the harbors, which make passage difficult and risky in rough weather.

Commercial fishing in Oregon, which occupies only 0.2 percent of the gainfully employed, is limited by several factors. Perhaps the most important is the limited market. Oregonians are not generally great fish eaters. Price is another factor. In recent years the price of salmon in the market has often exceeded that of beef. Other factors are the scarcity of the most desirable species, such as chinook salmon, the variability of the "run," and regulations, especially the short season, designed to conserve the fisheries.

The chinook season for commercial fishermen is quite short, usually one week early in March, one week after April 30, and a third season from August 10 to September 10. The coho season runs from August 10 to the end of October. Crabs may be taken from December 1 to August 15, shrimp from April 1 to October 15. Bottom fish and tuna can be taken the year round but rough weather in winter makes fishing difficult.

The re-establishment of the old Indian treaty, giving Indians unlimited fishing rights at certain points on the Columbia River, reduced the amount of fish available to the commercial and sports fishermen. On the other hand, the extension of United States territory in the ocean to the 200-mile limit eventually should improve commercial fishing. Previously Japanese and Russian fishermen, with their floating canneries, had fished just beyond the old 12-mile limit and sometimes within it. Their heavy trawls and other gear have taken a heavy toll of the fish resource and, in some areas, have permanently damaged the habitat of the bottom fish.

Sport fishing, although difficult to assess at dollar values, brings more income to the state than commercial fisheries. The numerous marinas on the estuaries, which supply boats, fishing gear, guides, and other services, and the hundreds of thousands of fishing licenses sold every year are evidence of the importance of this activity. With 400 miles of ocean shoreline, 62,000 miles of streams, and 1,600 lakes and reservoirs, sport fishing is available all year in Oregon. A variety of trout, striped bass, salmon, sturgeon, shad, perch, crappie, and catfish are among the fish taken. The industry of selling to and servicing the hundreds of thousands of sport fishermen is growing year by year.[18] The long-standing conflict between the sport and commercial fishermen is an uneven one — the sport fishermen have the votes.

MINERALS

Mining continued to play a minor role in Oregon's economy during this period.[19] Out of a total labor force of 1,020,000, only 1,800 were engaged in mining, mostly in the production of sand, gravel, stone, pumice, clay, and nickel. By value, the total production reached $88 million in 1975. Nickel was the only metal mined and processed in significant quantities (statistics on the amount produced are not available). Oregon was the only state producing primary nickel, and the search continues in the state for new deposits. The pro-

duction of sand, gravel, and stone declined, while pumice and clay production increased. It was becoming apparent for the first time that the supplies of sand and gravel in the state are not inexhaustible. Recent suburbanization has covered much land underlain by sand and gravel. With the energy crisis at hand, the economics and technology of coal mining in the Coos Bay area have been re-examined. As of 1975 it still did not appear feasible to reopen any of the mines.

In 1971 the Oregon Legislature passed a Mined Land Reclamation Act,[20] modified in 1975, requiring the registration of any surface mining (strip mining) operation for sand, gravel, pumice, rock, top soil, or other surface material. The law also requires that after the mining operation is completed, the surface be restored to approximately its original condition.

Extensive exploration and drilling for oil and gas in Oregon, both onshore and offshore, have revealed only small quantities of hydrocarbons. By 1975, 22 wells had been drilled in western Oregon and 12 in eastern Oregon, all dry holes.[21] Likewise, drilling offshore, both within and beyond the three-mile limit, has met with no success; the last well drilled offshore was in 1967. Exploration continues, however, especially in the Columbia Plateau; and promising wells recently have been drilled in Columbia County.

MANUFACTURING

During the period from 1950 to 1975 manufacturing continued to be the chief occupation in Oregon, as it had been for many years. By 1974 Oregon's labor force had grown to 1,020,000, of whom 76,000 were unemployed.[22] Manufacturing accounted for 197,400 employees in 1974, followed by wholesale and retail trade with 194,700; government services, 166,900; and general services, 140,900. Transportation, finance, and construction accounted for most of the remainder. The number of persons employed in manufacturing increased faster than the population in the period from 1947 to 1972, for which census data are available. The increases were uneven with respect to the different industries.

Most of the industries and more than half of the persons employed were in the three SMSAs (Standard Metropolitan Statistical Areas) — Portland (the only SMSA in Oregon in 1947), Salem, and Eugene — by 1972. Of these Portland was by far

184

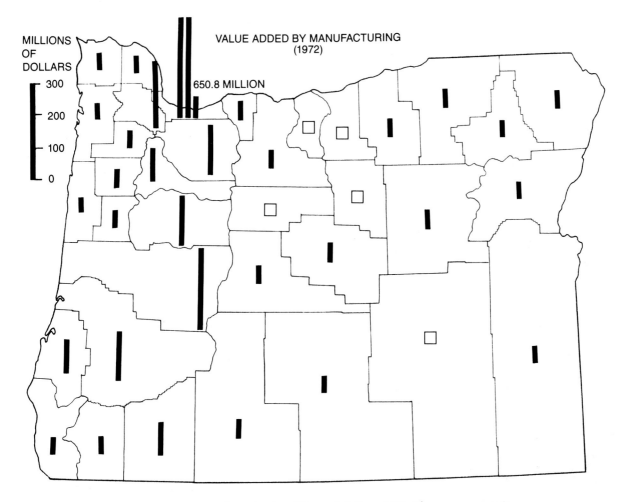

fig. 10.10   Value added by manufacturing in millions of dollars, 1972. The open squares indicate figures withheld. (Data from U.S. Bureau of the Census. Map modified
from William G. Loy, *Preliminary Atlas of Oregon*, 1972)

the largest and most diversified. Eugene was second and the least diversified, having nearly three-
fourths of its industrial employment in the wood
and paper industries. Most of the remaining industries in Oregon were also in the Willamette
Valley.

Although most industries grew substantially in
this period, furniture declined, food processing
grew only moderately, and the number of estab-

lishments actually declined. By counties, the distribution was much the same as in the previous
period, 1930–1950 (**fig. 10.10**), but within the
counties important changes occurred, especially
the migration of many industries to the suburbs.

The distribution of specific industries varied
widely, county to county,[23] based on location factors peculiar to each, such as availability of raw
materials, power supply, water supply, and trans-

TABLE 10:3

	Establishments		Employees (thousands)	
	1947	1972	1947	1972
Eugene	—	488	—	19.5
Portland	1,297	2,006	51.6	85.8
Salem	—	319	—	12.1
Totals	1,297	2,813	51.6	117.4

185

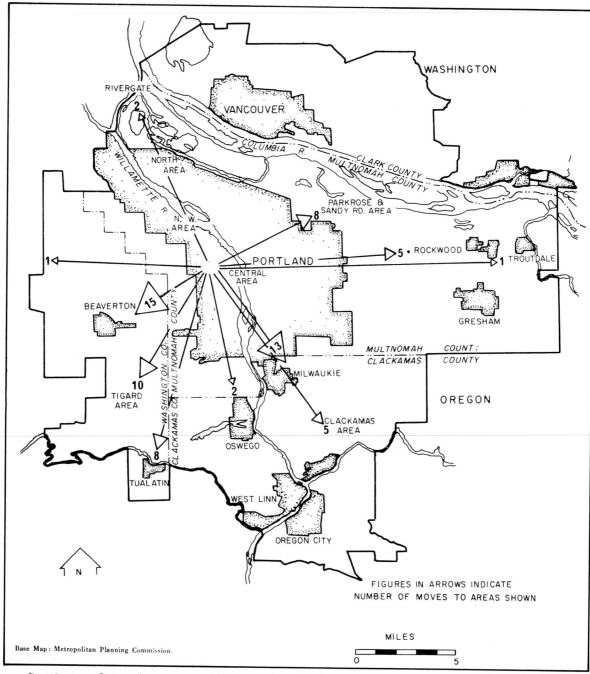

Base Map: Metropolitan Planning Commission.

FIGURES IN ARROWS INDICATE
NUMBER OF MOVES TO AREAS SHOWN

MILES
0   5

fig. 10.11   Outward movement of industries from Portland's central area to the suburbs, 1955-1969. In clockwise order, two industries moved to Rivergate, eight moved to Sandy Boulevard, five to Rockwood, one to Troutdale, thirteen to Milwaukie, five to Clackamas, two to Oswego, eight to Tualatin, ten to Tigard, fifteen to Beaverton, and one northwest of Beaverton. (From *Oregon Business Review*, August, 1971)

portation. Wood processing was widespread, all but a few counties having at least one lumber mill; but the bulk of the industry was concentrated in the southwest, in Lane, Douglas, Coos, and Jackson counties. Paper was best developed in Clackamas and Lane counties. In eastern Oregon, Klamath, Deschutes, Crook, and Umatilla counties led in wood products. The Willamette Valley was the site of most of the food-processing plants, especially Multnomah, Marion, and Lane counties, with some canneries, flour mills, and one beet-sugar factory in eastern Oregon. Primary metal refining included aluminum in the Portland area, rare metals at Albany, and nickel in Douglas County. Transportation equipment, mostly boat, truck, and bus bodies, was based largely in the Portland and Eugene areas.

The most dynamic change in Oregon's industry during this period was suburbanization,[24] the movement out of the central cities to the suburbs and satellite cities. The migration of industries stimulated the development of new shopping centers, schools, and residences. These changes were most marked in the Portland area, but the effects were also apparent in Salem and Eugene. The Portland migration for the period from 1955 to 1969 is shown on the map (**fig. 10.11**). The trend was toward the southwest, with the Beaverton area receiving the largest number of migrating industries, but there was also movement to the north, east, and southeast. During these years, 70 industries, with 9,400 employees, moved out of the central city. However, industries within the central cities continued to grow, but slowly.

TOURISM, RECREATION, AND RETIREMENT

Tourism, recreation, and retirement during the period from 1950 to 1978 were interrelated and difficult to separate. Together they rank third as a source of basic income in Oregon after wood products and agriculture. The same Oregon features—scenery, forests, parks, wild rivers, hunting, fishing, camping, and skiing—are of interest to tourists from outside the state as well as to Oregon residents. But hard facts about vacationers are hard to come by. It is estimated that the number of out-of-state tourists, traveling by automobile increased from 1,765,000 in 1955 to 3,331,000 in 1972.[25] Estimated tourist expenditures rose from $126 million to $370 million for the same period. As a measure of recreational participation by Oregon residents, 131,000 recreational vehicles were registered in Oregon in 1973, including campers, motor homes, travel trailers, and snowmobiles.

Still another measure of recreation is the use of state parks. In fiscal 1972–1973, the 160 developed state parks had 28 million day visitors and 1,770,000 camper nights. Most of the users of state parks are Oregonians; despite the addition to the camping facilities, the use is so heavy that reservations are necessary in summer. In recent years winter recreational activities have greatly increased and numerous ski lodges and resorts have been built in the Cascades, Siskiyous, and Blue Mountains.

A measure of retirement in Oregon is the number of persons over age 65, 226,000 in 1970, and their distribution throughout the state. It can be inferred that since about one-half of Oregon's population increase is from migration, a large share of the retirees are from outside the state. It should be noted also that a large proportion of the migrants are young people. Retired people are unequally distributed. The percentage is higher in cities and in a few special areas, notably along the coast, in southwestern Oregon, and in Deschutes County.

IMPACT ON THE LAND

The events and processes described above had a profound effect on the Oregon landscape, varying widely from region to region. Many of the changes have been gradual, scarcely noticeable from year to year, but, for the whole period, significant. The descriptions below are confined to what can be seen from the air, on the ground, or from airphotos. Obviously many subtle changes have occurred that cannot be seen or determined in a rapid overview, such as groundwater depletion, new property lines, underground pipelines, and cables. In chapter 2 the reader was taken on an imaginary flight over the state as an introduction to the major features, especially the natural landscape on which man has wrought so many changes. We will now repeat the flight described in chapter 2 (see **fig. 2.2**), to note some of the outstanding changes in the last 25 years.

In the Portland area, the spread to the suburbs is most striking. In 1950 the city was compact. Now the urbanized area extends beyond Vancouver, Washington, to the north; to the Sandy River on the east; beyond Oregon City to the south; and to Hillsboro on the west. In the center of the city, the high-rise buildings and the network of freeways and interchanges have transformed the landscape. To the south of Oregon City there is still the pleasing variety of pasture, cropland, and woodland, but the land use patterns have changed. There is more cropland in wheat and grass seed, and there are more irrigated fields. Here and there sprinklers are making dark, wet patches on the dry, brown fields. Looking closely we can see the effect of the decline of dairy farming; in some places only beef cattle are near the barns and silos.

Salem has spread beyond the old city limits of 1950, westward into Polk County, eastward and southward into the hills. Residential spread into the foothills was inevitable as the cities grew, but the cities have invaded the agricultural land also. In the southern part of the Willamette Valley, the checkerboard pattern of burning grass-stubble fields is visible, sending clouds of smoke into Eugene and sometimes into Corvallis and Salem, causing a bitter conflict between the farmers and the city people.

Continuing southward over Lane, Douglas, and Jackson counties, the most widespread change is the increased cut-over forest land. These counties have been the leading log producers for many years and the effects are apparent. A few areas have been burned over. On steep slopes erosion has occurred, especially on and near the logging roads. Also notable are the new U.S. Highway I-5 and the various developments along the way since 1950—filling stations, motels, restaurants, stores, and the very welcome rest stops with picnic facilities.

Turning westward over Josephine County we see the new state park on the Rogue River and, farther along, the new campsites and trails along the middle Rogue River to serve those tourists who hike or "run" this wild river. At Agness where the Illinois River joins the Rogue, numerous jet riverboats have replaced the single mail boat of 1950. Reaching the coast, we see the new jetties at Gold Beach, and turning southward for 30 miles we fly over the longest state park (Sam Boardman) and see the new harbor at Brookings. Much of the forest near the coast has been cut over since 1950 and many thousands of trees were blown down during the Columbus Day Storm of 1962. Hugging the steep shoreline is the new scenic route of U.S. Highway 101 with its many deep cuts and broad fills, open invitations to landslides.

Northward from Curry County, the highway in many places is relocated, straightened, and widened. But the changes that catch the eye are the subdivisions, developments, marinas, the improved Marine Biology Station and the marina at Charleston on Coos Bay, and an expanded marina at Winchester Bay on the Umpqua River. Although few changes have yet appeared between Coos Bay and Florence, most Oregonians know that the new Oregon Dunes National Recreation Area takes in the coast and adjacent dunes. At Newport the jetties and harbor have been expanded and improved and the Oceanographic Institute established. At many places along the coast new golf courses have been constructed, along with hotels, condominiums, residences, and improved marinas. Much of U.S. Highway 101 farther north, in the vicinity of Pacific City, has not been improved; it is still narrow and crooked, ill-suited to the heavy traffic. From Tillamook to Astoria the first section of the Oregon Coast Hiking Trail is now marked and open.

Much of Tillamook Head has been cut over recently, and 10 miles to the east, the Saddle Mountain area is only now beginning to show significant regrowth. It was cut and burned over more than 25 years ago. At Astoria, the chief new feature in the landscape is the long bridge across the Columbia River, giving this old and static city access to a larger hinterland. High tolls, however, have restricted the traffic on the bridge. East of Astoria, large dredges have kept the channel of the river open to ocean freighters. Of the towns along the river, only St. Helens has grown much recently and a part of that growth is the result of construction of the Trojan nuclear plant, a prime focus of conflict as the arguments for and against nuclear power continue.

East of Portland, on the way to Barlow Pass, the development of tourist facilities at Government Camp and the new ski lifts on the slopes of Mt. Hood testify to the great increase in recreational activity here. Turning southeastward, the Warm Springs Indian Reservation shows some changes, particularly the expanded resort facilities at the Springs and the cut-over timber land on the mountain slopes.

Crossing the Cascades to eastern Oregon, one is tempted to say that in the last 25 years this part of the state has changed little. It is true that in most of the eastern counties the population has been nearly static, so far as numbers are concerned, but looking at specific areas, it is evident that significant changes have occurred. In the first place irrigation has been expanded, thanks to new types of sprinklers. Also numerous promotional real estate developments have appeared, modern equivalents of the homesteads at the turn of the century. In the usual pattern a large tract of cheap land is acquired and subdivided, often by out-of-state promoters. Some projects emphasize recreation and retirement but others promise a livelihood by irrigation from wells. A representative development, which promised both recreation and profitable agriculture, is Christmas Lake Valley in northern Lake County. In the early 1900s this area was homesteaded, as was adjacent Fort Rock Valley, but almost none of the homesteads survived.[26] Too little water, the hazard of summer frosts, and the small size of the holdings contributed to the failures. In recent years development has included surveys, road building, and the construction of a lodge, a golf course, and an artificial lake. Water in varying amounts is available in wells at depths from 30 to 1,000 feet, but some wells have not yielded usable amounts of water. However, several tracts have been under irrigation for a few years with no appreciable lowering of the water table. Since the eight-inch annual rainfall is not sufficient to recharge the wells, it is assumed that water seeps in from adjacent areas. Nevertheless, the prospect for agriculture, in the long run, is dim; apparently the promotion now is based mostly on recreation.

Other developments concerned mostly with recreation, especially those near mountains, are on a firmer basis. Some promise the buyers rental income from their condominium units but there is usually no thought that the land and houses purchased or leased will provide a living. A few such developments have appeared in the vicinity of Bend in recent years.

Bend has grown little within the city limits, but in the vicinity new houses, housing developments, condominiums, and motels, related to the great expansion of skiing on Mt. Bachelor as well as to the increase in summer tourists, dot the margins of the Deschutes River south of the city. Southwest of Bend, there are increased numbers of recreational facilities—motels, summer cabins, new camps, and new roads—on the eastern slopes of the Cascades

from Sparks Lake and Bachelor Butte to Crescent Lake, most of them in the Deschutes National Forest. South of Crescent Lake, to and including Crater Lake National Park, changes are less apparent, and to the east of Crater Lake the termination of the large Klamath Indian Reservation has caused, as yet, little change. Some of the area is in the Fremont National Forest and in a wildlife refuge. The city of Klamath Falls has changed little but the outlying areas have grown. As lumber declined, irrigation expanded. Northeast of Klamath Falls the greatest change is in the cut-over land of the Fremont National Forest. Large quantities of timber were cut on the Indian reservation before it was abolished. Beyond Summer Lake the country is little populated and very little changed. Around Harney and Malheur lakes and along Donner und Blitzen River the wildlife refuge has been extended and the facilities improved.

In the Vale-Ontario-Nyssa areas of Malheur County irrigation has expanded with waters from the Owyhee, Malheur, and Snake rivers. Some of the large land holdings have been subdivided into small farms. Hay and sugar beets are still in evidence and a variety of fruits and vegetables have been added. To the north, at Farewell Bend, is the upper end of the 100-mile-long reservoir backed up by Brownlee Dam. Gone are the small ranches and mines along the Snake River, and the railroad branch line that formerly reached Robinette, the site of which was drowned by the reservoir. A new gravel road leads along the rim of the canyon. Ten miles below Brownlee Dam is the low Oxbow Dam, with a small, modern power plant. Twenty miles further downstream is Hells Canyon Dam in the upper part of Hells Canyon proper. All three dams, Brownlee, Oxbow, and Hells Canyon, are primarily for power with a limited function as flood control. The reservoirs are used for recreation, but the dams have been disastrous for the salmon run.

West of the Snake River is Wallowa County, where the chief changes have been increased cut-over land, especially in the "shoestring" forest areas, and expanded cropland, particularly for wheat and hay. In spite of this, the plateau seems to be almost deserted—abandoned houses and even an almost abandoned town, Flora. In northern Umatilla County, McNary Dam has created a new reservoir and the adjacent lowland has been transformed. This is naturally one of the driest areas in Oregon, but with irrigation from the Columbia River it has become very productive. Seventy miles downriver is John Day Dam, the construction of which made it necessary to move the town of Arlington to higher ground, with considerable improvement in its appearance.

Thirty miles below John Day Dam is The Dalles Dam, with its accompanying industrial development and urban growth. The Dalles population was 7,600 in 1950, more than 11,000 in 1978. At The Dalles the river enters the gorge, where, in the last 25 years, great improvements have been made to U.S. Highway I-80N, in difficult terrain.

In summary it can be said that the period from 1950 to 1978 produced few innovative changes in Oregon, but the changes formerly in process were accelerated. To be sure, nuclear power was new and one installation, the Trojan plant, had produced some power but not enough to affect the economy very much. Cities were beginning to sprawl before 1950, but shortly thereafter the spreading accelerated. The central core of the cities also grew vertically, as the price of land soared. Related to this growth was the expansion of freeways and their ramps, which came to dominate the margins of cities. There were a few power dams before 1950 but afterward more than 100 dams—federal, municipal, and private—together with their reservoirs and radiating power lines became prominent features.

The expansion of housing, high-rise apartments, ranch houses, condominiums, mobile homes, and trailers accompanied new life styles; but all the new housing units were scarcely equal to the demand of the growing population. As the period closed, the two most pressing questions were concerned with energy and the environment—how to find more sources of the first (nuclear, solar, and geothermal perhaps)—and how to save the second in spite of the growing pressure on Oregon's limited resources, especially in the light of the increasing demands of recreation.

NOTES

CHAPTER 1

1. Warren L. Cook, *Flood Tide of Empire: Spain and the Pacific Northwest, 1543-1819* (New Haven, 1973), ch. 1.
2. Cook, *Flood Tide of Empire*, p. 78.
3. For reproductions of early maps of Oregon see Carl Irving Wheat, *Mapping the Trans-Mississippi West, 1540-1861* (San Francisco, 1957-63), vols. 2, 3.
4. Charles O. Paullin, *Historical Atlas of the United States* (Washington, D.C., 1932), p. 14, plate 28.
5. Meriwether Lewis and William Clark, *Original Journals of the Lewis and Clark Expedition, 1804-1806*, ed. Reuben G. Thwaites (New York, 1904-05), 3:319, 323, 324.
6. David Douglas, *Journal Kept by David Douglas during His Travels in North America, 1823-1827* (London, 1914), p. 62.
7. John C. Frémont, *Narrative of the Exploring Expedition to the Rocky Mountains in the Year 1842, and to Oregon and North California in the Years 1843-1844* (London, 1846), p. 213.
8. Peter Skene Ogden, *Peter Skene Ogden's Snake Country Journal 1826-27*, ed. K. G. Davies, Hudson's Bay Record Society, vol. 23 (London, 1961), pp. 70, 83.
9. Ogden, *Snake Country Journal*, pp. lxi, lxii.
10. Harrison C. Dale, ed., *The Ashley-Smith Explorations and the Discovery of a Central Route to the Pacific, 1822-1829*, rev. ed. (Glendale, Calif., 1941), pp. 264-70.
11. U.S., Congress, Senate, *Congressional Record*, 10th Cong., 2nd sess., 1828-29. Quoted in D. W. Meinig, *The Great Columbia Plain* (Seattle, 1968), p. 96.
12. U.S., Congress, House, *Annals of Congress*, 16th Cong., 2nd sess., 1821, pp. 958-59. See also 17th Cong., 2nd sess., 1823, pp. 396-409. Quoted in Archer B. Hulbert, *Where Rolls the Oregon: Overland to the Pacific* (Denver, 1933), pp. 45-54.
13. Samuel Parker, *An Exploring Tour beyond the Rocky Mountains in North America* (Dublin, 1840), p. 131.
14. Daniel Lee and J. H. Frost, *Ten Years in Oregon* (New York, 1844), pp. 96-97.
15. Harvey Kimball Hines, *Missionary History of the Pacific Northwest* (Portland, 1899), p. 225. Quoted in Charles H. Carey, *History of Oregon*, author's ed. (Chicago and Portland, 1922), p. 340.
16. Lansford W. Hastings, *The Emigrants' Guide to Oregon and California* (1845; reprint ed., Princeton, N.J., 1932), pp. 43, 46.
17. Zebulon Pike, *The Expeditions of Zebulon Montgomery Pike*, ed. Elliott Coues (New York, 1895), 2:525.
18. Eugène Duflot de Mofras, *Exploration du territoire de l'Orégon, des Californies, et de la mer Vermeille, exécutée pendant les années 1840, 1841, et 1842* (Paris, 1844), 2:247 (author's translation).
19. Samuel Bowles, *Across the Continent* (New York, 1845), pp. 169, 178.
20. James Neall, *A Down-Easterner in the Far West*, ed. Martin Schmitt and K. Keith Richard (Ashland, Ore., 1977), p. 69.
21. U.S., Congress, House, *Report of Lieut. Neil M. Howison, United States Navy, to the Commander of the Pacific Squadron; Being the result of an examination in the year 1846 of the coast, harbors, rivers, soil, productions, climate, and population of the Territory of Oregon*, by Neil M. Howison, 30th Cong., 1st sess., 1848, H. Misc. Doc. 29. Also published in *Oregon Historical Quarterly* 14 (March 1913): 55-56.
22. Peter H. Burnett, *Recollections and Opinions of an Old Pioneer* (New York, 1880), pp. 180-81.
23. Lewis A. McArthur and Lewis L. McArthur, *Oregon Geographic Names*, 4th ed. (Portland, 1974).
24. Hulbert, *Where Rolls the Oregon*, pp. 160-61.
25. David Newsom, *David Newsom: The Western Observer, 1805-1882* (Portland, 1972), pp. 43, 44, 59, 60.

CHAPTER 3

1. Carl Johannessen et al., "The Vegetation of the Willamette Valley," *Annals of the Association of American Geographers* 61 (June 1971): 286–302.
2. Carl O. Sauer, "A Geographical Sketch of Early Man in America," *Geographical Review* 34 (1944): 529–73.
3. David Douglas, *Journal Kept by David Douglas during His Travels in North America, 1823–1827* (London, 1914), pp. 214–15.
4. Nellie B. Pipes, ed., "Journal of John H. Frost, 1840–43," *Oregon Historical Quarterly* 35 (1934): 260.
5. Warren N. Vaughan, "Journal, 1851–1854," Ms. no. 213:3, Oregon Historical Society, Portland, Ore.
6. Harrison C. Dale, ed., *The Ashley-Smith Explorations and the Discovery of a Central Route to the Pacific, 1822–1829*, rev. ed. (Glendale, Calif., 1941), p. 275.
7. Meriwether Lewis and William Clark, *Original Journals of the Lewis and Clark Expedition, 1804–1806*, ed. Reuben G. Thwaites (New York, 1904–05), 5:133, 311, 312.
8. Charles Wilkes, *Narrative of the United States Exploring Expedition* (Philadelphia, 1845), 5:141.
9. L. S. Cressman, *The Sandal and the Cave: The Indians of Oregon* (Portland, 1962), pp. 40–54. See also A. L. Kroeber, *Cultural and Natural Areas of North America* (Berkeley, 1939), pp. 28–29.
10. Lewis and Clark, *Original Journals*, 3:194. See also Paul Kane, "The Chinook Indians, 1846–1847," in *The Columbia Wanderer, 1846–1847*, ed. Thomas Vaughan (Portland, 1971), pp. 31–33.
11. Lewis and Clark, *Original Journals*, 3:347.
12. Cressman, *The Sandal and the Cave*, pp. 32–33. See also Thomas M. Newman, "Native Peoples and Shelters," in *Space, Style and Structure*, ed. Thomas Vaughan and Virginia Guest Ferriday (Portland, 1974), pp. 5–29.
13. Cressman, *The Sandal and the Cave*, p. 42.
14. Joel V. Berreman, *Tribal Distribution in Oregon*, American Anthropological Association Memoir no. 47 (Menasha, Wis., 1937), p. 55. See also F. W. Hodge, *Handbook of the American Indians North of Mexico* (Washington, D.C., 1907–10); William G. Loy, *The Atlas of Oregon* (Eugene, Ore., 1976), pp. 6, 7.
15. Berreman, *Tribal Distribution*, p. 57.
16. Verne F. Ray, "The Chinook Indians in the Early 1800s," in *The Western Shore*, ed. Thomas Vaughan (Portland, 1975), pp. 166, 167.
17. Elsie Frances Dennis, "Indian Slavery in the Pacific Northwest," *Oregon Historical Quarterly* 31 (1930): 68–81, 181–95, 285–96.
18. Berreman, *Tribal Distribution*, p. 64.
19. Samuel N. Dicken, "Oregon Geography before White Settlement, 1770–1840," in Vaughan, *The Western Shore*, p. 15.

CHAPTER 4

1. Warren L. Cook, *Flood Tide of Empire: Spain and the Pacific Northwest, 1543–1819* (New Haven, 1973), pp. 31–32.
2. Meriwether Lewis and William Clark, *Original Journals of the Lewis and Clark Expedition, 1804–1806*, ed. Reuben G. Thwaites (New York, 1904–05), 3:301.
3. James Cook, *The Journals of Captain James Cook on His Voyages of Discovery: The Voyage of the Resolution and Discovery, 1776–1780*, ed. J. C. Beaglehole (Cambridge, Eng., 1967), pt. 1, p. 289.
4. George Vancouver, *A Voyage of Discovery to the North Pacific Ocean* (London, 1798), vol. 1, bk. 2, ch. 3, p. 209.
5. "John Boit's Log of the Columbia—1790–1793," *Oregon Historical Quarterly* 22 (1921): 309.
6. J. N. Barry, "Columbia River Exploration, 1792," *Oregon Historical Quarterly* 33 (1932): 31–42, 143–55.
7. Julian P. Boyd, ed., *The Papers of Thomas Jefferson* (Princeton, N.J., 1952), 6:204–206. See also Charles H. Carey, *History of Oregon*, author's ed. (Chicago and Portland, 1922), pp. 163–64.
8. Donald Jackson, ed., *Letters of the Lewis and Clark Expedition, 1783–1854* (Urbana, Ill., 1962), pp. 669–72.
9. H. A. Washington, ed., *The Works of Thomas Jefferson* (New York, 1884), 4:516.
10. From a letter to Nemesio Salcedo from Casa Calvo, New Orleans, March 5, 1804. Quoted in Cook, *Flood Tide of Empire*, p. 455. See also James Ripley Jacobs, *Tarnished Warrior: Major-General James Wilkinson* (New York, 1938), pp. 205–206.
11. Lewis and Clark, *Original Journals*, vols. 3 and 4.
12. Paul R. Cutright, *Lewis and Clark, Pioneering Naturalists* (Urbana, Ill., 1969). See also Raymond D. Burroughs, ed., *The Natural History of the Lewis and Clark Expedition* (East Lansing, Mich., 1961).
13. Gabriel Franchère, *Narrative of a Voyage to the Northwest Coast of America in the Years 1811, 1812, 1813, and 1814*, ed. and trans. J. V. Huntington (New York, 1854), p. 102. See also Washington Irving, *Astoria*, Holly ed. (London, 1895), 1:110–26.
14. P. A. Rollins, *The Discovery of the Oregon Trail* (New York, 1935), pp. 197–239.
15. Peter Skene Ogden, *Peter Skene Ogden's Snake Country Journal 1826–27*, ed. K. G. Davies, Hudson's Bay Record Society, vol. 23 (London, 1961), pp. lvii–lxi, 143–63.
16. Ogden, *Snake Country Journal*, pp. lix–lxiii.
17. David Douglas, *Journal Kept by David Douglas during His Travels in North America, 1823–1827* (London, 1914), pp. 56–59.
18. Ogden, *Snake Country Journal*, pp. 69–107.
19. Harrison C. Dale, ed., *The Ashley-Smith Explorations and the Discovery of a Central Route to*

the *Pacific, 1822–1829*, rev. ed. (Glendale, Calif., 1941), pp. 265–80.

20. Ogden, *Snake Country Journal*, pp. xxvi, 20, 21, 24–27, 33, 116.
21. Douglas, *Journal*, pp. 189–95.
22. Washington Irving, *The Adventures of Captain Bonneville* (London, 1837), 2:220–21.
23. Carl I. Wheat, *Mapping the Trans-Mississippi West, 1540–1861* (San Francisco, 1957–63). In volumes 1 and 2 many old maps of Oregon are reproduced with commentary. See especially 2:80, 146, 159, 165–68, 178, 194–96.

CHAPTER 5

1. Samuel N. Dicken, *Pioneer Trails of the Oregon Coast* (Portland, 1971), p. 7.
2. Charles Wilkes, *Narrative of the United States Exploring Expedition* (Philadelphia, 1845), 4:141, 292, 296, 306.
3. Nellie B. Pipes, ed., "Journal of John H. Frost, 1840–43," *Oregon Historical Quarterly* 35 (1934): 235–62, 348–56.
4. John C. Frémont, *Memoirs of My Life* (Chicago, 1887), pp. 255ff.
5. U.S., Congress, House, *Report of Lieut. Neil M. Howison, United States Navy, to the Commander of the Pacific Squadron; Being the result of an examination in the year 1846 of the coast, harbors, rivers, soil, productions, climate, and population of the Territory of Oregon*, by Neil M. Howison, 30th Cong., 1st sess., 1848, H. Misc. Doc. 29, pp. 23–25. This document is cited below as Howison, *Report*. Also published in *Oregon Historical Quarterly* 14 (1913): 1–60.
6. William A. Bowen, "The Oregon Frontiersman: A Demographic View," in *The Western Shore*, ed. Thomas Vaughan (Portland, 1975), p. 184. See also William A. Bowen, *Willamette Valley: Migration and Settlement on the Oregon Frontier* (Seattle, 1978).
7. Peter Burnett, *Recollections and Opinions of an Old Pioneer* (New York, 1880), pp. 97–98. See also *Oregon Historical Quarterly* 5 (1904): 64–65.
8. Charles H. Carey, *History of Oregon*, author's ed. (Chicago and Portland, 1922), pp. 324–56. See also Daniel Lee and J. H. Frost, *Ten Years in Oregon* (New York, 1844); and D. W. Meinig, *The Great Columbia Plain* (Seattle, 1968), pp. 125–51.
9. Carey, *History of Oregon*, pp. 420–21.
10. Carey, *History of Oregon*, pp. 435ff.
11. Keith Clark and Lowell Tiller, *Terrible Trail: The Meek Cutoff, 1845* (Caldwell, Idaho, 1966), pp. 95, 122–32.
12. Burnett, *Recollections*, p. 175.
13. Howison, *Report*, p. 28.
14. Hubert H. Bancroft, *History of Oregon* (San Francisco, 1886–88), 2:39. See also A. J. Allen, *Ten Years in Oregon: Travels and Adventures of Doctor E. White and Lady, West of the Rocky Mountains* (Ithaca, N.Y., 1848), p. 220.
15. O. B. Sperlin, "The Indian of the Northwest as Revealed by the Earliest Journals," *Oregon Historical Quarterly* 17 (1916): 1–38.
16. Carey, *History of Oregon*, pp. 788–95. See also William G. Loy, *The Atlas of Oregon* (Eugene, Ore., 1976), pp. 42, 43.
17. Charles L. Camp, *James Clyman: Frontiersman*, 2nd ed. (Portland, 1960), pp. 136–37.
18. Theodore Talbot, *The Journals of Theodore Talbot, 1843 and 1849–52* (Portland, 1931), pp. 88, 133. See also Randall V. Mills, *Stern-wheelers Up Columbia* (Palo Alto, Calif., 1947), p. 13.
19. Bancroft, *History of Oregon*, 2:28.
20. Bancroft, *History of Oregon*, 1:531–33.
21. Carey, *History of Oregon*, p. 682.
22. Robert J. Loewenberg, *Equality on the Oregon Frontier: Jason Lee and the Methodist Mission, 1834–43* (Seattle, 1976), pp. 14–35, 195–228.
23. Dorothy O. Johansen, "The Role of Land Laws in the Settlement of Oregon," in Genealogical Forum (Portland), *Genealogical Material in Oregon Donation Land Claims* (Portland, 1957), vol. 1, unpaged.
24. Bancroft, *History of Oregon*, 2:42–52.
25. U.S., Dept. of the Interior, Census Office, *Seventh Census of the United States, 1850: Statistics of the Territories* (Washington, D.C., 1853), pp. 988–1013.
26. William A. Bowen, "Mapping an American Frontier: Oregon, 1850," *Annals of the Association of American Geographers*, Map Supplement no. 18 (March 1975).
27. Howard M. Corning, *Willamette Landings*, 2nd ed. (Portland, 1973), pp. 7–16. See also Eugene E. Snyder, *Early Portland: Stump-Town Triumphant; Rival Towns on the Willamette, 1831–1854* (Portland, 1970), pp. 18–35; and Howison, *Report*, p. 24.
28. Samuel N. Dicken, "Oregon Geography before White Settlement, 1770–1840," in Vaughan, *The Western Shore*, p. 25.
29. Bancroft, *History of Oregon*, 2:41.

CHAPTER 6

1. F. G. Young, "The Oregon Trail," *Oregon Historical Quarterly* 1 (1900): 370.
2. Howard C. Brooks and Len Ramp, *Gold and Silver in Oregon* (Portland, 1968), Oregon Dept. of Geology and Mineral Industries Bulletin 61, pp. 45–69, 165–69.
3. Harvey W. Scott, *History of the Oregon Country* (Cambridge, Mass., 1924), 1:332; Verne Bright, "Blue Mountain Eldoradoes: Auburn, 1861," *Oregon Historical Quarterly* 62 (1961): 216ff.
4. Brooks and Ramp, *Gold and Silver*, p. 8.
5. Brooks and Ramp, *Gold and Silver*, p. 167.
6. Brooks and Ramp, *Gold and Silver*, p. 43.
7. Brooks and Ramp, *Gold and Silver*, pp. 8, 9; Ar-

thur L. Throckmorton, *Oregon Argonauts* (Portland, 1961), pp. 275–76.

8. Charles H. Carey, *History of Oregon*, author's ed. (Chicago and Portland, 1922), pp. 658ff; Glenn T. Edwards, Jr., "Oregon Regiments in the Civil War Years: Duty on the Indian Frontier" (M.A. thesis, University of Oregon, 1960).

9. Gunther P. Barth, ed., *All Quiet on the Yamhill: The Civil War in Oregon: The Journal of Corporal Royal A. Bensell* (Eugene, Ore., 1959), pp. 183–84.

10. U.S., Dept. of the Interior, Census Office, *Ninth Census of the United States, 1870* (Washington, D.C., 1872), 1:241–43.

11. Donald G. Holtgrieve, "Historical Geography of Transportation Routes and Town Populations in Oregon's Willamette Valley" (Ph.D. diss., University of Oregon, 1973), pp. 74–80.

12. Carey, *History of Oregon*, pp. 788–888.

13. David Newsom, *David Newsom: The Western Observer, 1805–1882* (Portland, 1972), p. 66.

14. Pacific Northwest River Basin Commission, *Climatological Handbook, Columbia Basin States* (Vancouver, Wash., 1968, 1969), 1:8, 2:3.

15. *Ninth Census, 1870,* 2:720–21.

16. Hubert H. Bancroft, *History of Oregon* (San Francisco, 1886–88), 2:726–29.

17. Bancroft, *History of Oregon*, 2:733–34; Mary Goodall, *Oregon's Iron Dream* (Portland, 1958), pp. 43ff.

18. Alfred L. Lomax, *Pioneer Woolen Mills in Oregon* (Portland, 1941), pp. 97ff. See also his *Later Woolen Mills in Oregon* (Portland, 1974).

19. Bancroft, *History of Oregon*, 2:483.

20. Holtgrieve, "Historical Goegraphy," pp. 35–74. See also Randall V. Mills, *Stern-wheelers Up Columbia* (Palo Alto, Calif., 1947), pp. 29–66, 94–97; and Howard M. Corning, *Willamette Landings: Ghost Towns of the River* (Portland, 1947), pp. 24–25.

21. Holtgrieve, "Historical Geography," pp. 74–80; Bancroft, *History of Oregon*, 1:531–32.

22. Carey, *History of Oregon*, pp. 443, 512–513, 534, 682, 813.

23. W. Turrentine Jackson, "Federal Road Building Grants for Early Oregon," *Oregon Historical Quarterly* 50 (1949): 2–29; Robert Carlton Clark, "Military History of Oregon," *Oregon Historical Quarterly* 36 (1935): 53, 54.

24. Quoted in Mary S. Barlow, "History of the Barlow Road," *Oregon Historical Quarterly* 3 (1902): 79–80.

25. Scott, *History*, 3:182–86.

26. Scott, *History*, 3:187–88.

27. Harlow Z. Head, "The Oregon Donation Land Claims and Their Patterns" (Ph.D. diss., University of Oregon, 1971), pp. 9–12, 19–20; William G. Loy, *The Atlas of Oregon* (Eugene, Ore., 1976), pp. 8–9.

28. Bancroft, *History of Oregon*, 2:247–50, 268–75.

29. Head, "Oregon Donation Land Claims," p. 75.

30. George Davidson, *The Coast Pilot of California,*

Oregon, and Washington (Washington, D.C., 1869). See also subsequent editions, especially 1889.

CHAPTER 7

1. U.S., Dept. of the Interior, Census Office, *Twelfth Census of the United States, 1900* (Washington, D.C., 1901–02), vol. 1, pt. 1, p. 36.

2. Charles H. Carey, *History of Oregon*, author's ed. (Chicago and Portland, 1922), p. 828.

3. Hubert H. Bancroft, *History of Oregon* (San Francisco, 1886–88), 2:558.

4. U.S., Congress, Senate, *Reports of Explorations and Surveys to Ascertain the Most Practicable and Economical Route for a Railroad from the Mississippi River to the Pacific Ocean,* 33rd Cong., 2nd sess., 1855, S. Ex. Doc. 78, vol. 1, ch. 1; also 6:37–55.

5. *Reports of Explorations and Surveys,* 6:48.

6. Bancroft, *History of Oregon*, 2:697.

7. Carey, *History of Oregon*, p. 688.

8. William G. Loy, *The Atlas of Oregon* (Eugene, Ore., 1976), pp. 10–11, 84–85.

9. Randall V. Mills, *Railroads down the Valleys* (Palo Alto, Calif., 1950), pp. 32–70; also Richard L. Price, *Newport, Oregon, 1866–1936* (Newport, Ore., 1975), pp. 15–20.

10. Donald G. Holtgrieve, "The Effects of the Railroads on Small Town Population Changes: Linn County, Oregon," *Yearbook of the Association of Pacific Coast Geographers* 35 (Corvallis, Ore., 1973): 87–102.

11. Harold L. Throckmorton, "The Interurbans of Portland, Oregon, a Historical Geography" (M.A. thesis, University of Oregon, 1962), p. 22.

12. Carey, *History of Oregon*, p. 780.

13. W. Turrentine Jackson, "Federal Road Building Grants for Early Oregon," *Oregon Historical Quarterly* 50 (1949): 11–23.

14. Carey, *History of Oregon*, p. 803.

15. *Twelfth Census, 1900,* vol. 6, pt. 2, pp. 855–57.

16. J. Orin Oliphant, *On the Cattle Ranges of the Oregon Country* (Seattle, 1968).

17. David Newsom, *David Newsom: The Western Observer, 1805–1882* (Portland, 1972), pp. 237–39.

18. Carey, *History of Oregon*, p. 410. See also Bancroft, *History of Oregon*, 2:730–31.

19. Howard C. Brooks and Len Ramp, *Gold and Silver in Oregon* (Portland, 1968), Oregon Dept. of Geology and Mineral Industries Bulletin 61, p. 36.

20. J. E. Allen and E. M. Baldwin, *Geology and Coal Resources of the Coos Bay Quadrangle, Oregon* (Portland, 1944), Oregon Dept. of Geology and Mineral Industries Bulletin 27, pp. 51–62.

21. *Twelfth Census, 1900,* vol. 8, pt. 2, pp. 732–41.

22. Carey, *History of Oregon*, p. 856.

23. *Twelfth Census, 1900,* vol. 8, pt. 2, pp. 732–41.

24. Bancroft, *History of Oregon*, 2:745.
25. *Twelfth Census, 1900*, vol. 8, pt. 2, pp. 732–41.

CHAPTER 8

1. *Oregon Blue Book, 1975–1976* (Salem, Ore.), p. 125.
2. U.S., Dept. of Commerce, Bureau of the Census, *Fifteenth Census of the United States, 1930* (Washington, D.C., 1932), vol. 3, pt. 2, p. 609.
3. Jerry A. O'Callaghan, *The Disposition of the Public Domain in Oregon*, 86th Cong., 2nd sess., printed for the use of the Senate Committee on Interior and Insular Affairs (Washington, D.C., 1960), pp. 97–101. See also Dorothy O. Johansen, *Empire of the Columbia*, 2nd ed. (New York, 1967), pp. 373–74; and Phil F. Brogan, *East of the Cascades* (Portland, 1964), pp. 84, 85, 93, 94, 96.
4. Quoted on O'Callaghan, *Disposition*, p. 16.
5. Oregon State Board of Agriculture, *The Resources of the State of Oregon*, 3rd rev. ed. (Salem, Ore., 1898), p. 166.
6. Hugh M. Hoyt, Jr., "The Good Roads Movement in Oregon, 1900–1920" (Ph.D. diss., University of Oregon, 1966), pp. 48ff.
7. Quoted in *Oregon Historical Quarterly* 74 (1973): 350–51.
8. Isaiah Bowman, *The Pioneer Fringe* (New York, 1931), p. 102.
9. Oregon State Highway Commission, *State of Oregon Showing Proposed System of State Roads* (Salem, Ore., 1914).
10. Oregon State Highway Commission, *Highway Plan Map* (Salem, Ore., 1918).
11. Rand McNally and Co., *Auto Road Atlas of the United States, 1926*, reprint ed. (Chicago, 1974); William G. Loy, *The Atlas of Oregon* (Eugene, Ore., 1976), pp. 80–81.
12. Oregon State Highway Commission, *Highway Map of Oregon, 1918* (Salem, Ore., 1918).
13. Oregon State Highway Commission, *Highway Map of Oregon, 1930* (Salem, Ore., 1930).
14. Randall V. Mills, "A History of Transportation in the Pacific Northwest," *Oregon Historical Quarterly* 47 (1946): 281–301. The author is indebted to Donald T. Smith and Gilbert Hulin for specific information on Oregon's railroads.
15. Randall V. Mills, "Early Electric Interurbans in Oregon," *Oregon Historical Quarterly* 44 (1943): 386–96.
16. Harold L. Throckmorton, "The Interurbans of Portland, Oregon, a Historical Geography" (M.A. thesis, University of Oregon, 1962), pp. 22–127.
17. U.S., Dept. of the Interior, U.S. Geological Survey, *Index to the Topographic Maps of Oregon* (Washington, D.C., 1928). See later issues for later maps.
18. Johansen, *Empire*, pp. 375–76.
19. Johansen, *Empire*, pp. 384–98. See also O'Callaghan, *Disposition*, pp. 17–18.
20. *Fifteenth Census, 1930*, vol. 2, pt. 3, pp. 490–92.
21. *Fifteenth Census, 1930*, vol. 2, pt. 3, pp. 490–91.
22. Federal Cooperative Extension Service, *Oregon's First Century of Farming* (Corvallis, Ore., 1959), pp. 27–33; Dale C. Eggleston, "Harney County: Some Aspects of Sequent Occupancy and Land Use" (M.A. thesis, University of Oregon, 1970); Peter K. Simpson, "A Social History of the Cattle Industry of Southeastern Oregon" (Ph.D. diss., University of Oregon, 1973).
23. Johansen, *Empire*, pp. 405–408.
24. Howard C. Brooks and Len Ramp, *Gold and Silver in Oregon* (Portland, 1968), Oregon Dept. of Geology and Mineral Industries Bulletin 61, p. 10.
25. Warren D. Smith, ed., *Physical and Economic Geography of Oregon* (Salem, Ore.: Oregon State Board of Higher Education, 1940), p. 235. See also U.S., Dept. of Commerce, Bureau of Mines, *Mineral Resources of the United States*, pt. 2 (Washington, D.C., 1930), pp. 112ff.
26. Smith, *Physical and Economic Geography*, p. 258.
27. Smith, *Physical and Economic Geography*, pp. 224–26.
28. Johansen, *Empire*, p. 402.
29. Charles H. Carey, *History of Oregon*, author's ed. (Chicago and Portland, 1922) p. 694.
30. *Fifteenth Census, 1930*, 3:438.
31. Smith, *Physical and Economic Geography*, p. 264.

CHAPTER 9

1. U.S., Dept. of Commerce, Bureau of the Census, *Sixteenth Census of the United States, 1940: Population* (Washington, D.C., 1943), vol. 2, pt. 5, pp. 963ff.
2. Malcolm Clark, Jr., "The Second Hundred Years," in *The Western Shore*, ed. Thomas Vaughan (Portland, 1975), p. 305.
3. Otis W. Freeman and Howard M. Martin, eds., *The Pacific Northwest*, 2nd ed. (New York, 1954), p. 451.
4. George McMath, "Buildings and Gardens," in *Space, Style and Structure*, ed. Thomas Vaughan and Virginia Guest Ferriday (Portland, 1974), 2:484–85.
5. *Sixteenth Census, 1940: Population*, vol. 2, pt. 5, pp. 963ff.
6. Donald G. Holtgrieve, "Historical Geography of Transportation Routes and Town Populations in Oregon's Willamette Valley" (Ph.D. diss., University of Oregon, 1973), pp. 148–49, 186.
7. *Oregon Blue Book, 1930–1940* (Salem, Ore.), p. 235.
8. Oregon State Highway Commission, *Casual and Factual Glimpses at the Beginning and Development of Oregon's Roads and Highways* (Salem, Ore., 1950), p. 62.
9. Kenneth A. Ericksen, "Morphology of Lumber

Settlement in Oregon and Washington" (Ph.D. diss., University of California, Berkeley, 1965), p. 315.

10. Warren D. Smith, ed., *Physical and Economic Geography of Oregon* (Salem, Ore.: Oregon State Board of Higher Education, 1940), p. 282.

11. Elisabeth Walton, "Auto Accommodations," in Vaughan and Ferriday, *Space, Style and Structure*, 2:518–41.

12. Smith, *Physical and Economic Geography*, pp. 183–284.

13. Federal Cooperative Extension Service, *Oregon's First Century of Farming* (Corvallis, Ore., 1959), pp. 37–97.

14. U.S., Dept. of Commerce, Bureau of the Census, *Fifteenth Census of the United States, 1930: Agriculture* (Washington, D.C., 1932), vol. 2, pt. 3, pp. 474, 476. See also U.S., Dept. of Commerce, Bureau of the Census, *Census of Agriculture, 1950* (Washington, D.C., 1952), vol. 1, pt. 32, pp. 270–74.

15. Freeman and Martin, *Pacific Northwest*, p. 193. See also Smith, *Physical and Economic Geography*, p. 218.

16. U.S., Dept. of the Interior, Bureau of Mines, *Minerals Yearbook, 1950* (Washington, D.C., 1953), vol. 1, pp. 568, 571.

17. Richard M. Highsmith, ed., *Atlas of the Pacific Northwest* (Corvallis, Ore., 1953), plate 46.

18. U.S., Dept. of Commerce, Bureau of the Census, *Census of Manufactures, 1954* (Washington, D.C., 1957), vol. 3, sec. 136, pp. 5–8. See also *Fifteenth Census, 1930: Manufactures* (Washington, D.C., 1933), vol. 3, pp. 437–38; and *Sixteenth Census, 1940: Manufactures, 1939* (Washington, D.C., 1942), vol. 3, pp. 848–51.

CHAPTER 10

1. Wallace Kay Huntington, "Parks and Gardens of Western Oregon," in *Space, Style and Structure*, ed. Thomas Vaughan and Virginia Guest Ferriday (Portland, 1974), 2:684; William G. Loy, *The Atlas of Oregon* (Eugene, Ore., 1976), pp. 46–55.

2. U.S. Dept. of Commerce, Bureau of the Census, *Characteristics of the Population* (Washington, D.C., 1973), vol. 1, pt. 39, Oregon, pp. 39–45.

3. *Eugene Register-Guard*, 16 December 1975, p. 15A.

4. Bureau of Governmental Research and Service, University of Oregon, *1940–1970 Population and Housing Trends, Cities and Counties of Oregon* (Eugene, Ore., 1971), pp. 58–77.

5. Vaughan and Ferriday, *Space, Style and Structure*, especially 2:548, 552, 628–72, 684–705.

6. Steven W. Belcher, *Oregon's Mobile Homes: Housing by Any Other Name* (Boulder, Colo., 1974), pp. 7–9, 70–72.

7. U.S., Dept. of the Interior, Bonneville Power Administration, *The Electric Energy Picture in the Pacific Northwest* (Portland, 1971), pp. 7–11;

Loy, *Atlas of Oregon*, pp. 74–79.

8. Edwin J. Cohn, Jr., *Industry in the Pacific Northwest and the Location Theory* (New York, 1954), pp. 109–10.

9. Donald A. Hull and V. C. Newton, Jr., "Geothermal Activity in 1975," *The Ore Bin* (Oregon Dept. of Geology and Mineral Industries), vol. 38, no. 1 (January 1976): 10–17.

10. Barry Commoner, "Energy," *New Yorker*, 9 February 1976, pp. 55–77.

11. *Oregon Blue Book, 1975–1976* (Salem, Ore.), p. 125; Loy, *Atlas of Oregon*, pp. 80–89.

12. U.S., Dept. of Agriculture, Pacific Northwest Forest and Range Experiment Station, *1973 Oregon Timber Harvest* (Portland, 1974), U.S.D.A. Forest Service Resource Bulletin PNW–55; see also Bureau of Business Research, University of Oregon, *Oregon Economic Statistics, 1975* (Eugene, Ore., 1975) p. 80.

13. Robert E. Wolf, *The Douglas Fir Region Timber Supply Situation and Log Export Regulation as Proposed by H.R. 5544* (Washington, D.C.: Library of Congress, Congressional Research Service, 1975). See also U.S., Dept. of Agriculture, Pacific Northwest Forest and Range Experiment Station, *Timber Resource Statistics for Oregon*, by Patricia M. Bassett and Grover A. Choate (Portland, 1974), U.S.D.A. Forest Service Resource Bulletin PNW–56; and John H. Beuter, K. Norman Johnson, and H. Lynn Scheurman, *Timber for Oregon's Tomorrow* (Corvallis, Ore., 1976), Forest Research Laboratory, Oregon State University, Research Bulletin 19.

14. U.S., Dept. of Commerce, Bureau of the Census, *Census of Agriculture, 1969* (Washington, D.C., 1972), vol. 1, pt. 47, sec. 1, p. 2. Or see Bureau of Business Research, *Oregon Economic Statistics, 1975*, p. 71; U.S., Dept. of Commerce, Bureau of the Census, *Census of Agriculture, 1974* (Washington, D.C., 1977), vol. 1, pt. 37, ch. 1, table 10.

15. Everett G. Smith, Jr., "Fragmented Farms in the United States," *Annals of the Association of American Geographers* 65 (March 1975): 59–60.

16. *Census of Agriculture, 1969*, vol. 1, pt. 47, sec. 2, p. 2. See also U.S., Dept. of Commerce, Bureau of the Census, *Census of Agriculture, 1950* (Washington, D.C., 1952), vol. 1, pt. 32, p. 281.

17. Bernd H. Künnecke, *Distribution of Irrigation in Eastern Oregon* (Corvallis, Ore.: Water Resources Institute, 1974), table 4, p. 6. See also Loy, *Atlas of Oregon*, pp. 66, 67.

18. *Oregon Blue Book, 1975–1976*, p. 160.

19. Ralph S. Mason, "Oregon's Mineral and Metallurgical Industry in 1975," *The Ore Bin* 38, no. 1 (January 1976): 1–3.

20. Ralph S. Mason, "Oregon's Mineral and Metallurgical Industry in 1973," *The Ore Bin* 36, no. 1 (January 1974): 3. See also Standley L. Ausmus, "Mined Land Reclamation," *The Ore Bin* 38, no. 1 (January 1976): 3–5.

21. V. C. Newton, Jr., "Oil and Gas Exploration in

1974," *The Ore Bin* 37, no. 1 (January 1975): 4–7.

22. U.S., Dept. of Commerce, Bureau of the Census, *Census of Manufactures, 1972* (Washington, D.C., 1975), vol. 3, pt. 2, sec. 38, pp. 3, 7–10. See also U.S., Dept. of Commerce, Bureau of the Census, *Census of Manufactures, 1947* (Washington, D.C., 1950), vol. 3, p. 504.

23. *Census of Manufactures, 1972*, vol. 3, pt. 2, sec. 38, pp. 12–15; Loy, *Atlas of Oregon*, p. 92.

24. Jack D. Lesch and Thomas J. Maresh, "Industrial Suburbanization in Portland, Oregon," *Oregon Business Review* 30 (August 1971): 1–5.

25. Bureau of Business Research, *Oregon Economic Statistics, 1975*, p. 69.

26. James S. Buckles, "The Historical Geography of Fort Rock Valley" (M.A. thesis, University of Oregon, 1959).

INDEX

d=diagram; m=map; $o.f.$=overflight; p=photograph; t=table

Abert, John J., 11, 62, 63
Abert Lake, 28o.f., 29p
Abert Rim, 28o.f., 29p
Abiqua Creek, 12
Across the Continent (Bowles), 11
Adams Point, 49m, 53m
Aerial photography, 14, 161-62, 163p
Agency Lake, 28o.f.
Agriculture, 12, 75-77, 156, 164t, 165m
　development, 92-93, 117-25, 145-51, 182-83
　farms, 164, 165, 182, 182m
　methods & machinery, 83, 119-21, 135, 139, 146-47
Albacore, 166
Albany, 18o.f., 94, 99, 111, 118, 144
　population, 92, 159
Alfalfa, 150
Allegany, 96
Almota Landing, 76p
Alsea Bay, 24o.f.
Alsea Indians, 42m
Alsea River, 55
Al Serena mine, 88
Aluminum, 167
American Bottom, 82
"American West," 8, 13
Amity, 144
Ankeny Bottom, 82
Annie Faxton (steamer), 76p
Antimony, 127
Applegate, Jesse, 72, 111
Applegate, Lindsay, 78
Applegate River, 56, 86
Applegate Trail, 84, 96, 115
Apples, 117
Arago, Cape, 22o.f.
Architecture, 174
Arlington, 143, 190
Arrowsmith, Aaron, 65
Ashland, 106, 111
Ashland, Mount, 20
Ashland Sheet, 131-32
Astor, John Jacob, 52
Astor Column, 4p

Astoria, 4p, 24, 52, 54-55, 64, 77, 78, 176
　economy, 94, 116, 128, 183
　on maps, 9, 49m, 61, 63, 65, 66m, 102m
　population, 68, 81, 106, 137
　site, 53m, 82-83
　transportation, 95, 99, 108, 188
Astoria (Irving), 10
Astoria & Columbia R.R., 112
Astor party, 54, 57
Auburn, 88, 89, 92
Automobiles, 134, 138p, 139, 156, 179, 187
　effects, 144, 161, 170
Aviation, 161, 179

Baker, 58, 89, 92, 99, 128
Baker Basin, 31o.f.
Baker County, 84, 88, 124, 152, 165, 174
Bald Mountain, 22
Bancroft, Hubert H., 77, 95
Bandon, 106
Banks, 144
Bannock Indians, 42, 108
Baptist Church, 81
Barley, 149
Barlow, Samuel, 78
Barlow Road, 26o.f., 70-71m, 73, 78, 84, 96, 99
Barron mine, 88
Bartholomew Brothers, 124
"Basin of the Columbia," 13
Basin-Range Region, 4, 15m, 26-28
Basques, 31, 123, 137
Bates, Edward, 8
Bayocean, 144, 145p
Beaches, 21, 22, 24, 86, 115, 117
Bear Creek (Jackson Co.), 20, 86
Beaver, 4, 7, 52, 55-58
Beaver Creek (Coos Co.), 44
Beaverton, 101m, 144, 171m, 174
"Beeswax" ship, 48
Belknap Springs, 178
Bend, 27, 106, 143, 189
Ben Franklin (keel boat), 77
Bensell, Royal A., 55, 91

198

Benton County, 78-80, 93, 159, 164
"Benton's Log-Cabin Bill," 78
Bicycles, 170, 179
Biggs, 143
Birds, 52, 58
Bitterroot Mountains (Montana), 44
Blacks, 136-37
Blanco, Cape, 1, 2p, 3, 6, 22, 63
Blue Mountains, 15m, 28-33o.f., 32p, 46, 115, 123
   exploration, 55, 57-60, 68
   mapped, 11, 60, 61m, 65
   mining & geology, 84, 88-89, 126
Boardman, 33o.f.
Bohemia Mine, 88
Boise River (Idaho), 60
Bonneville, Benjamin L. E., 50, 60-62
Bonneville Dam, 167, 176
Bonneville Power Administration (BPA), 177p
Boone, Alphonso, 68
Boone, Jesse, 68
Boring, 144
Boundaries, 80, 84
Bowen, William A., 81
Bowles, Samuel, 11
Bowman, Isaiah, 139
Breitenbush, 178
Bridgeport, 89
Bridges, 4p, 21, 81, 188
Britain, 7, 8, 55, 64, 78
Brookings, 21, 94, 100, 183
Broughton, William, 49
Brownlee Dam, 176, 189
Brownsville, 94, 113
Brubaker, Howard, 162
Bryant, William Cullen, 8
Buffalo, 58, 59
Bull Run, 144
Bureau of Land Management, 155, 180
Burlington, 144
Burnett, Peter H., 11, 70, 72, 73
Burns, 143
Burnt River, 31, 58, 60, 88
Bush, Asahel, 92

Cabrillo, Juan Rodriguez, 2
Calapooya Mountains, 19, 111
Calapuya Indians, 38, 42m, 43, 74, 90
California, 11, 76
"California Isle," 3
Camas, 39, 43, 60
Camp Clatsop, 53m
Camp Colfax, 90
Camp Henderson, 90
Camp Logan, 90
Camp Maury, 90
Camp Polk, 90
Camp Warner, 90
Canadians, 105, 137
Canby, 174
Canemah, 94, 95
Cannon Beach, 43, 51, 53m, 144

Canoes, 35, 37, 39p, 43, 49, 64, 77
Canyon City, 88, 92, 94
Canyon Toll Road, 96
Capitol, 19p
"Captain Jack" (Keintpoos), 108
Carey, Paul J., 10
Carolina (steamer), 77
Carver, Jonathan, 3, 8
Cascade Head, 22, 24o.f.
Cascade Range, 15m, 16, 26-28, 42, 60, 61m, 63, 65,
   87, 111, 153
Cascade Rapids, 95
Cascades Indians, 42m, 43
Cascades Region. see Cascade Range
Catholic Church, 81
Catlin, George, 37
Cave Junction, 19o.f.
Cayuse Indians, 42m, 44
Cayuse War, 77
Cazadero, 144
Cedar, 40
Celilo Falls, 40p, 95, 151
Central Pacific R.R., 125m
Central Point, 87
Champoeg, 16, 64, 73, 77, 78, 91, 95
Champoeg County, 65, 72, 78
Champoeg District, 65m
Chehalem Valley, 75
Chemult, 143
Cherries, 117
Chetco Indians, 42m, 44
Chetco River, 117, 179
Chief Joseph, 108
Chinese, 105, 113, 125, 126, 136, 160
Chinook Indians, 38, 43
Christmas Lake Valley, 189
Chromium, 89, 126
Cities, 81-83, 92, 137, 158-59, 170, 173-74. see also
   specific cities
Civilian Conservation Corps (CCC), 157
Civil War, 89
Clackamas County, 65, 72, 78-80, 117, 171, 183
Clackamas District, 65m
Clackamas Indians, 42m, 43
Clackamas River, 43
"Clamet" (Rogue) River, 63
"Clammite" River, 57
Clark, George Rogers, 50-51
Clark, William, 3, 4, 48, 53, 60
Clark's (Columbia) River, 12
Clatskanie Indians, 42m
Clatsop County, 72, 76, 78-80, 105
Clatsop Indians, 42m, 43
Clatsop Plains, 4p, 9, 10, 24, 51, 64, 66, 100
Clawson, Marion, 157
"Claymouth River." see Klamath River
Clear Lake, 24
Climate, 4, 10, 19, 74, 83, 92, 111, 148, 180, 188
Clyman, James, 76
Coal & coal mining, 22, 89, 94, 100, 126, 127, 178,
   184

Coast Fork Willamette River, 18, 19
Coast Pilots, 103
Coast Range, 15*m*, 16, 22-26, 55, 60, 66, 115, 153
Coast Range Region. *see* Coast Range
Coast Reservation, 107
Coglar Rim, 28*o.f.*
Coleman Rim, 28*o.f.*
"Columbia," 13
Columbia (Robert Gray's ship), 49
Columbia (steamer), 77
Columbia County, 84
Columbia River, 4*p*, 15*o.f.*, 22, 33, 39, 43, 56, 57, 75, 84, 117
    dams, 167, 169, 176, 177, 188-90
    early explorations & descriptions, 2, 48-49, 51, 59, 64, 68
    entrance, 95, 96, 108, 116
    fishing, 126, 127*p*, 151, 167
    frozen, 83, 95
    gorge, 26, 27*m*, 34*p*, 108, 111
    mapped & surveyed, 6, 60, 62-64
    shipping, 77, 95, 179
Combines, 147
Condon, 143
Congregational Church, 81
Conners Creek, 88
Cook, Capt. James, 48
Coos Bay, 19, 22, 44, 92, 93, 96, 99, 100, 106, 117, 143, 188
    on early routes, 55, 57
    products & manufacturing, 89, 118, 126, 129, 178, 183
Coos County, 84
Coos Indians, 42*m*, 44
Coos River, 44, 95, 96
Copper, 89, 126
Coquille, 94
Coquille Indians, 56
Coquille River, 7, 22, 44, 56, 86, 95, 96, 100, 117, 126
Corn, 75, 93, 150
Cornelius, 111
Cortes, Hernando, 48
Corvallis, 18*o.f.*, 96, 99, 112, 114, 117, 144, 159
Covered wagons, 73*p*
"Cow Column," 72
Coxcomb Hill, 26, 102*m*
Cram, George F., 131
Cranberries, 22, 117
Crater Lake National Park, 26, 28, 84, 145, 189
Crescent City (Calif.), 87
Creswell, 161
Crook County, 107, 124, 134, 136, 158
Crops, 22, 33, 93, 117, 118, 122, 146*m*, 148-50, 182-83, 189. *see also* specific crops
Crown Point, 34*p*
"Cumberland" (Columbia) River, 12
Curry County, 57, 84, 172, 174

d'Aguilar, Martin, 3, 5
Dairies, 16, 93, 150-51, 188
    products, 21, 22, 76, 118, 122, 156

Dallas, 96, 113
Dalles, The, 9, 26*o.f.*, 33*o.f.*, 64, 65, 177*p*
    exploration & transportaion, 58, 68, 70-71, 89, 95, 99, 143
    population, 106, 190
Dalles Dam, The, 151, 176, 190
Dalles Military Road, The, 115
Dams, 152, 167, 189. *see also* specific dams, or Columbia River, dams
Davidson, George, 103
Davis, H. L., 137-38
Dayton, 113
de Mofras, Eugène Duflot, 11
Denio, 59
Depoe Bay, 24*o.f.*, 183
Deschutes County, 106, 124, 134, 158
Deschutes National Forest, 189
Deschutes R.R., 143
Deschutes River, 27*o.f.*, 27*m*, 33*o.f.* 58, 60, 109, 176
Deschutes-Umatilla Plateau, 15*m*, 26-28, 33-34*o.f.*, 58, 118, 124, 146, 147*p*, 176
Devil's Backbone, 71*m*
Devil's Half Acre, 71*m*
Devils Lake, 55
Diamond Lake, 26
Dickinson, Robert E., 170
Disappointment, Cape, 49*m*
Diseases, 43, 70, 74, 88
Dominis, Capt. (*Owyhee*), 126
Donation Land Claim Act, 79, 98*m*, 99-101
Donner und Blitzen River, 29*o.f.*, 189*o.f.*
Dooley Mountain Road, 99
Douglas, David, 3-4, 50, 56, 59
Douglas County, 84, 92, 93, 117, 122*p*, 181, 188
Douglas fir (*pinus taxifolia*), 56
Drake, Sir Francis, 2, 3
Dredging, 26
Dufur, 143
Dunes, 24, 24*o.f.*, 188*o.f.*
Durkee, 31*o.f.*

East Side Interurbans, 142*m*
Ecola Creek, 53*m*
Economic conditions, 79, 128, 157
Education, 157
E-eu-col Creek, 53*m*
El Dorado Ditch, 88
Elgin, 68, 94, 143
Elk, 40, 73
Elk Creek (Clatsop Co.), 53*m*
Elk Creek (Douglas Co.), 19, 56, 57
Elkhorn Mountains, 31*o.f.*
Elkton, 24, 57, 81
Ellensberg. *see* Gold Beach
Ellice, Point (Washington), 53*m*
Elmira, 96
Emigrant Hill, 33*o.f.*
Emmons, George, 50
Empire, 87, 89, 96, 106
Energy, 94, 170, 175-79, 190
English, 105, 137

Environment, 190
Eola Hills, 16
Estacada, 144
Eugene, 18, 99, 176, 184-85
    population, 92, 137, 159
    suburbanization & urbanization, 174, 187
    transportation, 111, 114, 117, 143, 144, 179
Exploration, 4, 7, 48-68
    journals, 50-60
    land, 50m (see also individual explorers)
    sea, 1, 2, 48 (see also individual explorers)
    secrecy, 1, 2
Exports, 89, 94, 96, 128, 130, 134, 149, 151, 153, 156, 157. see also trade

Faith, Hope and Charity Springs, 71m
Falcon, Cape, 24
Fall City, 143
Fall Creek mine, 88
Farewell Bend, 31o.f., 54, 189o.f.
Farnham, Thomas J., 1
Ferrelo, Cape, 3p, 44
Ferries, 24, 68, 114, 115, 143
Finnish, 105, 137, 160
Fish & fisheries, 21, 24, 39-40, 52
    canneries, 126, 128
    commercial species, 151, 166
    conflicts, 151-52, 183-84
    value, 151, 166, 183
Fish wheels, 126, 127p
Flax, 117
Floods, 94-95, 157
Flora (Wallowa Co.), 189o.f.
Florence, 24o.f., 106, 143
Flour Mills, 81, 94, 128, 129, 129m
Flowers, 22
Floyd, John, 8
"Folly Farm," 12
Food processing, 134, 156, 168-69
Forest Grove, 144
Forests & forestry, 64, 65, 111, 169, 179-81
    forestry practices, 24, 181, 188
    patterns, 16, 22, 32p
    products, 155, 156, 168, 180
    species, 22, 35, 52, 56, 57, 68, 180
    see also logging
Fort Astoria, 62m, 63
Fort Boise (Idaho), 31o.f., 60, 99
Fort Clatsop, 54
Fort Colville (Wash.), 65
Fort George (Astoria), 49m, 55
Fort Kootenai (British Columbia), 65
Fort Langley (British Columbia), 65
Fort Okanogan (British Columbia), 65
Fort Stevens, 113
Fort Umpqua, 24, 56, 57, 62m, 63
Fort Vancouver, 57, 59, 68, 74, 93, 94
    HBC headquarters, 55, 75p, 82
    on maps, 9, 61m, 63, 65
Fort Walla Walla, 61m, 63-65
Foulweather, Cape, 24o.f.

Franchère, Gabriel, 50, 54
Freeways, 190. see also roads, state highways, or U.S.
    Highways
Frémont, John C., 1, 3, 4, 10, 28, 50m, 68
Fremont National Forest, 189o.f.
French Canadians, 11, 16, 59, 73, 100m
French Prairie, 16, 81, 82, 100m
Frost, John H., 10, 37, 50m, 66
Fruit, 22, 31, 39, 40, 92, 117
Fulton, R. L., 133
Fur Trades & trappers, 1, 8, 24, 48, 49, 55-57, 59,
    59m, 74, 75, 87

Galice, 87
Gardiner, 24, 96, 106, 143
Garibaldi, 183
Gearhart, 162p
General Land Office, 162
Geographical Sketch of the Part of the Country Called
    Oregon (Carey), 10
Geographic names: sources, 11, 87
Geology, 28, 29, 31, 52, 84-85
George, Henry, 105
Geothermal energy, 177-78
Germans, 105, 137
Gill, J. K. & Co., 131
Gilliam County, 136, 174
Glass Buttes, 29
Gold Beach, 21, 21p, 87, 92, 100, 106
Gold Hill, 87
Gold mining, 84-89
    diverted labor, 99, 100
    impact, 79, 83-86, 88, 89
    methods, 85, 88, 88p, 126, 152, 152p
    production, 85, 152
Good Roads Assoc., 114, 139
Goose Lake, 28, 46, 58
Grain, 16, 182. see also specific crops
Grand Coulee Dam, 167, 177
Grande Ronde Basin, 31o.f., 54, 60, 65, 68, 89, 118
Grande Ronde River, 31, 60
Grand Ronde Indian Reservation, 90m, 91
Granite (Grant Co.), 88, 89
Grant County, 84, 88, 152, 174
Grants Pass, 19o.f., 20p, 57, 87, 96, 106, 159
Grass seed, 150, 188
Gray, Robert, 48
Grazing, 123, 124, 151, 165
Great Northern R.R., 125m
Great Sandy Desert (High Lava Plains), 28o.f.
Great Southern R.R., 143
Greeley, Horace, 64
Gresham, 144, 171m, 174
Grindstone, 71m
"Grub lands," 125, 126
Gutkind, E. A., 14

Harbors, 21, 33, 24, 87, 95-96
"Hardscrabble Creek" (Linn Co.), 11-12
Harney County, 138, 164
Harney Lake, 29o.f., 58, 189o.f.

Harriman, Edward H., 143
Hart Mountain, 28o.f.
Hastings, Lansford, 10
Hawaiians, 55, 93
Hay, 22
Head, Harlow, 101
Headlands, 21, 22
Heceta Head, 22, 24, 55
Hells Canyon, 31o.f.
Hells Canyon Dam, 176, 177, 189
Heppner, 59
Hezeta, Bruno, 2
High Cascades. see Cascade Range
High Lava Plains, 15m, 26-29o.f.
Highways, 161, 179. see also roads, state highways, or
   U.S. Highways
Hill, James J., 143
Hillsboro, 142m, 144, 159, 171m, 174
Hines, Harvey K., 10
Historical geography, 14, 34
Hobson, John, 48
Homestead Acts, 137, 138
Homesteads & homesteaders, 137-38, 147-48, 155, 189
Hood, Mount, 16o.f., 49, 178, 188
   mapped, 27m, 62, 63
   pictured, 17p, 18p, 75p
Hood River County, 106, 134, 165
Hood River Indians, 42m, 43
"Hooverville," 157
Horses, 55, 76, 93, 151
   Indian use, 12, 36, 37, 46
Housing, 82p, 83, 157, 179-75
Howison, Neil M., 1, 3, 11, 68, 73-79
Hudson's Bay Co. (HBC), 1, 4, 8, 11, 15, 55-60, 64,
   72, 74-76, 78, 82, 126
Humboldt ("Ogden's") River, 63
Humbug Mountain, 21o.f.
"Hungry Hill" (Josephine Co.), 12
Hunt, Wilson Price, 57
Hunting, 56, 58, 60
Huntington, 31o.f.
Hydroelectric power, 81, 153, 167, 176-77, 189, 190.
   see also specific dams

Idanha, 113
Illinois River, 19, 86
Immigrants, 1, 8, 11, 72
Immigration, 1, 10, 26, 172
   principal routes, 70-71
   sources, 68-70, 84, 104
   years:
      1842, 1, 72
      1845, 72
      1846, 72
      1847, 73
      1850-1870, 104
      1900-1930, 134
Imnaha River, 60, 61
Income, 125, 129
Independence, 144
Industries, 187

Indians, 4, 19, 68
   affected by whites, 38, 46-47, 63, 74-75, 81, 84, 91
   canoes, 35, 37, 39p, 43, 49, 64, 77
   conflicts & wars, 8, 20, 35, 37, 38, 46, 57, 74-75,
      78, 89-91, 107-109
   dwellings & villages, 40, 43-46, 49
   fire as tool, 35, 36, 43, 46, 50, 56-58
   fishing, 39, 40, 43, 44, 126, 151, 184
   food, 39-43, 46, 58, 60, 73
   guides, 36-37, 55, 56, 59, 60, 66
   migration, 35, 36m
   population, 10, 38-39, 43-44, 80, 107-108, 136, 160
   reservations, 24, 27, 42, 49, 90m, 91, 107, 189
   slavery, 43, 46
   timber, 180, 188, 189
   trails, 7, 87, 96
   tribal boundaries, 11, 35, 42-46, 66m
   tribes. see specific tribes
Interurban rail lines, 142m, 143-44
Irish, 100m, 123, 137, 160
Iron, 94
Irrigation, 30, 31, 33, 72, 120, 150, 188o.f., 189o.f.
   acreage, 147, 148m, 166m
   effect, 135, 136, 158, 159
   expansion, 121-22, 156, 183, 189
Irving, Washington, 10, 62
Isthmus Slough (Coos Bay), 44

Jackson County, 84, 86, 87, 117, 152, 171, 174,
   188o.f.
Jacksonville, 20, 106
James P. Flint (steamer), 95
Japanese, 136, 160
Jefferson, Thomas, 48, 50, 51
Jefferson County, 106, 124, 134, 159, 172
Jefferson, Mount, 16, 26o.f., 62, 63
Jenny (schooner), 49
Jetties, 21p, 96, 153, 188
   Columbia River, 4p, 116
   Rogue River, 117, 179
   Siuslaw River, 24, 116p
   Tillamook Bay, 117, 179
John Day, 89, 92
John Day Canyon, 27, 27m, 58
John Day Dam, 176, 190o.f.
John Day River, 33o.f., 60, 85, 88
Jordan Valley (Malheur Co.), 31o.f., 123
Joseph, 143
Josephine County, 84, 117, 152
Josephine Creek, 86
Juan de Fuca, Strait of, 6

Kathlamet Indians, 42m, 43
Keizer Bottom, 82
"Kellymoux" (Tillamook) River, 55
Kerby, 19o.f., 87
Kilchis River, 66
Killemooks. see Tillamook Indians
"Killemouk" (Tillamook) River, 62
"Killimoux River," 63
Kinzua, 143

Klamath County, 107, 156, 158, 165, 183
Klamath Falls, 28, 106, 137, 143, 178, 189
Klamath Indian Reservation, 90m, 91, 189
Klamath Indians, 42m, 46
Klamath Lake, 46, 58, 61m, 109, 147
Klamath Marsh, 28o.f., 68
Klamath Mountains, 15m, 18-20, 84-87, 89, 115, 126, 153
Klamath River, 26, 57, 61m, 63
Klamath Sheet, 131, 132m
Klikitat (Klickitat) Indians, 38
Kone, Rev., 10

Labor, 127, 128, 155, 156, 169, 184
Lafayette, 81, 96
Laframboise, Michel, 55
La Grande, 31, 58, 89, 92, 94, 128, 143
Lake County, 138, 158
Lake Oswego, 167, 174
Lakes, 24, 28. see also specific lakes
Lakeview, 106, 123
Landforms, 15m, 26-28, 31, 32p, 35, 42, 43, 52, 82, 111, 114-15
    coastal, 3p, 21, 22, 24
Land ownership, 37, 78-79, 99, 133, 137, 139, 147, 154-55
Landslides, 140
Land use, 83, 125-26, 134-35, 148, 189, 190
Lane County, 84, 174, 175, 188
    agriculture, 93, 117, 164, 183
    population, 92, 171
Lead, 89, 127
Lebanon, 161
Lee & Frost, 9
Lee, Daniel, 10
Lee, Jason, 10, 72
Lemert farm, 182
Lewis & Clark Expedition, 1, 8, 15, 26, 36-38, 43, 44, 48, 50m-52, 56, 73
Lewis, Meriwether, 3, 4
Lewis, S., 6
Lewis's (Snake) River, 12
Lewiston (Idaho), 117
Lime, 167
Lincoln, Abraham, 134
Lincoln County, 107
Linkville, 28
Linn City (West Linn), 81, 95
Linn County, 78-80, 92, 93, 117, 118, 183
Linnton, 78, 144
Little Deschutes River, 58
Little Nestucca River, 66
Livestock, 72
    cattle, 66, 76, 122, 122p, 150m, 151, 165
    grazing, 83, 121
    horses, 66, 123, 165
    number & value, 76, 93, 121m, 122-25, 150-51, 183
    sheep, 123, 123m, 165
    swine, 76, 123
Logging, 104, 128, 155p, 161, 168, 180, 181m, 188. see also Forests & forestry

Long Tom Creek Indians, 42m, 43
Lookingglass Valley, 56
Lookout, Cape, 24o.f., 48, 49, 62, 63
Lookout Point Dam, 176
Lot Whitcomb (steamer), 77
Louisiana Purchase, 7m, 8, 48
Lower Coquille Indians, 42m
Lower Klamath Lake, 28o.f., 46
Lower Umpqua Indians, 42m, 43
Lowland Takelma Indians, 42m, 43
Luckiamute Indians, 42m, 43
Lumber, 77, 94, 116, 128, 134. see also Sawmills
Lytle, Elmer E., 143

"McCleods" (Rogue) River, 63
McCredie Springs, 178
McGilvray's (Kootenay?) River, 12
McKenzie, Donald, 58
McKenzie Pass, 18, 26, 27
McKenzie River, 18, 62m, 63, 88, 177
McLeod, Alexander R., 7, 50m, 55-56
McLoughlin, John, 15, 75
McLoughlin, Mount, 11, 20, 28, 62m, 63
McMinnville, 144
McNary Dam, 176, 189
Madras, 143
Malaria, 74
Malheur County, 88, 139, 158, 183, 189
Malheur Lake, 29o.f., 58, 59, 189o.f.
Malheur River, 11, 31, 58, 60, 189
Malheur River Indian Reservation, 90m, 91
Malpass farm, 182
Manson, Donald, 55
Manufacturing, 81, 118, 127-30, 153, 156, 157, 167-69, 184
    value added by, 168m, 185m
Mapleton, 96
Maps & charts, 15m, 16m, 86m, 129m, 171m, 175m, 182m
    cropland, 118m, 146m, 149m, 165m
    energy, 176m, 178m
    early & explorers', 2-3, 10-11, 49, 50m, 60-63, 65m, 100m, 130m
        Abert, 62m
        Bonneville, 61m, 62-63
        Broughton, 49m
        Carver, 3
        Lee & Frost, 9m
        Lewis & Clark, 51m, 53m, 60
        Lewis, S., 6m
        Müller, 3, 5m
        Ogden, 59m
        Stewart, 54m
        Wilkes, 64, 66m
    hydrographic & topographic, 27m, 103, 132m
    Indians, 36m, 60, 90m, 103
    irrigation, 120m, 148m, 166m
    land claims, 98m, 100m, 103
    livestock, 121m, 123m, 125m, 150m
    manufacturing, 168m, 185m, 186m
    mapping, 131-32, 140, 161-64

Maps & charts (cont.)
  population, 69m, 79m, 85m, 106m, 135m, 136m,
    158m, 159m, 172m
  surveys, 101m, 102, 103
  timber, 154m, 172m
  transportation:
    railroads, 109m, 110m, 113m, 142m
    roads, 70-71m, 97m, 110m, 141-143
Marcola, 144
Marine Biology Station, 188o.f.
Marion County, 78-80, 92, 93, 117, 171, 174, 183
Marshfield (Coos Bay), 87, 94
Marys Peak, 16o.f.
Mary's River Indians, 42m, 43
Massachusetts (steamer), 77
Meares, Cape, 24o.f., 49
Medford, 19o.f., 20, 88p, 93, 106, 114, 137, 159
Meek, Stephen H., 38p
Meek Cutoff Trail, 85
Mercury, 89, 126, 127
Methodists, 72, 81
  missions, 10, 72, 78
Metsker Map Co., 164
Mexicans, 136
Miami River, 66
Michaux, André, 51
Middle Fork Willamette River, 18
Migration, 157
Military roads, 115
Mill City, 144
Mill Creek, 94
Milton, 82
Milwaukie, 81, 94
Mining & minerals, 28, 126-27, 153, 167
  effects, 21, 87, 89, 109, 115
  gold, 20, 21
  production & value, 152-53, 189
Minorities, 100m, 104, 134, 136-37
  distribution, 105, 159
Mission Bottom, 16
Mobile homes, 175m
Modoc Indians, 42m, 46, 108
Modoc Scarp, 28o.f.
Mogul (keel boat), 77
Molalla, 144, 161
Molalla Indians, 42m, 43
Molalla River, 87
Mormon Basin, 88
Morrow County, 138
Moses Columbia Indians, 42m
Mountain passes, 18, 20, 22. see specific passes
Mt. Angel, 144
Müller, Gerhardt, 3, 5
Mules, 76
Multnomah (steamer), 95
Multnomah County, 84, 92, 117, 159, 164, 171
Multnomah Indians, 42m
"Multnomah" (Willamette) River, 12, 56, 57, 60, 61m,
  62m
Myrtle Point, 94, 96, 144

Natural gas, 179, 184

Neahkahnie Mountain, 66, 67p
Neall, James, 11
Necanicum River, 53m
Nehalem Beach, 48
Nehalem Indians, 43
Nehalem River, 117, 126
Neptune State Park, 41p
Nestucca Indians, 43
Nestucca River, 18, 55, 126
Netarts Bay, 24o.f.
New Albion, 3
Newauna Creek, 53m
Newberg, 144
Newport, 24o.f., 95, 106, 114, 143, 144, 183, 188o.f.
Newsom, David, 12, 92, 125
Nez Perce Indians, 42m, 44, 108
Nickel, 126, 167
North Bend, 87, 94, 106, 143, 176
Northern Pacific R.R., 108, 125m
Northern Paiute Indians, 42m, 46
North Plains, 144
Northwest Airlines, 161
North West Co., 55, 57
Northwest Passage, 1, 48
Norwegians, 105, 137
Nuclear power, 178
"Nuevo Mexico," 3
Nuts, 43, 117

Oakridge, 174
"Oasis," 12
Oats, 149
Ogden, Peter Skene, 7, 80m, 56-59m, 77
Okanogan River, 60
Ontario, 31o.f., 58, 106, 143
Orchards, 12, 16, 76
"Oregon," 13
Oregon:
  name: early usage, 8
  perception of, 1-13, 48, 49, 83, 132-33
Oregon (Wyeth), 10
Oregon Agricultural College (O.S.U.), 93
Oregon & California R.R., 110m, 111, 112p, 131
Oregon & California Revested Lands, 111, 154-55
Oregon-California Trail, 19-20, 64, 86, 115, 130m
Oregon Central Military Road, 115, 115m, 139
Oregon City, 15, 65, 78, 95, 171m, 188o.f.
  manufacturing, 94, 128
  population, 68, 72, 81, 92
  transportation & communication, 70m, 77, 99, 114,
    117
Oregon Country, 8, 12, 13, 16, 51m, 57, 62, 65m, 78
Oregon Dunes National Recreation Area, 24o.f.,
  188o.f.
Oregon Electric Interurban Line, 146, 172m
"Oregon from the Air," 14-34, 187-90
Oregon Hotel (Oregon City), 95
Oregonian Railroad, 113
Oregon Railway & Navigation Co., 112
Oregon Short Line, 112, 129
Oregon State Dept. of Geology & Mineral Industries,
  162

Oregon State Fair, 120
Oregon State Highway Commission, 140, 162
Oregon State Highway System, 140
Oregon Steam & Navigation Co., 108, 112
Oregon Territory, 1, 7, 10, 63, 66m
Oregon Trail, 8, 10, 33, 54, 58, 65, 68, 70-72
Oregon Trunk R.R., 143
"Origan," 3
Oswego, 94
Overland Monthly, 132, 133
Owyhee (brig), 126
Owyhee Reservoir, 30p
Owyhee River, 31o.f., 60, 189
Owyhee Upland Region, 15m, 31
Oxbow Dam, 177, 189

Pacific City, 183
Pacific Mail Company, 77
Pacific Railroad Reports, 108
Paiute Indians, 42, 46
Palmer, Joel, 89
Palouse Hills, 33o.f., 59
Parker, Samuel, 1, 10, 65
Parks, 187, 188
Pasco (Washington), 108
Paulina Lake, 58
Paulina Mountains, 28o.f.
Paulina Peak , 28
Payette River(Idaho), 60
Pears, 117
Peas, 33
Pendleton, 33o.f., 58, 92, 106, 159
Pengra Pass. *see* Willamette Pass
Peoria Party, 72
Perpetua, Cape, 22, 23p, 24o.f.
Petroleum products, 179
Pilcher, Joshua, 12
Pike, Zebulon, 11
"Pit Lake." *see* Goose Lake
Pitt River, 109
Placer, 87
Plateau Indians, 42
Pocahontas, 88
Pocatello (Idaho), 55
Poker Jim Ridge, 28o.f.
Polk County, 78, 79, 93
Pollution, 170, 181
Population, 69m, 133, 135, 173t, 187
    by counties, 79m, 85m, 135m, 172m
    distribution & density, 16, 81, 105-107, 136m
    foreign-born, 70, 80, 84, 92
    increases, 84, 91-92, 105-108, 136, 156-60, 170-73
    Indians, 65, 107
    ratios, 72, 80, 107d, 160d
Portages, 95
Portland, 26o.f., 99, 174, 176
    industry & employment, 94, 128, 167, 184-85t, 186m
    location, 15, 17p, 81
    population, 68, 81, 92, 137, 158-59
    transportation, 15, 95, 112, 114, 114p, 144, 161, 179
    urbanization & suburbanization, 171m, 187-88

Portneuf River (Idaho), 55
Port Orford, 21-22, 87, 94, 100, 183
Port St. Francisco, 5
Port St. Francis Drake, 5
Postal Service, 77, 78, 92, 99, 161
Postroads, 78
Potatoes, 118, 150
Powder River, 60, 85, 88
Power plants, 176m
Powers, 144
Prairie City, 89, 92
Prairies, 16, 57, 64
Prices:
    agricultural goods, 126, 164, 164t
    fish, 49, 126
    goods & services, 49, 83, 99
    land, 126, 128, 147, 154, 155
    tolls, 70, 96
Prineville, 106
Printing, 128
Provisional government, 78, 79
Prunes, 117
Pudding River, 12
Pudding River Indians, 42m
Pyramid ("Battle") Lake, 63

Quartzville, 88
Quicksand, 24
"Quicksand" Bay. *see* Tillamook Bay
"Quicksand" (Sandy) River, 63

Railroads, 20, 24, 26, 31o.f., 81, 108-109, 111-14, 124, 128, 142m-45, 159, 155, 161, 179. *see also* specific railroads
Rainfall, 93, 94, 96
Randolph, 87
Ray's Landing, 113
Recreation, 151, 161, 170, 187-89
Red Deer River, 56
Reedsport, 19, 24, 143
Reptiles, 52
"River of the West," 3, 5, 8
Rivers, 18, 22, 117, 179. *see also* specific rivers
Roads, 67p, 68, 79, 97m, 125m
    construction & maintenance, 96, 99, 114, 138p, 140, 152-53
    development, 78, 114-16
    military, 96, 99
    toll, 96, 99
    wagon, 115
    see also highways, state highways, or U.S. Highways
Robinette, 189
Rockwell, Cleveland, 102
The Rocky Mountains (Irving), 62
Rocky ("Stoney") Mountains, 6, 63
Rogue (Tututni) Indians, 44
Rogue River, 20p, 21p, 43, 63, 85, 86, 188
    canyon, 21
    early descriptions, 56, 57
    jetties, 117, 179
    valley., 7, 19, 20, 92, 100
Rome, 31o.f.

Roseburg, 19, 81, 87, 93, 96, 99, 111
Ross, Alexander, 50
Ross Island, 82
"Rouge" (Rogue) River, 63
Row River, 88
Russia, 5m, 8
Russians, 137, 160
Rye Valley, 88

Saddle Butte, 31o.f.
Saddle Mountain, 16o.f., 49, 188
Sagebrush, 31, 83
Sahaptin Tribes, 42m
Saint Helens, 82, 94, 188
Saint Joseph, 112, 144
Saint Louis (Missouri), 55
Saint Paul, 73
Salem, 19p, 68, 143, 144, 176
  capital, 18, 82
  growth, 174, 187, 188
  industry & employment, 94, 118, 128, 184, 185t
  population, 81, 92, 137, 159
  site, 16, 18, 82
  transportation, 95, 99, 114, 179
Salem Hills, 16
Salmon, 12, 126, 167, 189
  Indian use of, 39, 40, 43, 44
Salmon Indians, 43
Salmon River (Idaho), 44, 60
Salmon River (Lincoln Co.), 18, 24, 55
Salmon River Range ("The Perpetual Snows"), 63
Sand & gravel, 126, 167
San Francisco Xavier (galleon), 48
Sanson (map), 3
Santiam Indians, 42m, 43
Santiam Pass, 18, 26, 27, 113
Santiam River, 18, 43, 87, 94, 176
Sauer, Carl, 35
Sauvie Island, 75, 93
Sawmills, 83, 127, 128, 135, 155p, 157, 179. see also
  Lumber
  sites, 12, 81, 93-94, 154m, 155
Scandinavians, 126
Scottish, 137
Scott, Levi, 78
Scottsburg, 87, 95, 96, 99
Sea Lion Caves, 24
Sea Lion Point, 55
Sea otter, 43, 52
Seaside, 113, 144
Sebastian, Cape, 3, 21o.f.
Settlement, 19, 20, 22, 31, 64-83, 84, 96
  effects, 43, 46, 47, 83
Settlements, 69, 66m, 81, 97m
Seven Devils, 22, 57
Shaniko, 143
Shark (schooner), 68
Sharks, 166
Shasta Costa Indians, 42m
Shasta Indians, 42m
Shasta ("Shasty"), Mount, 9, 62m, 63
"Shastie" (Applegate) River, 56

Sheep, 76, 93, 94, 124f, 151
Shellfish, 39, 126
Shell mounds, 41p
Sheridan, 113
Shipbuilding, 94, 96, 129, 134, 157
Shipping, 26, 83, 95
Shipwrecks, 22, 48, 96
Shoshone Indians, 42, 43, 46, 58
Siletz Bay, 24o.f.
Siletz Indians, 42m
Siletz Reservation, 44, 90m, 91
Siletz River, 126
Siltcoos Lake, 24
Silver, 89, 126, 127, 152
Silverton, 99, 113
Silvies River, 29o.f., 58
Siskiyou Mountains, 19, 20o.f., 56, 111
Siskiyou Pass, 20, 56, 96, 109
Siuslaw Indians, 42m, 43
Siuslaw River, 18, 24, 55, 94, 96, 116p, 117
Sixes River, 56
Skilloot Indians, 42m, 43
Skipanon (Warrenton), 94
Smith, Jedediah, 7-8, 22, 37, 50m, 57, 65
Smith, Sebastian, 66
Smith River, 86
Snake Indians, 58
Snake River, 31o.f., 54-60, 63, 68, 76p, 84, 117, 176,
  177, 179, 189
Snake River Country, 56, 58
Soils, 1, 4, 24, 52, 92
Solar energy, 179
Soto (Spaniard?), 54
Southern Pacific R.R., 111, 113, 143, 144, 154
Southern Pacific Red Electric, 142m
South Pass (Rocky Mts.), 55
South Slough (Coos Bay), 22, 44, 55
South Umpqua River, 86
Spain, 7, 8, 51, 84
Spokane (Washington), 65
Spokane Portland & Seattle R.R., 108
Sprague River, 28o.f., 46
Springfield, 18, 113, 159, 161, 179
Stagecoaches, 95, 99, 115
State highways, 24, 26, 27, 140-41, 141m. see also
  highways, roads, or U.S. Highways
Steamships, 77, 95, 117
Steens Mountain, 29o.f., 31, 59, 123
Stevens, Isaac I., 108
Streetcars, 114, 114p
Stuart, Robert, 8, 54-55
Suburbanization, 161, 173-74. see also specific cities
Sugar beets, 150
Sugar pine (pinus lambertiana), 56
Sullivan Gulch, 157
Summer Lake, 28, 68, 189o.f.
Sumpter, 88, 152p
Surveys, 100-104, 108, 109
Susanville, 88
Swan Flat, 28o.f.
Swan Island, 15
Swedish, 137

Sweet Home, 144, 161
Swine, 76, 123, 151

Table Mountain, 49
Table Rock, 20, 87
Tahkenitch Lake, 24
Takelma Indians, 43
Tanner, Henry S., 62
Taxes, 140
Taylor Grazing Act, 165
Telegraph lines, 99
Tenino (Warm Springs) Indians, 42, 44
Tenmile Lake, 24
Tenny, W.A., 132
Ten Years in Oregon (Lee & Frost), 10
Thanatopsis (Bryant), 88
Thermal power plants, 176, 177
"The Territory of Oregon," 13
Thielson, Mount, 28o.f.
Thompson, David, 55
Three Fingered Jack, 26o.f.
Three Sisters, 26o.f., 28o.f.
Tigard, 144, 174
Tillamook, 25p, 92, 99, 100, 106, 122, 143, 176, 183
Tillamook Bay, 24, 43, 49, 63, 66, 145p
    harbor, 22, 95
    jetties, 117, 179
    products, 94, 118, 126
Tillamook Burn, 169
Tillamook County, 84
Tillamook Head, 4, 22, 24, 36, 42, 43, 53m, 188o.f.
Tillamook Indians, 42m, 43
Tillamook River, 66
Timber harvest, 180d
Timberline Lodge, 161
Timber species, 52, 134, 153
Toledo, 96, 135
Tollgate Pass, 59, 68, 115
Tolowa Indians, 42m
"Too-to-nez" (Rogue) River, 63
Touchet River (Washington), 75
Tourism, 144, 156, 161, 187-89
Trade, 12, 87, 89, 94, 96, 130-31, 153, 156, 157, 164.
    see also exports
Trails, 31o.f., 33, 55, 57-60, 64, 78
    Barlow, 26, 70-71m
    coastal, 22, 24, 66
    Coast Range, 22, 24, 56
    Oregon-California, 56, 57, 87, 96
    see also specific trails and roads
Transportation, 77-78, 95-97, 99, 104, 160-61, 179
Trask River, 66
Trojan power plant, 188, 190
Troutdale, 144
Truck registration, 179
Trullinger, 101
Tualatin, 78, 144
Tualatin Indians, 42m, 43
Tualatin Valley, 72, 81, 99
Tuality County, 78
Tuality District, 65m
Tule Lake, 28o.f., 46

Tututni (Rogue) Indians, 42m, 44
Tygh Valley, 68

Umatilla, 58, 92, 95
Umatilla County, 84, 93, 107, 138, 183, 189
Umatilla Indians, 42, 44
Umatilla Reservation, 44, 90m, 91
Umatilla River, 33, 60
"Umpaquah." see Umpqua
Umpqua County, 84
Umpqua Indians, 43
Umpqua Mountains, 111
Umpqua River, 24, 43, 95, 126
    explored, 8, 19, 24, 55-57
    mapped, 61m, 62m, 63
    navigation, 87, 95, 96, 117
Umpqua Valley, 19, 81, 92, 100, 147
"Umqua." see Umpqua
Union, 31, 92, 94
Union County, 84, 152
Union Pacific R.R., 33, 112, 143
United Air Lines, 161
United Railways, 142m, 144
U.S. Army, 75, 77, 90, 108
U.S. Army Corps of Engineers, 145, 162
U.S. Bureau of Census, 133
U.S. Coast and Geodetic Survey, 103
U.S. Forest Service, 162, 180
U.S. Geological Survey, 131, 142, 162
U.S. Government, 8, 64, 78, 111, 140, 154
U.S. Highways:
    Highway 20, 20o.f., 27, 140
    Highway 26, 26o.f., 140
    Highway 30, 26o.f., 140
    Highway 97, 26o.f., 140
    Highway 99, 140
    Highway 101, 21o.f., 23p, 24o.f., 115, 140, 188o.f.
    Highway 199, 87
    Interstate-5, 20, 140, 188o.f.
    Interstate-80N, 31o.f., 33o.f., 34p, 115, 140, 190o.f.
    see also highways, roads, or state highways
Unity, 89
Upland Takelma Indians, 42m
Upper Coquille Indians, 42m
Upper Klamath Lake, 28o.f.
Upper Umpqua Indians, 42m

Vale, 31o.f.
Valsetz, 143
Vancouver, George, 3, 48-49
Vancouver, Mount. see Jefferson, Mount
Vancouver (Washington), 15, 26, 82, 114, 171m, 187-88o.f.
"Vancouvre." see Fort Vancouver
Vanport, 157
Vaughan, Thomas, 13
Vaughan, Warren, 37
Vegetation, 33, 39, 46, 57, 73
    changes in, 36, 63, 83, 125
    noted by explorers, 8, 12, 56, 60
Villard, Henry, 112

Wagons, 77
Wagontire Mountain, 29o.f.
"Walamet." see Willamette
Waldo, Daniel, 72
Waldo, 87
Waldo Hills, 72, 81
Waldport, 24o.f., 143
"Walla Matte." see Willamette
Walla Walla River, 33, 55, 59
Wallowa County, 44, 174, 189
Wallowa Mountain, 31o.f., 123
Wapato, 39, 43
Warm Springs Reservation, 27o.f., 44, 90m, 91, 107, 188
Warm Springs (Tenino) Indians, 42
Warner Valley, 28o.f., 59
Wasco, 92
Wasco County, 84, 93, 107, 117, 134, 136, 172
Wascow Indians, 42m
Washington County, 78-80, 171, 174, 183
Washington, Mount, 26o.f.
Waterways, 77, 116-17, 162
Waverly Country Club, 144
"Web Feet," 11
Weiser River, 60
West Linn, 174
"West Side Line," 111
Weyerhaeuser Co., 154
Whaling, 8, 39
Wheat, 31o.f., 33o.f., 93, 116, 124
  acreage, 118m, 148, 149m
  production, 27, 76, 83, 89, 118, 119p, 146-47p, 164
Wheeler County, 174
Whisky Run, 56, 87p
White, Elijah, 74
Whitman Mission, 33, 64, 71, 73, 74
Wildhorse Creek, 33o.f.
Wildlife, 28, 36, 46, 52, 58, 60, 73-74
Wilkes, Charles, 1, 3, 50m, 78
  map, 11, 66
  reports, 10, 38, 43, 64-65
Wilkinson, James, 51
Willamette Falls, 9
Willamette Farmer, 119
Willamette Pass (Pengra Pass), 18o.f., 26
Willamette River, 15, 17p, 18, 19, 176
  mapped, 9, 60, 61m, 62m
  navigation, 77, 81, 95, 117
Willamette University, 19p
Willamette Valley, 11, 13, 15-18o.f., 18p, 66, 68, 99, 125, 187-88o.f.

Willamette Valley (cont.)
  agriculture, 75, 76, 92, 93, 117-18, 120, 122, 146
  cities & towns, 81-83, 91m
  Indians, 43, 56, 74
  maps, 15m, 63
  population, 91-92, 133, 135, 159
  transportation, 111, 143, 144
Willamette Valley & Cascade Mountain Road, 110m, 115
Willamette Valley Southern, 142m
Willamina, 143, 161
"Williamete." see Willamette
Williamson River, 46, 58
Willow Creek, 58
Wilson River, 66, 163p
Wilsonville, 18p, 144
Winchester Bay, 183, 188
Wind River Range (Idaho), 55
Winter Ridge, 68
Woahink Lake, 24
Wolves, 74
Women, 80
Woodburn, 113, 174
Wool, 89, 94, 128, 156
Works Progress Administration (WPA), 157
World War I, 134, 156
World War II, 157
Wyeth, John B., 10
Wyeth, Nathaniel, 50

Yachats, 55
Yainax Butte, 28o.f.
Yamhill, 99, 144
Yamhill County, 72, 78-80, 117, 133
Yamhill District, 65m
Yamhill Indians, 42m
Yamhill River, 18, 55
Yaquina (steamer), 113
Yaquina Bay, 22
Yaquina Head, 22, 24o.f., 43
Yaquina Indians, 42m
Yaquina River, 55, 96, 117
Yawhee Plateau, 28o.f.
Yoncalla Indians, 42m
Young, Ewing, 50, 75, 76
Youngs River, 24
Youngs River Bay, 24

Zinc, 89, 127
Zinc Creek, 88

This book is typeset in Compugraphic's Paladium, an Oldstyle, Aldine-French typeface based on Herman Zapf's Palatino. The book is printed on 70 lb. Paloma Matte. The softcover copies are bound in Zelco cover, and the hard cover copies with Holliston Crown Linen. The typesetting was done by Harrison Typesetting, Inc., the printing by Glass-Dahlstrom Graphic Press, the lamination by Northwest Bookbinding Co., the softcover copies were bound by American Bindery, and the hardcover copies by Lincoln & Allen (all firms located in Portland, Oregon). The book was designed by Bruce T. Hamilton.